CHRISTOPHER BUCK is a Pennsylvania
attorney and independent scholar who has taught
at Michigan State University, Quincy University,
Millikin University, and Carleton University.
His publications include *Alain Locke: Faith and
Philosophy*; *Paradise and Paradigm: Key Symbols in Persian
Christianity and the Bahá'í Faith*; *Symbol and Secret:
Qur'an Commentary in Bahá'u'lláh's Kitáb-i-Íqán*, as
well as a number of book chapters, journal articles,
and encyclopedia articles.

Religious Myths and Visions of America

How Minority Faiths Redefined America's World Role

Christopher Buck

PRAEGER

Westport, Connecticut
London

Library of Congress Cataloging-in-Publication Data

Buck, Christopher, 1950–
    Religious myths and visions of America : how minority faiths redefined America's world role /
Christopher Buck
        p. cm.
    Includes bibliographical references (p.) and index.
    ISBN 978–0–313–35959–0 (alk. paper)
1. United States—Religion. 2. United States—History—Religious aspects. 3. Mythology—Political
aspects—United States—History. I. Title.
BL2525.B84 2009
200.973—dc22   2008046765

British Library Cataloguing in Publication Data is available.

Library of Congress Catalog Card Number: 2008046765
ISBN: 978–0–313–35959–0

First published in 2009

Praeger Publishers, 88 Post Road West, Westport, CT 06881
An imprint of Greenwood Publishing Group, Inc.
www.praeger.com

Printed in the United States of America

The paper used in this book complies with the
Permanent Paper Standard issued by the National
Information Standards Organization (Z39.48-1984).

10 9 8 7 6 5 4 3 2 1

Contents

Acknowledgments

On November 1, 2007, Suzanne I. Staszak-Silva (formerly Senior Editor, ABC-CLIO, Praeger, Greenwood—now editor at Rowman & Littlefield Publishers) invited me to submit a book proposal based on a course I had designed and taught at Michigan State University for the 2003–2004 academic year—*Religious Myths of America* (IAH 211C, Area Studies and Multicultural Civilizations). In August 2003—when I created the syllabus for *Religious Myths of America*—I had no inkling that, four years later, I would be asked to turn this rather novel and unique course into a book for Praeger Publishers. Praeger is an imprint of Greenwood Publishing Group (now owned by ABC-CLIO, America's largest publisher of print and online reference resources), and publishes Greenwood's line of scholarly and professional books in the social sciences and humanities.

From proposal to publication, I have had the pleasure of working productively with Ms. Staszak-Silva as my editor over the course of the writing, editing, and production process. I am also indebted to Kathy Breit, Project Manager, BeaconPMG, Ashland, Ohio, for her professional oversight of the copyediting, typesetting, and proofreading of this book, for her assistance in the indexing, and for maintaining high production standards in the publication of this book.

There are some other extraordinary people whom I would like to thank, who also helped make this book possible. First, I wish to thank the following scholars for their respective endorsements of *Religious Myths and Visions of America:*

- Bruce E. Johansen, Frederick W. Kayser Professor, School of Communication, University of Nebraska at Omaha—author of *Forgotten Founders: Benjamin Franklin, the Iroquois, and the Rationale for the American Revolution* (1982) and (with Donald A. Grinde, Jr.) *Exemplar of Liberty: Native America and the Evolution of Democracy* (1991)—most notably for his overall commendation: "*Religious Myths and Visions of America* is an intellectual feast, sparkling with original interpretations of how many religions have helped shape America's national character, from the Iroquois origin story, to Christian, Mormon, Bahá'í, and Black Muslim beliefs, among others. This book will provoke insights and controversy for years to come."

- Todd Lawson, Professor of Islamic Studies, Department of Near and Middle Eastern Civilizations, University of Toronto—author of *Gnostic Apocalypse in Islam: The Qur'an and the Bábí Movement* (2009) and *The Crucifixion and the Qur'an: A Study in the History of Muslim Thought* (2009)—most significantly for his evaluation of this book's methodological contribution: "An experiment on the 'idea of America' with engaging results, this book examines the role of ten religions in redefining America's world role—a topic of importance given America's influence in world affairs. On the premise that America is both 'nation and notion,' this project is a breath of methodological fresh air. *Religious Myths and Visions of America* is a novel, imaginative, and rigorously scholarly contribution to comparative religion, worthy of serious attention and debate. Of general contemporary and historical interest to students, scholars, and thinking people everywhere."

- William E. Paden, Professor of Religion, University of Vermont—author of *Religious Worlds: The Comparative Study of Religion* (1988/1994), and *Interpreting the Sacred: Ways of Viewing Religion* (1992/2003)—especially for his comment on the timely relevance of the book: "Christopher Buck's new book is a timely and highly readable consideration of the way American religions have continued to remythologize the country. To this theme the author brings impressive research and notable facility in the comparative study of myth while at the same time presenting the material in an entirely accessible, lucid, and interesting manner. Few topics are more relevant today, in a time when the self-definition of Americans is such an influential force on the global stage."

- Jay Parini, D. E. Axinn Professor of English and Creative Writing, Middlebury College—author of *Promised Land: Thirteen Books That Changed America* (2008)—particularly for his insight that "America's idea of itself" is "central to our national psyche" and is therefore a key issue in American studies: "In this remarkable book, Dr. Buck examines the key religious ideas that have shaped America's idea of itself. It's a broadly informed and beautifully written work that reveals the various strains in American mythology and religion. This country has always had a visionary aspect, a sense of the numinous; this impulse has taken many different forms. I can think of no subject in American studies more central to our national psyche. This is an important, interesting, thought-provoking work."

- Andrew Rippin, Professor of History (Specialist in Islamic Studies with an interest in the Qur'an and the history of its interpretation), Dean of the Faculty of Humanities, University of Victoria, Canada—author of *Muslims: Their Religious Beliefs and Practices* (2005), and editor of *The Blackwell Companion to the Qur'an* (2006) and *The Islamic World* (2008)—for his welcome assessment: "This is an ambitious and unique work, covering a broad range of religious visions of America in their global context. Buck's firm theoretical framework and rigorous documentation make this a significant contribution to contemporary discussions of the place, role, and future of the diversity of religions that make up America today."

- Richard W. Thomas, Professor of History, Michigan State University—author of *Racial Unity: An Imperative for Social Progress* (1993) and *Understanding Interracial Unity: A Study of U.S. Race Relations* (1996)—most illuminatingly for calling attention to the connections between religion and race in the American context: "For those of us who have yearned for a more readable and scholarly book on the multifaceted ways in which minorities, be they racial, cultural, or religious, have 'redefined America's world role,' Christopher Buck's most recent book is a welcome addition to the fields of racial, cultural, and ethnic studies. Using myths and visions of minority faiths, Buck has introduced an engaging and fresh new approach to understanding and appreciating the influence of these faiths on America's role in the world. He does this by bringing these minority faiths from the periphery of scholarly discourse to the center of a new, more inclusive scholarly discourse. Scholars have always known about the impact of race and ethnicity on religion throughout American history, but Buck's contribution is in the way that he explains the historical connections between race and religion and in the process of shaping America's role in the world. Above all, Buck keeps the reader engaged and intrigued in a study that reads like a good novel by a warm fire on a cold winter evening."

For their assistance with the manuscript itself, I would like to acknowledge the contributions of these scholars as well:

- Imam Abu Laith Luqman Ahmad, for his kind permission to publish excerpts from his essay and social commentary, "Islam American Style" (2004).

- Andrew Rippin, Professor of History, Specialist in Islamic Studies (with an interest in the Qur'an and the history of its interpretation) and Dean of the Faculty of Humanities, University of Victoria, for his assistance with Chapter 9, "Islamic Myths and Visions of America."

- Jonathan Sarna, the Joseph H. and Belle R. Braun Professor of American Jewish History at Brandeis University and Director of its Hornstein Jewish Professional

Leadership Program, for his assistance with Chapter 3, "Jewish Myths and Visions of America."

- Robert Stockman, Director of the Research Office at the U.S. Bahá'í National Center and Instructor of Religious Studies at DePaul University, for access to his Harvard dissertation cited in Chapter 11, "Bahá'í Myths and Visions of America."

And, last but not least—for their variously personal and professional support of this project—I am indebted to the following individuals:

- Nahzy Abadi Buck—my beloved wife of 25 years—for patiently and persistently urging me, for well over a decade, to turn the course I designed and taught at Millikin University (1997–1999)—*God and Apple Pie: Visions of America's Spiritual Destiny*—into a book. I am especially indebted to Nahzy for making possible my Ph.D. (University of Toronto, 1996) and my Juris Doctor (2006) degrees—which provided the requisite skill set and acumen needed to write this book—as well as for raising two fine sons, Takur and Taraz, in a treasured family environment that made this project psychologically possible.
- Takur Buck—senior, Psychology/Pre-Med, University of Pittsburgh—for his steadfast encouragement, for his moral and stalwart religious support, and for the model of manly determination and academic discipline that he exemplifies.
- Taraz Buck—3rd-year Ph.D. student, Ph.D. candidate, Computational Biology, Carnegie Mellon University—for the sunshine of his intermittent interest, for his occasional technical troubleshooting in the inevitable computing jams I would find myself in, and for his model of academic achievement that continues to amaze me.
- Jason Buck—3rd-year student, Computer Science, University of Alaska, and my son—for his virtual and welcome interest as well.
- Victor Pribanic—senior partner of Pribanic & Pribanic (the law firm where I work as an associate attorney) in White Oak and one of Pennsylvania's most respected medical malpractice trial lawyers—for his "out of the box" mentorship and for his empowering encouragement, both professionally and personally.
- My students at Michigan State University—who enrolled in my *Religious Myths of America* course in fall 2003 and spring 2004—for their intrinsic interest, beyond grades, in the subject matter of the course itself; for their uncanny, critical questions; for their creative, multimedia group presentations; and for their engaged and lively discussions.

Christopher Buck
Pittsburgh, Pennsylvania

CHAPTER 1

America: Nation and Notion

Nations provoke fantasy.

—Lauren Gail Berlant (1991)[1]

America is not a geographic so much as a visionary concept and entity.
—Kevin Lewis (1999)[2]

Any vital myth does not hide in the hinterland of a "realm of ideas" but impinges upon the life of a people as a spring of their action. To give serious attention to the myth of American destiny in its various forms is to heed the concrete courses of action that are excited by it and that in turn affect it.
—Conrad Cherry (1998)[3]

This book is about an unusual *religious* topic: the United States of America ("America"), past and present. "America" is, at once, nation and notion, country and creed, republic and rhetoric, entity and ideology, sovereignty and salience. In other words, "America" is real and abstract. There are *secular* ideas about America, and then there are *religious* perspectives on America. Given America's preeminent position in the world today, the present volume treats the relationship of the *supernatural* world to the world's *superpower*. In fine, this book is about *Providence* and *principle*—as these relate to America.

The proverbial idea of "God and country"—as applied to America—is presented in a wide array of religious texts that are the subject of this study. The idea of America, as a religious concept, is an intriguing social phenomenon—one that has received considerable scholarly attention in terms of American Protestantism, but yet remains to be fully explored with respect to America's other religions, which have been termed by James H. Moorhead as America's "minority faiths." The study of how minority faiths have redefined America's sense of national purpose is what *Religious Myths and Visions of America* is about.

The fact that America is presented in a somewhat novel way in this study is perhaps the main claim for the book's originality and contribution to American studies. Beyond presenting these religious views of America, an effort will be made to make sense of them. What significance, if any, do these religious ideas about America have for the twenty-first century? Patterns will be identified and compared. At a deeper level of analysis, meaningful connections will be made, and a web of significance will emerge. At the end of this book, the reader will see America in a new light.

As the epigraph above says, "Nations provoke fantasy." Myths and visions of various nations are nothing new. Throughout history, peoples have had visions of their origins, destiny, and mission, as Donald White points out: "For Romans, the worldview was a Pax Romana embodied in a divine Caesar; for Arabs, it was Islam; for Englishmen, it was the imperialism of the 'White Man's Burden'; for Soviet Russia, it was Marxist communism."[4] In much the same way, visionary "America" has served as a source of social cohesion and has imbued the country with a sense of national purpose. "America" is a word that has taken on mythic proportions.

"America" is not in the Bible, nor in the Qur'an (the holy book of Islam), nor in the vast majority of the scriptures of the great world religions. Yet "America" today pulsates with religious significance. How is that possible? This is because some religions, in the modern context, have invested America with religious significance. As a survey of religions that have attached some kind of spiritual meaning to America—that is, "a theology of America"—it is precisely this ideological and social phenomenon that has determined the selection process for which religions have been included with the scope of this study, to the exclusion of others.

Not every religion in America has a religious view of America. Such faith-communities as the Quakers, the Amish, the Seventh-day Adventists, Lutherans, Hindus, Jains, Sikhs, and Zoroastrians, to name a few, have not been represented in this book. The reason is simple: most religions do not have identifiably religious convictions about America. Those that do have been included in this book. Ten religions have been selected for their distinctive perspectives on America: (1) Native American religion (Iroquois); (2) Protestant Christianity (the Puritans); (3) Roman Catholicism; (4) Judaism (Orthodox, Conservative, Reform, and Reconstructionist); (5) The Church of Jesus Christ of Latter-day Saints (the Mormons); (6) Christian Identity (White nationalists); (7) Black Muslim (Black nationalists); (8) Islam (especially Radical Islamists and Progressive Muslims); (9) Buddhism (Tibetan and Soka Gakkai); and (10) the Bahá'í Faith. These ten religions were not chosen because of *what* they say about America, but simply because they have something to say *about* America. If more such religions come to light, then a revised and expanded edition of *Religious Myths and Visions of America* may be called for. This book therefore invites serious reflection on what it means to be an American, particularly from a religious perspective.

The selection process, in the planning stages of this book, was not easy. The ten religions privileged from study neither have the same beliefs about America nor hold those beliefs with the same degree of religious conviction. American Judaism, for instance, exemplifies what is referred to as "Jewish Americanism" or what Jonathan Sarna calls the "cult of synthesis."[5] Apart from various prayers for America, however, there is little by way of any Jewish *doctrine* regarding America. Where are actual religious doctrines regarding America to be found? Clearly, the Church of Jesus Christ of Latter-day Saints (the Mormons) and the Bahá'í Faith have clearly enunciated beliefs about the spiritual destiny of America. What most, but not all of these ten religions do share is a sense of America's mission—or the "world role" to which America should aspire.

To recapitulate, the single most important criterion for the selection of a religion for inclusion in this study is that it must have something to say about America, whether positive or negative. One would think that this would include all of the religions that have specifically American origins. In the case of the Seventh-day Adventists, which is one of the most successful of America's indigenous religions, a conscious effort has been made by Adventists to distance the religion from any hint of American religious nationalism: "In Adventism, the American dream is reinterpreted; in Mormonism, Christianity is reinterpreted. Adventists have become un-American in an effort to be more truly American."[6] The result was a decidedly dark apocalyptic vision of America—a vision that, theoretically speaking, is germane and otherwise within the scope of this book. For instance, one Adventist, in 1851, interpreted the "two horns like a lamb"—a description of the Beast in Revelation 13—as denoting "the civil and religious power of this nation [America]—its Republican civil power, and its Protestant ecclesiastical power."[7] American religious power was viewed as corrupt for having instituted Sunday rather than Saturday Sabbath, which is a central issue considering the Sabbatarianism that has indelibly stamped Adventist identity.

Very late in the writing of this book, the author came across this dissertation: Dawn L. Hutchinson, "Antiquity and Social Reform: Religious Experience in the Unification Church, Feminist Wicca and the Nation of Yahweh" (2007).[8] But it was really far too late to include these religions in the present volume. Therefore, a very brief mention will be made here of their respective visions of America. "The Unification Church," Hutchinson relates, "offered a way to purify the morally corrupt American society and the rest of the world through perfected families." [9] The Unification Church's vision of America was most optimistic in 1976, when America was celebrating the bicentennial of the Declaration of Independence: "[Rev. Sun Myung] Moon saw the celebration of the bicentennial of America as an opportunity to stress the providential destiny of America." [10]

"Feminist Wicca," Hutchinson continues, "proposed a vision of a peaceful American society in which women and men shared power equally." [11] "The Nation of Yahweh," says the author regarding this separatist religion, "meant . . . to wage a war against the white establishment in the United States, one action at a time, dismantling the power structure of the persecutors of African-Americans." [12]

In *Myths America Lives By,* Richard T. Hughes, a Distinguished Professor of Religion and the Director of the Center for Faith and Learning at Pepperdine University, presents five foundational myths of America: (1) the Myth of the Chosen Nation; (2) the Myth of Nature's Nation; (3) the Myth of the Christian Nation; (4) the Myth of the Millennial Nation, and (5) the Myth of the Innocent Nation. [13] These are powerful social myths that have largely shaped mainstream American identity. Moreover, these fives myths are predominantly representative of what may be called the Protestant master myth of America. Indeed, both Hughes himself and the writer of the foreword, Robert Bellah, write from a decidedly *Christian* perspective: "Richard Hughes writes as a Christian and so do I." [14] These foundational myths form what is called American civil religion, which may be defined as follows:

American civil religion is an institutionalized set of beliefs about the nation, including a faith in a transcendent deity who will protect and guide the United States as long as its people and government abide by his laws. The virtues of liberty, justice, charity, and personal integrity are all pillars of this religion and lend a moral dimension to its public decision-making processes quite different from the realpolitik that presumably underlies the calculations of states not equally favored by divine providence. American civil religion is clearly an offshoot of the Judeo-Christian tradition, but it is not confined to conventional denominational categories. [15]

While *Myths America Lives By* is a framing statement about American civil religion, the present volume treats a wider array of myths of America. The Native American, Protestant, Catholic, Jewish, Mormon, Christian Identity, Black Muslim, traditional Muslim, Buddhist, and Bahá'í religions each has its own special metaphorics (ideating images) of "the American experiment." These are communicated through religious *myths* and *visions* of America.

At the outset, it is important to define what is meant by religious "myths" by defining what myths are *not*. For our purposes, myths are not merely "tall tales" or travesties of truth. Rather, religious myths are tapestries into which the woof of social truths are woven into the warp of sacred narrative. In other words, religious myths are spiritual and social ideals are enshrined in narrative form. A religious myth, if not literally true, can therefore be called a "true lie." This is because the function of storytelling is not to rehearse *historical fact,* but to convey *spiritual truth.* Just as Aesop's fables each had a "moral" to the story, religious myths are vehicles of moral values. This accords with Peter D. Salins's definition: "Myths are not mere fantasies or untruths. Myths are exaggerated or simplified representations of human traits and situations, paradigms of society and morality, that are based on some underlying truth." [16]

The "myth of America" exists in a variety of forms. Closely associated with the "myth of America" is a sense of national purpose, or "mission." Historically, the dominant myth of America has been the Protestant "master myth" of America. For instance, there were two biblical motifs that formed the historic taproot of America's sense of destiny: America's identification with ancient Israel and the Kingdom of God.[17] Beginning with the Puritans, the Protestant mission in America was to *colonize,* to *Christianize,* and to *civilize.* The Puritans have vanished, but vestiges of the religious meaning that they invested in America persist to this day. These religious visions of America, and the ideals that they enshrine, are part of a process that may be thought of as *the symbolic construction of America.* The idea of America has been summed up in this succinct statement:

> America's sense of itself always had a self-conscious, even ideological, side. First, the United States, founded by a rebellion against legitimate authority, had to explain and justify that rebellion to mankind. Then, the growing nation had to justify taking over a continent from its previous owners. Finally, it had to persuade the immigrants arriving on that continent that, in assimilating to the American nation, they were not being false to themselves, that Americanism was in some sense a universal creed to which all could be admitted.[18]

Common to most of these religious visions of America is some sort of belief in "God and country." Any belief that links God with America can rightly be called a "theology of America." Dean Hoge was the first to coin the neologism, "theology of America." [19] And so a religiously inspired perspective on America is typically a "theology of America," although this would certainly not hold true for a nontheistic religion like Buddhism. Thus, except for nontheistic religions such as Buddhism, religious views of America may generally be described as "theologies of America," as Hoge explains:

"Any living religious community has theological views about many things, and these things include the nation. In America such views might be called 'theology of America.' " [20]

Obviously, there is no single religious idea or "theology of America." Just as there are different religions in America, so there are sundry religious visions of America. By presenting a range of religious perspectives on America, this book invites serious reflection on what it means to be an American. However, it is not enough merely to catalog these views on America. It is important to make sense of them as well. And in order to make sense of competing ideas about America, one may ask if these ideas reflect any *patterns*. If so, can these patterns be explained? This is where comparative method generally comes into play. This is a challenge since there is no well-defined "method" to follow, as Americanist Donald White points out: "The study of social myth has lacked coherent method." [21] Notwithstanding, the lack of consensus on method should not deter such a study from being undertaken. Often, the topic under study—and the questions that interrogate it—suggest an approach and method that intrinsically arise out of the very subject matter itself. That is the case in the present study.

In a word, America was founded on religious ideals and continues to be reshaped by them. The reader will discover that some of today's minority religions offer fresh ideas about America that enrich our understanding of the significance of America today, particularly as regards its place in the world today. To the extent that the minority faiths, as presented in this study, offer new ideas regarding America, one can say that *religions remythologize America*. In order to appreciate this concept of remythologizing, it will be necessary to relate minority religious visions of America to the Protestant "master myth" of America.

CIVIL MYTHS OF AMERICA AND CIVIL RELIGION

The *notion* of a nation is *nationalism*. American nationalism is an idealization of the character of America. The "idea of America"—to use academic parlance—has taken on mythic proportions. America has a national mythology, anchored in history but embellished by idealization. That mythic idealization has played a formative and sustaining role in "the construction of American nationhood." [22] Just as the American national character changes over time, as a function of social change, so do America's myths and symbols. Thus the late Canadian Americanist Sacvan Bercovitch wrote of "transformations in the symbolic construction of America." [23]

Nationalism and religion often combine to form religious nationalism, which typically takes on mythic proportions. "Religious nationalism is the fusion of nationalism and religion such that they are inseparable," according to Barbara-Ann J. Rieffer.[24] "It is a community of religious people or the political movement of a group of people heavily influenced by religious beliefs who aspire to be politically self-determining."[25] Religious nationalism can make great use of myth. "Myth is the primary language of historical memory," writes Richard Slotkin, "a body of traditional stories that have, over time, been used to summarize the course of our collective history and to assign ideological meanings to that history."[26] Political theorist George Schöpflin treats myths as an element in the formation and maintenance of national identities, America being no exception. National myths function on both personal and social levels, according to Schöpflin, "so that individuals may construct their identities as individuals and simultaneously as members of a community."[27]

Nationalism incorporates myth.[28] Just as nationalism is an invented doctrine, so are myths. Myths are "true lies." The "lies" are the tall tales that myths tell, while mythic "truths" are the social precepts these tales convey. In other words, myths are fictions that serve as vehicles of truth. From this perspective, Mary Fulbrook states that "myths are stories which are not necessarily true, nor even believed to be true, but which have symbolic power."[29] Anthony D. Smith states that, "Modern nationalism can be seen in part as deriving from powerful, external, and premodern traditions, symbols, and myths, which are then taken up and recast in the nationalist ideologies of national mission and destiny as these emerge in the crucible of modernization"; Smith even speaks of "a symbiosis and even a fusion between the earlier religious myths and the nationalist ideal."[30] That symbolic power reinforces national ideology and thus national identity. As mythographer William Doty states: "Myths provide 'charters' insofar as they justify and exemplify the social order."[31] Myths capture social truths. While those truths are not the whole truth, they are the truths of a whole people.

Civil myths of America often have a religious dimension, reflecting a fusion of "God and country." Their hybridization has been noted by Anthony D. Smith.[32] Smith argues that nationalism "draws much of its passion, conviction and intensity from the belief in a national mission and destiny; and this belief in turn owes much to a powerful religious myth of ethnic election."[33] America, broadly speaking, has its myths of origin, myths of mission, and myths of destiny—the "master myth" being the collective Protestant myth of America, most famously secularized as American exceptionalism.[34] Thus one can speak of religious visions of America as a species of national myth. Traditionally, Protestant myths of America have served as the stained-glass windows of national ideals. They form a master myth of American destiny.[35] Protestant visions of America are a hybrid of religious and national myth, combining to form what has been termed "American civil religion."[36]

Sociologist Dean Hoge has outlined three basic civil visions of America, the first two of which originate in American Protestantism. The first vision of America is that of a model nation, a Puritan vision that "focused on making America an example to the world, a model society to show all the world what a godly and free nation can be." [37] The second vision "saw America as a chosen people with an obligation to work actively in the world to win others to American principles and to safeguard those principles everywhere." [38] Although weak at first, this vision was the direct precursor of the doctrine of Manifest Destiny: "It was clearly stated in the doctrine of Manifest Destiny, that America's destiny was to settle the whole continent—and later, to bring freedom and civilization to all peoples." [39] Hoge also notes that this "activistic vision" of America "was a motivating source of the world Christian mission movement and of American expansionism in the late nineteenth century" in that "America would save the world for Christ or for democracy." [40] "A third vision of America's mission," Hoge goes on to say, "calls for internationalism based not on messianic ideas but on a posture of openness and cooperation, assuming that others have legitimate interests and identities and equally valid perceptions of truth." [41] Hoge connects this third ideal with Robert Bellah's ideal of a "world civil religion" [42]—a concept that the present writer will expand on in the "Conclusion" (Chapter 12). Examples of each of these three basic types of religious and civil visions of America appear throughout this book.

RELIGIOUS MYTHS AND VISIONS OF AMERICA

Sociofunctionalism recognizes the fact that myths convey social and moral values. In the same vein, one may define a "religious myth of America" as an *"idealized narrative exemplifying key precepts and practices."* This is true insofar as the myth incorporates and conveys social values in an effective way. When a story is told, a truth is told. A narrative that is *descriptive in form* may be *prescriptive in function.*

America's national myth has Puritan origins, and religion has helped shape American identity ever since. A prime example is the doctrine of Manifest Destiny (the right of America to *conquer, colonize, and Christianize* the continent of North America). Nearly every American student learns of "Manifest Destiny" [43]—the American imperial myth. Manifest Destiny is the doctrine that Euro-Americans had a God-given right to conquer and colonize North America, and eventually to civilize and imperialize Hawaii, Cuba, Puerto Rico, Guam, and the Philippines. Manifest Destiny is a salient theme in American history that runs through the Indian Wars, the Mexican-American War, the Spanish-American War, the wars across the Arc of Rimland Asia, and beyond.

The present study treats religious *myths* and religious *visions* as complementary categories. The two typically go together. There is certainly overlap between religious myths and religious visions of America. Such myths, as previously said, are *descriptive in form* yet may be *prescriptive in function*. These myths are *thought-orienting,* whereas visions of America are typically *action-orienting.* That is to say, such visions are prescriptive in both form and function.

The Protestant myth of America—which has long reigned as America's master myth—is arguably being reshaped by religious visions of America held by minority faiths, as historian James Moorhead has suggested: "But the point is that minority faiths themselves played no small part in the weakening of white Protestant hegemony. Their creativity in adapting and reinterpreting the symbols of American destiny broadened the framework of discourse within which citizens explained national identity." [44] While the religious "master myth" of America is Protestant, this myth is being improvised upon by alternative myths of America held by religious minorities, who have altered America's religious landscape, and by Protestants themselves. The question is *how?* How have minority religions dealt with the Protestant myth of America? First, according to Moorhead, minority faiths strove to understand the meaning of America and their place in it. Second, minority faiths could turn ideas originally derived from Protestantism to their own uses. Third, minority religions and the Protestant mainstream engaged in a complex pattern of contests and negotiations as together they redefined American identity. Minority religious visions of America have thus broadened—and continue to reshape—American identity.

A study in the new religious dimensions of American identity is one whose time has come. The myths and visions of America, as held by minority faiths covered in this volume, are productive of a view of America that is essentially reactive to the Protestant mything of America. These competing myths of America have been as undertheorized as they have been inadequately surveyed and compared.

RACIAL MYTHS AND VISIONS OF AMERICA

Perhaps the most salient theme among these minority myths of America is that of race. Indeed, the theme of race stands out as a defining feature of these visions and myths. In a sense, this was already predicted by David Wills, who has suggested that the "central themes" of American religious history are pluralism, Puritanism, and the encounter of black and white. [45]

The process of racializing and redefining race affords a prime example of this flux in American identity and religious thought over time. Although not useful as a biological category, race has operated and still does operate as a central determinant of social identity. According to Paul Harvey, Christianity was a major catalyst in racializing America: "Christianity necessarily was central to the process of *racializing* peoples—imposing categories of racial hierarchies upon groups of humanity or other societies." [46] One may say that religions in America have dealt with racial categories in various ways. This is really a modern phenomenon, and one that is refracted in various religious communities as an epiphenomenon of the whole notion of "race." For purely illustrative purposes, while disclaiming any attempt to essentialize religions, certain patterns with respect to American religions and race begin to fall into focus once their respective visions of America are studied and then compared. On comparative grounds, therefore, one may venture the following "operative hypotheses," to be elucidated, tested, and refined throughout the course of this book.

Tentatively, one may say that Protestant Christianity had set a racial agenda during the colonial period. At the risk of oversimplifying, American Protestantism—by rationalizing and institutionalizing slavery in the South, and by formulating opposing rationale in the North—set the stage for racial ideologies that had social consequences of world-historical proportions. To this history and its persisting legacy, minority faiths have tended to "react" to the problem of race in their own ways. As for the minority faiths surveyed in this book, the Nation of Islam has idiosyncratically racialized America by mythologizing Blacks as "original" and thus superior. Equally as idiosyncratically as well as invidiously, Christian Identity has racialized America by mythologizing Whites as racially "pure" and thus superior. The Mormons have racialized America by mythologizing Native Americans as transplanted Whites, but since darkened, and Blacks as once cursed, but now eligible for priesthood (males). However, since 1978, the Church of Jesus Christ of Latter-day Saints has now adopted a much more egalitarian stance. And the Bahá'í Faith has reacted to a racialized America by representing race as America's most challenging issue, the solution to which is to harmonize the races and thus ultimately deracialize America. Egalitarianism continues to act as an equalizing force, and religions are increasingly playing a role in overcoming the problems that historically resulted from the influence of racial doctrines, as religiously rationalized.

An operative thesis may be ventured in the chapters to follow: Over the course of American history, religious myths and visions of America tend to reflect an ever-changing American civil society, whether as a *function* of its social evolution or as a *catalyst* of it. That is to say, in the survey of religions undertaken in this book, the following operative hypothesis may be tested: *Religions remythologize America.* And further: *Religions re-envision America.*

CHAPTER 2

Native American Myths and Visions of America

A voluntary Union entered into by the Colonies themselves, I think, would be preferable to one impos'd by [the British] Parliament. . . . It would be a very strange Thing, if Six Nations [the Iroquois Confederacy] of ignorant Savages should be capable of forming a Scheme for such an Union [of the American colonies], and be able to execute it in such a Manner, as that it has subsisted Ages, and appears indissoluble; and yet that a like Union should be impracticable for ten or a Dozen English Colonies, to whom it is more necessary, and must be more advantageous; and who cannot be supposed to want an equal Understanding of their Interests.

—Benjamin Franklin (1750)[1]

The first New World democracy, as alluded to by Benjamin Franklin in the epigraph above, was the Iroquois Confederacy—a consensus-based system of governance established by Deganawidah and Hiawatha (whether during the eclipse of 1142 or 1451[2]), who will be discussed further in this chapter. Among the other "firsts" attributable to Native Americans, the first visions of America were those of Native American visionaries and culture heroes. This only makes sense: the first religious mythologies of America, in which a view of the land was not yet called "America," were originated and handed down by Native Americans. Of these, the Iroquois (or *Haudenosaunee*)[3] myths and visions of America are as representative as they are preeminent. They are also arguably foundational, in the sense that Iroquois civilization gave rise to the first New World democracy.

THE TURTLE ISLAND MYTH AND THE MYTH OF "MOTHER EARTH"

Before America became "America," one of the original names for North America was "Turtle Island." Historically, "Turtle Island" probably designated the region of the Northeast United States and contiguous territories in nearby Canada. While the geographical reference is real, the name itself, "Turtle Island," is mythical. Today, the myth of Turtle Island is universally familiar to all Native Americans, but not to most non-Native Americans. Nevertheless, the idea of Turtle Island (but not necessarily knowledge of the myth itself) is becoming increasing familiar to the American public. Turtle Island is now part of American popular culture. Once exclusive to Native American folklore, the myth of Turtle Island has now been assimilated as a part of American folklore. Understandably, it is the idea or the metaphor of Turtle Island that has taken root in American popular culture, rather than the story itself. To supplement this lack of common awareness as to the underlying narrative itself, the myth may be generally described as follows.

Of the Founding Fathers, Thomas Jefferson (1743–1826), third president of the United States (1801–1809), was certainly aware of the original vision of America as Turtle Island. On January 10, 1802, Thomas Jefferson told a delegation of Wyandot, Ottawa, Chippewa, Powtewatamie, and Shawanese chiefs: "Your blood will mix with ours, and will spread, with ours, over this great island." [4] The expression, "this great island" was not an appellation for America current among Euro-Americans. In other words, it was definitely *not* a widely used euphemism for the United States. One must look elsewhere for the meaning of this term and for whatever allusions it likely evoked in the minds of the audience. Here, Thomas Jefferson, in ostensibly encouraging fraternity (and even intermarriage) between the Creeks and the Euro-Americans, was evidently referring to Turtle Island. To this day, in fact, virtually all Iroquois still call North America "Turtle Island," as do most, if not all, Indian Nations. While certainly not the case in Jefferson's day, the Turtle Island myth is one of the best known of all Native American myths. And the myth of Turtle Island is closely aligned with the concept of "Mother Earth."

"Turtle Island" is an Edenic narrative about the origin of a sacred land, whether part or all of North America. A standard Eastern Woodland creation myth, the story of Turtle Island is the Iroquois' foundation myth. It is "history" in the form of a "story." It is a Haudenosaunee origin story—and perhaps the original religious myth of America. It has been a widespread myth practically from its exception. Historically, the basic elements of this myth are common to the Iroquis and Algonquin Nations of the Northeast, among others, such as the Tuskegee and Blackfoot, as well as the Inuit and the Athabascans of the Arctic and the Far North.

The Turtle Island myth is a variation of what anthropologists have termed "the Earth Diver Creation" myth, found throughout the eastern region of North America and even in California. The story of the Earth Diver is a common theme in North American Indian creation mythology, in which land is first formed from a mere handful of mud taken from the ocean floor by a heroic animal spirit that must dive to great depths for it. After the animal spirit succeeds in extracting this mud from the sea bed, the sediment itself is transformed into an island—land that emerges from the primordial deep. In an article that is now considered a classic, Gladys A. Reichard has provided an analysis and a study of the diffusion and distribution of the Earth Diver myth. She cites documented versions of this myth from the ethnographies of a considerable range of Indian nations.[5]

Of all of these variations on the same basic myth, the Iroquois myth of Turtle Island itself exists in some 25 versions. These versions, notwithstanding their variants, share a core of nine essential elements: (1) Sky Woman, who dwells in the Sky World, becomes mysteriously pregnant; (2) in jealous outrage, her husband uproots the Tree of Light, the *axis mundis* of the Sky World; (3) and casts down Sky Woman, who plummets through the vasty space, her fall cushioned by birds, and who lands on the back of a giant Tortoise, swimming atop the primal sea; (4) after taking council, the animal spirits dive to wrest mud from the ocean floor, and the precious sediment is brought to the surface; (5) this generative soil is then transplanted on Turtle's back, and burgeons into a vast island; (6) Sky Woman's daughter begets twins, Good Minded and Evil Minded; (7) as an Iroquois culture hero, Good Minded liberates animals pent up by Evil Minded and then secures corn; (8) the Good Twin and the Evil Twin engage in a cosmic duel, an archetypal battle fought with deadly weapons—rushes or maize versus flint or antler; and, finally (9) Good Minded vanquishes Evil Minded, who is banished, while Sky Woman and Good Minded return to the Sky World, promising to return on the last day of the world.[6] The first five elements of the core narrative may be summarized in more detail as follows.

(1) *The Sky World:* The original forebears of the Iroquois were the sky People. They dwelled in *Karionake,* "The Place in the Sky," otherwise known as the Sky World. The Sky World was a physical place that floated among the stars. The Sky World was the celestial prototype of Iroquoia, with the same geography. The familiar flora and fauna had their spiritual counterparts in the Sky World. There is a good reason for this: "The bedrock assumption of eastern cultures is that everything that exists, exists by halves. The cosmos is seen as naturally dividing into its two, complementary parts—sky and Earth—which interact for harmony." [7] As above, so below.

There may be another principle at work in this myth as well. Consider the fact that the social order of the Sky World greatly resembled later Iroquois society.[8] Here, one clearly sees *cosmogony as sociogony*—that is, the Iroquois creation cycle is not so much an account of the creation of the physical world as it is an account of the establishment of Iroquois society, of its folkways and social mores. This essential function of Iroquois myth is noted by William Nelson Fenton: "The great cosmological myth spells out the duties that each was assigned to perform for the benefit of humankind; it tells how the first human beings on earth learned to adjust to the situation as they found it, and how they responded to crises later on." [9] Fenton's insight here is specific to the myth itself; it is not generalized to all myth. But, on comparative grounds, the function of cosmogony as sociogony can be seen as fairly universal. In other words, accounts of the creation of the physical world from primeval chaos are representations of the functioning of ordered societies as bulwarks against social chaos.

(2) *Uprooting of the Tree of Light:* In the center of the Sky World was a sacred Tree. Atop the tree was a luminous orb that gave off light, illumining the Sky World. In the Onondaga version, this tree was called "Tooth," possibly alluding to the yellow dog-tooth violet. This light was soft, not harsh. Its light was not bright, but resembling twilight, with the half-light of dawn or dusk. The sacred Councils of the Sky World were held beneath the branches of Tooth. Without rehearsing the details of how she became pregnant, Sky Woman's pregnancy aroused the jealous outrage of her husband, the Keeper of the Tree of Light. In blind rage, he uproots the great Tooth, which creates a gaping cavity. Through this giant hole, the husband casts Sky Woman into the chasm of the world below.

(3) *Sky Woman Falls to Earth:* While Sky Woman was hurtling through the abyss toward the primeval sea below, the Sky People set Tooth, the Tree of Light, back into its place. Plunging precipitously without protection, Sky Woman was in great peril. As she hurtled through the mid-space between earth and sky, Heron and Loon came to her rescue. By interlocking their wings, they nestled Sky Woman in their feathery embrace and gently carried her as she descended to the world below. However, since that world was covered in water, there was no place to live, no land on which to hunt or cultivate. Without intervention, Sky Woman would not be able to survive.

(4) *Animals Dive to Bring Earth to the Surface:* Meanwhile, a giant turtle swam the primal seas. Alive to the danger that Sky Woman faced, the Great Tortoise summoned the Elder Animals to an emergency council. He offered his carapace as a dwelling place for Sky Woman. Among the Elder Animals, the valiant few who would exert themselves in their quest to save Sky Woman included Muskrat, Otter, Toad, and/or Beaver. They each made their dives in the watery depths. Rather than diving for pearls, they were diving for grains of dirt. In order to bring up mud from the ocean floor, each of these heroic spirits risked his life. In the Mohawk version, only Muskrat succeeded in

retrieving a handful of this precious mud. But, in doing so, Muskrat sacrificed his life.

(5) *Earth Established on Turtle's Back:* The mud was then placed on Turtle's back. This spot of earth now in place, Heron and Loon could now set Sky Woman safely on her new abode below. Magically (that is, mythically), wherever Sky Woman ventured, the earth would keep spreading out before her, opening new vistas far and wide. As the land kept expanding, so every kind of plant sprouted up before her as well. This is how Turtle Island came into being.

Since this myth depicts the creation of earth, or at least the creation of an inhabitable land, one might be tempted to regard Sky Woman as an incarnation of "Mother Earth," who is described in the next section of this chapter. However, Sky Woman is not the same as Mother Earth. Perhaps she might be thought of as the *mother of Mother Earth.* This would be a logical way to harmonize what are really two disparate myths. Suffice it to say that myths lead independent lives. They can inhabit the same spiritual universe. Each myth is the bearer of its own moral and social truths. And so the Myth of "Mother Earth" really bears no formal relation with the myth of the Sky Woman. Sky Woman is Edenic. Mother Earth is environmentalist.

The Myth of "Mother Earth"

The reverential idea of "Mother Earth" has become increasingly familiar in American popular culture. "Mother Earth" embodies what might be called a "gospel of environmentalism." It is a gospel without a narrative—morally rich and ethically sound—but without discernible roots in pre-Colonial American Indian mythology. "Mother Earth" is not a person but a symbol. Furthermore, "Mother Earth" is a myth without a story—and more metaphor than myth. The essence of this myth is that Planet Earth is our collective mother. Mother Earth transcends America itself. Mother Earth has geographic boundaries, but no national borders. It is one country. Just as we should respect our own mothers, by virtue of the fact that our mothers gave birth, nourished, protected, and raised us, so also should one respect Mother Earth, who, after all, is the source of being and sustainer of all life on earth.

The myth of Mother Earth—ostensibly a venerable, pan-Indian belief—is not ancient, but modern. It appears to be largely a relatively recent invention promulgated by scholars, popularized by the American press, and further promoted by Native Americans themselves. In a quest to find the historical roots of the belief in Mother Earth, anthropologist Sam D. Gill searched over 1,300 ethnographic records. He found only three sources for a Native American belief in a Mother Earth goddess. These were the sources from which the concept of Mother Earth was largely "invented" as the product of promoting and popularizing a once-obscure idea: "It seems that Mother Earth as a major goddess of the Indians of North America is a reality, but that she has become so only during the twentieth century." [10] Thus "Mother Earth" is more of a myth *about* Native Americans than it is a myth *by* Native Americans.

If Gill is right, then here is a dramatic example of American religious myth-making, suggesting that the promotion of Mother Earth is a post-contact phenomenon.[11] Yet there is evidence that Native Americans anciently regarded the earth as a common mother. Consider, for instance, this statement by Iroquois Chief Cornstalk who, on June 1, 1776, remarked: "Our white Brethren who have grown out this same Ground with ourselves—for this Big Island being our common Mother, we and they are like one Flesh and Blood." [12] A reply, in kind, came from the American Commissioners for Indian Affairs to Delawares, Senecas, Munsees, and Mingos:

> We are sprung from one common Mother, we were all born in this big Island; we earnestly wish to repose under the same Tree of Peace with you; we request to live in Friendship with all the Indians in the Woods. . . . We call God to Witness, that we desire nothing more ardently than that the white and red Inhabitants of this big Island should cultivate the most Brotherly affection, and be united in the firmest bands of Love and friendship.[13]

What is remarkable here, from both Chief Cornstalk and the American Commissioners for Indian Affairs, is the common vocabulary, evidencing the interrelationship—indeed, the very confluence—of the myths of "Turtle Island," "Mother Earth," and "Great Tree," the last myth being the topic of the next section of this chapter.

The next section transitions from the myths of "Turtle Island" and "Mother Earth" to the legend of Deganawidah. Here, the distinction between "myth" and "legend" is that myth is ahistorical, while legend presumably has a historical kernel, overlaid by mythical embellishments.

THE DEGANAWIDAH LEGEND

> I am Dekanawidah and with the Five Nations' Confederate Lords I plant the Tree of the Great Peace. . . .
>
> I name the tree the Tree of the Great Long Leaves. Under the shade of this Tree of the Great Peace we spread the soft white feathery down of the globe thistle as seats for you, Adodarhoh, and your cousin Lords. . . .
>
> Roots have spread out from the Tree of the Great Peace, one to the north, one to the east, one to the south and one to the west. The name of these roots is The Great White Roots and their nature is Peace and Strength. . . .
>
> We place at the top of the Tree of the Long Leaves an Eagle who is able to see afar. If he sees in the distance any evil approaching or any danger threatening he will at once warn the people of the Confederacy.[14]

This famous passage comes from one of the versions of the Deganawidah Epic, which is the second of three grand cycles of tradition among the Iroquois. Traditional Iroquois history is divided into three epochs represented by three epic narratives: (1) the *myth* of Sky Woman; (2) the *legend* of Deganawidah; and (3) the *history* of Handsome Lake, the late eighteenth- and early nineteenth-century Seneca prophet. The first epic, that of Sky Woman, was presented earlier in this chapter. The Deganawidah "myth" itself is quintessentially an origin-of-government narrative. The Deganawidah epic is properly considered a "legend" in that there is a general consensus that "the Peacemaker" was a historical figure. While this legend exists in an estimated 24 recensions,[15] the most authoritative version is known as *Concerning the League,* which is said to be the original legend, or the most authoritative account, of the League of the Iroquois, otherwise known as the Iroquois Confederacy.

The Iroquois Confederacy—which began as the union of five Iroquois Nations, to which a sixth was later added, evidently included a total of ten nations at later points in history. The Iroquois "League of Nations" united the Mohawks, Onondagas, Senecas, Oneidas, and Cayugas. In 1714, the Tuscaroras were adopted and, in 1753, the Nanticokes and Tuteloes were incorporated, expanding the League into eight Nations.[16] There is evidence that the Saponi and Conoy Nations were added later, enlarging the League into ten Nations—with the Delawares being given Iroquois protection, but without formal adoption. Historian Jay Hansford Vest explains: "Although the Hodenosaunee were never referred to as the Seven, Eight, or Nine Nations following the admission of other nations, including the Tuteloes and Nanticokes, it was referenced as the Six Nations after the Tuscaroras were added to the Longhouse in 1714."[17] This League was remarkable in that it was probably the New World's first democracy. And, if not, certainly the Confederacy was the New World's preeminent and most influential democracy. Its greatest influence is said to have been its impact on the formation and structure of American democracy itself. In scholarly parlance, this idea that American democracy has roots in Iroquois democracy is called the "Iroquois influence thesis." While the Iroquois influence thesis remains controversial, even dubious, among the majority of scholars, it is a widespread belief among Native Americans. Whether the idea of Iroquois influence has merit or not, this much one knows to be true: Deganawidah was the founder of the League of the Iroquois. Deganawidah is revered in Iroquois tradition. His name is ineffable; that is, it is deemed too sacred to pronounce. Therefore, Deganawidah is commonly referred to, in oral discourse, as "the Peacemaker."

Huron by birth and Mohawk by adoption, Deganawidah was a prophet, statesman, and lawgiver who, along with his cohort and spokesman, Hiawatha, established the Iroquois "League of People of the Longhouse"

(*Haudenosaunee*), also known as the "Great League of Peace" (*Kaianere-kowa*). This League, in actual practice, was vested in a council of 50 peace chiefs, or "sachems" (a term used to distinguish these from other chiefs). Each successor to a League chief was chosen by a "clan mother" presiding over the lineage in which the title was held. The governing council required unanimous consent to render each of its decisions. The symbol of the League was the Great White Pine, or White Tree of Peace, on the top of which perched a farsighted eagle. The historicity of the League of Five Nations is not in dispute, nor is the existence and role of Deganawidah himself in the formation of the original Iroquois confederacy. The traditional legend, which survives in several versions, has variations that pose no serious challenge to the unity of the narrative. Mythic elements, of course, give the legend its charm and symbolic depth.

The story, in its basic form, is as follows: In ancient times, Tarenyawagon ("The Holder of the Heavens") saved the Five Nations from onslaught of the stone Giants. He conquered monsters and put the world in order. He gave laws for men to follow, taught the art of war, and provided for good fishing. Over time, the five tribes had a disagreement, and went their separate ways. Among the ancestors a child was born to a Huron virgin near the Bay of Quinte near Kingston, Ontario. This child was an incarnation of Tarenyawagon, entrusted with a great mission of peace. His first task was to cure the Iroquois of rampant cannibalism and revenge warfare ("mourning wars").

Tradition holds that Deganawidah was born in what became Canada—near present-day Kingston, Ontario, on what is now the Thayendanaga or Deseronto Reservation—*circa* 1450 CE Deganawidah. The sacred name "Deganawidah" means "two river currents flowing together." [18] His mother, a virgin, was told by a heavenly messenger in a dream that the child she bore was destined to plant the Tree of Peace at Onondaga (Syracuse, New York). On reaching manhood, Deganawidah told his mother of the mission that the Great Spirit had chosen him to undertake, which was to bring the message of "Righteousness, Peace, and Power" to men, to establish peace founded upon justice, backed by force when needed to enforce law and order.

The time came for Deganawidah to set out on his mission in a canoe, carved from white stone. (This may be a "miracle" that was added later to the legend as an embellishment under putative Christian influence, because an earlier version has Deganawidah traveling in a canoe made of birch.) And so Deganawidah crossed Lake Ontario. On the far shore, he set foot in the land of the Onondagas. There he found hunters whose village had been razed. They spoke of interminable warmongering, of the indiscriminate and heartless slaughter of innocents, and of horrific cannibalism. Deganawidah then visited Djigonsasa, the Mother of Nations, who fed warriors traveling through. He told her to cease supporting the war parties, and then imparted to the Mother of Nations his gospel of Righteousness, Peace, and Power: "I carry the Mind of the Master of Life, and my message will bring an end to the wars between east and west. The word that I bring is that all peoples shall love one another and live together in peace. This message has three parts: Righteousness and Health and Power." This was a powerful Message, one that claimed to be divine.

In his first missionary journey before becoming a statesman, Deganawidah came to one cannibal's lodge, that of an Onondaga warrior. Deganawidah climbed the bark roof of the cannibal's dwelling and lay, chest down, by the smoke hole. Looking down, Deganawidah's face was reflected on the surface of the water in the kettle below. After the cannibal had brewed his grisly stew of human remains, and as the warrior was about to eat his meal from a bowl made of bark, he suddenly beheld, in the boiling kettle, a face of striking handsomeness and serenity. Having no clue that this face belonged to another, the cannibal thought he saw a reflection of himself. This gave him pause for thought. On reflection, the warrior was struck by the nobility of the visage he saw, and how brutal was the life he had been living. Then and there, the warrior decided not to eat his victim. In utter revulsion, the cannibal emptied the kettle. By the fire, he brooded.

Then Deganawidah climbed down, and entered the cannibal's dwelling. They talked. As they held converse, Deganawidah convinced the warrior that eating other men was evil and vile. Together, they buried the victim's remains. Deganawidah and the warrior hunted a deer and partook of the venison together. Deganawidah then taught the warrior the gospel of Righteousness, Peace, and Power—and won over his first convert. Together, the two made plans to embark on a mission to bring the local nations into a peaceful confederacy. Deganawidah told the warrior that the Great Spirit had ordained that antlers be worn as a sign of authority. And so the former cannibal accepted to work alongside "the Peacemaker."

The greatest obstacle to the confederacy was Atotarho, chief of the Onondagas. Powerful and primal, Atotarho was a tyrant. Hideous to behold, Atotarho's body had seven crooks in it. His hair seethed with serpents. Deganawidah then named his disciple, "Hiawatha" ("He Who Combs"), for Hiawatha's mission would be to comb the snakes out of Atotarho's hair. First, Deganawidah and Hiawatha successively won the allegiance of the Mohawks, Oneidas, Cayugas, and Senecas. This is how Deganawidah presented his Message:

Thereupon Tekanawita [Deganawidah] stood up in the center of the gathering place, and then he said: First I will answer what it means to say, "Now it is arriving, the Good Message." This, indeed, is what it means: When it stops, the slaughter of your own people who live here on earth, then everywhere peace will come about, by day and also by night, and it will come about that as one travels around, everyone will be related . . .

Now again [?], secondly I say, "Now it is arriving, the Power," and this means that the different nations, all of the nations, will become just a single one, and the Great Law will come into being, so that all now will be related to each other, and there will come to be just a single family, and in the future, in days to come, this family will continue on.

Now in turn, the other, my third saying, "Now it is arriving, the Peace," this means that everyone will become related, men and also women, and also the young people and the children, and when all are relatives, every nation, then there will be peace. . . . Then there will be truthfulness, and they will uphold hope and charity, so that it is peace that will unite all of the people, indeed, it will be as though they have but one mind, and they are a single person with only one body and one head and one life, which means that there will be unity. . . . When they are functioning, the Good Message and also the Power and the Peace, these will be the principal things everybody will live by; these will be the great values among the people.[19]

Deganawidah then led the four Nations, now united under these powerful sociomoral principles, to the powerful sorcerer-chief of the Onondaga, Atotarho. In addition to his vile appearance and tyrannical abuse of power, Atotarho was also a cannibal. In order to transform Atotarho, Deganawidah and Hiawatha sang the Peace Hymn. As the procession reached the Onondaga, Deganawidah exorcised Atotarho of his evil spirits. Atotarho then accepted the Great Law of Peace (*Gai Eneshah Go' Nah*). Now the Iroquois Confederacy could finally be established. Deganawidah and Hiawatha got Atotarho to agree to be the firekeeper of the newly formed League. Where formerly Atotarho was the principal opponent, he would now preside as its principal chief and could wield veto power at will. Furthermore, Deganawidah and Hiawatha designated Onondaga as the capital of the Five Nations' territory. After enlisting Atotarho's support, Deganawidah planted the Great Tree of Peace in what is now Syracuse, New York, thus fulfilling the dream that was given to his mother.

There, Deganawidah planted the great Tree of Peace: a great white pine with white roots extending in the four sacred directions, to guide men everywhere who desired to trace peace to its source. Atop the Tree, he placed the farsighted eagle, ever vigilant and watchful of any approaching danger. Beneath the Tree of Peace, Deganawidah opened a cavern into which he cast weapons of war. This was the culmination of his mission. No matter how visionary, resourceful, and effective, Deganawidah's work was not merely the product of enlightened statesmanship and effective diplomacy. It was a sacred undertaking. He had achieved the sacred purpose for which he was commissioned by the Great Spirit.

In solemn ceremony, Deganawidah then placed antlers on the heads of the 50 chiefs (sachems) representing the Five Nations. The respective names of each of these chiefs would be passed on to the chiefs who succeeded them). Deganawidah then delivered to the sachems the canons of the Great Law, the Constitution of the Five Nations. In assessing the historical and cultural significance of the legend of Deganawidah, Paul A. W. Wallace had this to say:

> The legend that grew up about him [Deganawidah] long served as a guide to Iroquois conduct, at home and abroad. In its various recorded versions it now appears a strange medley of religion, mythology, constitutional law, wisdom literature, animal lore, and folk custom. But the core of the narrative, which describes the practical steps taken by Dekanahwideh [*sic*], the Heavenly Messenger, to establish a firm League of Nations under the Tree of Peace, *has a grandeur of conception unsurpassed in popular tradition anywhere in the world.*[20]

To this day, the Confederacy is officially known as *Kayanerenh-kowa* ("the Great Peace"), a term that describes its sacred purpose. The League is also known as *Kanonsionni* (the "Longhouse"), a designation that describes both its constitutional structure and its geographical extent. This Longhouse is highly symbolic: Typically, the Iroquois longhouse is a dwelling built of saplings and bark, in dimensions of some 80 to 100 feet in length. Although each was within its own bark-partitioned section, several families of the same lineage occupied it. At the center of the longhouse was a hearth fire. All relatives of the extended family were under the watchful supervision of an elder matron of the lineage. By analogy, the Five Nations took counsel together in the sacred longhouse as though they were members of one family. Their meetings were actuated and guided by a pervasive sense of unity. And so it is that the social and political organization of the Five Nations is traditionally ascribed to Deganawidah.

THE IROQUOIS INFLUENCE THESIS: MYTH OR HISTORY?

The "Iroquois Influence Thesis" has been advanced by several scholars—with Donald A. Grinde and Bruce Johansen[21] in the forefront—and by segments of the popular media. As stated in the previous section, the Iroquois (a French name) or Six Nations (an English name) Confederacy (who called themselves *Haudenosaunee,* "People of the Longhouse") maintained a federal league of nations for several hundred years before Europeans arrived in their homeland. Their example was not lost on Benjamin Franklin, who cited their model approvingly about the time he proposed the Albany Plan of Union (1754), a precursor to the Articles of Confederation and U.S. Constitution. This example, along with copious use by Franklin and other U.S. Founders of the *Haudenosaunee* and other Native people as exemplars of liberty, have led to a pointed debate in our own time over their role in the evolution of democracy on a worldwide scale. Advocates insist that this example should be studied in the context of other influences, while opponents often argue that the Iroquois are being incorrectly advanced as a singular example. The Iroquois influence thesis holds that the Iroquois Confederacy, founded by Deganawidah, helped shape American democracy. More to the point, the Iroquois influence thesis asserts that the U.S. Constitution was partially modeled on the Iroquois Constitution. As the reader might expect, this thesis has sparked a vigorous scholarly debate. On what evidence is the Iroquois influence thesis based?

While it was the product of Constitutional Convention in 1787, the U.S. Constitution itself evolved from earlier constitutional agreements. A key figure in that process was Benjamin Franklin, who was greatly impressed by the Iroquois Confederacy. Franklin's advocacy of the League as a prospective model of governance begins with a speech by an Iroquois notable, which Franklin published. In 1742, at the council of Lancaster (Pennsylvania), colonists succeeded in gaining the friendship of the Iroquois, and agreed to treaty. Two years later, in confirming their treaty, the colonists were advised by Canassatego, an Iroquois chief of the Six Nations and one of the 50 sachems of the League, to unite. On Friday, July 4, 1744, in his closing speech, Canassatego recommended that British colonists form a union based on the League of the Iroquois:

> WE have one Thing further to say, and that is, We heartily recommend Union and a good Agreement between you our Brethren. Never disagree, but preserve a strict Friendship for one another, and thereby you, as well as we, will become the stronger.
>
> OUR wise Forefathers established Union and Amity between the Five Nations; this has made us formidable; this has given us great Weight and Authority with our neighbouring Nations.
>
> WE are a powerful Confederacy; and, by your observing the same Methods our wise Forefathers have taken, you will acquire fresh strength and Power; therefore whatever befals you, never fall out one with another.[22]

The official name of the treaty concluded at Lancaster was *A Treaty Held at the Town of Lancaster, By the Honourable the Lieutenant Governor of the Province, and the Honourable the Commissioners for the Province of Virginia and Maryland, with the Indians of the Six Nations in June, 1744.*[23] Both the Treaty and Canassatego's speech were published by Benjamin Franklin.

In 1751, Franklin wrote to James Parker, his New York City printing partner, with this comment on the Iroquois League:

> It would be a very strange Thing, if six Nations of Ignorant Savages should be capable of forming a Scheme for such an Union, and be able to execute it in such a Manner, as that it has subsisted Ages, and appears indissoluble; and yet that a like Union should be impracticable for ten or a Dozen English Colonies, to whom it is more necessary, and must be more advantageous; and who cannot be supposed to want an equal Understanding of their Interests.[24]

Although Franklin called the Iroquois "Ignorant Savages," let us see what he really meant by this term:

> SAVAGES we call them, because their manners differ from ours, which we think the Perfection of Civility; they think the same of theirs. . . . Having frequent Occasions to hold public Councils, they have acquired great Order and Decency in conducting them. . . . He that would speak, rises. The rest observe a profound Silence. When he has finished and sits down, they leave him five or six Minutes to recollect, that if he has omitted anything he intended to say, or has anything to add, he may rise again and deliver it. To interrupt another, even in common Conversation, is reckoned highly indecent. How different this from the Conduct of a polite British House of Commons, where scarce a Day passes without some Confusion that makes the Speaker hoarse in calling *to order;* and how different from the mode of Conversation in many polite Companies of Europe, where if you do not deliver your Sentence with great Rapidity, you are cut off in the middle of it by the impatient Loquacity of those you converse with, and never suffer'd to finish it.[25]

Following the Declaration of Independence in 1776, the fledgling Republic was governed by the Articles of Confederation. It is here that the Iroquois influence thesis finds its greatest claim, because the Articles were based on an earlier document, known as the Albany Plan of Union. In 1754, Benjamin Franklin formalized his 1751 recommendation to James Parker in the "Albany Plan of Union," which was an important precursor to the U.S. Constitution. Franklin proposed the Albany Plan of Union as a model of governance under which the colonies might be united.

The Albany Congress was held from June 19 to July 10, 1754. As the name indicates, the Congress was held in Albany, New York. Benjamin Franklin was the most influential of the delegates present. Besides Franklin's presence and prestige, several Iroquois attended the Congress as well. Among these was a certain "Hendrick" (known as "Tiyanoga" among the Iroquois), who served as one of the principal representatives of the Six Nations at the Albany Congress.

Prior to leaving Philadelphia to attend the Congress in Albany, besides gaining the support of the leading political figures of his day, Franklin saw the need to rally public opinion behind his Plan for Union. He published an article, datelined Philadelphia, May 9, 1954, in his newspaper, the *Pennsylvania Gazette,* urging the need for a union of the colonies and pointing to the fact that "our enemies have the great advantage of being under one direction, with one council, and one purse." This is a transparent reference to the Iroquois Confederacy. In a historic moment in journalist history, Benjamin Franklin illustrated the article by printing a political cartoon: a woodcut of a snake segmented into parts, representing the colonies, with the motto beneath: "JOIN OR DIE." This motto, "Join or Die," was used again to launch the American Revolution.[26]

Franklin began his Plan of Union proposal with this recommendation: "1. That the said General Government be administered by a President General, to be appointed and Supported by the Crown; and a Grand Council, to be Chosen by the Representatives of the People of the Several Colonies, met in their respective Assemblies."[27] Proponents of the Iroquois influence thesis hold that Franklin's Plan of Union was loosely modeled on the Iroquois Confederacy. His proposed "Grand Council" was similar to the Iroquois Great Council, with 48 representatives, close to the 50 sachems of Iroquois. In fact, James de Lancy, acting governor of New York, expressed to those assembled his hope that there would emerge an agreement to form a union of states as powerful and prominent as the Iroquois League itself.[28]

While Franklin's proposal was approved by the Albany Congress, the Albany Plan of Union was not ratified by the colonial legislatures. Thus it never took effect. While Franklin's Plan was not ratified, it later served as the basis for the Articles of Confederation, which was, as mentioned earlier, a precursor to the U.S. Constitution. Thus, the Albany Plan of Union was a significant milestone in the evolution of the U.S. Constitution. At that stage in the events leading up to the adoption of the Constitution, Iroquois influence was arguably present. The debate is over just how influential that Iroquois presence really was.

Even if the Iroquois influence thesis is a myth without historical foundation, this myth has influenced the Congress of the United States of America. Indeed, the fact that the Iroquois influence myth has enjoyed popular support is reflected in a Congressional resolution, passed in 1988. On September 16, 1987, Senator Daniel Inouye (D-Hawaii) introduced S.Con.Res. 76. On July 11, 1988, similar legislation was introduced by Representative Morris Udall (D-Arizona) in the House of Representatives as H.Con.Res. 331. On October 4, 1988, the House passed H.Con.Res. 331—*A concurrent resolution to acknowledge the contribution of the Iroquois Confederacy of Nations to the development of the United States Constitution and to reaffirm the continuing government-to-government relationship between Indian tribes and the United States established in the Constitution*—by a vote of 408–8. By voice vote, the Senate agreed to H.Con.Res. 331 on October 21, 1988. That resolution reads, in part:

> Whereas the original framers of the Constitution, including, most notably, George Washington and Benjamin Franklin, are known to have greatly admired the concepts of the six Nations of the Iroquois Confederacy; Whereas, the Confederation of the original Thirteen Colonies into one republic was influenced by the political system developed by the Iroquois Confederacy as were many of the democratic principles which were incorporated into the Constitution itself; . . . *Resolved by the House of Representatives (the Senate concurring)*, That— (1) the Congress, on the occasion of the two hundredth anniversary of the signing of the United States Constitution, acknowledges contribution made by the Iroquois Confederacy and other Indian Nations to the formation and development of the United States.[29]

In 2007, U.S. Representative Joe Baca and U.S. Senator Daniel Inouye, respectively, introduced H.R. 3585 and S. 1852 to the House and Senate, to wit: *Native American Heritage Day Act of 2007,* "A bill to designate the Friday after Thanksgiving of each year as 'Native American Heritage Day' in honor of the achievements and contributions of Native Americans to the United States." This proposed legislation, in its current draft, acknowledges the contribution of the Iroquois League of Nations. This draft resolution reads, in part: "Congress finds that . . . the Founding Fathers based the provisions of the Constitution on the unique system of democracy of the six Nations of the Iroquois Confederacy, which divided powers among the branches of government and provided for a system of checks and balances."[30]

Here, to invoke the words of one historian commenting on eighteenth-century history, "the mystique of Iroquois unity and power had taken on a life of its own."[31] The Iroquois influence myth has indeed taken on a life of its own, as the Congressional resolution clearly illustrates. As one scholar notes: "Despite the highly speculative nature of the evidence, this misconception has become a shibboleth, one which has been given even the official imprimatur of the United States Senate (United States Congress, Senate Resolution No. 76 [Washington, DC: U.S.G.P.O., 1988])."[32]

The Iroquois influence thesis, in the estimation of one authority, "has become a revisionist narrative about the birth of the United States."[33] The purpose of this revisionist theory is that it allows for a multicultural understanding of how America came to be the republic that it is today. Whether revisionist or not, the "Iroquois Influence Thesis" represents a Native American vision of America. To the extent that the Great Spirit had commissioned

Deganawidah to establish the Iroquois League, then this revisionist vision of America has a religious dimension in addition to its primarily secular application. And to the extent that the Iroquois influence thesis has succeeded in gaining considerable popular support—as well as limited support in the Academy (that is, among a minority of scholars) and in Congress—then it has exerted its own influence on mainstream America.

To conclude, this chapter has treated Native American religious visions of America in four dimensions. It is safe to say that the myth of "Turtle Island" and "Mother Earth," as well as the Deganawidah legend and the "Iroquois Influence Thesis," have taken their rightful place in American popular culture, in the halls of Congress, and in the ivory tower of the Academy itself.

CHAPTER 3

Protestant Myths and Visions of America

Wee shall be as a Citty upon a Hill, the Eies of all people are uppon us.
—John Winthrop (1630)[1]

In the beginning was the word, "America," and the word was in the Bible, and the word was made flesh in the Americans, this new breed of humans, destined to build a shining city upon a hill.
—Sacvan Bercovitch (1982)[2]

Native American visions of America were succeeded by Protestant visions of America. Turtle's Back gave way to Plymouth Rock. The founding myths of America, therefore, are Puritan in particular and Protestant in general. These myths are as enduring as they were originative. Until recently, Protestant visions held sway as the dominant "master myth" of America. Essentially, the Protestant quest for a Christian America gave rise to a Protestant nationalism that united the dominant Protestant groups in a common vision of the spiritual mission and destiny of America. Consequently, most of the later religious visions of America may be broadly conceived as transformations of the foundational myths of America. Subsequent, non-Protestant visions of America typically presuppose their Protestant predecessors, if only because they are competing ways of understanding America's mission and destiny. There are splendid exceptions, to be sure.

And there is something decidedly "ethnic"—even racial—about these Protestant myths of America, as Eric Kaufmann explains:

> In the case of the United States, the national ethnic group was Anglo-American Protestant ("American"). *This was the first European group to "imagine" the territory of the United States as its homeland and traces its genealogy back to New World colonists who rebelled against their mother country.* In its mind, the American nation-state, its land, its history, its mission, and its Anglo-American people were woven into one great tapestry of the imagination. This social construction considered the United States to be founded by the "Americans," who thereby had title to the land and the mandate to mould the nation (and any immigrants who might enter it) in their own Anglo-Saxon, Protestant self-image.[3]

This nativist Protestant complex of myths and symbols springs out of shared experience and a common biblical heritage. In fact, biblical interpretations were projected onto the American experience—as though the Bible, reconditely, already had something to say about America. The Bible was a veritable quarry from which foundational and enduring social metaphors were hewn, and an edifice of the imagination was thereby constructed. In a word, "America" was God's new "Israel." America was the Promised Land—but only after the Canaanites of the New World (the Native Americans) were conquered and displaced.

THE PURITAN MYTH OF AMERICA

"In the beginning was the word, and the word was with the New England Way, and the word became 'America'," [4] wrote the acclaimed Americanist, Sacvan Bercovitch. The Puritans established what has come to be regarded as the foundational myth of America. Their vision generated the greater—and perhaps grander—Protestant master myth of America: "The Puritans provided the scriptural basis for what we have come to call the myth of America." [5] Again mimicking the style of the prologue of the Gospel of John, Bercovitch characterizes the Puritan myth of America so: *"In the beginning was the word, 'America,' and the word was in the Bible, and the word was made flesh in the Americans, this new breed of humans, destined to build a shining city upon a hill."* [6] Here, Bercovitch's reference to "city upon a hill" alludes to the first definitive Puritan discourse on America, "A Modell of Christian Charity" (1630), which is John Winthrop's speech to his fellow Puritans aboard the *Arbella,* on its voyage across the Atlantic to the Massachusetts coast. This homily was destined to become one of the most powerful, pervasive, and persistent visions of America—the doctrine of American exceptionalism.

The Puritan myth of America was first articulated by the Honorable John Winthrop, Esq. (1588–1649), who was appointed as the governor of the Company of the Massachusetts Bay. The good ship, *Arbella* (formerly called the *Eagle*) was the designated admiral of a fleet of 11 vessels that transported the Massachusetts Bay company across the Atlantic, with the celebrated *Mayflower* being among them. (The *Mayflower* had taken the first band of Puritans to America ten years earlier.) The *Arbella* weighed 350 tons, and carried 28 guns along with its 52 men. Tuesdays and Wednesdays were appointed to catechize the passengers. One such catechism, "A Modell of Christian Charity" (no date, except the year 1630, is associated with it) reads, in part:

> Thus stands the case between God and us. We are entered into a Covenant with Him for this work. We have taken out a commission. . . . For this end, we must be knit together, in this work, as one man. We must entertain each other in brotherly affection. We must be willing to abridge ourselves of our superfluities, for the supply of other's necessities. We must uphold a familiar commerce together in all meekness, gentleness, patience, and liberality. We must delight in each other; make other's condition our own; rejoice together, mourn together, labor and suffer together, always having before our eyes our commission and community in the work, as members of the same body. So shall *we keep the unity of the spirit in the bond of peace.* The Lord will be our God, and delight to dwell among us, as his own people, and will command a blessing upon us in all our ways. So that we shall see much more of his wisdom, power, goodness and truth, than formerly we have been acquainted with. We shall find that the God of Israel is among us, when ten of us shall be able to resist a thousand of our enemies; when he shall make us a praise and a glory, that men shall say of succeeding plantations, "The Lord make it likely that of *New England.*" For we must consider that we shall be as a City upon a hill. The eyes of all people are upon us.[7]

Here, the "City upon a hill" alludes to one of the timeless sayings of Jesus from the Sermon on the Mount: "Ye are the light of the world. A city that is set on an hill cannot be hid."[8] By "City," Winthrop meant Puritan "society"—the salient characteristics of which may be briefly described as follows: Puritans were bound by a solemn "Covenant" to God and by their joint "commission" to further the commercial interests of the Massachusetts Bay company. Among these godly and enterprising pilgrims, the words (in their original italics), *"we keep the unity of the spirit in the bond of peace,"* were meant to foster bonds of unity, of corporate identity, and of collective purpose. In the fuller text of this homily, brief scriptural references are made, invoking biblical precedent for what was promoted as an exemplary Christian society. Governor Winthrop exhorts the community to aspire to such moral nobility and material success as to excite the admiration and envy of others, such "that we shall be as a City upon a hill. The eyes of all people are upon us." What was being promoted here—that the new society strive to be exemplary spiritually and materially—was all well and good. But this same sense of "mission"—which, in the words of the present writer, was to *conquer, Christianize, and civilize*—also contained the seeds of missionary expansion by conquest.

The Puritans frequently cited or alluded to passages of scripture, as though the Bible had foreordained the Puritan errand into the wilderness of America. This was possible to accomplish through constructing an exegetical bridge between the biblical past and the contemporary present. Puritans used the interpretative technique of *presentism,* aptly named, to apply the Israelite past to the American present. That is, the Puritans interpreted the Bible in the present tense. All events in the Bible were seen as *typological*—that is, as forecasts of things to come, as part of a divine drama in which the Puritans themselves played a central role.

Certain biblical motifs fall into focus here. Gary Gerstle traces "the origins of American mythology" to "biblical notions of Israelite persecution, chosenness, and deliverance." [9] The Puritans were fleeing religious persecution, were divinely elected (chosen by God) to establish an exemplary society in a New World, and were successfully delivered to America in furtherance of that mission. Hence, the Puritans' escape from persecution in the Old World to emancipation in the New World finds its scriptural prototype in the Exodus of the Hebrews from Egypt, where America becomes the Promised Land and "God's New Israel," which is the title of a major anthology of mostly Protestant visions of America, skillfully anthologized by Conrad Cherry. [10] A fuller description of the Puritan vision of America—Edenic and messianic—is epitomized by Gerstle so:

> [T]he Puritans who fled religious oppression in England ... conceived of America as their Promised Land. Their reference to the journey of the Israelites was hardly accidental or casual. The Puritans knew the Old Testament well and, in the persecution of the Israelites at the hands of Egyptian authorities, in their wanderings through the desert wilderness, in their embrace of God's covenant, and in their deliverance to the Promised Land of Israel, the Puritans found precedents for their own saga of suffering and redemption. Like the Israelites' settlement of Canaan, the Puritans' conquest of the American wilderness would yield a new society, a society so pure and blinding in its light, so special in its unique covenant with God, that the rest of God's creatures would turn to America for salvation. The Puritans believed that they, like the Israelites, had been chosen by God to carry a message of deliverance and renewal to the entire world. This deep sense of mission, which would in the 19th century come to be known as "Manifest Destiny," has been part of America's self-identity ever since. [11]

In other words, the Puritans' sense of mission, in time, evolved into the American expansionist doctrine of "Manifest Destiny," with its unabashedly imperialist aspirations. The Puritan myth of America is really a constellation of motifs, where several major subthemes coalesce: exodus, destiny, wilderness, and prosperity. The first two motifs—exodus and destiny—primarily relate to the idea of the Puritan *covenant,* while the latter two motifs—wilderness and prosperity—accentuate conquest and prosperity, as Szilvia Csábi explains:

> Conceptual metaphors and metonymies concerning America were often used in Puritan literary works. The various metaphors have different entailments, and they highlight and hide different aspects of Puritan experiences. The principal conceptual metaphors can be clustered under a "master metaphor": THE SET-TLEMENT OF AMERICA IS THE MOVEMENT OF THE JEWS FROM EGYPT TO ISRAEL. This master metaphor can be broken down into three basic submetaphors—AMERICA IS THE PROMISED LAND, AMERICA IS A WILDERNESS, and GOING TO AMERICA IS ENACTING A BUSINESS DEAL. Several excerpts from Puritan literary works will illustrate the coherent though flexible use of these metaphors: they lived by certain metaphors . . . These metaphors appear to be so powerful and appropriate in a wide variety of situations that they are used over several generations.[12]

The Protestant master myth of America is inflected by the great Puritan myth of the City on a Hill. America is a land specially favored by God. The conceptualization of America as the Promised Land was the best known and most elaborate Puritan metaphor for America.[13] The source domain of this conceptual metaphor is Canaan. The target domain is America.[14] Szilvia Csábi observes:

> Within the metaphor AMERICA IS THE PROMISED LAND, the mappings are systematic: America is the Holy Land, Canaan, and New England is the City of God; the Puritan settlers are the selected people of God. Interestingly, the terms the city of Jerusalem, the city of God, the Promised Land and the land of Canaan can be seen as "co-referential" in the sense that metaphorically they are equivalent or identical images of God's kingdom manifest on earth.[15]

This Puritan ideal soon proved contagious, for it excited the wider American imagination.

The impact of the Puritans' vision of America on subsequent American self-identity and political policy has been long-recognized by historians. John Winthrop's famous speech aboard the *Arbella* has had its own trajectory, down to the present. This is just one recent example of what has now come to be an accepted fact of American history: "John Winthrop's 1630 *Arbella* address to his fellow Puritans has evolved over the course of American history into a justification for American expansionism on missionary grounds." [16] In an important sense, the Puritan "myth of America"—the corporate ideal of a purified community of saints visibly identified with the national body politic—was mapped onto the consumer utopia of a "culture of abundance." [17] That is, if Americans were faithful to their spiritual covenant and were diligent in their material endeavors (i.e., their "commission"), then Providence would bless their affairs. In fine, the blending of Puritan literary texts clearly show that Puritans thought of America as God's "Promised Land."

For a local idea to catch on—and eventually to be taken up by a nation at large—how did the Puritan vision of America excite the popular imagination? The way in which the Puritan sense of America's mission and destiny was transmitted to the rest of Protestant America was through what is known as the Great Awakening (1725–1750), as Eric Kaufmann explains:

> New England's Puritan sense of election and mission, and its description of America as a New Canaan, or promised land, slowly came to infect the entire nation. Its vision also came to influence the American outlook through a nation-wide religious revival known as the Great Awakening (1725–50). John Armstrong has noted that religion provided one of the few vehicles of mass communication in the pre-modern era and it was religion that was largely responsible for American intercolonial integration in the eighteenth century." Led by Jonathan Edwards, amongst others, the Great Awakening spread like wildfire across the colonies from New England to Georgia, and is described by some as the first instance of American self-consciousness. [18]

It is from this point forward that the metaphor of America as a "redeemer nation" takes hold.

THE "MANIFEST DESTINY" MYTH

As already pointed out in Chapter 1, nearly every American student learns of "Manifest Destiny"—the American imperial myth. Simply put, the doctrine of Manifest Destiny translates American exceptionalism into action. Manifest Destiny is the doctrine that Euro-Americans had a God-given right to conquer and colonize North America, and eventually to civilize and imperialize Hawaii, Cuba, Puerto Rico, Guam, and the Philippines. Manifest Destiny is a salient theme in American history that runs through the Indian Wars, the U.S.–Mexican War, the Spanish-American War, the wars across the Arc of Rimland Asia, and beyond. The term "manifest destiny" was first coined in 1845 by John L. O'Sullivan (1813–1895), founder and editor of the *United States Magazine and Democratic Review,* in this editorial:

Why, were other reasoning wanting, in favor of now elevating this question of the reception of Texas into the Union, out of the lower region of our past party dissensions, up to its proper level of a high and broad nationality, it surely is to be found, found abundantly, in the manner in which other nations have undertaken to intrude themselves into it, between us and the proper parties to the case, in a spirit of hostile interference against us, for the avowed object of thwarting our policy and hampering our power, limiting our greatness and checking the fulfillment of *our manifest destiny* to overspread the continent allotted by Providence for the free development of our yearly multiplying millions.[19]

This phrase was contagious and quickly attached itself to official American expansionist ideology. One historian comments on the tremendous impact these words exerted: "Here was the powerful phrase that promoted continental expansion, resulting in a doubling of American territory in four years." [20] Soon after, the concept of Manifest Destiny was quickly introduced to Congress.

Robert C. Winthrop (1809–1894), Representative of Massachusetts, was a descendant of John Winthrop, first governor of Massachusetts Bay Colony, who was met in the previous section. While John Winthrop was the one who established the Puritan vision of America as a "City upon a hill," it was Robert Winthrop who first formally introduced the doctrine of "Manifest Destiny" in Congress. Although the existing literature, reviewed in preparation for this chapter, notes the blood relationship, the ideological relationship has not been directly connected. This is not to suggest that the genealogical ties by blood provides a direct genealogy of ideology, but it is quite curious that one of the earliest theorists of Manifest Destiny was a direct descendant of John Winthrop. This tantalizes the larger hypothesis that Manifest Destiny represents a further development of Puritan ideology. That is, America, after first aspiring to be a "City upon a hill," embarked on a conscious quest to, in effect, become "King of the hill." A word of caution here: although Robert C. Winthrop was the first to articulate the doctrine of Manifest Destiny before Congress, he cites the doctrine in order to oppose it. On January 3, 1846, in a speech in the House of Representatives, Representative Robert C. Winthrop of Massachusetts articulated the doctrine of Manifest Destiny, in what has been described as "first public utterance of the phrase," [21] of "manifest destiny"—albeit with sardonic disdain:

There is one element in our title [to Oregon], however, which I confess that I have not named, and to which I may not have done entire justice. I mean that new revelation of right which has been designated as *the right of our manifest destiny to spread over this whole continent.* It has been openly avowed in a leading Administration journal that this, after all, is our best and strongest title—one so clear, so pre-eminent, so indisputable, that if Great Britain had all our other titles in addition to her own, they would weigh nothing against it. The right of our manifest destiny! There is a right for new chapter in the law of nations; or rather, in the special laws of our own country; for I suppose the right to a manifest destiny to spread will not be admitted to exist in any nation except the universal Yankee nation!

To the extent that Winthrop has correctly represented the doctrine that he himself opposed, this is a remarkable statement. Note the repeated use of the word "right," as if for rhetorical emphasis. Without explicitly saying so, there is an elliptical sense that, by "right," a sense of divine prerogative or of a "God-given" right is meant. Also note the doctrine of American exceptionalism is part and parcel of this doctrine. As formulated here, the specific exception, legitimized by American exceptionalism, is that American domestic policy, if not foreign policy, requires and justifies a clear deviation from the prevailing "law of nations." To the extent that appropriation and annexation of Oregon to the territory of the United States is being legitimized by advocates of Manifest Destiny, technically this would fall under the rubric of "foreign policy." Two years after Winthrop's speech, President James Polk signed the Organic Act on August 14, 1848, thereby creating the Oregon Territory. This was a reflex of Manifest Destiny, legitimizing territorial expansion. In his speech, the article that Winthrop had alluded to, where Manifest Destiny was championed, had appeared only a week before, also addressing the "Oregon question" as part of a national debate:

> Our legal title to Oregon, so far as law exists for such rights, is perfect. There is no doubt of this. . . . [W]e have a still better title than any that can ever be constructed out of all these antiquated materials of old black-letter international law. Away, away with all these cobweb tissues of rights of discovery, exploration, settlement, continuity, etc. . . . And that claim is *by the right of our manifest to overspread and to possess the whole of the continent* which Providence has given us for the development of the great experiment of liberty and federated self-government entrusted to us. . . . The God of nature and of nations has marked it for us; with His blessing we will firmly maintain the incontestable rights He has given, and fearlessly perform the high duties He has imposed.[22]

In this editorial, the "rights of discovery, exploration, settlement, continuity, etc." are invoked, but these "rights" were not universal. They were the province of the Americans, whether nationally, ethnically, or racially defined. These rights were circumscribed. To state the obvious, they belonged exclusively to Euro-Americans, and not to the Native Americans. The enforcement of such rights by the "Americans" against the Native Americans necessarily deprived the latter of what the Declaration of Independence had, at least in theory, declared to be "inalienable." And all this was done with the putative blessing of "the God of nature and of nations." "Providence" had so decreed, it would seem. The "City upon a hill" became an "empire of right"—conquering, Christianizing, and civilizing by might, in the name of these self-arrogated "rights."

Let us now see how this doctrine was translated into American and world history. Mostafa Rejai, Distinguished Professor Emeritus at Miami University, Ohio, provides this clear overview across the horizons of history, in which Manifest Destiny had a direct impact on the destiny of vast territories and their peoples:

> Manifest destiny is going to refer, among other things, to the physical direction in which the country is going to be moving. Coming from the points we do, our natural direction of movement is toward the West. So, manifest destiny means, in the first place, that the new nation is bound to expand over the entire continent—and with it, the values of life, liberty, and pursuit of happiness will spread from coast to coast. Later on, we will have such expressions as "from sea to shining sea" and "from the mountains, to the prairies, to the oceans" to capture this aspect of manifest destiny. So, the westward movement is manifest destiny in action. The frontier is manifest destiny in action. The purchase of Louisiana is manifest destiny in action. The annexation of California and Texas is manifest destiny in action.
>
> Now, manifest destiny means much more. Having expanded over the entire continent, the new nation is bound to go across the seas. It is our preordained mission to go beyond the continent. Why? Because wherever we go, life, liberty, and the pursuit of happiness go with us. We have to bring the blessings of democracy to the less fortunate peoples of the world. Accordingly, the acquisitions of Cuba, Puerto Rico, Guam, Hawaii, Alaska, and the Philippines—these are all manifest destiny in action.[23]

From this succinct epitome of the range and reach of Manifest Destiny, the reader now has a clear impression of its vast historical impact. Manifest Destiny may be thought of as the American doctrine of conquest, as the ideology of American expansionism. Its ideological underpinnings, although secular, have markedly religious antecedents. In other words, Manifest Destiny is a quasi-religious concept. Baldly put, it urged the conquest of North America (and beyond), as ordained by divine will.

In his monograph on the ideology of Manifest Destiny, Anders Stephanson[24] charts a trajectory of Manifest Destiny over the course of American history and connects this history with its ideological justifications. Disclaiming any attempt to define "the meaning of America," Stephanson maintains that "manifest destiny is of signal importance in the way the United States came to understand itself in the world and still does."[25] As the ideology of American nationalism, Manifest Destiny reflected America's belief in a "providentially assigned role . . . to lead the world to new and better things." [26] At the heart of this ideology lies "an apparent paradox: a particular (and particularly powerful) nationalism constituting itself not only as prophetic but also [as] universal." [27] Manifest Destiny, which "crystallized most clearly in the moments of aggrandizement or intervention," [28] provided Americans with "a tradition that created a sense of national place and direction in a variety of historical settings." [29] Accordingly, the expansionist wars against Mexico in the 1840s and Spain in the 1890s were direct outcomes of this ideology translated into national policy.

Manifest Destiny arose during the Revolutionary and Federalist periods, when the 13 colonies, in their quest to forge an independent union and to preserve its sense of national purpose, required an ideology that would provide a coherent rationale. Lacking the unifying ethnic and cultural heritage that already unified other nation-states, Americans needed "a set of simple symbols . . . that would distill the past and at the same time proclaim the future." [30] In fashioning this sense of common heritage and purpose, a "peculiar fusion of providential and republican ideology that took place after the Revolution" emerged, imbuing the United States of America with a sense of divine mission.[31] Apart from acknowledged classical influences, Stephanson claims that "any genealogy . . . must begin with the religious sources." [32] Although regional, New England Puritanism proved to be the key catalyst in the formation and formulation of a national ideology. In other words, the Puritans were the precursors of Manifest Destiny. Admixed with other ideological alloys, Stephanson asserts that "the invaluable Puritan matrix could be projected onto more recent bourgeois models of enlightenment and profit, generating a modern nationhood of process and mission." [33]

Stephanson speaks of the "Jeffersonian Moment" as a critical turning point in the further development of Manifest Destiny. Expansionist aspirations—an agrarian vision in which the empire of liberty might enlarge—made territorial acquisition a necessity. This necessitated the infamous Indian Removal Act that triggered the Indian Wars, as America advanced its frontiers. Inevitably, this would lead to confrontation with European states as Americans overtook their colonial empires. Thus, the Jeffersonians' "dynamism and ideology of national aggrandizement" became "emblematic of the nineteenth century." [34] Over the course of the twentieth century, the United States developed to its current position as "world hegemon." [35]

One of the presumptions of Manifest Destiny is that Protestantism is superior to Catholicism. This allowed a country that was overwhelmingly Protestant to pretextually invade and annex half of the territory of Mexico in the 1840s. The U.S.–Mexican War of 1846–1848 was a prime example of how Manifest Destiny was exploited as justification for conquest. In a 2001 dissertation, *Crusade and Conquest: Anti-Catholicism, Manifest Destiny, and the*

United States–Mexican War of 1846–1848, John Christopher Pinheiro examines how anti-Catholic sentiment influenced public opinion regarding the war against Mexico. Pinheiro explores how, in the late 1830s and early 1840s, increased immigration and republican ideology allowed anti-Catholicism and nativism to fuse, with this result:

> Contrary to their usual anti-immigrant rhetoric, nativists also supported the annexation of Mexico in its entirety in the name of Manifest Destiny, and for racist and anti-Catholic reasons. . . . Voicing their opinions in republican language, many evangelicals saw the war as a Providential opportunity to evangelize Catholic Mexico with a "pure" gospel. To them, the Manifest Destiny of the United States included the spread of Protestantism as the necessary foundation of republican government. . . . Certain tenets of American republicanism were brought into play when the overwhelmingly Protestant United States waged war on Catholic Mexico. Located at the middle point in the growth of the antebellum anti-Catholic movement, the U.S.–Mexican War helped to hone the concept of American republicanism as an ideology that included Anglo-Saxonism and anti-Catholicism under the greater umbrella of Manifest Destiny.[36]

Succinctly put, Manifest Destiny allowed for the pretextual invasion and annexation of half of Mexico's land mass in the 1846–1848 war: "Expressing a hegemonic faith in the racial, moral, religious, and cultural superiority of the United States, Manifest Destiny legitimized the occupation of adjacent territorial zones and therefore affected Mexico directly."[37] Besides its anti-Catholic sentiment, Manifest Destiny entails a racial ideology as well. In *Race and Manifest Destiny: The Origins of American Racial Anglo-Saxonism,* Reginald Horsman characterizes Manifest Destiny as a "search for personal and national wealth" that was "put in terms of world progress, under the leadership of a supreme race."[38]

THE "CURSE OF HAM" MYTH

This is where the Protestant myth of America becomes overtly racial. Pro-slavery Americans tried their best to Christianize slavery. A favorite verse of Southern clergymen, for instance, was this: "Masters, give unto your servants that which is just and equal, knowing that ye also have a master in heaven."[39] Even more influential was the biblical account of the "Curse of Ham."[40] The verse, "Cursed be Canaan; a slave of slaves shall he be to his brothers" (Genesis 9:25), was invoked as a proof text for Christian legitimation of slavery throughout the South. The "Curse of Ham" was also known as the "Curse of Canaan." (Ham was Noah's youngest son, and Canaan was one of Ham's sons.) Canaan gets punished for Ham's delict. Because Africans were considered to be descendants of Ham, they were fated to be slaves, so that logic goes. This foregone conclusion—this perverse interpretation of a biblical story—transmogrified the biblical account into a racialized American Protestant myth.

This story played a prominent role in proslavery rhetoric. It theologically sanctioned slavery by means of a racialized exegesis of the biblical account of Noah, who planted a vineyard, got drunk, and was seen naked by one of his three sons, Ham, whom Noah then cursed. The immediate irony here is that Christianity stands for salvation—in justifying the sinner before God through the economy of Christ's redemptive work. Unfortunately, institutional Christianity (primarily in the Southern States), in order to justify slavery, found a powerful argument in favor of slavery in the Curse of Ham myth.

For much of the eighteenth, nineteenth, and twentieth centuries in the Christian West, in fact, the Curse of Ham was the foremost religious theory for making sense of racial differences within humanity. In fact, it served as the central religious justification of the "peculiar institution" of chattel slavery in America. Because one of Ham's descendants, Cush, was black (Genesis 10:6–14), the "Curse of Ham" has been interpreted racially in order to legitimate the slavery of people of African origin.

That is where a Bible story, racially interpreted, was transmogrified into a racial myth of polygenesis that gained almost universal assent among white nineteenth-century American Protestants.[41] In its treatment of the relationship of Noah's three sons—Japheth, Shem, Ham—the Curse of Ham myth provided the typology by which race relations among the three racial groups that Noah's three sons, respectively, represented (Caucasian, Asian, and African descent) could be differentiated and regulated. As one historian observes: "These relations were unsurprisingly a mirror of contemporary relations in 19th century—whites were dominant, indigenous peoples were marginalized, and blacks were subjugated."[42]

Protestant Americans were certainly not alone in reading race into scripture. Exponents of racial exegesis in Judaism, Christianity, and Islam exercised their influence in providing scriptural warrant for racial doctrines.[43] The "Curse of Ham"/"Curse of Canaan" refers to the following passage of scripture in the book of *Genesis:*

The sons of Noah who went forth from the ark were Shem, Ham, and Japheth. Ham was the father of Canaan. These three were the sons of Noah; and from these the whole earth was peopled. Noah was the first tiller of the soil. He planted a vineyard; and he drank of the wine, and became drunk, and lay uncovered in his tent. And Ham, the father of Canaan, saw the nakedness of his father, and told his two brothers outside. Then Shem and Japheth took a garment, laid it upon both their shoulders, and walked backward and covered the nakedness of their father; their faces were turned away, and they did not see their father's nakedness. When Noah awoke from his wine and knew what his youngest son had done to him, he said, "Cursed be Canaan; a slave of slaves shall he be to his brothers."[44]

After the Flood, Noah planted a vineyard, became drunk, and lay naked in his tent. The drunkenness and nakedness of Noah thus occasioned the violation by Ham. Ham's sin is that he beheld his father's nakedness. While Noah's other two sons (Shem and Japheth) were careful to avert their eyes, Ham gazed upon his drunken father's body—a shameful act that triggered Noah's curse: "Cursed be Canaan; a slave of slaves shall he be to his brothers." Note that it is not Ham who is cursed, but rather his son, Canaan, who is fated to perpetual slavery, as is his progeny. Nor is there any mention of skin color, as David Goldenberg points out: "This biblical story has been the single greatest justification for Black slavery for more than a thousand years. It is a strange justification indeed, for there is no reference in it to Blacks at all."[45]

The association with Blacks came later, as chronicled in David Goldenberg's masterful survey, *The Curse of Ham: Race and Slavery in Early Judaism, Christianity, and Islam.*[46] For our purposes, what matters is how this biblical understanding affected American history. Etymology begat etiology: "Ham" commonly came to mean "hot," "burnt," "swarthy," "dark," and "black." In the popular conception of it, the received meaning of "Ham" clearly pointed to Africa as the "hot" clime that produced the "black" race. Nothing could be more obvious, it would seem. Both in the North and in the South, Ham was universally regarded as the progenitor of black Africans: "In a study of the mythic world of the antebellum South vis-à-vis Blacks," Goldenberg explains, " . . . the notion of Blacks as 'the children of Ham' was a well-entrenched belief."[47] In nineteenth-century America, the sheer ubiquitousness of what came to be a commonplace assumption supports this conclusion, which can be stated with confidence: "It didn't matter whether one supported the institution of Black slavery or not, or whether one was Black or not; everyone in nineteenth-century America seemed to believe in the truth of Ham's blackness."[48] As pervasive as the Curse of Ham myth was in the nineteenth century, it persisted well into the twentieth century: "The Curse of Ham was commonly taught and believed in America up to recent times."[49] And so the myth of Canaan, as cursed by God with black skin, took root as a widespread religious myth of America. Its importance and pivotal influence cannot be overemphasized, a fact that Goldenberg accentuates:

As the Black slave trade moved to England and then America, the Curse of Ham moved with it. . . . There can be no denying the fact, however, that the Curse made its most harmful appearance in America, and there can be no denying the central role it played in sustaining the slave system. It was *the* ideological cornerstone for the justification of Black slavery, "the major argument in the proslavery arsenal of biblical texts," "certainly among the most popular defenses of slavery if not the most popular." Its place in American thought of the time was succinctly described in 1862 by Alexander Crummel, a man born in the United States to freed slaves. In a learned article he refers to "the opinion that the sufferings and the slavery of the Negro race are the consequence of the curse of Noah" as a "general, almost universal, opinion in the Christian world." [50]

Proslavery ideologues saw slaves as depraved by nature, since Ham, as the ancestor of Africans, embodied the debased character that drew Noah's wrath. Notwithstanding, Blacks withstood. Blacks took exception to American exceptionalism by means of reactionary Black anti-exceptionalism, or what one scholar has dubbed "double exceptionalism." [51] As a bulwark against the Curse of Ham, African Americans framed counter-myths that conveyed a covert theology of liberation from oppression.

THE AFRICAN AMERICAN EXODUS COUNTER-MYTH

Within Protestant Christianity itself, African Americans developed their own religious visions of America that served as viable alternatives to the white Protestant myths that helped rationalize and reinforce institutionalized racism in America, from slavery forward. Eddie S. Glaude notes that "religious myths remain central to the making of a new African American self and the location of that self in history." [52] While he does not use the term "counter-myth," Glaude clearly has the idea of a counter-myth in mind when he further observes:

> African American religious myths deployed in the struggles against white supremacy have produced particularly charged conceptions of history, identity, and memory (which range across the political spectrum). . . . But many uses of religious myths among African Americans reject identification with America. This rejection begins with a basic reconfiguration of historical beginnings that makes possible the construction of an identity that stands over and against "the idea of America." [53]

The preeminent African American counter-myth is the *Exodus* story. This is the subject of a 2007 dissertation, the information provided by which cannot be recapitulated here.[54] In brief, *Exodus* chronicles Israel's entrance into Egypt, liberation from slavery, and settlement in the Promised Land of Canaan. This biblical narrative contained the seeds of a theology of liberation. Once it was introduced to American slaves, they immediately recognized a parallel to their own plight, and seized upon it as a source of inspiration and hope for their own freedom from oppression:

> Exodus functioned as an archetypal myth for the slaves. The sacred history of God's liberation of his people would be or was being reenacted in the American South. A white Union Army chaplain working among freedmen in Decatur, Alabama, commented disapprovingly on the slaves' fascination with Exodus: "There is no part of the Bible with which they are so familiar as the story of the deliverance of Israel. Moses is their *ideal* of all that is high, and noble, and perfect, in man. I think they have been accustomed to regard Christ not so much in the light of a *spiritual* Deliverer, as that of a second Moses who would eventually lead them out of their prison-house of bondage." [55]

In this alternative religious myth of America, America is not "God's New Israel," as so many white Protestants, as far back as the Puritans, believed. Under its racial interpretation by Black slaves, America was the new oppressor. It was Egypt reenacted. Under the Exodus myth, therefore, America's mythic role is reversed. In "African Americans, Exodus, and the American Israel," Albert J. Raboteau explains this reversal of Biblical imagery:

> No single story captures more clearly the distinctiveness of African-American Christianity than that of the Exodus. From the earliest days of colonization, white Christians had represented their journey across the Atlantic to America as the exodus of a New Israel; slaves identified themselves as the Old Israel, suffering bondage under a new Pharaoh.[56]

Out of the Exodus story, two divergent American religious myths emerged: a White Exodus narrative and a Black Exodus story. Each told a different history. The first was the Puritans' escape from religious oppression to find religious freedom; the second was the struggle of African Americans to escape the oppression at the hands of the Puritans' descendants. A prime example of this motif is the dialect poem, "An Ante-Bellum Sermon" (1895), by African American poet Paul Laurence Dunbar (1872–1906)—excerpts from which will give the reader a fair impression of how the Exodus narrative was analogized to the new Egypt, America:

AN ANTE-BELLUM SERMON

We is gathahed hyeah, my brothahs,
In di howlin' wildaness,
Fu' to speak some words o comfo't
to each othah in distress.
An' we choose fu' ouah subjic'
Dis—we'll 'splain it by an' by;

"An' de Lawd said, "Moses, Moses,"
An' de man said, Hyeah am I.' "

*****

Now ole Pher'oh, down in Egypt
Was de wuss man evah bo'n,
An' he had de Hebrew chillun
Down dah wukin' in his co'n;
'Twell de Lawd got tiahed o' his foolin',
an' sez he: "I'll let him know'
Look hyeah, Moses, go tell Pher'oh
Fu' to let dem chillun go."

*****

"An' ef he refuse do it,
I will make him rue de houah,
fu' I'll empty down on Egypt
All de vials of my powah."
Yes, he did—-an' Pher'oh's ahmy
Wasn't wurth a ha'f a dime;
Fu' de Lawd will he'p his chillum,
You kin trust him evah time.

*****

An' you' enemies may 'sail you
In de back an' in de front;
But de Lawd is all aroun' you,
Fu' to ba' de battle's brunt.
Dey kin fo'ge yo' chains an' shackles
F'om de mountains to de sea;
But de Lawd will sen' some Moses
Fu' to set his chilun free.

*****

An' de lan' shall hyeah his thundah,
Lak a blas' f'om Gab'el's ho'n,
Fu' de Lawd of hosts is mighty
When he girds his ahmor on.
But fu' feah some one mistakes me,
I will pause right hyeah to say,
Dat I'm still a-preachin' ancient,
I ain't talkin' bout to-day.

*****

But I tell you, fellah christuns,
Things'll happen mighty strange;
Now, de Lawd done dis fu' Isrul,

An' his ways don't nevah change,
An' de love he showed to Isrul
Wasn't all on Isrul spent;
Now don't run an' tell yo' mastahs
Dat I's preachin' discontent.

*****

'Cause I isn't; I'se a-judgin'
Bible people by dier ac's;
I'se a-givin' you de Scriptuah,
I'se a-handin' you de fac's.
Cose ole Pher'or b'lieved in
slav'ry,
But de Lawd he let him see,
Dat de people he put bref in,
Evah mothah's son was free.

*****

An' dah's othahs thinks lak Pher'or,
But dey calls de Scriptuah liar,
Fu' de Bible says "a servant
Is worthy of his hire,"
An' you cain't git roun' nor thoo dat,
An' you cain't git ovah it,
Fu' whatevah place you git in,
Dis hyeah Bible too'll fit.

*****

So you see de Lawd's intention,
Evah sence de worl' began,
Was dat His almight freedom
Should belong to evah man,
But I think it would be bettah,
Ef I'd pause agin to say,
Dat I'm talkin' 'bout ouah freedom
In a Bibleistic way.[57]

Dunbar skillfully recreates a sermon, just as it might have sounded like in the days of Black folk preachers during the time of slavery. Through subversive use of dialect, Dunbar's preacher is a master of double entendre—the art of saying one thing and meaning another. The preacher invokes the past to address the present. After providing a detailed literary interpretation of this poem, David T. Shannon offers "An Ante-bellum Sermon" as an exemplar of African American hermeneutics:

The early African American sermons, of which Dunbar's poetic rendition is a remarkable remembrance, make a significant contribution to the development of an African American hermeneutic in several ways. They address the issues of (1) *contextuality,* (2) *correlation,* (3) *confrontation,* and (4) *consolation,* which, argues, are four significant modes of African American biblical interpretation.[58]

The Exodus myth is the leading example of African American counter-myths of America. Like this sermon, the destiny of African Americans is to expose Manifest Destiny for what it really is—a religious pretext for naked greed. The blessing of African Americans, moreover, is to counter the "Curse of Ham." This dialectic of religious myth and counter-myth is a dynamic that pervades religious myths of America generally, as part of a long and arduous struggle to overcome the past. In Chapter 1, it was suggested that the "central themes" of American religious history are pluralism, Puritanism, and the encounter of black and white.[59] In a sense, all three themes are interrelated. Puritanism, largely through the encounter of black and white, embarked on a tortuous, historic path that is leading to a healthy diversity unified by a grand sense of overarching pluralism. The encounter of black and white will prove to be a major theme in the religious visions of America to follow.

CHAPTER 4

Catholic Myths and Visions of America

Mr. President ... I wish to extol the blessing and gifts that America has received from God and cultivated, and which have become the true values of the whole American experiment in the past two centuries. ... The more powerful a nation is, the greater becomes its international responsibility, the greater also must be its commitment to the betterment of the lot of those whose very humanity is constantly being threatened by want and need. ... America needs freedom to be herself and to fulfill her mission in the world.

—John Paul II (1987)[1]

Given the diverse nature of "fissiparous Protestantism,"[2] there is no official Protestant vision of America. This is due, in large measure, to the lack of a central authority in Protestantism generally. Similarly, there is no official Catholic vision of America. But this is not for *lack* of a central authority, but because of the *presence* of it. The intervention of the papacy —the central authority of the Roman Catholic church—put an end to a movement known as the "Americanist controversy." The so-called Americanists argued that America has a divine destiny. William L. Portier, Distinguished Professor of Religious Studies of the University of Dayton, provides one of the clearest introductions as to who the Americanists were, and how the Americanists' vision of America relates back to that of the Puritans, and eventually to the "mythical" belief in "American exceptionalism" that is part of the American Protestant legacy:

Many of us live in the United States of America. Looking back to John Winthrop's fateful identification of the new land and covenanted people with the gospel "city upon a hill," there has been a strong tendency for citizens of the United States to sacralize their country, to see it as chosen by God. ... This mythical contrast often plays out politically and historically in "American exceptionalism," a fervent belief in the virtuous uniqueness of our political institutions and way of life.

This tendency to look upon our country as providential entered Catholic thought in the United States with Orestes Brownson. His 1855 essay, "Mission of America," founds what is sometimes called the tradition of Catholic "Americanism" and gives classic expression to the notion that there is a providential fit between Catholicism and American institutions. Think of the heroes of American Catholic historiography. They are the heroes of the Catholic Americanist tradition: Isaac Hecker, John Ireland and James Gibbons, John A. Ryan, and John Courtney Murray. The idea that Catholics have what America needs has increasingly had its counterpart in the idea that the Church needs America to do its work in the world.[3]

As will be explained in more detail further in this chapter, the Americanists were nearly pronounced heretics by papal decree. On January 22, 1899, Pope Leo XIII (1810–1903) promulgated an encyclical, known as *Testem Benevolentiae Nostrae,* addressed to "Our Beloved Son, James Cardinal Gibbons, Cardinal Priest of the Title *Sancta Maria,* Beyond the Tiber, Archbishop of Baltimore," in which the Supreme Pontiff, towards the end of his encyclical, expresses this concern: "From the foregoing it is manifest, beloved son, that we are not able to give approval to those views which, in their collective sense, are called by some 'Americanism.' "[4] Pope Leo XIII admonished Catholics, *inter alia,* to avoid (1) exalting "active" over "passive" virtues, (2) asserting the superiority of the "natural" to the "supernatural," and (3) reducing the Catholic faith to the surrounding culture. These warnings of the doctrinally dangerous tendencies of Americanism having been authoritatively proclaimed, the advance of the Americanist movement was effectively halted. Thus, Catholic Americanism has often been called a "phantom heresy," because it never developed to such an extent as to be branded an actual heresy. None of the Americanists was branded a "heretic." The immediate threat of Americanism was contained.

Yet certain features of Americanist beliefs regarding America's world role and divine destiny have, in fact, been echoed approvingly in some remarkable papal statements regarding America. These later papal remarks, primarily diplomatic in nature, have accorded America with extraordinary recognition. For this reason, one may begin with the most recent and relevant papal disquisitions on America, and then hark back to the roots of this Catholic discussion of the destiny of America, which began, in earnest, with the writings of

Orestes Brownson (1803–1876), then further developed by the Americanists themselves. In the several papal comments on America presented in the next section, the reader will note the purpose of these comments, which is, generally, to encourage American political leaders not to lose sight of America's potential and purpose in exercising its enormous influence in world affairs for the betterment of humanity.

PAPAL PRAISE OF AMERICA

Like dreams, some myths have the potential to become self-fulfilling—that is, capable of being actualized. Alive to America's vast potential, the Vatican has recently commented on America, in which the familiar rhetoric of America's mission and destiny is judiciously invoked for rhetorical effect. That approach, after all, is part and parcel of effective diplomacy. For instance, on Thursday, April 17, 2008, Pope Benedict XVI, speaking in the "Rotunda" Hall of the Pope John Paul II Cultural Center of Washington, D.C., had this to say about America:

> Americans have always valued the ability to worship freely and in accordance with their conscience. Alexis de Tocqueville, the French historian and observer of American affairs, was fascinated with this aspect of the nation. He remarked that this is a country in which religion and freedom are "intimately linked" in contributing to a stable democracy that fosters social virtues and participation in the communal life of all its citizens. In urban areas, it is common for individuals from different cultural backgrounds and religions to engage with one another daily in commercial, social and educational settings. Today, in classrooms throughout the country, young Christians, Jews, Muslims, Hindus, Buddhists, and indeed children of all religions sit side-by-side, learning with one another and from one another. This diversity gives rise to new challenges that spark a deeper reflection on the core principles of a democratic society. May others take heart from your experience, realizing that a united society can indeed arise from a plurality of peoples—"*E pluribus unum*": "out of many, one"— provided that all recognize religious liberty as a basic civil right.[5]

Note how the American secular value of religious freedom—one of the founding principles of America itself—is given religious approbation. Here, America is extolled as an exemplar that "others" should seek to emulate. Now, the American *motto*—"*E pluribus unum*"—is taken as a religiously approved *maxim*. This is consistent with previous papal statements. For instance, on Tuesday, January 27, 2004, Pope John Paul II received Vice President Dick Cheney, who represented President George W. Bush. This is what Pope John Paul II had to say:

Mr. Vice President,

I am pleased to welcome you and your family to the Vatican and to receive the cordial greetings which you bring from President Bush. The American people have always cherished the fundamental values of freedom, justice and equality. In a world marked by conflict, injustice and division, *the human family needs to foster these values in its search for unity, peace and respect for the dignity of all.* I encourage you and your fellow-citizens to work, at home and abroad, *for the growth of international cooperation and solidarity in the service of that peace which is the deepest aspiration of all men and women.* Upon you and all the American people I cordially invoke the abundant blessings of Almighty God.[6]

What the 2008 and 2004 statements have in common is an implicit sense of America's mission to promote international peace and religious freedom as a "basic civil right" and as one of the "core principles of a democratic society." This mission is not America's alone, however. So, while America is singled out as exemplary in this noble endeavor, America is not given a special status. Thus, America is *exemplary,* but not *exceptional.* As one may see, it was any Catholic countenance of *American exceptionalism* to which the Vatican has taken *official exception.* Even so, Pope John Paul II has come close to recognizing some sense of America's spiritual destiny:

To everyone I repeat on this occasion what I said on that memorable day in 1979 when I arrived in Boston: "On my part I come to you—America—with sentiments of friendship, reverence and esteem. I come as one who already knows you and loves you, as one who wishes you to fulfill completely your noble destiny of service to the world." ... And finally I come to join you as you celebrate the Bicentennial of that great document, the Constitution of the United States of America. I willingly join you in your prayer of thanksgiving to God for the providential way in which the Constitution has served the people of this nation for two centuries: for the union it has established, the tranquillity and peace it has ensured, the general welfare it has promoted, and the blessings of liberty it has secured.[7]

Note how the U.S. Constitution is praised as a "great document," and how "providential" was the way in which the Constitution had served to preserve the blessings of freedom for two centuries. Perhaps the fullest expression of papal praise of America was occasioned on the visit of Pope John Paul II to Vizcaya Museum, Miami, on Thursday, September 10, 1987, where he addressed President Ronald Reagan. Highlights of this extraordinary view of America, from the supreme authority of the Catholic church itself, are as follows:

Mr. President,

1. ... In addressing you I express *my own deep respect for the constitutional structure of this democracy,* ... I willingly pay honour to the United States for what she has accomplished for her own people, for all those whom she has embraced in a cultural creativity and welcomed into an indivisible national unity, according to her own motto: *E pluribus unum.* ... Also today, I wish to extol the blessing and gifts that America has received from God and cultivated, and which have become *the true values of the whole American experiment* in the past two centuries.

2. For all of you this is a special hour in your history: the celebration of *the Bicentennial of your Constitution.* It is a time to recognize the meaning of that document and to reflect on important aspects of the constitutionalism that produced it. It is a time to recall the original American political faith with its appeal to the sovereignty of God. To celebrate the origin of the United States is *to stress those moral and spiritual principles, those ethical concerns that influenced your Founding Fathers* and have been incorporated into the experience of America. ...

3. *Among the many admirable values of this nation* there is one that stands out in particular. It is freedom. *An experience in ordered freedom is truly a cherished part of the history of this land.* This is the freedom that America is called to live and guard and to transmit. She is called to exercise it in such a way that it will also benefit the cause of freedom in other nations and among other peoples. ...

   The effort to guard and perfect the gift of freedom must also include the relentless pursuit of truth. ...

4. ... In continuity with what I said to the President of the United States in 1979 I would now repeat: "Attachment to human values and to ethical concerns, which have been a hallmark of the American people, must be situated, especially in the present context of the growing interdependence of peoples across the globe, within the framework of the view that the common good of society embraces not just the individual nation to which one belongs but the citizens of the whole world. ... The more powerful a nation is, the greater becomes its international responsibility, the greater also must be its commitment to the betterment of the lot of those whose very humanity is constantly being threatened by want and need. ...

5. ... *America needs freedom to be herself and to fulfill her mission* in the world. ... *A new birth of freedom is repeatedly necessary:* freedom to exercise responsibility and generosity, freedom to meet the challenge of serving humanity, the freedom necessary to fulfill human destiny, the freedom to live by truth, to defend it against whatever distorts and manipulates it, the freedom to observe God's law—which is the supreme standard of all human liberty—the freedom to live as children of God, secure and happy: *the freedom to be America* in that constitutional democracy which was conceived to be "one Nation under God, indivisible, with liberty and justice for all."[8]

The reader should note that these papal remarks are not binding pronouncements. They are not issued *ex cathedra* ("from the chair" [of St. Peter]); that is, these statements are not binding upon Catholics. Like a Supreme Court ruling, these statements are merely *dicta, not decisions.* Similarly, these papal remarks are *dicta, not doctrine*. Still, papal comments on America are significant (to American Catholics, at least), yet do not rise to the threshold of a full-blown American exceptionalism.

THE AMERICANIST MYTH OF AMERICA

America, some Catholics believe, has a destiny. But that is not the same thing as Manifest Destiny. This is a crucial distinction. There were American Catholic writers and leaders, however, who did hold to a view of Manifest Destiny. Among these was Orestes Brownson,[9] who was an avowed supporter of Manifest Destiny.

In 1844, after a spiritual odyssey, Orestes Brownson converted to Catholicism. Prior to his conversion, Brownson had been, in turn, a Presbyterian, a Universalist, and agnostic Unitarian, a world-reformer, and a Transcendentalist.[10] From 1844 forward, Brownson's renown was that of a Catholic public philosopher. A gifted writer, Brownson's rhetorical style has been colorfully epitomized: "There is in Brownson's style a rhetorical habit of using the harsh blow of a miner's sledge when the tap of a carpenter's hammer would be more effective." Moreover, he had an "inclination to use a battle ax to crush a butterfly."[11] Here is Brownson's most well-known statement on Manifest Destiny:

> There is more than meets the eye in the popular expression, "Manifest Destiny." We have a manifest destiny, and the world sees and confesses it, some with fear and some with hope; but it is not precisely that supposed by our journalists, or pretended by our filibusters,—although these filibusters may be unconsciously and unintentionally preparing for its fulfillment. It may be our manifest destiny to extend our government over the whole American continent, but that is in itself alone a small affair, and no worthy object of true American ambition.... The manifest destiny of this country is something far higher, nobler, and more spiritual,—the realization, we should say, of the Christian ideal of society for both the Old World and the New.[12]

This unabashed support for Manifest Destiny did not reflect an official Catholic stance. Although Brownson was arguably the most influential Catholic philosopher of his era, his views were fairly idiosyncratic—some of them even extravagant. Moreover, Brownson did not represent a school of thought within the Catholic communion. Rather, he was a splendid individualist. Like his pre-Catholic peregrinations, Brownson's religious and political views were in a constant state of flux. For that reason, he is occasionally referred to in scholarly literature as a "weathervane."[13] Brownson's inclusion in this chapter is principally because he provides something of a bridge, or transition, to the Americanists, who were definitely a group representing what might well be regarded as a "school of thought," as it were. Orestes Brownson is significant because he was the immediate ideological precursor of the Americanists and had a direct influence on Archbishop John Ireland (1838–1918) of Baltimore, one of the principal leaders of the Americanist movement.

Brownson's view of Manifest Destiny, it should be added, cannot be reduced to specious patriotic jingoism, for it had a decidedly Catholic dimension to it. His essay, "The Mission of America," can be best understood if one attaches the word "Catholic" to it. Thus, the "Catholic" mission of America is for Americans to discover in Catholic values the highest expression of American ideals. In fine, the mission of America, as professed by Orestes Brownson, was its Catholic role in reforming civilization throughout the world. And herein lies a key to several of the other religious visions of America presented in this book: To understand what the "mission of America" is—from any particular religious perspective (that is, if America is generally regarded in a positive light)—one simply has to add that religion's name before the phrase, "mission of America," whether that mission may reflect a Bahá'í, Buddhist, Mormon, or other religiously nuanced vision of America. In his major work on America, *The American Republic* (1866),[14] Orestes Brownson speaks of the political separation of church and state operationally, but of the necessity of the fusion of church and state at the level of principle:

> But the United States have a religious as well as a political destiny, for religion and politics go together. Church and state, as governments, are separate indeed, but the principles on which the state is founded have their origin and ground in the spiritual order—in the principles revealed or affirmed by religion—and are inseparable from them. There is no state without God, any more than there is a church without Christ or the Incarnation. An atheist may be a politician, but if there were no God there could be no politics. Theological principles are the basis of political principles. . . . The effect of this mission of our country fully realized, would be to harmonize church and state, religion and politics, not by absorbing either in the other, or by obliterating the natural distinction between them, but by conforming both to the real or Divine order, which is supreme and immutable.[15]

Thus, in Brownson's view, America can fulfill its "Catholic" mission by becoming more "catholic" in promoting a secular application of religious principles. One would think that, to a lesser degree at least, other countries could contribute, each in its own way, to this larger sense of humanitarian and divine mission—that is, of "Providence, or God operating through historical facts."[16] Not so:

> Of all the states or colonies on this continent, the American Republic alone has a destiny, or the ability to add any thing to the civilization of the race. Canada and

the other British Provinces, Mexico and Central America, Columbia and Brazil, and the rest of the South American States, might be absorbed in the United States without being missed by the civilized world. They represent no idea, and the work of civilization could go on without them as well as with them. If they keep up with the progress of civilization, it is all that can be expected of them.[17]

It is undoubtedly such parochial provincialism that the Catholic church found so unacceptable, with respect to the tendencies of the later "Americanists" who were the ideological heirs of Orestes Brownson. This leads us to ask, what is "Americanism" in the American Catholic context—considering the fact that Brownson was the great precursor to the Americanist movement, although not one of the principals themselves? The simplest explanation is that the Americanists, following in Brownson's ideological footsteps, believed in "God and country"—that is, that America has a divine destiny, and that, together, the alliance of America and Catholicism would redound to the advancement of both. To this end, the Americanists sought rapport between Catholicism and America. The Americanists held that a harmony—potentially, if not essentially—exists between American values and Catholic ideals. Even more than striking a harmony, the ultimate goal of the Americanists was that Catholicism might prove to be a catalyst in America's mission to reform civilization.

What largely precipitated the Americanist controversy was the influence of the vehemently and violently anti-Catholic "Know-Nothings." Antipathy to Catholicism traces back to the Reformation. Reflecting the bias prevalent in mother England, anti-Catholic sentiments were transferred from Europe to America during the course of colonization of the New World. Anti-Catholicism persisted in America on the false assumption by many Protestants who assumed that Catholic loyalty to Rome undermined democracy. Around 1850 Charles B. Allen founded the Order of the Star Spangled Banner. This was a secret society bent on wresting political power away from immigrants and inflicting reprisals on those elected officials who catered to Catholics. By 1854, this secret order became more commonly known as the "Know-Nothing Party" or "American Party." This order was responsible for a surge of nativist, anti-Catholic rhetoric and concomitant violence.

Largely in response to the national pandemic of anti-Catholic sentiment aimed at the Irish and other Catholic immigrants, the Americanists argued that the principles of American democracy were compatible with Catholic doctrines and that Catholicism could, and should, provide strong support for the Republic. Americanists sought a rapprochement between the Roman Catholic church and American culture. They championed religious freedom, praised democracy, and saw the separation of church and state in a positive light. The Americanists favored accommodation, and encouraged Catholic immigrants to learn English and adopt American cultural values. The Americanists supported labor unions as institutions promoting social justice for workers, and recommended that Catholics align their educational institutions with American models.

Who were the acknowledged leaders of the Americanist movement? First and foremost is James Cardinal Gibbons, Archbishop of Baltimore. "Cardinal" was not his middle name, but rather reflects the fact that, on June 7, 1886, Gibbons was elevated to the position of a cardinal, the second American so honored. Gibbons was the leader of the Americanist hierarchy, which included, *inter alia,* the following prelates: Archbishop John Ireland, of St. Paul, Minnesota; Bishop John Keane, of Richmond, Virginia, and later the first rector of the Catholic University; Monsignor Denis O'Connell, rector of the North American College in Rome; and John Lancaster Spalding of Peoria.[18] These ecclesial and intellectual leaders of the American Catholic church made reconciliation with the America's political principles—particularly that of religious freedom—a priority. As such, the Americanists, although unsuccessful in the short run, were a catalyst in the Americanization of Catholic doctrine, especially in the furtherance of progressive social ideals.

One prime example of this rapprochement between Catholicism and progressive American social ideals will illustrate. John Ireland, who was the first archbishop of St. Paul, Minnesota, delivered his famous address, "The Catholic Church and Civil Society," on Monday, November 10, 1884, before the Third Plenary Council of Baltimore, in which he proclaimed:

> Republic of America, . . . Thou bearest in thy hands the brightest hopes of the human race. God's mission to thee is to show to nations that man is capable of the highest liberty. . . . *Esto perpetua! . . .* [N]o hands will be lifted up stronger and more willing to defend, in war and peace, thy laws and institutions than Catholic hands. *Esto perpetua!*[19]

Beyond these noble aspirations and lofty sentiments, what principles were the Americanists trying to promote? And to what extent, one may ask, were Catholic ethical and moral teachings and American social principles found to be congruent? What cross-fertilization did the Americanists envision? While there is no definitive "creed" of the Americanist platform, the principal Americanist beliefs can be distilled from the leading speeches and essays of the Americanists themselves. In fine, what was the Americanist myth of America? In answer to this question, John Ireland is not of much help, beyond general asseverations that Catholic values are compatible with American ideals. One prime example of this will suffice to exemplify the point. In his essay, "The Church in America," Ireland writes:

The Church of America has the world-wide duties which the world-wide influence of the American Republic has thrust upon it. Wherever goes the flag of
America, wherever go the power and prestige of America, there should the
Church of America be known, there should its influence for good be felt and recognized. A special mission of the Catholic Church in America will always be to
demonstrate how congenial is the freedom of democracy to the religion of
Christ, how naturally from the teachings of Christ's Gospel proceed the principles of democracy liberty, equality and brotherhood. It is because of this special
mission that the American Catholic Church is so anxiously watched by thinking
men all over the world. Humanity is entering upon a new phase of its social and
political history. To what degree will the Church of nineteen centuries find itself
at home in this new world? It is to the American Church to give the answer.[20]

One is hard put to find a definitive expression of the Americanist agenda. It
is largely a set of platitudes with little substance, and of diffuse principles
with little real application. Americanism is a Catholic apologetic that largely
failed.

PAPAL RESPONSES TO THE AMERICANIST MYTH OF AMERICA

As mentioned at the beginning of this chapter, Pope Leo XIII officially con-
demned Americanism in his apostolic letter, *Testem Benevolentiae Nostrae:
Concerning New Opinions, Virtue, Nature And Grace, With Regard To
Americanism,* issued on January 22, 1899) and addressed to Cardinal James
Gibbons (1834–1921) of Baltimore:

From the foregoing it is manifest, beloved son, that we are not able to give
approval to those views which, in their collective sense, are called by some
"Americanism." But if by this name are to be understood certain endowments
of mind which belong to the American people, just as other characteristics
belong to various other nations, and if, moreover, by it is designated your political condition and the laws and customs by which you are governed, there is no
reason to take exception to the name. But if this is to be so understood that the
doctrines which have been adverted to above are not only indicated, but exalted,
there can be no manner of doubt that our venerable brethren, the bishops of
America, would be the first to repudiate and condemn it as being most injurious
to themselves and to their country. For it would give rise to the suspicion that
there are among you some who conceive and would have the Church in America
to be different from what it is in the rest of the world.[21]

In instant obedience to Pope Leo XIII's decree, James Gibbons,
St. Patrick's Day, 1899, publicly renounced "Americanism" as named and
characterized in the encyclical: "This doctrine, which I deliberately call
extravagant and absurd, this Americanism as it is called, has nothing in

common with the views, aspirations, doctrine and conduct of Americans."[22] Does this mean that Cardinal Gibbons repudiated his own personal views, or simply the caricature of "Americanism" was delineated in *Testem Benevolentiae Nostrae?*

In keeping with the spirit of this encyclical, later pontiffs were careful to praise "certain endowments of mind which belong to the American people" while eschewing any temptation to elevate America's endowments—along with whatever mission and destiny America might have in God's plan, as it were—to the status of some kind of special doctrinal position and prerogative.

As suggested in the beginning of this chapter, the Vatican, while having officially rejected Americanism as a doctrine,[23] has accorded great significance to certain aspects of that doctrine. In the American Catholic context, the legacy of Americanism is of both historical importance and contemporary relevance. This is seen in later papal pronouncements on America and democracy—without endorsing Americanism—indicating that America still has a special purpose in the divine scheme of things, even though a theology of America has no place in official Catholic doctrine. On December 16, 1997, for instance, Pope John Paul II officially stated that America "carries a weighty and far-reaching responsibility, not only for the well-being of its own people, but for the development and destiny of peoples throughout the world." Yet "the continuing success of American democracy," the Pontiff added, "depends on ... a free society with liberty and justice for all ... if the United States is to fulfill the destiny to which the Founders pledged their 'lives ... fortunes ... and sacred honor.' "[24]

CAN THE AMERICANIST MYTH OF AMERICA BECOME A REALITY?

Can a vision, if well-defined and if possible to act upon, be realized? Can the Catholic Americanist myth of America become a reality? Whether phantom heresy or cherished hope, can a dream become true, even if partially? To what degree are Catholic aspirations for America even possible? These questions invite contemporary Catholic reflections on the moral compass of America, on what direction America should follow, on what future course it should track, and on how Catholic values might serve as a guide.

Can a Catholic vision of America be defined? To this end, Cardinal Joseph Bernardin's *A Moral Vision of America* affords a prime exemplar.[25] Archbishop of Chicago from 1982 to 1996 after having served as archbishop of Cincinnati from 1972 to 1982, Joseph Cardinal Bernardin (1928–1996) was promoted to cardinal by Pope John Paul II in 1983 and was awarded the Presidential Medal of Freedom in 1996. For some 20 years, Cardinal Bernardin was the most influential U.S. Catholic bishop. In *A Moral Vision of America,* Bernardin develops his central theme, a "consistent ethic of life." This is a comprehensive ethical system, a moral framework that structures and unifies his vision of America, which is really Cardinal Bernardin's Catholic vision for the world. Although it is one man's vision, it is probably shared by a great number of Catholics. Without recapitulating his views on such controversial topics as abortion and capital punishment, Cardinal Bernardin has contributed enormously to clarifying and promoting his moral vision for America.

Another noteworthy Catholic commentary on America is John Courtney Murray's 1960 collection of essays, *We Hold These Truths: Catholic Reflections on the American Proposition,* and reprinted by Georgetown University Press in 2005.[26] When this book first appeared, Father Murray (1904–1967) himself was pictured on the cover of the December 12, 1960, issue of *Time* magazine, in a portrait drawn by artist Boris Chaliapin.[27] This *Time* piece, a cover feature story, could truly be called a "Catholic moment" in the Catholic impact on America. In the "Critical Introduction," Peter Lawler characterizes Father Murray's book as "one of two astute and comprehensive books written by American Catholic citizens about their country." "The other great Catholic book on America written by an American Catholic," Lawler adds, "is Orestes Brownson's *The American Republic* (1866)."[28]

Catholic Reflections on the American Proposition is not a simplistic, flag-waving paean to America by a Catholic leader. "The Catholic may not, as others do," writes Father Murray in his preface, "merge his religious and his patriotic faith, or submerge one in the other."[29] For Catholicism itself is far more historic and universal than America itself: "He must reckon with his own tradition of thought, which is wider and deeper than any that America has elaborated."[30] Murray's primary "message," as it were, is that Catholic values are harmonious with American ideals. This evades the real issue as to whether the Catholic church actually has, or can exert, any appreciable influence on the course of American thought and culture itself.

Retrospectively, however, Catholic visions of America have failed to have much decisive impact. The rhetoric was there, but not the results, according to Catholic sociologist Joseph Varacalli. In *Bright Promise, Failed Community* (2000), Varacalli explains why Catholic America essentially failed to shape the American Republic in any significant way.[31] Varacalli's concluding chapter is disappointing, however, being the afterthought of just one single page in this very short book.[32] One has to look elsewhere for a more forward-looking perspective. Prospectively, in an article that appeared in the Catholic popular journal, *Homiletic and Pastoral Review* in 2004, and reprinted in *Ignatius Insight* in May 2005, Varacalli elaborates further on the analysis he presented in *Bright Promise, Failed Community,* but with a view to the future of Catholicism in America. Varacalli articulates this vision in the following 12 "Propositions and Principles," which the present writer distills as follows:

Proposition One: Patriotic sentiments are principally realized at the level of the nation; such patriotism may soon be mediated through a kind of globalism. Either way, the key question is how Catholic citizens should relate to America.

Proposition Two: It is "idolatrous," however, to exalt a national interest above a religious concern. That is to say, faithful adherence to the practice of the Catholic religion must take precedence: "For all of its virtues, America is, at best, a means to some higher end such as human liberty," Varacalli states.

Proposition Three: Varacalli hastens to add that patriotism, per se, is neutral: "Patriotism, in and by itself, is neither good nor bad; the issue is the nature of what one is patriotic towards." Accordingly, a good Catholic must develop a healthy patriotism and not be "patriotic" for its own sake. For, to do so, would be tantamount to a blind patriotism. One should not be patriotic merely for the sake of patriotism.

Proposition Four: American society is in flux. Since the "America" that is the focus of our patriotism is constantly changing, therefore our own patriotism has to be adjusted accordingly.

Proposition Five: Its precipitous moral decline notwithstanding, Varacalli believes that, "all things considered, this country was a better place to live in fifty years or so ago."

Proposition Six: From a Catholic perspective, America is positive and negative.

Proposition Seven: The natural consequence of Proposition Six is that a Catholic view of America must be realistic, and must mediate between idealizing America, on the one extreme, and belonging to the "America hating club," on the other: "Fairness, realism, and the Catholic worldview, then, should acknowledge the ambiguous cultural reality of the present situation in the United States," Varacalli writes.

Proposition Eight: In many ways, this proposition is the key to Varacalli's Catholic vision of America, where "the possibility of reversing this society's descent into the culture of death or, conversely, building a society based on love and human solidarity depends on the implementation in American society of ideas either derived from, or consistent with, Catholic social teachings." From his own perspective as a devout Catholic, Varacalli's vision of America, in his own words, essentially boils down to this:

> The Catholic defense of the fundamental dignity of all human life, including the unborn; its positing of truth and the exercise of reason; its promotion of the intact, nuclear, traditional family; its insistence that the purpose of government is to serve the common good; its position that workers and employees have the right to organize for a decent spiritual and material existence; its claim that

creative and dignified work is constitutive of the anthropology of mankind; and its argument that the true development of nations and individual lives involves the furthering of both body and soul, are just a few examples of what I've referred to as the "bright promise" contained within Catholic social thought and the natural law. Simply put, the saving and further perfection of the American experiment lies primarily with the ability of the Catholic Church to serve as a leaven for our society and culture. Put another way, and translated into the central concern of my presentation, a great way to be a patriotic American is to be a serious, educated, and committed Catholic American.

Proposition Nine: Realistically, the Catholic Church in America is not currently positioned or equipped "to effectively lead the restoration of American society and culture," Varacalli admits. "As I've argued in my book, *Bright Promise, Failed Community: Catholics and the American Public Order,*" Varacalli explains, "the Catholic Church in the United States has suffered a massive 'secularization from within' during the post-Vatican II era." In other words, the American Catholic church has, unfortunately,

> allowed itself to be co-opted by corrupting secular influences, thus losing her ability not only to serve as a leaven for our society and culture but also her ability to evangelize her own community of slightly less than twenty-five percent of the American population. Simply put, the Church can't save America if she can't first save herself.

Proposition Ten: Given this critique, Varacalli advances what may well be considered his American Catholic manifesto: "The first task for the Catholic Church, then, is to restore integrity to the Catholic house through an intensive emphasis on authentic Catholic evangelization, catechesis, socialization, and education. In the language of sociology, the Catholic Church must rebuild its 'plausibility structure' or series of social institutions" in order to effectively regain any kind of measurable influence on American society.

Proposition Eleven: "The keys to creating and sustaining an orthodox Catholic institution capable both of socializing effectively its members and evangelizing successfully outside its walls is," Varacalli proposes, (1) maintaining the Catholic tradition "in all its majesty and sophistication"; (2) maintaining "high standards of professionalism and competence"; and (3) "reinforcing communication and social interaction." "Simply put," Varacalli proposes, American Catholics should "invest less time with American mass culture and more time in an authentically Catholic milieu."

Proposition Twelve: Finally, Varacalli exhorts American Catholics, in words of Jesus, to be "innocent as a dove and as wise as a serpent." Here, American Catholics need to look to contemporary role models. "One such role model," Varacalli proposes, "is Mel Gibson, whose film, *The Passion of the Christ,* represents a major victory for those who believe that Christians have a right to attempt to contribute and shape the contours of our culture and society." "Mel Gibson is a Christian who has made a difference in American public life," Varacalli explains, "by enriching it with the Gospel message. He is a true American patriot and a true Christian American."

Varacalli concludes that "the simple and stark fact is that United States of America needs the Catholic worldview more than the Catholic faith requires the American experience." The test of whether American Catholics have succeeded in their mission to positively influence America in realizing its own mission is simply this: "If this county of ours, which we love so much and which has done so much good for so many, is to escape further descent into the culture of death, it will be because of the presence, witness, and actions of a revitalized Catholic Church in the United States of America."[33]

Can the Catholic Americanist myth of America become a reality? With the sexual abuse scandal having significantly undermined faith in the Catholic priesthood, and with America's wider unmooring from the traditional harbors of morality, decency, and traditional American values, the answer to that question is likely this: Not on its own. Visions of America that can translate American ideals into reality will take other shapes and forms, as will be described throughout the remainder of this book. To the extent that a shared vision may be found, and common ground gained, the alternative visions of America that are most viable will probably be so because they reveal a grander vision. A much different, yet complementary vision of America will unfold in the chapters to come, beginning with Jewish visions of America.

CHAPTER 5

Jewish Myths and Visions of America

Behold America, the land of the future! ... The land of promise for all persecuted!
—Kaufmann Kohler (1911)[1]

We thank Thee, O God, for having taught the founders of our Republic laws that safeguard the equal rights of all citizens and impose equal obligations upon all.
—Mordecai Kaplan (1945)[2]

"Americanism" simply refers to an ideology of America—its identity, mission, and destiny. In the preceding chapter, one finds that Catholic visions of America—particularly the positive valuations of America by the so-called "Americanists" and, later, *inter alia,* by Pope John Paul II and Pope Benedict XVI—presupposed Protestant visions of America. To some degree, these eulogizing encomia of America were Catholicized, yet deracialized, echoes of the Protestant master myth of America. "Americanism" is also part of the common heritage of American Jews and served *Jewish* interests by serving *American* interests. Jewish Americanism was a "hyphen" that mediated between the extremes of ethnic ghettoism and total assimilation, thus allowing Jewish communities to have faith in America while "keeping the faith" as Jews.

Described as "a common feature in the history of all sectors in the American Jewish population," Americanism has been "the sociocultural and political creed of several million Jews" and "should be reexamined as a Jewish form of self-defense and legitimation."[3] Although noticeably ideological in *form*, Jewish visions of America are mythical in *content*, to the extent that these, in some ways, *reshape the Protestant myth of America by universalizing it*. By universalizing America's identity, mission, and destiny, the interests of the American Jewish community, are, reflexively, benefited. In American Judaism, therefore, one sees a transformative process at work. "As minority faiths strove to understand the meaning of America and their place in it," writes James Moorhead, "minority faiths themselves played no small part in the weakening of white Protestant hegemony. Their creativity in adapting and reinterpreting the symbols of American destiny broadened the framework of discourse within which citizens explained national identity."[4]

Jewish visions of America are directly linked to Jewish survival and identity. That is to say, the degree to which America takes on a religious significance is roughly coefficient with the extent to which America furthers Jewish interests. This is not a matter of expediency, but is directly connected with the future of Judaism in America itself. However, since America cannot, constitutionally speaking, directly advance Jewish interests by way of "state action," those interests will be indirectly furthered so long as fundamental human and civic rights prevail and are held to be inviolable. What is good for all is certainly good for one. What promotes freedom of religion for all faiths, in general, redounds to the benefit of American Judaism in particular. What benefits all Americans will surely benefit American Jews.

Americanism is expressed in a wide array of ways. In "The New Covenant: The Jews and the Myth of America," Sam B. Girgus asks whether a decidedly *religious* Jewish myth of America even exists.[5] In this chapter, key speeches by American Jewish leaders and related texts will be cited, not as *definitive*, but as *representative* of Jewish visions of America. Even if there were definitive Jewish religious perspectives on America, they would be necessarily plural, since there is no chief rabbi in America, and no central Jewish authority. Consider the fact that American Jews now have an Orthodox Pentateuch, a Conservative Pentateuch, and a Reform Pentateuch. While the Hebrew text is the same, the translations are different, and so are the commentaries.[6] Similarly, while the historical context of American Jews is roughly the same, the interpretations of that experience are different. However, these interpretations do reflect certain patterns, a description of which may be helpful in presenting a coherent overview of Jewish visions of America.

This positive regard for America finds greater expression in Jewish civil religion than it does in the Jewish religion itself. What unifies the range of Jewish myths of America is the American experience itself. Despite backlashes of anti-semitism, America has afforded immigrant Jews a land of refuge and of opportunity, as well as a place to maintain Jewish identity and continuity, even though assimilation ("Americanization") has been seen as a real threat to the American Jewish communities. Reciprocally, American Jews have contributed enormously to American thought and culture.

Jewish uniqueness is largely an issue of cultural and religious survival:

> "The key tenets of Jewish civil religion," according to Jonathan Woocher, are "concern for Jewish survival, the belief in collective action on the behalf of both Jewish interests and Jewish values, a devotion to Israel as a unique expression of Judaism's understanding of the meaning of and route toward redemption, and an acceptance of the community's right to make certain demands on us [as Americans]." [7]

In this sense, the preservation of uniqueness necessarily requires the presence of equality, with all of the safeguards it affords. A Jewish civil religion of America proceeds from American core values of equality. Here is where efforts were made by certain American Jewish leaders to integrate civil religion within the American Jewish communal experience.

JEWISH VISIONS OF AMERICA AS A MIRROR OF JEWISH IDEOLOGIES

Jewish visions *of* America developed as a result of the Jewish experience *in* America. The first Jewish community in America was New Amsterdam— later known as New York, when, in 1664, the British took over the Dutch colonies and split the land into New York and New Jersey. These "Sephardic" Jews hailed from Spain and Portugal. Not long after, they were joined by "Ashkenazic" Jews from Germany and Europe. Here, the Jews enjoyed a newfound religious freedom, although not without suffering anti-semitism, which was transplanted from the Old World into the New World. Notwithstanding, the 1776 Treaty of Breda gave full rights of trade, worship, and other rights to the settlers, including Jews. As popular support for the position that *freedom* of religion has been interpreted by Jewish Americans as *equality* of religion, Jonathan Sarna cites Article 11 of a 1797 treaty between the United States and the Bey and subjects of Tripoli, which states: "The government of the United States of America is not in any sense founded on the Christian religion." Authored by American diplomat Joel Barlow in 1796, the Treaty of Peace and Friendship between the United States and the Bey and subjects of Tripoli of Barbary was read aloud from the floor of the Senate, June 7, 1797, during the session of the Fifth Congress, where it was unanimously approved and later signed by President John Adams, who proclaimed it to the nation on June 10, 1797. Article 11 states, in full:

> As the Government of the United States of America is not, in any sense, founded on the Christian religion; as it has in itself no character of enmity against the laws, religion, or tranquillity, of Mussulmen; and, as the said states never entered

into any war, or act of hostility against any Mahometan nation, it is declared by the parties, that no pretext arising from religious opinions, shall ever produce an interruption of the harmony existing between the two countries.[8]

This particular statement has often been cited by American Jewish leaders "to reassure the faithful that *no* religion obtains special treatment in America."[9] Thus, a natural affinity has developed between the right to be a Jew and civil rights for all peoples, giving rise to expressions of a Jewish civil religion of America. Trade-offs between *integration* and *identity*—that is, being accepted as Americans while maintaining their distinctive identity as Jews—are at the heart of Jewish perspectives on America. Since ethnic otherness has always stood in tension with American assimilation, a key to Jewish survival is to be forged—*but not melted*—in the "melting pot" of America. Before examining some of these prayers for the government, recited in American Jewish liturgies, it will be useful to establish a context for the Jewish myth of America as "The Promised Land," followed by a brief overview of the Jewish myth of Columbus.

THE JEWISH MYTH OF AMERICA AS "THE PROMISED LAND"

For over 200 years, prominent Jewish leaders and writers have acclaimed America as the "Promised Land" or, alternatively, as the "Land of Promise."[10] Several examples will serve to illustrate this ideological and social phenomenon. Elected to the South Carolina state legislature in 1810, Myer Moses II (1779–1833)—in a speech delivered in Charleston in 1806—exuberantly exclaimed: "The Almighty gave to the Jews what had long been promised them, namely a second Jerusalem! . . . I am so proud of being a sojourner in this promised land."[11] In December 1898, the Union of American Hebrew Congregations adopted a resolution that proclaimed: "America is our Zion. Here in the home of religious liberty, we have aided in founding of this new Zion, the fruition of the beginning laid in the old."[12] And in 1987, Jewish historian and Conservative Rabbi Jacob Neusner was quite explicit in affirming that America is indeed the Promised Land for Jews:

> It is time to say that America is a better place to be a Jew than Jerusalem. If ever there was a Promised Land, we Jewish Americans are living in it. Here Jews have flourished, not alone in politics and the economy, but in matters of art, culture and learning. Jews feel safe and secure here in ways that they do not and cannot in the State of Israel.[13]

Traditionally, exile and return is a powerful organizing principle of Jewish history. It has served as a hermeneutical prism of the American Jewish experience as well. Indeed, Jewish visions of America have arisen out of the

American Jewish experience in a reciprocal interplay of Jewish and American identities, shaped also by the motif of "Holocaust and Redemption," which, according to Jacob Neusner, still operates as *the generative myth by which the generality of Jewish Americans make sense of themselves and decide what to do with that part of themselves set aside for 'being Jewish.'*"[14]

Certainly the most poignant and tragic moment of the 2,000-year Exile was the Holocaust. In the aftermath of the Holocaust, the subsequent return of Jews to their ancestral homeland of Israel (i.e., the *Kibbutz Galuyot,* the "ingathering of the exiles") and the formation of the state of Israel in 1948 is part of the "Redemption" of Jews. Thus it comes as no surprise that the Holocaust and the State of Israel are dominant themes that defined American Jewish identity in the latter half of the twentieth century, although less so in the twenty-first century. Within the American experience itself, Jonathan Sarna sees a pattern of *exile* and *return* to Judaism—in which American Judaism *waxes* and *wanes*—with perpetual tension between these polarities.[15]

Jewish Americans are understandably concerned more about the biblical Promised Land—Israel—than about America, which, prior to the establishment of the State of Israel in 1948, offered its own promise as a virtual and, perhaps, surrogate "Promised Land." Different from American Protestants—who looked to America as God's New Israel—the ancestral Jewish homeland and the modern state of Israel remain a powerful orientation for nearly all Jews. Jewish Americans have a *home* in America and a *homeland* in Israel. While America is still home to the world's largest Jewish community, the Jewish homeland of Israel—not America—is the *axis mundis* of the Jewish world.

As Israel's most powerful ally, America has played a key role in strategically protecting the biblical Promised Land. It would seem that such a role, in the eyes of Jewish Americans at least, would have invested America with some kind of transcendent purpose, since America has providentially safeguarded the Holy Land. Ironically, while one might expect that this singular fact should have taken on some *religious* significance, one is hard-pressed to find a definitive "theology of America" within an American Jewish framework itself. Instead, Jewish visions of "America" are articulated in a number of less-pronounced ways.

There is no question that Jewish patriotism for America is healthy and vibrant, in a secular sense. But does America have any *religious* significance for Jewish Americans? Is America exceptional, in any way, just as the Jews themselves are regarded as exceptional, as a "chosen people"? Are Jewish Americans a "chosen people" within a "chosen" nation? There is American exceptionalism and then there is Jewish exceptionalism. The two are obviously not the same. From Jewish perspectives, American exceptionalism is coefficient with America's ability to preserve and promote Jewish exceptionalism. And so it is that Jewish Americans have been described as "A Unique People in an Exceptional Country." [16]

In thinking about the religious significance that America may hold for Jewish Americans, one must keep in mind that American Judaism is composed of multi-synagogue communities that primarily include Orthodox, Conservative, Reform, and Reconstructionist groups, not to mention religiously unaffiliated and "other" Jews, reflecting a *de facto* religious pluralism within American Judaism. Since there are four normative branches of Judaism in the United States today—Orthodox, Conservative, Reform, and Reconstructionist Judaism—Jewish Americanism has been variously expressed, and not without controversy. One aspect of this is the Jewish myth of Columbus, in which it is said that Jews accompanied Christopher Columbus in his discovery of America.

THE JEWISH "MYTH OF COLUMBUS"

In 1492, when Christopher Columbus discovered America, Jews were expelled from Spain. Notwithstanding, when Columbus sailed from Old World Spain to the New World, Luis de Torres, a Jewish interpreter, accompanied him. Thus, Jews can claim to have played a role in America from the very moment America was discovered. The Jewish experience in America, therefore, reaches as far back as the discovery of America itself. Imagine if Christopher Columbus himself was a Jew. If so, then Jewish Americans could rightly claim that they are as authentically "American" as any other American, since the discoverer of America was himself a Jew. It is for this reason that the figure of Columbus has taken on mythic proportions in American Judaism, albeit in a secular rather than a religious sense.

The Jewish myth of Columbus was developed as part of an overarching survival strategy and as a means of gaining American respect. The popular Jewish myth that Columbus himself was crypto-Jew served as a bulwark against rising nativism in America.[17] "Other ethnic groups in America claimed founder status based on their putative roles as discoverers of the new world," observes Jonathan Sarna. "Jews, I believe, are the only group which has claimed status based on ties to the Indians, the Puritans, and Columbus, as well." [18] By associating themselves with the founding myths of America, Jewish Americans could prove that they, like the Indians, were original Americans and played a role in America's origins.

JEWISH PRAYERS FOR AMERICA: COMMUNAL VISIONS OF AMERICA

Historically, nearly all Jewish prayer books in America have included a prayer for the welfare of the government. This is part of a long-standing

Jewish practice around the world, as Gordon M. Freeman explains: "In fact, a prayer for the government is a feature of every type of prayer book of every land of the Jewish diaspora irrespective of the specific religious movement of the community." [19] This is an ancient Jewish obligation and a venerable tradition that has carried over to the Jewish experience in America. In the rabbinic commentary, *Pirke Avot,* Jews are enjoined to "Pray for the welfare of the government, because were it not for the fear it inspires, every man would swallow his neighbor alive" (3:2). Jews have maintained this time-honored practice from the time of the Second Temple. Alexander the Great, it is said, claimed that the priests in the temple prayed for his well-being.

While prayer does not have scriptural status, it is a conduit of religious ideology. Since there is no Jewish scripture regarding America, one therefore looks to Jewish prayer books for some communal Jewish perspectives on America. Prayer books, after all, are not simply liturgy. They are communal performances of doctrine in a spirit of devotion. "Second only to the Torah, the *siddur* (prayer book)," states one Reform rabbi, *"expresses the ideology of our people."* [20] As a congregation prays, so it believes.

As ideology evolves, so do prayer books. As such, they are documents of the history of ideas within religious contexts. Liturgical texts, as Jonathan Sarna demonstrates, offer a window into history: "Prayer, while unquestionably a part of the American experience, is not a phenomenon that most American historians study. Yet, liturgical texts—as well as other aspects of prayer—may be subjected to historical analysis." [21]

While there is no communally held doctrine of America among Jews in the United States today, Jews have ritually included prayers for the U.S. government in various prayer books. In other words, American Judaism has what might be called a "liturgy of America," although this aspect of Jewish worship is admittedly minor. A study of these prayers, therefore, will reveal some ways in which Jews incorporate the secular into the sacred, partly through a process of *sacralizing the secular.* American Jewish prayer books are a testament to the Americanization of Judaism.

ORTHODOX JUDAISM'S TRADITIONAL PRAYER FOR THE GOVERNMENT

What may be the first Jewish prayer for the U.S. government is a handwritten manuscript dated 1784, although neither would the U.S. Constitution be ratified nor George Washington elected as the nation's first president until 1789. This prayer, preserved in the Jacques Judah Lyons Collection of the American Jewish Historical Society, is a prayer of thanksgiving for the successful conclusion of the American War for Independence. The prayer itself is attributed to Hendla Jochanan van Oettingen, a *hazzan* (reader) of New York's Congregation *Shearith Israel,* the country's first Jewish congregation. The prayer mentions the names of both General George Washington, commander in chief of the American Army, and Governor George Clinton, chief magistrate of New York. The prayer reads, in part:

> Mayest Thou grant intelligence, wisdom and knowledge to our lords, the rulers of these thirteen states. . . . As Thou has granted to these thirteen states of America everlasting freedom, so mayest Thou bring us forth once again from bondage into freedom.[22]

In 1826, however, the version of *Hanoten Teshua* published in New York blesses the president and the vice president, the Senate, the House of Representatives, the governor, the lieutenant governor, and the magistrates of New York City.[23]

The most explicitly nationalist of these Orthodox prayers for the American government is one that was rediscovered by Jonathan Sarna. The prayer, *Ribbon Kol Ha-olamim,* rendered into English, reads, in part:

> Master of the Universe, Lord of all Works, Who extends peace like a river, and the glory of nations like a rapid stream. Look down from Your holy dwelling and bless this land, the United States of America, whereon we dwell. Let not violence be heard in their land, wasting and destruction within their boundaries, but You shall call its walls "Salvation" and its gates "Praise." . . .
>
> Pour down the bounty of Your goodness upon the President, and the Vice President of the United States. Let their prosperity be like a river, their righteousness like the waves of the sea. In their days may kindness and truth meet each other, righteousness and peace kiss. Great shall be their honor; through Your help and in Your strength they will greatly exult. Amen. . . .
>
> Ordain Your blessings also upon the Governor and the lieutenant Governor of the state and the Mayor and the Common Council of this City. Teach them the good way wherein they should walk so as to judge the entire people rightly, the entire nation justly, and all will see it and delight themselves from the abundance of peace. Send Your salvation also to the City of New York and all its inhabitants. Spread over them the canopy of Your Peace and remove from them every ailment and mishap. . . .[24]

Sarna, who ascribes the authorship of this unique prayer to Rabbi Max Lilienthal (1814?–1882),[25] observes that particular prayer "did much to signify to them that America was different—if not actually Zion then the closest thing to it." [26] This prayer is no longer in use. One reason is that this was a purely local innovation. It was atypical of Orthodox Judaism generally.

Of the four forms of contemporary American Judaism, Orthodox liturgy is the least amenable to change, as Ruth Langer notes:

> The contemporary Orthodox world defines itself by adherence to traditional *halakhah,* including the received liturgical text, and by varying degrees of opposition to the outside world. Therefore, its core Hebrew and Aramaic prayer

texts are nonnegotiable. At the most liberal end of the spectrum, modern Ortho-doxy seeks cultural accommodation within the bounds of *halakhah,* which still creates a community that sees itself as religiously rigorously separate. Accom-modation to modernity occurs in the esthetic presentation of the liturgy, in the printed translations or commentaries, and sometimes in the choices of *piyyutim* or other non-halakhic elements of the service.[27]

By way of a very brief introduction, Orthodox Judaism accepts, without reservation, the doctrine: "The Torah is from Heaven." [28] Orthodox Jews thus see themselves as "Torah-true." They manifest complete loyalty to the Jewish past. Basically, Orthodoxy represents faithfulness to the practices of Judaism as enshrined in the *Halakhah* in its traditional formulation. That is, an Orthodox Jew is one who obeys the rules promulgated in the standard Code of Jewish law, the *Shulhan Arukh.* Orthodox Judaism rejects the notion advo-cated by Reform Judaism that, in the light of modernity, Judaism needs to be "reformed." This "old-time religion" is good enough for Orthodox Jews.[29] There are, however, a range of Orthodox worldviews, from the ultra-Orthodox to neo-Orthodoxy.[30] Notwithstanding, Orthodox Jews are unified in rightly claiming that theirs is the Judaism of tradition as practiced in the premodern era.[31] In contrast to Reform Judaism, which sought to place ethi-cal monotheism at the center of Jewish life, Orthodox Judaism placed the Torah at the center of Jewish life.

Common to Orthodox Judaism and Reform Judaism, however, is the fact that both integrated prayer in support of the government in their respective lit-urgies. The traditional Orthodox Jewish prayer for the government is known as the *Hanoten Teshu'ah.* From its origins in the fifteenth century, the *Han-oten Teshu'ah* became the most popular prayer for the government until the twentieth century. An Americanized version of this Orthodox prayer reads as follows:

PRAYER FOR THE GOVERNMENT
Hanoten Teshu'ah
The reader takes the Torah and recites:

He who granted victory to kings and dominion to princes, his kingdom is a king-dom of all ages; he who delivered his servant David from the evil sword, he who opened a road through the sea, a path amid the mighty waters—may he bless and protect, help and exalt:

THE PRESIDENT AND THE VICE PRESIDENT
AND ALL THE OFFICERS OF THIS COUNTRY.

May the supreme King of kings, in his mercy, sustain them and deliver them from all distress and misfortune. May the supreme King of kings, in his mercy, inspire them and all their counselors and aides to deal kindly with us and with all Israel. In their days and in our days Judah shall be saved, Israel shall dwell in security, and a redeemer shall come to Zion. May this be the will of God; and let us say, Amen.[32]

There is nothing remarkably "American" about this prayer, except for its recognition of the fact that the leaders of the American government are the U.S. president and vice president. Although assumed, the United States is not named. In his 2006 paper, "Who is an American Jew?," Michael Walzer, of The Institute for Advanced Study's School of Social Science, Princeton University, comments on this prayer in the American context:

> This is an extraordinary prayer for citizens to recite, given that the president and vice president must come to them and ask for their votes. In fact, the prayer isn't written in the common language of democratic citizenship, but in a much older language. It reflects an exilic sense of marginality and danger. For centuries, we were radically dependent on the kindness of kings, but our relation to presidents is, or ought to be, different. Perhaps the subtext of the orthodox prayer is skepticism about that difference. The people who recite it, assuming that they mean what they say, are still living in the imaginative space of exile, where "all the world is against us." They are in fact citizens of the United States but in their own minds, they are something else.[33]

During the Vietnam years, "chauvinistic prayers from an earlier era rang hollow." [34] From then until now, the traditional Jewish practice of praying for the welfare of the government—a tradition with a rich and venerable history going back to the medieval period—has experienced widespread decline. It was during the post-Vietnam era when traditional prayers for America largely fell silent, with the result that this practice has largely disappeared, as Sarna observes: "Impressionistic evidence suggests that even where prayer books did include a regular prayer for the government, congregations recited it less frequently." [35] A prime example of this trend is that a popular Orthodox *siddur,* known as *The Complete ArtScroll Siddur* (1984), includes no prayer for the government at all, with only a footnote that perfunctorily explains that "in many congregations, a prayer for the welfare of the State is recited." [36] Ironically, this would appear to be a break from the Orthodox tradition of offering prayers for the government, throughout the Diaspora.

CONSERVATIVE JUDAISM'S VISION OF AMERICA

Conservative Judaism occupies the middle ground between Orthodoxy and Reform. With its center in the United States, Conservative Judaism is the largest of the four movements in America. Jewish Theological Seminary in New York (with branches in Los Angeles and Jerusalem) is the primary institution for the training of Conservative Rabbis, who are organized as the Rabbinical Assembly of Conservative Rabbis. Zachariah Frankel and Solomon Schechter are the two key thinkers of Conservative Judaism.[37] While Schechter was Conservative Judaism's most illustrious personality, the leading ideologist of Conservative Judaism in the Schechter era was Israel Friedlaender. In 1907, Friedlaender presented his vision of America within the broader context of Zionism: "The only place where such a Judaism has a chance of realization is America." [38]

Conservative Jews have a new prayer book (*siddur*), the *Sim Shalom for Shabbat and Festivals,* edited by Rabbi Lawrence Cahan. The previous *siddur,* also titled *Sim Shalom,* was edited by Rabbi Jules Harlow, but contains services for weekdays, along with Sabbath and festivals. The prior *Sim Shalom* was first published in 1985. The first Conservative *siddur* appeared in 1927. That *siddur* introduced a "Prayer for Our Country," which was considered an innovation. Of all Jewish prayers for the American government, the most perdurable is "A Prayer for Our Country," composed by the great rabbinic scholar, Louis Ginzberg (1873–1953). As Rabbi David Golinkin states: "In 1927, when the Conservative movement published its first prayer book for festivals, Prof. Louis Ginzberg composed the prayer for the government. This version is no longer based on *Hanoten Teshua* which was intended for a monarchy. It is a brand new prayer expressly written for a democracy." [39]

First published both in Hebrew and in English translation in the *Festival Prayer Book* of the Conservative movement (1927), this prayer was subsequently reprinted in standard Conservative Jewish prayer books and in older Reconstructionist prayer books as well.[40] All major Conservative prayer books contain this prayer, which is essentially the same text in Hebrew, but with varying English paraphrases.[41] The so-called "Silverman Siddur" (with black bindings), was edited by Rabbi Morris Silverman and first published in 1946. Silverman intended the "Prayer for Our Country" as a replacement for the ancient prayer for the government. The "Silverman Siddur" was standard in the Conservative movement for nearly 40 years, and is still in use at some synagogues today. In 1962, Rabbi Silverman composed "A Prayer for Our Country," published in the *High Holiday Prayer Book.* This prayer reads, in part:

A PRAYER FOR OUR COUNTRY

May all the peoples that make up this great Commonwealth consecrate their efforts, under Thy guidance, to the cause of liberty, equality, and justice. May we remain united in purpose, respecting each other's rights and striving together with resolute hearts and willing hands for the welfare of all the inhabitants of our land.[42]

The *Sim Shalom for Shabbat and Festivals* is only for Sabbath and festivals, with no liturgy for weekday services. However, the new *Sim Shalom for Shabbat and Festivals* continues the regular use of Louis Ginzberg's prayer for America:

A PRAYER FOR OUR COUNTRY

Our God and God of our ancestors: We ask Your blessings for our country—for its government, for its leaders and advisors, and for all who exercise just and rightful authority. Teach them insights from Your Torah, that they may administer all affairs of state fairly, that peace and security, happiness and prosperity, justice and freedom may forever abide in our midst.

Creator of all flesh, bless all the inhabitants of our country with Your spirit. May citizens of all races and creeds forge a common bond in true harmony, to banish hatred and bigotry, and to safeguard the ideals and free institutions that are the pride and glory of our country.

May this land, under your providence, be an influence for good throughout the world, uniting all people in peace and freedom—helping them to fulfill the vision of your prophet: "Nation shall not lift up sword against nation, neither shall they experience war any more" (Isaiah 2:4). And let us say: Amen.[43]

As explained by Ruth Langer, "our country" in American Reform liturgies through the mid-twentieth century always referred to the United States.[44] In Sarna's translation, the prayer reads, in part: "May citizens of all races and creeds forge a common bond in true harmony to banish all hatred and bigotry." The universalism of this prayer is also evident in this passage: "Plant among the peoples of different nationalities and faiths who dwell here, love and brotherhood, peace and friendship."[45] Ginzberg's vision of America—liturgically shared by Conservative and Reconstructionist Judaism—represents what Sarna terms a "universalistic peroration."[46] It is a prayer that transcends sectarian boundaries and creedal differences.

REFORM JUDAISM'S VISION OF AMERICA

In 1830, the Reformed Society of Israelites in Charleston, South Carolina, published an English prayer book that contained a "Prayer for the Government in English," to be recited during "The Service on Sabbath Morning." This prayer follows immediately after the "Reading of the Sanctification of the Sabbath and the Sh'ma in English by the Minister With Responses by the Congregation."[47] This "Prayer for the Government in English"—composed by David N. Carvalho—is described by Jonathan Sarna as follows:

Written entirely in English, the new prayer had none of the regal language of its traditional counterpart. Rather than "exalting" the President and other federal and state officials, for example, it simply asked God to "bless," "preserve," and (a reflection of their highest ideal) "enlighten" them. Then, in an expression of patriotic piety not previously encountered in an American Jewish prayer book, it thanked God for having "numbered us with the inhabitants of this thy much favoured land . . . where the noble and virtuous mind is the only crown of distinction, and equality of rights the only fountain of power," for having removed from the republic "the intolerance of bigotry," and for freeing its people "from the yoke of political and religious bondage." Finally, it sought divine blessings upon "the people of these United States," called for charity, friendship and unity among them, and prayed that "the lights of science and civilization . . . defend them on every side from the subtle hypocrite and open adversary." The hope for Jewish redemption that closed the traditional prayer for the government went unmentioned.[48]

For Reform Jews, America is the "Land of Promise"—just as Israel is the "Promised Land." [49] After Reform spread from Germany to America, Isaac Mayer Wise (1819–1900) became the redoubtable architect of Reform Judaism in the United States. In 1875, the Hebrew Union College was established, by Wise, in Cincinnati for the training of Reform Rabbis.[50]

How does Reform Judaism define itself? It does so by periodically *redefining* itself. On four occasions throughout its American history, the Reform rabbinate has adopted principles statements that have guided the thought and practice of the Reform movement. In 1885, fifteen rabbis promulgated the *Pittsburgh Platform,* a set of principles that piloted Reform Judaism for the next 50 years. In 1937, a revised set of principles—the *Columbus Platform* —was adopted by the Central Conference of American Rabbis. In 1976, a third set of rabbinic guidelines, the *Centenary Perspective,* was proclaimed on the occasion of the centenary of the Union of American Hebrew Congregations and the Hebrew Union College–Jewish Institute of Religion. Then, in the 1999 Pittsburgh Convention, the Central Conference of American Rabbis adopted "A Statement of Principles for Reform Judaism." Thus, the 1999 *Pittsburgh Platform* represents quite an evolution of Reform doctrine beyond the original 1885 *Pittsburgh Platform.* So, on the one hand, Reform Jews are part and parcel of the people of Israel: "We are Israel, a people aspiring to holiness, singled out through our ancient covenant and our unique history among the nations to be witnesses to God's presence." On the other hand, Reform Jews in America are part and parcel of the people of America: "We embrace religious and cultural pluralism as an expression of the vitality of Jewish communal life in Israel and the Diaspora." [51] America is obviously part of that Diaspora. Therefore, Reform Jews—as with Jewish Americans generally—may be regarded as a *dual-authority* polity. As one might expect, the corresponding ideology would have both Jewish and American interests at heart.

In the Reform view, Judaism is a universal religion, a "light unto the nations." Reform sees itself as part of the "Jewish mission" to mankind.[52] For Reform Jews, as previously stated, America is the "Land of Promise"— just as Israel is the "Promised Land." Perhaps this was little more than an ideology for Jewish survival in America.[53] Rabbi Isaac Mayer Wise believed Judaism first had to be modernized, democratized, and Americanized before it could be universalized as a religion that would enlighten the world. America would play a pivotal role in the destiny of Judaism. In 1869, Rabbi Isaac Mayer Wise proclaimed:

> History is Providence realized. . . . The destiny which a nation realizes in the designs of Providence, is its place in history. . . . The people of the United States, on accepting this Constitution, had formally and solemnly chosen its destiny, to be now and forever the palladium of liberty and its divinely appointed banner-bearer, for the progress and redemption of mankind. . . . Freedom to all nations; freedom to every man, this is our country's place in history; liberty in the name of my God and my country.[54]

Reform Judaism has used a succession of three major prayer books: (1) *The Union Prayer Book* (1894); (2) *Gates of Prayer* (1975);[55] and (3) the *Mishkan T'filah* ("Tabernacle of Prayer" or "Sanctuary of Prayer") (2007). Reform Judaism's first official prayer book, *The Union Prayer Book for Jewish Worship, Seder Tifilos Yisroel, 1894–1895,* was first published in 1894. The predecessor of the *Union Prayer Book* was *Minhag America,* edited by Isaac Mayer Wise. Curiously, *Minhag America* did not contain a prayer for the welfare of the government.[56] Nor was the *Union Prayer Book* modeled on *Minhag America,* but rather on Dr. David Einhorn's radical *Olat Tamid* prayer book, a reworked liturgy in German with Hebrew selections reading from left to right, for Sunday morning services.[57] The *Union Prayer Book* features the following prayer for America:

FOR OUR PEOPLE AND OUR NATION

Bless, O God, this congregation, those who lead and serve it, those who contribute to its strength. Bless all who enter this House, that the worship offered within its walls may be worthy of Your greatness and Your love, and that all who seek Your presence here may find it. For the joy of community, the gift of diversity, and the vision of harmony, we offer our grateful thanks.

Bless our land and all its inhabitants. Prosper us in all our undertakings. Be with those whom we have chosen to lead us, that they may strive to establish justice and opportunity for all, and labor to bring peace to the family of nations.

Bless the household of Israel wherever they dwell. Be with us here, where we worship You in freedom. And may those who live under oppressive rule find release and liberty speedily, in our own day.

May Your favor rest upon Israel, her land, her people. Protect her against hatred and war. Grant that the promise of her beginning may ripen into fulfillment, bringing comfort to those who seek refuge, light to those who dwell in darkness, new hope to all humanity. And let us say: Amen.

The successor to the *Union Prayer Book* was the *Gates of Prayer*—a liturgy said to be a "unique blending of Jewish tradition and the American spirit." Notwithstanding the merits of this prayer for America in the *Union Prayer Book,* Sarna observes that the replacement prayer was perfunctory in comparison, comprising just four lines:

The new Reform Jewish prayer book, *Gates of Prayer* (1975), for example, abandoned the fervent supplication that was for so long a staple of Reform Jewish worship, replacing it with an occasional prayer, divorced from the regular liturgy, that covered the nation, its inhabitants, and its leaders in four short lines.[58]

In 1994, the Reform movement introduced its gender-inclusive liturgy, *Gates of Prayer for Shabbat and Weekdays: A Gender Sensitive Prayer Book.* Under *Gates of Prayer,* plain text is what the rabbi or leader reads; text in italics is what the congregation reads. The *Gates of Prayer* was phased out in 2007, as was the four-line prayer for America. The *Mishkan T'filah—A Reform Siddur* ("Tabernacle of Prayer" or "Sanctuary of Prayer") is the new Reform *siddur.* It has no italics, and thus does not differentiate rabbi from congregant as to what is recited. The current Reform prayer for America is as follows:

FOR OUR COUNTRY

THUS SAYS ADONAI, This is what I desire:
To unlock the fetters of wickedness, and untie the cords of lawlessness;
To let the oppressed go free; to break off every yoke.
Share your bread with the hungry, and to take the wretched poor into your home.
When you see the naked, give clothing, and do not ignore your own kin.
If you banish the yoke from your midst, the menacing hand, the evil speech;
If you offer compassion to the hungry and satisfy the famished creature—
Then your light shall shine in darkness.

[Isaiah 58:6–7, 9–10]

O GUARDIAN of life and liberty,
may our nation always merit Your protection.
Teach us to give thanks for what we have
by sharing it with those who are in need.
Keep our eyes open to the wonders of creation,
and alert to the care of the earth.
May we never be lazy in the work of peace;
and honor those who have died in defense of our ideals.

Grant our leaders wisdom and forbearance.
May they govern with justice and compassion.
Help us all to appreciate one another,
And to respect the many ways that we serve You.
May our homes be safe from affliction and strife,
and may our country be sound in body and spirit.
Amen[59]

This Reform prayer for America may be regarded as a meditation on Isaiah 58:6–7, 9–10. Here, the social ethic that Isaiah enjoins on the individual is generalized to the leaders of America. If guided by the principles of Isaiah, then America will "govern with justice and compassion" as a reflex of "wisdom and forbearance." While peace remains the overarching ideal, there appears to be a doctrine of just war "in defense of our ideals." Rather than idealizing America's world role in the community of nations, there seems to be a greater emphasis on "protection" and "defense." Might the emphasis of this prayer be a response, in part, to the terrorist attacks of September 11, 2001? What is clear and manifest is that this Reform prayer for America is infused with prophetic ideals.

In light of this decline in Reform liturgical support for America, one wonders if this kind of claim can withstand scrutiny: "Certainly no movement," one historian observes, "exceeded Reform in alluding to America's chosenness." [60] Historically, Reconstructionist Judaism is certainly a close rival.

RECONSTRUCTIONIST JUDAISM'S VISION OF AMERICA

Briefly, Reconstructionism is an American movement with branches abroad. Reconstructionism views Judaism as a "civilization"—replete with its own religion, culture, music, literature, art, mores, and folkways. Founded by Mordecai Menaheim Kaplan (1881–1983), Reconstructionists seek to revitalize Judaism in the modern world.[61] Reconstructionism, having developed as a fourth Jewish movement in the United States, has established its own seminary, the Rabbinical College in Wyncote, Pennsylvania, founded in 1957. While a small number of Reconstructionist synagogues have also been established, Reconstructionist Rabbis serve in Reform and Conservative congregations as well.[62] Liturgical creativity has been a hallmark of Reconstructionism.[63]

Mordecai M. Kaplan founded Reconstructionism in an effort to bridge the divisions of Orthodox, Conservative, and Reform Judaism.[64] In this, he did not succeed. However, he established, for his followers at least, democracy as a religious value. Kaplan has come to be valued more highly now as compared to then: "Mordecai M. Kaplan is rightly acclaimed as the greatest Jewish thinker to have emerged from the American Jewish context." [65] Born in Lithuania in 1881, arriving in the United States at the age of nine, in 1934, Mordecai M. Kaplan published his *magnum opus* and what would certainly be his most enduring work: *Judaism as a Civilization: Toward a Reconstruction of American-Jewish Life.*[66]

The title of this masterwork could be transposed to reflect a subthesis: *America as a Civilization: Toward a Reconstruction of American Life.* While the transformation of this title is the present writer's, it does reflect some recent scholarship on Kaplan: "Scholars and Jewish thinkers alike have much to learn from Kaplan's efforts to save Judaism by reconstructing the common understanding of American civilization." [67] For this analysis, the following statement by Kaplan shows that, ideally, Judaism would exercise a beneficial influence on America by transforming America's democratic nationalism into a civilizational nationalism—one that adumbrates the civic virtues of democracy, while allowing for the reciprocal influence of religious values:

> America is destined to depart from the strict logic of democratic nationalism and to achieve a new cultural constellation in which historical civilizations, or churches, may be permitted to conserve the finest products of their experience and contribute them to the sum total of American culture and civilization.[68]

Jewish Americans, in Kaplan's view, have a mission to widen America's profession and practice of democracy:

> Kaplan clung tenaciously to an unwavering belief in the promise of America. Steadfast faith in the ideal of American democracy served as a cornerstone of his program for the Jewish future, the American future, and the relationship between the two. He repeatedly stressed that the fate of Jews was "bound up with that of genuine democracy." But the notion that Jewish survival rested on the security provided by American democracy represents only one (perhaps the most obvious) element of Kaplan's philosophy. Kaplan also posited a specific mission for Jews in America. In one of the many sentences that he tended to italicize in order to signal their importance to the reader, he insisted that, "By staking our fortune upon the ultimate establishment of true democracy, we are contributing to that consummation." Democracy, as the foundation of American civil religion, had for Kaplan a spiritual component, capable of providing "a source of inner peace" for all Americans; moreover, he claimed that Jews had a particular role in bringing American democracy to its fullest expression.[69]

Noam Pianko argues that Kaplan's use of the term "civilization" plays two disparate functions in Kaplan's thought. His original purpose was to equate Judaism with the highest values of America, regarded as one of the world's premier "civilizations." Later, "Kaplan appropriated the term civilization in order to present Jewish nationalism as an important corrective to totalizing claims of American nationalism prevalent in the years leading up to the publication of his magnum opus" [70] in 1934.

Kaplan later translated this ideology into liturgy, both for Americans in general and for Jewish Americans in particular. In 1951, Mordecai Kaplan and two other editors edited a now-forgotten anthology, *The Faith of America: Readings, Songs and Prayers for the Celebration of American Holidays.*[71] *The Faith of America* was composed as a liturgy for American civic celebrations, as Kaplan himself writes: "This book is designed to foster faith in American democracy through the observance of our national holidays. Each holiday becomes not only a day for recreation but a means for deepening our democratic faith." [72] Kaplan goes on to explain how the lofty principles of Judaism should exert an edifying influence to elevate to America's civil religion:

> An illustration of the way those principles should be incorporated in American institutional life is afforded by *The Faith of America.* That book contains programs for the religious observance of American holidays. . . . Given the wish to survive as a segment of the Jewish people, that wish is bound to seek an outlet in some effort that would give to our persistence as Jews not merely the significance of inertia but rather the lift that comes from being dedicated to a high purpose. That high purpose should be to contribute to the spiritual life of America the kind of civic religion that will place America in the spiritual forefront of the world, as she is now in the political and economic.[73]

While the anthology itself failed to attract a following in the wider American society, six years earlier, Rabbi Kaplan's civic commemorations had already entered the Reconstructionist *Sabbath Prayer Book,* published in 1945. The *Sabbath Prayer Book* incensed the American Orthodox rabbis. The last section of this prayer book is dedicated to American civic festivals, reflecting "Kaplan's desire to have Jews internalize civic commitment and to lend that commitment a religious dimension." [74] Historian Beth Wenger cites a few examples from the *Sabbath Prayer Book:*

> Kaplan hoped that including patriotic sentiments in prayer would encourage Jews to internalize devotion to American ideals as a religious obligation. The prayer books of other Jewish movements contained various readings about America, including the American anthem and a prayer for the government, but Kaplan's innovation was to create organized services for national holidays. On Independence Day, worshippers actually rose to recite in unison two paragraphs from the Declaration of Independence, beginning with, "We hold these truths to be self-evident." Nowhere is the essence of Kaplan's ideology more apparent than in a lengthy reading for Thanksgiving Day that celebrates "God's Goodness" in four parts, beginning with "The Testament on Nature," then moving to

"The Testament of Man," then to "The Testament of Israel" (here, the people Israel), and finally concluding with "The Testament of America." In a clearly formulated teleology, Kaplan takes God's plan from nature, to human beings, to the Jewish people, to the United States of America.[75]

A quick glance at the table of contents of the *Sabbath Prayer Book: With A Supplement Containing Prayers, Readings and Hymns and With A New Translation*[76] reveals that "God's Goodness—the Testament of America" appears on pages 559–560, which reads as follows:

> God's Goodness—the Testament of America
>
> Thy goodness is revealed in the *Testament of America.* Into this land there have assembled the outcast and the weary of the older nations of the world. Here they dreamed a new dream of a nation founded on the truth, that all men are created equal, that they are endowed by their Creator with certain inalienable rights, that among those rights are life, liberty and the pursuit of happiness.
>
> And because Thou hast been with us and Thy goodness has kept us strong, the freedom which they won is still ours. May we ever be worthy of our American heritage; may we ever treasure our liberties, not for ourselves alone but for all our fellowmen; and may our country become a guiding light to all mankind.

In the words of Abraham Lincoln:

> With malice toward none, with charity for all, with firmness in the right as God gives us to see the right, let us strive to finish the work we are in.
>
> To do all which may achieve and cherish a just and lasting peace among ourselves and with all nations.
>
> Why should there not be a patient confidence in the ultimate justice of the people?
>
> Is there any better or equal hope in the world?[77]
>
> In founding the United States, our fathers brought forth upon this continent a new nation, conceived in liberty and dedicated to the proposition that all men are created equal.
>
> It is for us to be here dedicated to the great task remaining before us. We here highly resolve that the dead shall not have died in vain.[78]
>
> That this nation under God shall have a new birth of freedom, and that government of the people, by the people, and for the people shall not perish from the earth.[79]

Reader and Congregation

For all these, O Lord Our God, we thank Thee: for Thy goodness as maintained in Nature, in the human spirit, in Israel's Torah, and in America's promise. Embolden our hearts so that, surmounting discouragement and despair, we may learn to see clearly Thy bounties, and seeing them, make them manifest to all the world. Amen.

Here, America's world role is envisioned (i.e., "America's promise").

"America the Beautiful" is printed on page 561 of the *Sabbath Prayer Book*. Moreover, on Brotherhood Sabbath (celebrated on the Sabbath between Washington's and Lincoln's birthdays), the following prayer is to be recited: "We thank Thee, O God, for having taught the founders of our Republic laws that safeguard the equal rights of all citizens and impose equal obligations upon all." [80] This prayer, in effect, sacralizes American governance as divinely sanctioned. Kaplan had included the American *Declaration of Independence* as a supplementary prayer book reading. Four years earlier, Kaplan, in *The New Haggadah*—co-edited with Ira Eisenstein and Eugene Kohn— included a reference to the "sacred rights" of "life, liberty, and the pursuit of happiness." [81] Eric Caplan provides an even fuller description:

> Kaplan included services for all major American civic holidays in the supplement, a clear outgrowth of his belief that Jewish Americans should identify fully with their country's history, heroes, culture, and ideals. The text for Brotherhood Sabbath associates God with developments in American history ("We thank Thee, O God, for having taught the founders of our Republic laws that safeguard the equal rights of all citizens and impose equal obligations upon all" [p. 539]) and reflects well Kaplan's view that all things that contribute to human moral progress are the product of divine forces. The association of God with American history is reinforced further by the use of "El Male" Rahamim to commemorate the American war dead. The service for Memorial Day expresses the hope that the example of those who were willing to die for the protection of the United States "impel us to make our country great, its laws just and wise, its culture deep and true, its economy productive, equitable and free, and its religion profound and pure. . . . Then will no sacrifice for preserving the nation be too high a price to pay" [pp. 541–542]. These services show the same concern for ethical issues evident throughout the Sabbath Prayer Book, and the linking of God to America gives the quest for American civil rights a religious significance that helps render responsible American citizenship fully compatible with Jewish values.

The prayer in the *Sabbath Prayer Book* makes American democracy sacred. In June 1945, the Union of Orthodox Rabbis of the United States and Canada not only excommunicated Kaplan—by invoking the *cherem,* the ancient ban of excommunication—but burned the *Sabbath Prayer Book* as well. [82] This was reported in a story published in *Time* magazine:

In solemn session in Manhattan last week, the Union called the prayer book a compound of "atheism, heresy and disbelief . . . " and hurled at Dr. Kaplan (who is not a member of the Union) a proclamation of excommunication—first in its history. Then, after Rabbi Israel Rosenberg, president of the Union, banned the Kaplan-edited prayers from all synagogues, an excited young rabbi set fire to a copy of the book.

This is one of several issues that brought Mordecai Kaplan into conflict with Orthodox Judaism.[83] This tension continues to this day. For instance, in 1990, Arthur Green, a scholar of Hasidism and president of the Reconstructionist Rabbinical College, stated the Reconstructionist position that belief in the Jews as the "chosen" people was "mythic":

> I certainly do not want to say that our ancestors were lying to me when they asserted chosenness, or that they were inaccurately recording their impressions of the relationship they had with God . . . [but] I cannot give them more than that. . . . "God has chosen Israel" *is a mythic statement.* . . . This is the shared private religious speech of the Jewish People . . . [not] a historical reality.[84]

The *Sabbath Prayer Book* has since been superseded, first by the old *Kol Haneshamah,* and now by the new *Kol Haneshamah* series. The prayer for America in the old *Kol Haneshamah* is as follows:

TORAH SERVICE: PRAYER FOR THE COUNTRY

Sovereign of the universe, mercifully receive our prayer for our land and its government. Let your blessing pour out on this land and on all officials of this country who are occupied, in good faith, with the public needs. Instruct them from your Torah's laws, enable them to understand your principles of justice, so that peace and tranquility, happiness and freedom, might never turn away from our land. Please, WISE ONE, God of the lifebreath of all flesh, waken your spirit within all inhabitants of our land, and plant among the peoples of different nationalities and faiths who dwell here, love and brotherhood, peace and friendship. Uproot from their hearts all hatred and enmity, all jealousy and vying for supremacy. Fulfill the yearning of all the people of our country to speak proudly in its honor. Fulfill their desire to see it become a light to all nations. Therefore, may it be your will, that our land should be a blessing to all inhabitants of the globe. Cause to dwell among all peoples friendship and freedom. And soon fulfill the vision of your prophet: "Nation shall not lift up sword against nation. Let them learn no longer ways of war." And let us say: Amen.[85]

The old *Kol Haneshamah* has since been replaced by the new "*Kol Haneshamah Siddurim Sets.*" The new *Kol Haneshamah* prayer book series includes Louis Ginzberg's prayer for America. Although Ginzberg's name does not appear after this prayer for the American government (yet remains a universal prayer that may be invoked on behalf of any just government), "A Prayer for our country" [sic] appears on page 148:

> Our God and God of our ancestors: We ask Your blessings for our country—for its government, for its leaders and advisors, and for all who exercise just and rightful authority. Teach them insights from Your Torah, that they may administer all affairs of state fairly, that peace and security, happiness and prosperity, justice and freedom may forever abide in our midst.
>
> Creator of all flesh, bless all the inhabitants of our country with Your spirit. May citizens of all races and creeds forge a common bond in true harmony, to banish hatred and bigotry, and to safeguard the ideals and free institutions that are the pride and glory of our country.
>
> May this land, under Your providence, be an influence for good throughout the world, uniting all people in peace and freedom—helping them to fulfill the vision of Your prophet: "Nation shall not lift up sword against nation, neither shall they learn war any more." And let us say, Amen.[86]

This prayer is immediately followed, on page 149, by "A prayer for the State of Israel (*Siddur Sim Shalom,* page 149)" [sic].

JEWISH AMERICANISM: THE "CULT OF SYNTHESIS"

Jewish prayers for America have a living resonance. Various siddurs were surveyed in this chapter, for the simple reason that "one of the most comprehensive and authoritative (but not systematic) statements of Jewish theology is embedded in the *siddur.*"[87] Earlier in this chapter, a Reform rabbi was cited, who said: "Second only to the Torah, the *siddur* (prayer book) *expresses the ideology of our people.*"[88] The results of the present writer's survey of Jewish prayers of America has yielded this unexpected result: From the fact that Louis Ginzberg's "A Prayer for Our Country" is recited in every Conservative synagogue every Sabbath,[89] and presumably also in every Reconstructionist Sabbath service, it would appear that the American Jewish vision of America was best expressed by this singular prayer. If the present writer can take this liberty, then the Jewish vision of America that Ginzberg's prayer translates into may be reduced to the following principles:

JEWISH AMERICANS' VISION OF AMERICA

1. As faithful Jews, we are, each and all, loyal Americans.
2. We have the best interests of America at heart.
3. We call upon our government officials to be just and right in their exercise of legitimate authority.

4. We encourage our leaders to draw upon the wisdom enshrined in the Torah.

5. May peace and security, happiness and prosperity, justice and freedom, one day, reign supreme in America.

6. We seek God's blessings on all Americans, irrespective of creed.

7. In America, may all races and creeds live in true harmony.

8. We seek to banish all forms of hatred and bigotry.

9. We seek to safeguard our country's ideals and free institutions—the pride and glory of America.

10. May America be an influence for good throughout the world, uniting all people in peace and freedom.

11. May Providence guide America in realizing Isaiah's vision of universal peace.

These Jewish principles, expressed as universals, are all consonant, and indeed resonate, with cherished American values. They exemplify Jewish Americanism at its finest.

Jonathan Sarna describes the phenomenon of Jewish Americanism, in which American Jews today merge their American and Jewish identities, which he calls the "cult of synthesis." [90] By "cult," Sarna means "a collective veneration or worship . . . in which the collectivity is defined and united by its common devotional practice." [91] Noting the synergy between American Judaism and American civil religion, Sarna develops his thesis of the "cult of synthesis," and adduces abundant evidence for it:

> This understanding of the American Jewish experience—the belief that Judaism and Americanism reinforce one another, the two traditions converging in a common path—encapsulates a central theme in American Jewish culture that may be termed "the cult of synthesis." Dating back well over a century, it reflects an ongoing effort on the part of American Jews to interweave their "Judaism" with their "Americanism" in an attempt to fashion for themselves some unified, "synthetic" whole. Anyone even remotely connected with American Jewish life is familiar with this theme, which has elsewhere been described as a central tenet of American Jewish "civil religion." [92]

Sarna's thesis, in part, is that "such diverse American Jewish religious leaders as Leo Jung, Samuel Belkin, Abba Hillel Silver, Jacob Rader Marcus, Nelson Glueck, Louis Finkelstein, Simon Greenberg, and Robert Gordis all argued in various ways for the compatibility of Judaism and American democracy." [93] Mordecai Kaplan—who "at one point, explicitly sought to redefine America from a Jewish perspective"—echoed the same idea in this memorable way: "The American religion of democracy has room for Judaism, and Jewish religion has room for American democracy." [94]

Among others, Sarna singles out for distinction Horace Kallen[95]—the father of "cultural pluralism" (now known as "multiculturalism"). Horace Kallen (1882–1974), a Jewish pragmatist philosopher, invented the term "cultural pluralism" in 1907 at Oxford University, in conversations that he had with Alain Locke (1885–1954, member of the Bahá'í community since 1918), who, earlier that year, had won national acclaim as the first African American Rhodes Scholar. Kallen reports that "we had a race problem because Rhodes Scholars from the South were bastards," who "had a Thanksgiving dinner which I refused to attend because they refused to have Locke." Traumatized, Locke mused: "What difference does the difference [of race] make? We are all alike Americans." And so, "in arguing out those questions the formulae, then phrases, developed—'cultural pluralism,' 'the right to be different,'" writes Kallen. Yet it was not until 1924 when the term "cultural pluralism"—the antipode of "the melting pot"—first appeared in print. In *Culture and Democracy in the United States* (in which Kallen's essay, "Democracy versus the Melting Pot" is reprinted, with minor changes), Kallen states: "Cultural Pluralism . . . is the view that democracy is an essential prerequisite to culture, that culture can be and sometimes is a fine flowering of democracy, and that the history of the relation of the two in the United States exhibits this fact." The counter-metaphor that Kallen proposes is that of the philharmonic. "American civilization" may be envisioned as "the perfection of coöperative harmonies" of "European civilization"—a "multiplicity in a unity, an orchestration of mankind" in which "every type of instrument has its specific *timbre* and *tonality*" to create a veritable "symphony of civilization."[96]

The phenomenon of Jewish Americanism cuts across all major forms of American Judaism. In other words, Jewish Americanism is not the preserve of one Jewish movement within the United States. Sarna cites the late eminent sociologist, Charles Liebman, who, in discussing the "major ideas, symbols, and institutions arousing the deepest loyalties and passions of American Jews," declared: "There is nothing incompatible between being a good Jew and a good American, or between Jewish and American standards of behavior. In fact, for a Jew, the better an American one is, the better Jew one is."[97] So pervasive is the cult of synthesis that it "actually permeated all of the major movements and ideologies of American Judaism."[98] Sarna registers this point absolutely and emphatically: "All shared the firm belief that Americanism and Judaism reinforced one another."[99]

To be sure, significant differences exist among American Jews today as to precisely how this salutary cultural symbiosis works best, in that American Jews "take it as an article of faith that 'American' and 'Jew' *can* be reconciled. What they debate is how the grand synthesis may best be accomplished, not whether it is achievable in the first place." [100] To what extent Jewish Americanism has influenced other faith-communities is hard to say. What can definitely be said is that American Judaism has, at heart, wholly embraced American values. In fact, Jewish Americanism is a salient characteristic of American Judaism generally. The two go hand-in-hand.

CHAPTER 6

Mormon Myths and Visions of America

I established the Constitution of the land, by the hands of wise men whom I raised up unto this very purpose.

—Jesus Christ (in Mormonism)[1]

The city of Zion spoken of by David, in the one hundred and second Psalm, will be built upon the land of America.

—Joseph Smith (1833)[2]

eaders of the previous five chapters will, in this chapter, encounter some rather exotic and engaging mythic and visionary accounts of America, as collectively held by "Mormons"—the popular name for followers of the Church of Jesus Christ of Latter-day Saints (LDS). (LDS is the "revealed" name of the church.) LDS was founded by the prophet Joseph Smith (1805–1844) in 1830. Since that time, the Mormon church, by virtue of its missionary zeal, has spread to many parts of the world, its far-flung membership thus constituting a global community. On June 24, 2007, President Gordon B. Hinckley (the fifteenth Mormon president), addressing the New Mission Presidents' Seminar, announced that LDS church membership had reached 13 million (the official 2007 figure is 13,193,999),[3] with more Mormons residing outside the United States than within, thus reflecting the global breadth and diversity of its worldwide membership.[4] As the fourth largest "church" in the United States by some accounts,[5] the Mormons are a sizable body of religious adherents who communally share religious convictions about America.

What is Mormonism? One may answer this question through introducing three major dimensions of Mormon doctrine and praxis: (1) restorationism; (2) perfectionism; (3) millenarianism. *Restorationism* (also known as primitivism) is the reestablishment of the original Christian church, as indicated in Article 6 of the *Articles of Faith,* a Mormon creed: "We believe in the same organization that existed in the Primitive Church, namely, apostles, prophets, pastors, teachers, evangelists, and so forth."[6] *Millenarianism* is the belief in a future, 1,000-year reign of Christ on earth, as taught in Article 6 of the *Articles of Faith:* "We believe in the literal gathering of Israel and in the restoration of the Ten Tribes; that Zion will be built upon this [the American] continent; that Christ will reign personally upon the earth; and that the earth will be renewed and receive its paradisiacal glory."[7] *Perfectionism* is basically a doctrine of eternal progression, of becoming more divine (God-like) in the process—i.e., the possibility of man becoming equal with Christ and God—as promised in *Doctrine and Covenants:* "Wherefore, as it is written, they are *gods,* even the *sons of God*—";[8] "And then shall the angels be crowned with the glory of his might, and the saints shall be filled with his glory, and receive their inheritance and be made *equal* with him."[9] Mormon restorationism has been analyzed, *inter alia,* by Jan Shipps,[10] Mormon millenarianism by Grant Underwood,[11] and Mormon perfectionism by John Brooke.[12] These categories will be variously applied throughout this chapter. A brief explanation of each category follows.

Restorationism: The Church of Jesus Christ of Latter-day Saints arose during the season of revivals known as the Second Great Awakening. (The first Great Awakening, 1725–1765, was followed by the Second Great Awakening, 1795–1860.) Established in 1830, the Church of Jesus Christ of Latter-day Saints presents itself as true Christianity restored. This is a form of primitivism, which is belief in the necessity of restoring Christ's apostolic or "primitive" church. As an end-times religion, Mormonism sees itself as "that old-time religion."

In nineteenth-century America, the time became ripe for the great Restoration commenced by Smith and his followers, supported by LDS restoration scriptures, especially the *Book of Mormon.* The Restoration was long overdue, for Christianity is said to have undergone a "Great Apostasy" during the apostolic age.[13] Preparations for the Restoration began in 1820, through the appearance of two divine personages to Joseph Smith, then a youth, on his family's farm near Palmyra, New York.[14] In this First Vision (also called the "Grove Experience"), both God the Father and Jesus personally appeared to Joseph Smith. (In Joseph Smith's original 1832 version of the First Vision, however, only one Personage, the Son, appeared to the young seer.)[15] The First Vision may be seen as an "Annunciation," preparing the youthful Smith for a prophetic vocation. In this vision, the 14-year-old youth was told not to join any churches of the day. This, in and of itself, implied that Jesus did not recognize any current form of Christianity as fully authentic. Other contemporary movements were making similar claims.

The First Vision is foundational, for it not only establishes Joseph Smith's prophetic credentials in the eye of Mormons, but discloses the reality and nature of God as well. The significance of the First Vision in Mormon belief is paramount, as one Mormon historian notes: "Its importance is second only to belief in the divinity of Jesus of Nazareth." [16] God the Father and Jesus Christ appeared to Joseph Smith as celestial human beings. This apparition was real and underscores Mormon perfectionism, which is related to the Restoration. In one sense, the First Vision may be viewed as a restoration of the true knowledge of God. There was a restoration of the priestly office and its charismatic prerogative as well. This took place on May 15, 1829.

The Restoration is "the signal event of the post-biblical age." [17] On April 6, 1830, Joseph Smith is said to have completed the process of restoring the true church to its pristine form. This was an ecclesiastical restoration. According to Shipps, there were actually three types of restoration: (1) restoration of church and priesthood; (2) restoration of Israel; and (3) "the restoration of all things," referring to the final overlay of perfectionist tenets in the closing years of Joseph Smith's ministry. [18] Here, one sees the three major dimensions used in this framework of analysis: Mormon restorationism, millenarianism, and perfectionism.

Because of its paramount importance, a brief overview of Mormon priestly orders is needed. One Mormon historian's description of the restoration of the priesthoods that purportedly existed in primitive Christianity, which the Mormon church has now restored, illustrates this key LDS truth claim:

> This restoration was effected by the Lord through the Prophet Joseph Smith, who, together with Oliver Cowdery, in 1829, received the Aaronic Priesthood (the Levitical priesthood) under the hands of John the Baptist; and later the Melchizedek Priesthood under the hands of the former-day apostles, Peter, James, and John. [19]

Of these two orders, that of Melchizedek is greater, having the same authority as the righteous king and high priest after whom the priesthood was named.

In the LDS Church, however, there are actually three grand orders of priesthood: the Melchizedek, the Aaronic, and the Patriarchal. [20] As the name implies, the patriarchal order includes the right of worthy, ordained fathers to preside over their descendants for all time. Women are not ordained into priesthood. The issue of Mormon priesthood takes on added significance, considering the priesthood ban for all black males—a policy that was rescinded (but not repudiated)—by a divine revelation in 1978. This racial dimension to the Mormon priesthood will be discussed later in this chapter. Both the Aaronic Priesthood[21] and the Melchizedek Priesthood[22] are considered essential to theocracy, or the government of God, which takes place in the Millennium.

Millenarianism: Mormonism has introduced America into the millennial scheme of things. Today—which is to say, in these "latter days"—the first church is now the last church, being the Church of Jesus Christ of Latter-day Saints. Because it sees itself as the restoration of original Christianity, Mormonism is the only true church: "The Latter-day Saints declare their high claim to the true Church organization, similar in all essentials to the organization effected by Christ among the Jews." [23] Embodying both the doctrine and ecclesial structure of the apostolic church, the primitivism of the LDS church is both normative and jurisdictional. Through his millennialism, Joseph Smith's primitivism became, in fact, a full-blown dispensationalism, transforming all traditional notions of Christianity.

Perfectionism: As the term implies, perfectionism (also known as Hermeticism in relation to Mormonism) is the belief in the perfectibility of human character and nature. Typically, this refers to the quest for immortality, both spiritual and physical. LDS doctrine teaches a progressive path to deification. As Joseph Smith himself states: "Every man who reigns in celestial glory is a God to his dominions." [24] "Hermeticism," in Brooke's view, "explains the more exotic features of the inner logic of Mormon theology." [25] Despite some of the features it has in common with perfectionism generally, Brooke asserts that "the Mormon claim of a revealed restoration ideal has few parallels, and the combination of temple ritual, polygamous marriage, three-tiered heavens, the coequality of spirit and matter, and promise of godhood is essentially unique." [26]

Latter-day Saints view God the Father in anthropomorphic terms. In a literal reading of Genesis 1:26, man is created in the "image and likeness" of God. Therefore, God must have an image and form as well. According to Joseph Smith, "The Father has a body of flesh and bones as tangible as man's; the Son also; but the Holy Ghost has not a body of flesh and bones, but is a personage of Spirit." [27] God is an exalted man. He stands as the prototype of human potential for perfection. The path to this perfection was not previously known, nor could it be followed, until the true gospel had been restored. This was Joseph Smith's mission. By means of the Restoration, people can now embark on the path of perfectionism. The primary scriptural source for Mormon perfectionism is the King Follett Discourse (April 7, 1844, funeral sermon preached by Joseph Smith on behalf of Mormon notable Elder King Follett), in which Joseph Smith states, in part:

God Himself who sits enthroned in yonder heavens is a Man like unto one of yourselves—that is the great secret! ... For I am going to tell you how God came to be God and what sort of a being He is. For we have imagined that God was God from the beginning of all eternity. I will refute that idea and take away the veil so you may see. ... The first principle of truth and of the Gospel is to know for a certainty the character of God, and that ... He once was a man like one of us and that God Himself, the Father of us all, once dwelled on an earth the same as Jesus Christ himself did in the flesh and like us.[28]

Put more succinctly, this doctrine is expressed in the oft-quoted couplet by Lorenzo Snow (fifth president of the Church of Jesus Christ of Latter-day Saints): "As man now is, God once was; as God is now man may be."[29] Atonement assures resurrection, but not exaltation. "In its final form," Brooke concludes, "the Mormon doctrine of salvation made the gift of grace through faith in Christ's atonement a necessary condition for salvation but not a sufficient condition."[30] Mormon soteriology makes a "critical distinction ... between simple salvation and divine exaltation."[31] Beyond salvation is exaltation (deification). Exaltation is ultimate salvation.[32]

With this three-dimensional framework of analysis for Mormon doctrine and praxis in place, one can now introduce the *Book of Mormon*—the central Mormon scripture—in which some of the key Mormon myths and visions of America are enshrined.

The Book of Mormon: The central Mormon scripture is the *Book of Mormon: Another Testament of Jesus Christ.* While acknowledging the traditional Holy Land as, indeed, holy, the *Book of Mormon,* along with other Mormon scriptures, has recast America (and the Americas, that is, the New World as a whole) as a sacred landscape. In other words, in the Mormon view of it, America is the new Holy Land. So what makes America holy, in the Mormon conception of it?

Joseph Smith is said to have both discovered and produced the *Book of Mormon,* which is purportedly "an account written by the hand of Mormon upon plates taken from the Plates of Nephi," as the title page of the *Book of Mormon* proclaims. These are "gold plates" revealing the "history" of ancient America. This history begins with the prophet Lehi, a Jerusalem-born descendant of Joseph, said to have left Israel and ultimately founded a colony in the New World, some 600 years before Christ. Thus Lehi, not Christopher Columbus, discovered America, as the *Book of Mormon* implies. The subsequent history of Lehi's progeny in America, the appearance of Jesus Christ in America, and the pre-Columbian history of the American Indians are chronicled in the *Book of Mormon,* which was indelibly, if unintelligibly, inscribed on golden plates.

Shortly after Lehi's party's arrival in the New World, family quarrels fragmented clans into two warring nations. Over the 1,000-year period that the *Book of Mormon* chronicles, the saga of these two nations' decline and fall is told. The signal moment of peace and prosperity came as the result of a visit by the risen, resurrected Jesus Christ to the peoples of ancient America, where He established His church, as in the Old World. For nearly 200 years following Christ's visit, the church flourished. Over time, however, apostasy set in, as the Christianized inhabitants of ancient America precipitously abandoned Christ's teachings. Wickedness prevailed, war ensued, and extermination resulted.

Over the course of these centuries, meticulous records were said to have been kept on metal plates. One of the last of these historians was Mormon, an ancient American prophet who abridged this history and inscribed it on gold plates. The last of the ancient American prophets and sole survivor of his now-extinct nation, Moroni, protectively buried the gold plates—which are gilded history, quite literally—in the fifth century. Moroni buried the plates in a hillside, today called the Hill Cumorah, located in Palmyra, New York. While Moroni's burial of this book reportedly preserved this sacred history, it remained hidden for 14 centuries. How Joseph Smith came to discover this sacred history of America—and how he came to decipher the ancient language it contained—is explained, in Mormon belief, as a divinely inspired series of events.

Born on December 23,1805, in Sharon, Vermont, Joseph Smith, Jr., was troubled, as a teenager, by the maelstrom of competing faiths and religious conflicts that plagued the churches in America. In 1820, at the age of 14, the young Smith experienced a theophany, or vision of God, which Mormons commonly refer to as "the First Vision." In 1823, Moroni returned and led young Joseph Smith to the hidden plates. These gold plates were in the temporary custody of Joseph Smith, who, according to Mormon accounts, permitted three men to actually see them and another eight men to handle them. The written testimony of these witnesses follow the *Book of Mormon*'s introduction.

Joseph translated the plates in about three months after which he returned them to the angel Moroni. In June 1829, Joseph Smith completed his translation of the plates by means of the Urim and Thummim, a device which, in biblical times, a high priest would wear on his breastplate and by means of which that priest would divine the will of God.[33] Described as "two stones in silver bows,"[34] the Urim and Thummim enabled the prophet to interpret the engravings on the gold plates. It evidently functioned much like a seer stone. The *Book of Mormon* was first published in 1830, with a print run of 5,000 copies at a cost of $3,000.[35]

When people think of the Mormons, they typically do not think first of Mormons' beliefs about America. True, the Church of Jesus Christ of Latter-day Saints has its distinctive doctrines—of restoration, progression, revelation, ordinances, patriarchy, Jesus Christ, and the heavens. In addition to these, Mormonism also has a rich fund of what can properly be called religious myths and visions of America. One could write an entire book on this topic. One Mormon author, E. Douglas Clark, has compiled a book of relevant Mormon texts on the topic of America.[36] The Mormon myth of America covers its past, present, and future. Generally, however, Mormon sources consistently portray the destiny of America as glorious. To inquiring minds, while the Mormon vision of America may be "too good to be true," the existence of such beliefs about America is a fascinating social phenomenon.

The LDS Church has exhibited a duality of attitudes towards America. As historian Richard Bushman succinctly states: "The American land was given an honored place in *Book of Mormon* sacred history, but American civilization was not."[37] Moreover: "Mormon optimism arose not from romantic hope for America but from the faith grounded in the *Book of Mormon* that God would redeem the land from the evil that prevailed there."[38]

America, in Mormon belief, has spiritual roots, a divine mandate for the present, and a theocratic future. In the words of one scholar, Mormons added "to the disembodied outline of the millennial dream the firm contours of America."[39]

THE GARDEN OF EDEN MYTH

Unique as it is, the LDS Church is not without precedents. Primitivism inspired restorationist churches in America, such as the Churches of Christ (also known as "Campbellites") and the Disciples of Christ. That the Church of Jesus Christ of Latter-day Saints sees itself as the one, true church is obviously a truth claim that raises center-and-periphery issues with respect to mainstream Christianity. Mormon primitivism is not simply a restoration of the primitive Church as conceived by Joseph Smith. LDS primitivism extends as far back as the Garden of Eden, where salvation history begins.

America, in Mormon belief, has had a special place in salvation history since primordial times. America was once Paradise. Brigham Young, who succeeded Mormon prophet-founder Joseph Smith after the latter was assassinated in 1844, disclosed that the Garden of Eden was located in the heart of ancient America: "In the beginning, after this earth was prepared for man, the Lord commenced his work upon what is now called the American continent, where the Garden of Eden was made."[40] A direct link between the Latter Days and creation resides in the Mormon belief that the Garden of Eden was located in what is now Independence, in Jackson County, Missouri.

"Independence was to be the location of Enoch's city," Brooke writes, "because it had once been Paradise itself. From this Garden of Eden, centrally located in the North American continent, Adam had been expelled to 'Adam ondi Ahman,' where he gathered his posterity, and from where Noah had sailed his ark to Palestine during the Flood.[41] Official LDS statements back this claim: President Heber C. Kimball (1801–1868), former counselor in the First Presidency, pinpointed Eden's precise location: "The spot chosen for the garden of Eden was Jackson County, in the state of Missouri, where [the city of] Independence now stands; it was occupied in the morn of creation by Adam." [42]

THE LOST TRIBES MYTH

The Mormon myth of America's pre-Columbian history is also racial. The *Book of Mormon* is at once a history of the Native Americans and a history of Israel in America,[43] because Indians were Israelites unawares (but not at first unaware of the Israelite heritage, according to LDS doctrine). "Independence was to be the location of Enoch's city," Brooke writes, "because it had once been Paradise itself. From this Garden of Eden, centrally located in the North American continent, Adam had been expelled to 'Adam ondi Ahman,' where he gathered his posterity, and from where Noah had sailed his ark to Palestine during the Flood. Thus three waves of Old World immigrants—Jaredites, Nephites, and Euro-Americans—had come to the New World in search of Paradise." [44]

Prior to Smith's discovery and translation of the *Book of Mormon*, efforts had been made to historicize the legend of the ten Lost Tribes, Jews who the Assyrians exiled in 722 BCE and who mysteriously vanished from history. In the biblical account, all Jewish tribes, except for Judah and Benjamin, were exiled to Halah and Habor by the River Gozan.[45] There has been much speculation ever since as to the fate of these Ten Tribes, but the most famous has been their identification with Native Americans, as conjectured by the Amsterdam Rabbi Manasseh ben Israel in his *Hope of Israel* (1650). The same idea stood at the center of Ethan Smith's work, *View of the Hebrews, or the Tribes of Israel in America* (1823).[46]

Given this background, it is evident that the *Book of Mormon* has a context. But the *Book of Mormon* does not speculate on their fate beyond the simple conjecture that the ten Lost Tribes had probably migrated to the northern climes.[47] "And they who are in the north countries," Joseph Smith proclaimed, "shall come in remembrance before the Lord" where "their prophets shall hear his voice" and "shall smite the rocks, and the ice shall flow." [48]

The *Book of Mormon* focuses, not on the ten Lost Tribes, but on the Jewish prophet Lehi,[49] from the Tribe of Joseph through his son Manasseh. Lehi is said to have departed for America with a tiny band of Jews, who left from Jerusalem, not Assyria, 125 years after the Assyrian conquest. Indians are therefore Israelites. According to the *Book of Mormon,* America was first populated by three groups of emigrants: the Jaredites, the Nephites, and the Mulekites. The Jaredites cames first, followed by the Nephites and Mulekites. The Jaredites were led by a prophet known only as the "brother of Jared." After the dispersion that followed the Tower of Babel, around 2250 BCE by some Mormon estimates (the date is not essential), the Jaredites set sail in "barges" towards the "Promised Land" (America).

Evidently, there were eight such vessels, each illuminated by two luminescent stones, "white and clear," [50] placed fore and aft. By this mysterious technology, these ships had to withstand all the vicissitudes of an arduous, transoceanic journey that lasted 344 days. After the Jaredites came the Nephites. They were led to America by the Hebrew prophet Lehi, around 589 BCE.[51] According to the *Book of Mormon,* soon after his resurrection, Jesus Christ appeared in America to both the Nephites (descendants of Nephi, a great prophet who lived around 600 BCE) and the Lamanites. Jesus said: "And behold, this people will I establish in this land, unto the fulfilling of the covenant which I made with your father Jacob; and it shall be a New Jerusalem. And the powers of heaven shall be in the midst of this people; yea, even I will be in the midst of you.' " [52] By asserting Israelite origins for Native Americans, with Jesus Christ having appeared to them, the *Book of Mormon* has succeeded in establishing America as another Holy Land.

By this mysterious technology, these ships had to withstand all the vicissitudes of an arduous, transoceanic journey that lasted 344 days. They had to endure tempests and fierce winds, stirring up "mountain waves" that buffeted and, quite literally, "buried" the ships.[53] To make a long story short, the Jaredites became extinct, due to their wickedness, around 590 BCE. The last great Jaredite prophet and chronicler was Ether, whose history, *The Book of Ether,* was recorded on 24 gold plates.[54] Ether foretold the future establishment of "a New Jerusalem upon this land [America]." [55] But this vision concerned another people entirely, for the Jaredites were on the brink of extinction.

After the Jaredites came the Nephites. They were led to America by the Hebrew prophet Lehi, around 589 BCE.[56] Rival claims to prophetic office advanced by Laman, eldest son of Lehi, and by Nephi, Lehi's designated successor, led to an eventual division between the Lamanites and Nephites (named after these two sons of Lehi). The Nephites had first occupied the southern climes, while the "Land of Mulek" (after descendants of Mulek, the "son of Zedekiah") was to the north. Internal divisions split the Nephites into the Nephites and Lamanites. Nephi became the founder of a flourishing civilization of farmers and city builders. But Laman broke away and led a nomadic band of outlaws who continually menaced the Nephites, in consequence of which the Lamanites were cursed with dark skin.[57] The Mulekites eventually merged with the Nephites. The inhabitants of the New World were believed to have all been the direct descendants of the patriarch Joseph.

According to the Book of Mormon, soon after his resurrection, Jesus Christ appeared in America to both the Nephites (descendants of Nephi, a great prophet who lived around 600 BCE) and the Lamanites. Jesus said: "And behold, this people will I establish in this land, unto the fulfilling of the covenant which I made with your father Jacob; and it shall be a New Jerusalem. And the powers of heaven shall be in the midst of this people; yea, even I will be in the midst of you.' "[58] In his synopsis of the writings of Ether, the prophet Moroni writes: "Behold, Ether saw the days of Christ, and he spake concerning a New Jerusalem upon this land [America]."[59]

Distant traces of historical memory of Christ's appearance in the Americas are said to have been preserved in selected ethnographic accounts of culture heroes, especially those myths surrounding the Toltec civilizer, Quetzalcoatl.[60] A Mormon film, *Christ in America,* treats the legend of Quetzalcoatl as an ancient memory of Christ's visitation to the New World as sober fact. LDS apologists still have to contend with skeptics and critics, who point to alleged anthropological anachronisms in the text (horses, wheat, steel swords, etc.). But faith in both the *Book of Mormon* and Joseph Smith's inspired translation of it sustain the authority of the text. This faith is undergirded by perceived evidences of ancient Judaic characteristics that the *Book of Mormon* exhibits, independent of any apologetic approach.

Eventually, the savage Lamanites slaughtered the Nephites. Subsequently, the Lamanites "became dark in skin and benighted in spirit."[61] Native Americans are said to be their descendants. The last set of records of the Nephites was written by Mormon (c. 333 CE) and buried in the Hill Ramah (Jaredite name for Hill Cumorah). The record of these peoples is contained in abridged form in the *Book of Mormon,* said to have been written in "reformed Egyptian" and inscribed on gold plates, which Joseph Smith translated. It was Mormon's son, Moroni (whom Mormons identify as the angel of Revelation 14:6, although Bruce McConkie and others hold that this verse could refer to other angels as well), who appeared to Joseph Smith to lead him to discover where the plates had been hidden. They were deposited in a stone vault and buried in the Hill Cumorah, near the village of Manchester, New York. The prophet came into possession of these gold plates on September 22, 1827. A facsimile of the characters exists in a circular published with the heading, "Stick of Joseph taken from the Hand of Ephraim: A Correct Copy of the Characters taken from the Plates [of] the *Book of Mormon.*"[62] This "stick of Joseph" was added to the "stick of Judah"—a euphemism for the Bible.

The *Book of Mormon* describes America as "the land of promise"[63] for a Jewish remnant, who would traverse "across the great deep into the promised land"[64]:

> And behold, this people [Jewish remnant = Nephites/Lamanites] will I establish in this land [America], unto the fulfilling of the covenant which I made with your father Jacob; and it shall be a New Jerusalem. And the powers of heaven shall be in the midst of this people; yea, even I [Jesus Christ] will be in the midst of you.[65]

America would also be home to "Gentiles" who "were white, and exceedingly fair and beautiful."[66] Together, the Jews and Gentiles of America will work together to build the New Jerusalem: "And then shall they [Gentiles = Euro-Americans] shall assist my people [remnant of Jacob = Lamanites = Native Americans] that they may be gathered in, who are scattered upon all the face of the land, in unto the New Jerusalem."[67]

By asserting Israelite origins for Native Americans, with Jesus Christ having appeared to them, the *Book of Mormon* has succeeded in establishing America as another Holy Land. As the saga of the Nephites and Lamanites, the *Book of Mormon* purports to be a faithful and inspired account of the history of Native Americans. They were thus among the first to be evangelized in the "Latter Day." In October 1830, Joseph Smith sent Oliver Cowdery, Parley P. Pratt, Peter Whitmer, and Ziba Peterson on the Church's first mission to the Lamanites.[68] They preached to the Cattaraugus in western New York, to the Wyandots of western Ohio, and to the Delawares and Shawnees in eastern Kansas.[69] Proselyting among the American Indians would hasten the promised conversion of all Israel.[70]

THE COLUMBUS MYTH

Apart from a single verse, Christopher Columbus has no religious significance for Mormons. His inclusion here is because of the scriptural allusion. The *Book of Mormon,* Latter-day Saints generally believe, foretells the 1492 voyage of Christopher Columbus:

> And I looked and beheld a man among the Gentiles, who was separated from the seed of my brethren by the many waters; and I beheld the spirit of God, that it came down and wrought upon the man; and he went forth upon the many waters, even unto the seed of my brethren, who were in the promised land.[71]

The "promised land," as the reader might expect, alludes to America. Columbus's discovery of America, accordingly, fulfills Nephi's prophecy.[72]

THE CONSTITUTION MYTH

Generally, Latter-day Saints see the hand of Providence at work in the founding of America. An important feature of the Mormon theology of America is the conviction that the Constitution of the United States of America was divinely inspired. This derives, in part, from the following revelation given to the prophet Joseph Smith, in which Jesus Christ states: "And for this purpose have I established the Constitution of this land, by the hands of wise men whom I raised up unto this very purpose, and redeemed the land by the shedding of blood." [73] That is not to say that God revealed the Constitution, but that there is a dimension of sacred purpose infused within it. One might characterize this influx of spiritual genius within the Constitution as the presence of an invisible, divine signature above the flourish of John Hancock. Jesus Christ, moreover, is believed to teach that constitutions, generally, are important for the good governance of a nation: "And that law of the land which is constitutional, supporting that principle of freedom in maintaining rights and privileges, belongs to all mankind, and is justifiable before me." [74] The freedoms enshrined by that document—not the least of which is the freedom of religion—is seen as part of a divine preparation for America's destiny as the bearer of the restored Gospel.

Without America, in fact, there would be no restored Gospel. According to LDS teachings, God has chosen America for a glorious destiny. While that destiny will not ultimately be forfeited, it can be frustrated. America's destiny can and is being subverted by godlessness. Only by reforming its ways and by realigning its values and aspirations can America live up to its potential and fulfill its mission in the divine scheme.

THE FOUNDING FATHERS MYTH

If there is something sacred about the U.S. Constitution, then might there be something divine about the Declaration of Independence as well? If so, then the hands that affixed their signatures to it—the Founding Fathers—were also fulfilling God's purpose. During the Fourth of July celebration in 1854, in the Mormon Tabernacle in Salt Lake City, Elder Orson Hyde (d. 1878) delivered a patriotic speech, as would befit the occasion. A few years earlier, Hyde had assumed the office of the president of the Quorum of the Twelve Apostles on December 27, 1847. Elder Hyde extolled the men who "had not only the moral courage to sign the Declaration of our nation's Independence, but hearts of iron and nerves of steel to defend it by force of arms against the fearful odds arrayed against them." They braved all danger for a noble cause, as they went on "to raise the standard of liberty, and unfurl its banner to the world as a warning to oppressors, as the star of hope to the oppressed." Elder Hyde went on to say:

In those early and perilous times, our men were few, and our resources limited. Poverty was among the most potent enemies we had to encounter; yet our arms were successful; and it may not be amiss to ask here, by whose power victory so often perched on our banner? It was by the agency of that same angel of God that appeared unto Joseph Smith, and revealed to him the history of the early inhabitants of this country, whose mounds, bones, and remains of towns, cities, and fortifications speak from the dust in the ears of the living with the voice of undeniable truth. This same angel presides over the destinies of America, and feels a lively interest in all our doings. He was in the camp of Washington; and, by an invisible hand, led on our fathers to conquest and victory; and all this to open and prepare the way for the Church and kingdom of God to be established on the western hemisphere, for the redemption of Israel and the salvation of the world.

Simply put, America's destiny and the Mormon mission are intertwined. There is an interesting—call it mystic—connection between the two. Wilford Woodruff (1807–1898) was the fourth LDS president, succeeding his predecessors, Joseph Smith, Brigham Young, and John Taylor. In 1877 (the year he assumed leadership of the Church as the senior member of the Quorum of the Twelve Apostles upon the death of President John Taylor), according to Woodruff's own journal entry for April 1898, George Washington, John Wesley, Benjamin Franklin, and Christopher Columbus appeared to Woodruff in the Saint George Temple (in Saint George, Utah) and requested baptism for the dead (that is, for themselves), in recompense for their role in helping prepare the way for the restoration of the gospel.[75] "Every one of those men that signed the Declaration of Independence with General Washington called upon me as an apostle of the Lord Jesus Christ in the temple at Saint George," Woodruff recounts in the following spoken memoir:

> I am going to bear my testimony to this assembly, if I never do it again in my life, that those men who laid the foundation of this American government ... were the best spirits the God of heaven could find on the face of the earth. These were choice spirits, not wicked men. General Washington and all of the men that labored for the purpose were inspired of the Lord .... Every one of those men that signed the Declaration of Independence with General Washington called upon me as an apostle of the Lord Jesus Christ in the temple at St. George two consecutive nights and demanded at my hands that I should go forth and attend to the ordinances of the House of God for them .... Brother McAllister baptized me for all of those men, and then I told those brethren that it was their duty to go into the temple and labor until they had got endowments for all of them. They did it. Would these spirits have called on me, as an elder in Israel, to perform this work if they had not been noble spirits before God. They would not.[76]

This is clearly an instance of the "Mormonization" of America's founding fathers. So religiously significant is this topic that Brigham Young University Press, in a commemorative volume, published a collection of essays exploring Mormon appreciation for the Constitution.[77] Space does not permit an analysis of other Mormon scriptures that are also interpreted as references to America.[78] It is this last verse that brings us to the America as Zion myth.

THE THEODEMOCRACY MYTH

Another Mormon myth of America regards the future government of America. On January 29, 1844, Joseph Smith and the Twelve Apostles decided that the prophet would run for president. This decision followed Smith's unsuccessful mission to elicit assurances from the five presidential candidates, then running for U.S. president, that the constitutional rights of all citizens, particularly the Mormons—who were the recurring targets of persecution in a country that advocated, as a founding principle, freedom of religion—were experiencing. For instance, on October 27, 1838, Missouri Governor Lilburn Boggs (1796–1860) had issued Missouri Executive Order 44, to expel or exterminate the Mormons from Missouri. This was in response to the 1838 Mormon War and a subsequent assassination attempt on the governor's life (allegedly by Orin Porter Rockwell, a close associate of Joseph Smith). It was not until 137 years after being signed that Boggs's extermination order was formally rescinded by Governor Christopher S. Bond on June 25, 1976.

Smith had asked each of the contenders—among who were John C. Calhoun, Henry Clay, and Martin Van Buren—to offer "an immediate, specific, and candid reply to *What will be your rule of action relative to us as a people, should fortune favor your ascension to the chief magistry?*"[79] Their position on this question was clearly unsatisfactory. Since none of the existing candidates would safeguard Mormon interests, Smith decided to run for president himself. It was during his campaign for president of the United States that Smith first coined the term "theodemocracy" on April 15, 1844. This neologism first appeared in a widely reprinted letter in a nineteenth-century Latter-day Saint periodical, *Times and Seasons* (published monthly or twice monthly) in Nauvoo, Illinois. America should (and, in the future, would) become a "theodemocracy":

> As the "*world is governed too much*" and as there is not a nation or dynasty, now occupying the earth, which acknowledges Almighty God as their law giver, and as "crowns won by blood, by blood must be maintained," I go emphatically, virtuously, and humanely, for a THEODEMOCRACY, where God and the people hold the power to conduct the affairs of men in righteousness. And where liberty, free trade, and sailor's rights, and the protection of life and property shall be

maintained inviolate, for the benefit of ALL. To exalt mankind is nobly acting the part of a God; to degrade them, is meanly doing the drudgery of the devil. *Unitas, libertas, caritas esto perpetua.*[80]

What were some of the elements of this theodemocracy, which Joseph Smith envisioned? On the thorny issue of slavery, Smith advocated freeing the slaves and reimbursing their masters through revenues generated by the sale of public land. An ardent expansionist, Smith advocated the annexation of Texas, opposed British claims to Oregon, and, if undertaken peacefully, favored the annexation of both Canada and Mexico as well. On economic reform, Smith called for the reestablishment of a national bank, with branches in every state. To reduce parasitic bureaucracy, Smith urged that Congress be reduced to half its size, and each Congressman's pay be reduced to two dollars a day, plus board: "That is more than a farmer gets, and he lives honestly." The president of the United States, Smith argued, should be given the authority to suppress mobs and protect the constitutional rights of all citizens (including the rights of the Latter-day Saints themselves, who continued to face persecution). Smith urged that all convicts be freed, with the injunction to "go thy way and sin no more."[81]

Instead of being elected president, Joseph Smith was assassinated on June 27, 1844, by an anti-Mormon mob, which stormed a jailhouse in Carthage, Illinois, in which Joseph Smith and his brother, Hyrum, were incarcerated, murdering both. As historian Kenneth Winn rightly observes, "The Mormons came to their millenarianism, in large part, through their bleak republican assessment of the state of the nation."[82] In the fullness of time, when the Church would fulfill its mission, theodemocracy would become possible. Not only that, it would become part and parcel of a world government.

THE AMERICA AS ZION MYTH

In the LDS creed known as the *Articles of Faith,* Article 10 explicitly claims that Zion will be built on North American soil: "We believe in the literal gathering of Israel and in the restoration of the Ten Tribes; that Zion will be built upon this [the American] continent; that Christ will reign personally upon the earth; and that the earth will be renewed and receive its paradisiacal glory."[83] What is this "Zion" and what is its connection with America?

Mormon sources say that the prophet Enoch built a magnificent city called Zion, a holy city, which was, together with Enoch himself, translated into heaven.[84] This city is idealized in *The Pearl of Great Price:* "And the Lord called his people Zion, because they were of one heart and one mind, and dwelt in righteousness; and there was no poor among them,"[85] thus providing an ideal type for Latter-day Saints. In the fullness of time, Enoch foresaw that his Zion would descend to unite with another Zion, to be established by a people drawn from the world over, which would be known as the "New Jerusalem." [86] "Zion will extend, eventually, all over this earth," prophesied Brigham Young. "There will be no nook or corner upon the earth but what will be Zion. It will all be Zion." [87] Notwithstanding this later expansion of Zion, Joseph Smith himself made it clear: "The city of Zion spoken of by David, in the one hundred and second Psalm, will be built upon the land of America." [88]

Latter-day Saints actually believe in two end-time "Zions"—one in Israel (Jerusalem) and the other in America (Independence, Missouri). This is based on a literal interpretation of such verses as Isaiah 24:23, who foresaw a day "when the Lord of hosts shall reign in mount Zion, and in Jerusalem, and before his ancients gloriously." Rather than understanding this dual reference as a common biblical parallelism, Joseph Smith, according to a revelation, gave this interpretation: "Let them, therefore, who are among the Gentiles flee unto Zion. And let them who be of Judah flee unto Jerusalem, unto the mountains of the Lord's house." [89] There is thus a certain eschatological symmetry in Mormon texts between East and West, expressed as a complementarity. While Jerusalem would be the place for the regathering of the Jews, "Zion" in America would be for the gathering of Gentile and Native Americans (as descendants of New World Jews, the Lamanites).

In the New World, the New Zion is also the New Jerusalem. The *Book of Mormon,* which echoes King James diction, speaks of a New Jerusalem,[90] but did not specify its location.[91] That information came with a later revelation. In 1831, Joseph Smith identified the town of Independence (now a suburb of Kansas City, Missouri, more than 900 miles west of Kirtland, Ohio) as the site of the new Zion:

> This land, which is the land of Missouri, is the land which I have appointed and consecrated for the gathering of the saints. Wherefore, this is the land of promise, and the place for the city Zion. . . . Behold the place which is now called Independence is the center place; and a spot for the temple is lying westward, upon a lot which is not far from the courthouse. Wherefore, it is wisdom that the land should be purchased by the saints . . . that they may obtain it for an everlasting inheritance.[92]

Commenting on this pronouncement, which was a signal turning point in Mormon eschatology, Richard Bushman, a contemporary Mormon historian, writes:

> The sacred history of the past at that point flowed into the Mormon present, soon after Joseph Smith received that vision. Oliver Cowdery trudged through the snow to Missouri to find the place for the holy city, the New Jerusalem, where Enoch and modern Mormons were to be united.[93]

Joseph Smith himself had drawn up his own plans for the eschatological city and its Temple complex. These plans are still extant. On August 3, 1831, Joseph Smith, together with his associates in the priesthood, personally dedicated the temple site.[94] The Mormon community in Independence grew to around 1,200 people.[95] But, within two years, the saints had excited the anger of their neighbors, and were driven out of Jackson County at gunpoint. The Mormons were forced to abandon Zion, which has yet to become the New Jerusalem. Today, the "temple lot" is owned by the Church of Christ (formerly the Reorganized Church of Jesus Christ of Latter-day Saints), a Mormon splinter group.[96] When Christ returns to establish the Kingdom of God on Earth, the two capitals of the new empire will be "Jerusalem in the east and Zion in the west." [97]

American Zion will be the scene of the return of "Enoch's Zion." "The City of Zion spoken of by David in Psalms 102," Joseph Smith proclaimed, "will be built upon the Land of America." [98] In the words of one scholar, Mormons added "to the disembodied outline of the millennial dream the firm contours of America." [99] America was once Eden, is now Zion under construction, and will become the New Jerusalem (American Zion) completed in the fullness of time. Sacred history will go full circle, in that Mormon eschatology engages in "marrying millennium and primordium" [100] by envisioning an end-time return to Paradise, in which the earth would be "renewed and receive its paradisiacal glory." [101]

THE MARK OF CAIN MYTH

As in other religious myths of America, the issue of race typically comes up.[102] It is a pivotal theme in the American religious experience. Let us trace this development in Mormon history and doctrine.

While the Mormon message is universal in principle, in practice it was not, for the simple reason that Blacks were barred from the priesthood. The policy was first proclaimed publicly by Brigham Young in 1852. In 1852, and in spite of Joseph Smith's abolitionist leanings later in life, Brigham Young legalized slavery in Utah. For the record, it should be noted that, for years, Mormon scholars, most notably Lester Bush, argued that God had never ordained the priesthood ban in the first place, and that the so-called "Negro doctrine" lacks official sanction by revelation.[103] It would, however, take a direct revelation from God to eventually overturn Brigham Young's decree.[104]

What was the origin of this priesthood ban? Was it Brigham Young's own prejudice, or was there scriptural warrant for it? There are, in fact, several Mormon texts that might have served as a pretext for the priesthood ban, which was based on what may be termed the Mormon "curse of Cain myth," which is a further development of the Protestant "curse of Ham" myth.

In the *Book of Mormon,* dark skin was represented as a curse—the consequence of unrighteousness. In 1 Nephi 12:23, the Lamanites (a term that refers to Native Americans), because of their unbelief, "became a dark, and loathsome, and a filthy people, full of idleness and all manner of abominations." Unbelief and waywardness effected the curse. But why did the curse take the form of color? The reason is given in 2 Nephi 5:21, which relates: "And he had caused the cursing to come upon them, . . . wherefore, as they were white, and exceedingly fair and delightsome, that they might not be enticing unto my people the Lord God did cause a skin of blackness to come upon them." Verse 23 makes the Lamanites even more undesirable: "And cursed shall be the seed of him that mixeth with their seed; for they shall be cursed with the same cursing." The curse, however, may be reversed. As 2 Nephi 30:6 promises, when these lost Jews, the Lamanites, believe in Christ, they shall become "a pure and delightsome people." In the original text of the *Book of Mormon,* the word "pure" had read "white." Under President Kimball's administration, the text was revised. "The *Book of Mormon* made the white race morally superior to the red," according to Brooke, "and the Book of Abraham subordinated blacks." [105] Furthermore, in the Book of Moses, black skin was associated with the progeny of Cain: "The seed of Cain were black." [106] This racialized reading of the curse of Cain equates divine disfavor with dark skin. Naturally, Cain's descendants were heirs to the curse, such that "a blackness came upon all the children of Canaan, that they were despised among all people." [107] Said to be under the "curse of Canaan," black males were thus barred from the Mormon priesthood.

It was the Book of Abraham, however, that "stood as the scriptural basis of Mormon racism" [108] by excluding blacks from the priesthood, beginning with Pharaoh ("Pharaoh being of that lineage").[109] Pharaoh and the Egyptians, as descendants of Ham and Canaan, are represented in the Book of Abraham as the progenitors of people of African descent. The same Mormon scripture states that the heirs of the Canaanites and Noah's son Ham "preserved the curse in the land" and that Noah "cursed him [Ham] as pertaining to the priesthood." [110]

A dramatic reversal of the Mormon racial policy was announced on June 8, 1978. As the result of a personal revelation—witnessed by high-ranking Church authorities—President Herbert Spencer Kimball announced that "all worthy male members of the Church may be ordained to the priesthood without regard for race or color." [111] Kimball's decision, said to have been actuated by his desire to erect a temple in Sao Paulo, Brazil, assumed the status of revelation and was thus included in *Doctrine and Covenants,* immediately following the text of Wilford Woodruff's antipolygamy Manifesto of October 6, 1890 (canonized in *Doctrine and Covenants* in 1908). A witness to that signal event, Elder Bruce R. McConkie, described the Kimball revelation as "one which would reverse the whole direction of the Church, procedurally and administratively." [112] Reflecting on its tremendous impact, the current LDS president, Gordon B. Hinckley, who assumed office in 1995 and serves as the Church's living prophet, had this to say about the revelation: "I need not tell you of the electric effect that was felt both within the Church and without. There was much weeping, with tears of gratitude. . . . Gone is every element of discrimination." [113]

Ever since the "priesthood revelation," Mormons have actively proselyted Blacks. The symbolism of this sea change within the Mormon hierarchy was seen in the elevation of a Black, Brazilian believer, Helvecio Martins, who became the first Saint of African descent to become a General Authority. From 1990–1995, Martins served in the Second Quorum of the Seventy. According to some critics within the Church, however, the 1978 Declaration did not address the theological background that had given rise to the "older race theology" in the first place. [114] Notwithstanding, it is significant that current President Gordon Hinckley spoke on race relations before a regional conference of the NAACP in 1998. [115]

The Church of Jesus Christ of Latter-day Saints has racialized religious beliefs about America by mythologizing Native Americans as transplanted Whites, but who have since darkened, and Blacks as once cursed, but now eligible for priesthood (males). Sacred Mormon scriptures idealize—that is, sacralize—America, as well as criticize, racialize, and ultimately deracialize it. In principle and in practice, Mormon myths of America have evolved as a direct result of a progressive unfoldment of Mormon self-understanding. The Church of Jesus Christ of Latter-day Saints began with the revelation of the *Book of Mormon* and its ancillary texts. Later revelations were needed to demythologize some of the racial aspects of these same Mormon myths. Like the Nation of Islam, the racial doctrines in the early history of the religion have softened over time, with increasing egalitarianism evolving Mormon doctrine as a reflection of America's overall social evolution into an increasingly diverse society with a corresponding ideology of multiculturalism.

In fine, LDS belief holds that America was once Eden, is now Zion under construction, and will become the New Jerusalem (American Zion) completed in the fullness of time. Sacred history will go full circle, in that LDS eschatology engages in "marrying millennium and primordium" [116] by envisioning an end-time return to Paradise, in which the earth would be "renewed and receive its paradisiacal glory." [117] Promising deification (perfectionism) through restoration of true Christianity (primitivism), Joseph Smith prepared his followers for the apocalypse (millenarianism), and revalorized America in the process. Viewing Mormonism three-dimensionally, as a complex of primitivism, millenarianism, and perfectionism, however, does not adequately account for its uniqueness.

For Latter-day Saints, there is the revelatory signature of Joseph Smith himself. In *The American Religion: The Emergence of the Post-Christian Nation,* non-Mormon author Harold Bloom (who is widely regarded as America's foremost literary critic), credits the Mormon prophet in stating that Joseph "Smith was an authentic religious genius, unique in our national history." [118] Joseph Smith's "genius" is to be seen in his rejection of the received traditional interpretation of Genesis:

> Smith's insight could have come only from a remarkably apt reading of the Bible, and there I would locate the secret of his religious genius . . . . So strong was this act of reading that it broke through all the orthodoxies—Protestant, Catholic, Judaic—and found its way back to elements that Smith rightly intuited had been censored out of the stories of the archaic Jewish religion. [119]

Of its myths of America, Mormon racial myths would prove to be the most controversial. [120] Yet the Mormon theology of America has undergone significant transformations with respect to its original doctrines of polygamy and priesthood. Gone is polygamy. Gone is the priesthood ban against Black males. Mormonism thus reflects the social evolution of America, in which professed racism has given way to professed egalitarianism. "It was a religious version of the American dream," as Ostling and Ostling have observed, "Everyman presented with unlimited potential." [121] Clearly, the LDS theology of America has contributed enormously to its evangelical success. The gold plates of Mormon (who edited and abridged the plates of Nephi)—nicknamed the "Gold Bible" by non-Mormons [122]—have thus gilded America. America, the beautiful, becomes America the beatified.

CHAPTER 7

Christian Identity Myths and Visions of America

America will be delivered. God says: . . . "There is going to be a might[y] attack from the air. There will be great Hail Stones. There will be storms and strong winds will sweep the world. . . . War is going to save America. Battling in the streets of the cities is going to say [save] your civilization from mongrelization and this battling is going to save you from being absorbed forever.
—Dr. Wesley A. Swift (1966)[1]

"Christian Identity" is a racial faith that advocates an American racial destiny. As an umbrella term, Christian Identity refers to a constellation of White supremacist groups unified by theology of hate. Christian Identity sects promote a gospel of racism in the name of Christ. Identity is not the only religion of racial hate. According to Betty A. Dobratz, Professor of Sociology at Iowa State University, three religious belief systems—Christian Identity, World Church of the Creator (WCOTC), and Odinism—have played key roles in the construction of White racial identity and in the maintenance of White privilege.[2] These White supremacist organizations have succeeded in harnessing the power of the Internet. As such, they are primarily a virtual community, with a larger-than-life Internet presence that might otherwise belie the marginality of this extremist population. Of the three, Christian Identity is the most influential.

The second most influential racist religion in America is the WCOTC (now known, since 2003, as the Creativity Movement), which boldly proclaims: "CREATIVITY is a *racial religion* whose prime goal is the survival,

expansion and advancement of the White Race." [3] Founder Ben Klassen's
The White Man's Bible offers a "powerful Racial Religion." [4] Odinism, the
third major White supremacist religion, is a pagan belief in Norse mythology
that serves as an alternative spiritual basis for White solidarity. Like the Creativity Movement, Odinism is anti-Christian. Of the three, Christian Identity
sects have the greatest presence on the Internet, as a 2001 study has found:
"Of the religious oriented groups, Christian Identity appears to be the most
common (73) with Creativity representing a small proportion of sites (7)
and only one (1) designated as explicitly Odinist." [5] White supremacy, in fact,
has become a White cyberculture, with Christian Identity as its principal
"religion."

What distinguishes Christian Identity groups from politically oriented
White supremacy groups is its success in using *religion*—that is, Christianity—to legitimatize racialist views. Identity theology provides a unifying
ideology that effectively networks White supremacist groups. Christian Identity is really "skin identity," since the color of one's skin seems to be more
critical than one's religious identity. "Identity links biology and theology,"
remarks Stephen Shaw, "One's virtue is found in one's skin color." [6] Besides
linking genes with creed, Christian Identity furnishes a cohesive ideology that
serves to form a common bond among sundry White supremacist groups, as
Dobratz and Shanks note: "Identity provides religious unity for various racialist organizations and exposes people with such religious orientations to the
racialist aspects of the movement." [7] In fine, Christian Identity has become
the "religion" of choice for the Ku Klux Klan, Aryan Nations and local
branches of Aryan Nations, White Aryan Resistance, Southwest Aryan Sepa-
ratists, and other White nationalist hate groups.

There are a number of enclaves within the Identity movement. They promulgate their literature both online and in print, as well as in the air. The
"Church of True Israel," for example, offers immediate access to the "sermons" of "Dr. Wesley A. Swift," a major Identity ideologue.[8] In the print
world, *The Jubilee,* a bimonthly Identity-affiliated newspaper published in
Midpines, California, and edited by Paul Hall, is the nation's leading White
supremacist newspaper. *The Jubilee* sponsors a syndicated radio program
entitled, *NewsLight.* All of these groups share a common belief system, with
minor exceptions. Christian Identity Web sites function primarily as dissemination venues for racialist literature.

Another Christian Identity group, "Kingdom Identity Ministries," [9] oper-
ates out of Harrison, Arkansas. Of all the Christian Identity sects, Kingdom
Identity presents itself most fully as a religion, replete with its own "Doctrinal
Statement" that adduces its proof texts from various passages in the Bible.[10]
Kingdom Identity is significant in that it is more focused and organized in
promoting its "religious" views than the Church of Jesus Christ Christian/

Aryan Nations. Kingdom Identity claims to promulgate its message by these means: "We proclaim the Gospel of the Kingdom (government according to God's Law) through books, tracts, tapes, videos, the American Institute of Theology Bible Correspondence Course, our international Herald of Truth Radio Broadcasts, a Prison Ministry, Biblical Counseling, Seminars, and other means." [11] The "Herald of Truth" programs are short wave broadcasts emanating from three power stations—located in Monticello, Maine, and Nashville and Manchester, Tennessee—as well as by satellite. Past broadcasts are archived on the Web.[12]

Briefly, the history of Christian Identity may be summed up as follows: In 1946, Wesley Swift (d. 1970) established the first Christian Identity church in Lancaster, California. Wesley's "church" was first called the "Anglo Saxon Christian Congregation," and then, soon after, the "Church of Jesus Christ Christian," reflecting his view that Jesus was not a Jew. Ten years later, in 1956, Swift ordained William Potter Gale, who systematized Swift's teachings into a coherent ideology when, in 1963, Gale published the booklet, *The Faith of Our Fathers*.[13] In his booklet, *Racial and National Identity: A Sermon,* Gale performs a racialized exegesis of Genesis, drawing this moral:

> God's first commandment to Adam and Eve was for them NOT TO MONGREL-IZE THE HOLY SEED of God's family here on earth. This was the meaning of the command He gave them, not to partake of the fruit of the tree of KNOWL-EDGE of good and evil, and this is exactly what He meant. The only tree with KNOWLEDGE is a family or racial tree.[14]

Here, the politics of identity have a scriptural foundation, as strained as the interpretation may be.

To somewhat oversimplify, Identity succession runs from Wesley Swift (1913–1970) through William Potter Gale (1917–1988) to Richard Butler (1938–2004). "Dr." Richard Girnt Butler was one of Swift's foremost followers. In 1979, Butler established the "Church of Jesus Christ Christian/Aryan Nations"[15] on a 20-acre compound on the shores of Hayden Lake, deep in the forests of Northern Idaho. Butler formed the Aryan Nations as the political wing of the Church of Jesus Christ Christian, as a secular, rather than a religious, organization. (The Aryan Nations now maintains a separate Web site that opens with the slogan, "Stop the hate—segregate!"[16]) In 2000, Butler was forced to relinquish the Aryan Nations compound after he was bankrupted by a $6.3 million civil judgment in a lawsuit brought by the Southern Poverty Law Center on behalf of Victoria Keenan and her son.[17] After Butler's death, Christian Identity groups have further fragmented.

Shifting from history to ideology, Christian Identity is the polar opposite of racial universalism and egalitarianism. Not surprisingly, at the heart of

Identity is the doctrine of White supremacy: i.e., the doctrine that the White race is descended from Adam, Jews are the spawn of Satan, and other non-White races are the progeny of pre-Adamic, subhuman "mud peoples," according to Identity theology. Christian Identity believes that Whites, not Jews, are God's chosen people:

> WE BELIEVE the White, Anglo-Saxon, Germanic and kindred people to be God's true, literal Children of Israel. Only this race fulfills every detail of Biblical Prophecy and World History concerning Israel and continues in these latter days to be heirs and possessors of the Covenants, Prophecies, Promises and Blessings YHVH God made to Israel. This chosen seedline making up the "Christian Nations" (Gen. 35:11; Isa. 62:2; Acts 11:26) of the earth stands far superior to all other peoples in their call as God's servant race (Isa. 41:8, 44:21; Luke 1:54).[18]

Based on this information alone, Identity's "religious" visions of America are clearly racial myths of America. These myths include the Lost Tribes Myth, the Two-Seed Myth, the Mud Races Myth, the White Homeland Myth, and the Racial Holy War Myth. Identity's religious myths of America, therefore, have played a key role in "sanctioning racism and sanctifying it with an external religious authority." [19]

THE TWO-SEED MYTH

To provide scriptural warrant for its beliefs, Christian Identity engages in a racialized interpretation of the Bible. This is particularly evident in the Two-Seed Myth and the Mud Races Myth. These complementary myths are remythologized exegeses of the biblical account of the origin of man and his races. Craig Prentiss rightly argues that "the Christian Identity movement . . . filter[s] their biblical exegesis through the prism of racial imaginations shaped by American culture." [20] Through this prism, the colors of the racial spectrum are clearly delineated and differentiated. These myths, moreover, are two sides of the same ideological coin: both combine to show the inherent inferiority of non-White races.[21] To accomplish this, Christian Identity has formulated a doctrine of *polygenesis,* which means "many origins." There are three tines to this ideological trident: (1) the White race is the offspring of Adam; (2) the Jewish "race" is the spawn of Satan; and (3) the other races are sprung from subhuman ancestors. Identity's Two-Seed Myth, or "Serpent Seed" myth, simply put, makes Whites the Seed of Adam and Jews the "Seed of Satan," because Eve mated with Satan in the Garden of Eden. One of the most visible Christian Identity Web sites, Kingdom Identity Ministries, formulates its version of the Two-Seed Theory in its "Kingdom

Identity Ministries Doctrinal Statement of Beliefs," as follows:

> WE BELIEVE in an existing being known as the Devil or Satan and called the
> Serpent (Gen. 3:1; Rev. 12:9), who has a literal "seed" or posterity in the earth
> (Gen. 3:15) commonly called Jews today (Rev. 2:9; 3:9; Isa. 65:15). These chil-
> dren of Satan (John 8:44-47; Matt. 13:38; John 8:23) through Cain (I John 2:22,
> 4:3) who have throughout history always been a curse to true Israel, the Children
> of God, because of a natural enmity between the two races (Gen. 3:15), because
> they do the works of their father the Devil (John 8:38-44), and because they
> please not God, and are contrary to all men (I Thes. 2:14-15), though they often
> pose as ministers of righteousness (II Cor. 11:13-15). The ultimate end of this
> evil race whose hands bear the blood of our Savior (Matt. 27:25) and all the
> righteous slain upon the earth (Matt. 23:35), is Divine judgment (Matt. 13:38-
> 42, 15:13; Zech. 14:21).[22]

As part of a subtler Identity rhetoric, note that this creedal statement does
not explicitly state that the serpent, Satan, seduced Eve, thus spawning the
Jews. But Genesis 3:15 is referenced. The text reads: "And I will put enmity
between thee and the woman, and between thy seed and her seed; it shall
bruise thy head, and thou shalt bruise his heel."[23] One can see how the two-
seed line theory developed: there is Satan's "seed" and then there is Eve's
"seed," which is really Adam's seed under a patriarchal reading. From
Adam's seed the Whites descended, and from Satan's seed came the Jews,
according to this perversely racialized reading of Genesis 3:15. How does this
exegesis reach such an unexpected result? The answer is simple: It is Identity's racial lens that affords this idiosyncratic understanding of an otherwise
universal religious text. Here is a prime example of this racialized exegesis:
Wesley Swift, a former California Ku Klux Klan organizer and Methodist
minister's son, offers this commentary on Genesis 3:15:

> Rather, using only the Scriptures, I will show you that the Fall was brought on by
> an unholy sexual union between Satan and Eve. In Gen. 3:1, we read of a
> "serpent" appearing to Eve in the Garden of Eden. It's important to realize that
> the "serpent" spoken of here was not a literal snake, but rather Satan in human
> form. . . . Gen. 3:15 then tells us that two literal, biological seedlines are to come
> forth from Eve. They are the seedline of Satan and the seedline of the woman
> (through Adam). Verse 15 also tells us that the two seedlines would be in direct
> conflict with one another and in the end the Satanic seed will be crushed. . . .
> Finally, Eve was to have two literal seedlines come forth from her womb. One
> being the "serpents" (Satan in human form) and the other being hers through
> Adam. . . . But Jesus clearly traces the bloodline of the righteous only through
> the white Adamic race. In Matt. 23:33, Jesus calls the Jews "serpents." This is
> an obvious reference to their literal, biological father as spoken of in Gen. chap-
> ter three.[24]

While no less an authority than Michael Barkun (and those who cite him, like Cowan) holds the doctrine of Jews as the spawn of Satan to be a core Identity belief,[25] not all Christian Identity believers hold to this theory, but rather adhere to a "one-seed" theory, which is simply that Whites are the progeny of Adam. Thus, while Identity theology still maintains that Jews are of another (non-White) seed line, the Two-Seed theory is not a universally held tenet. The alternative doctrine is that Jews are descended from Esau (Edom), and that they, along with Blacks and other races, are "strangers in the land" of America.[26] It is possible that softening of the two-seed theory into a one-seed doctrine is simply a case of what sociologists call "stigma transformation"[27] as a means of impression management or "deviance disavowal" to avoid the social stigma of being known as an anti-semite.

THE MUD RACES MYTH

In Identity belief, the White race is the "chosen" race, endowed with spirit, as well as body and soul. This "spirit" is what gives the White man his superior intellectual endowments, according to Identity doctrine, to wit: "Adamic man [the White race] is made trichotomous, that is, not only of body and soul, but having an implanted spirit (Gen. 2:7; I Thes. 5:23; Heb. 4:12) giving him a higher form of consciousness and distinguishing him from all the other races of the earth (Deut. 7:6, 10:15; Amos 3:2)."[28] This is obviously a narrow, racialized reading of scripture—an interpretational framing of race theory. It is an unapologetic attempt to legitimate White supremacy through reference to the Bible, as though it was deciphered cipher—a secret code that Christian Identity has now made clear.

By this logic, if the White race is superior, it follows that "race-mixing" is forbidden, as it dilutes and pollutes it: "Race-mixing is an abomination in the sight of Almighty God, a Satanic attempt meant to destroy the chosen seedline, and is strictly forbidden by His commandments."[29] Note the abundant citations to scripture here, attempting to give biblical warrant to these racialist doctrines. White supremacists, generally, have a great fear and loathing of what they call "mongrelizing" (i.e., reproducing interracially). Besides forbidding marriage and physical intercourse with non-Whites, social intercourse is discouraged as well. As one may see, the ultimate White separatism is the call for a White homeland.

It is one thing to foster racial pride. Yet fostering racial pride seems to go hand-in-hand with fomenting racial hate. It is a commonplace, on the Internet, to see consistent references to Christian Identity groups calling non-White (and non-Jewish) races as "mud peoples" or "mud races." Obviously, "mud races" is a term of deprecation. Nothing more pejorative, and offensive, can scarcely be imagined. The term "mud peoples" evidently was coined by avowed atheist Ben Klassen, founder of the World Church of the Creator and author of two WCOTC scriptures, *Nature's Eternal Religion* and *The White Man's Bible*. The term then migrated to Identity enclaves, becoming part and parcel of the popular parlance of White supremacists generally.

THE LOST TRIBES MYTH

Christian Identity, and its theology-rooted racialism, has an ideological pedigree. A twentieth-century variation of British Israelism (also known as Anglo-Israelism), Identity holds that Whites are the true Jews because they are descendants of the ten lost tribes of Israel. As British Israelism was an ideology for an empire, Christian Identity became an ideology for a race.

British-Israelism began with John Wilson (d. 1871), with his book, *Lectures on Our Israelitish Origin* (1840), in which he argued that the ten lost tribes of Israel, over time, had migrated through Europe into Great Britain. But the classic tract of British-Israelism is Edward Hine's *Identity of the Ten Lost Tribes of Israel with the Anglo-Celto-Saxons,* which was a best seller in its day (having sold 250,000 copies!) and is still reprinted in Identity circles today. Beyond what Wilson had claimed, Hine (1825–1891) said that Britain, "the Island Nation," was itself the true home of the lost tribes of Israel. For the British, this idea had tremendous appeal. In 1884, Hine sailed to the United States, where he spread his ideas over the fertile soil of ethnocentric American exceptionalism during the course of his four-year visit.[30] Stock pseudo-linguist proofs are nearly universal in such tracts; for instance, when contracting the two words, "Isaac's sons," one comes up with the word, "Saxons."[31] Wesley Swift adapted this doctrine to America, and naturally it spread to other Christian Identity sects. As a prime example of how this doctrine is formulated and given scriptural warrant, the Kingdom Identity "Doctrinal Statement of Beliefs" states, in part:

WE BELIEVE that the United States of America fulfills the prophesied (II Sam. 7:10; Isa. 11:12; Ezek. 36:24) place where Christians from all the tribes of Israel would be regathered. It is here in this blessed land (Deut. 15.6, 28:11, 33:13–17) that God made a small one a strong nation (Isa. 60:22), feeding His people with knowledge and understanding through Christian pastors (Jer. 3:14–15) who have carried the light of truth and blessings unto the nations of the earth (Isa. 49:6, 2:2–3; Gen. 12:3). North America is the wilderness (Hosea 2:14) to which God brought the dispersed seed of israel, the land between two seas (Zech. 9:10), surveyed and divided by rivers (Isa. 18:1–2,7), where springs of water and streams break out and the desert blossoms as the rose (Isa. 35:1,6–7).[32]

In other words, America will be divinely established as a Christian Republic. Note here how the Bible is invoked for everything Aryan. And so it is that Christian Identity is a species of the broader Anglo-Israelite Myth, which popularized the idea that the White race in America (rather than the British Isles) was descended from the lost tribes of ancient Israel. As one Christian Identity tract proclaims, America is the true Israel: "Israel's new name America, the only founded Christian Nation," the "great Christian Kingdom." [33]

THE WHITE HOMELAND MYTH

In the previous section, one sees how America has been accorded a special destiny. Identity theology provides a political eschatology that holds out the hope and promise of an Aryan homeland sometime in the future. That is to say, not only will America be the site of God's kingdom on earth, America is also destined to become a White homeland. Consistent with other aspects of his racialist ideology, the idea of a White homeland was promulgated by Richard Butler. In brief, here is Richard Butler's story.

In 1968, the Lockheed Aircraft Company hired Richard Butler as a senior marketing engineer. His job was to help set up assembly lines to build the l-1011 jumbo jet. During this time, Butler took flying lessons and got a private pilot's license. Then he began making trips to the Pacific Northwest. Captivated by the beauty and grandeur of that country, Butler dreamed of establishing an Aryan homeland there.[34] As the co-inventor of a rapid repair system for the tubeless tire, Butler was able to retire early in life, at age 55. It was then that he moved to Hayden Lake in 1974. There he purchased an old farmhouse on a 20-acre parcel of land, where he posted a sign warning, "Whites Only." The compound was patrolled by German shepherds. In 1977, Butler established the Church of Jesus Christ Christian, and then the political wing, the Aryan Nations, in 1979.[35] This foothold in the Pacific Northwest was the first step forward in realizing Christian Identity's dream of a White homeland.

Ordained a "Christian" minister after his correspondence course from the American Institute of Theology in Arkansas, "Pastor" Butler, from his Hayden Lake compound, openly advocated establishing a Whites-only "homeland" in the Pacific Northwest. Butler called his vision the "Ten Percent Solution." The Pacific Northwest would be a Whites-only, exclusively heterosexual enclave within the borders of five states—Washington, Oregon, Idaho, Montana, and Wyoming. Later, the Aryan Nations would call this plan the "Northwest Territorial Imperative" (or simply "Northwest Imperative"). If this vision was ever to be realized—and the Pacific Northwest become a White bastion—where would the non-Whites go?

The formation of a White homeland would require the expulsion, or "repatriation," of all non-Whites. In 1984, David Duke, who established the

National Association for the Advancement of White People (NAAWP) in 1980 and later founded the National Association for European American Rights in January 2000, proposed specific regions of the United States where different races would be relocated. These proposals were originally published in the magazine, *Instauration,* and later reprinted in the December 1984 *NAAWP News.* Duke's proposal would redraw the map of the United States, roughly as follows:

> Blacks could live in a New Africa made up of parts of Georgia, Alabama, and Mississippi; Jews would dwell in West Israel, comprised of Long Island and Manhattan; the rest of the New York metropolitan area and southern Connecticut would be home to various "unassimilable minorities," including Puerto Ricans, southern Italians, Greeks, and immigrants from the southern Mediterranean littoral; Mexicans would get the Southwest, except for a slice of territory called Navahona, which would be reserved for American Indians; the Hawaiian Islands would be renamed East Mongolia and be set aside for Asians; Dade County, Florida would be the New Cuba. Anyone straying across their borders would be shot on sight.[36]

Currently, the most popular advocate of a White homeland or "Ethnostate" is Wilmot Robertson,[37] a "racially awake" activist fighting for a "territorial initiative." The role of Christian Identity in all of this is to provide religious sanction for what are essentially political aspirations.

Richard Butler's Hayden Lake compound was the crown jewel of the Aryan movement. It was the first concrete realization of the dream of a White homeland. On July 1, 1998, three of Butler's security guards allegedly assaulted seasonal berry picker Victoria Keenan and her son Jason. Dees argued that Butler owed the Keenans damages for the terror they suffered.[38] A lawsuit brought by Morris Dees and the Southern Poverty Law Center in 2000 against the Aryan Nations resulted in a $6.3 million civil judgment against him.[39] The case was captioned, *Keenan v. Aryan Nations,* No. CV-99-441 (Idaho 2000).[40] Enforcement of that judgment forced the sale of the Hayden Lake compound. The Keenans purchased the property at a U.S. Bankruptcy Court sale, and later resold it to a multimillionaire. The Aryan dream was shattered. But the Christian Identity myths of America live on.

THE RACIAL HOLY WAR MYTH

The Christian Identity vision of the *future* is a transparent revelation of what the world would be like *today*—if only Identity had the power to enforce its ideology. In other words, the time of the end is where Identity aspirations would be fully realized and come to full fruition. There are two sides to Identity's vision of the end, as with apocalyptic scenarios in general, as Kathleen

Stewart points out: "Apocalypticism and millennialism are the dark and light sides of a historical sensibility transfixed by the possibility of imminent catastrophe, cosmic redemption, spiritual transformation, and a new world order." [41] In this double vision of the end of time, Christian Identity envisions a racial apocalypse followed by a millennium in which the White race, led by Christ, will rule the earth. In the Identity apocalypse, Christ will take revenge on the Jews, who will be annihilated first: "The ultimate end of this evil race [the Jews] whose hands bear the blood of our Savior (Matt. 27:25) and all the righteous slain upon the earth (Matt. 23:35), is Divine judgment (Matt. 13:38-42, 15:13; Zech. 14:21)." [42] In a further elaboration on the American apocalypse, Identity further prophesies that Christ will return to bring judgment on the other non-White races as well:

> WE BELIEVE the ultimate destiny of all history will be the establishment of the Kingdom of God upon this earth (Psalm 37:9, 11, 22; Isa. 11:9; Matt. 5:5, 6:10; Rev. 21:2–3) with Yahshua our Messiah (Jesus Christ) reigning as King of kings over the house of Jacob forever, of this kingdom and dominion there shall be no end (Luke 1:32–33; Dan. 2:44, 7:14; Zech. 14:9). When our Savior returns to restore righteous government on the earth, there will be a day of reckoning when the kingdoms of this world become His (Rev. 11:15; Isa. 9:6-7) and all evil shall be destroyed (Isa. 13:9; Mal. 4:3; Matt. 13:30, 41–42; II Thes. 2:8).[43]

Here, "all evil shall be destroyed" can easily be understood to mean the non-White races. In the Kingdom Identity statement, Christ will mete out punishment. However, the WCOTC/Creativity apocalyptic scenario involves what may be characterized as an eschatological vigilantism, in which Whites will wage a "Racial Holy War" against Jews and Blacks, not to mention other races.

The term "Racial Holy War" was coined by the WCOTC. The WCOTC coined the phrase "RaHoWa" as a battle cry for "Racial Holy War," and it serves as an official greeting as well. The politics of digitality allows for this battle cry to echo on the Internet with impressive ubiquity. RaHoWa seeks the overthrow of ZOG (Zionist Occupation Government), which is part of the Christian Identity myth of a Zionist plot to destroy the White race through miscegenation.

The WCOTC/Creativity Movement has produced the *Little White Book,* which serves as a manifesto or bible. For the unsympathetic, this book is hard to stomach. Consider, for instance, how a massacre is heralded as a milestone in White history: "One hundred years ago, on December 29, 1890, at the battle of Wounded Knee Creek, South Dakota, the White Race finally and absolutely triumphed in America. Let us honor and celebrate this glorious day—THE DAY OF TRIUMPH OF WHITE AMERICA—every year." [44] If the Battle of Wounded Knee is glorified as an exemplar in the White supremacist mind, one can well imagine what RaHoWa would look like, if it was ever to be waged. The *Little White Book* ends with these words, on page 33: "A RACIAL HOLY WAR under the victorious flag of the one and only, true and revolutionary White Racial Religion—CREATIVITY—is the ONLY SALVATION for the White Race."[45]

Presumably, these are the words of WCOTC founder, Ben Klassen. While America is not mentioned here (presumably because RaHoWa would entail a global conflagration), this is, by far, potentially the most dangerous ideology we have encountered so far—the most virulent religious myth of America yet. (For many readers, the next chapter will prove equally disturbing.) Consider the case of Gabriel Carafa, a leader in the World Church of the Creator—now known as the Creativity Movement—and a skinhead group called the Hated. On May 5, 2006, Carafa pleaded guilty in federal court in Camden, New Jersey, to selling 11 stolen guns to an informant. The *Philadelphia Inquirer* account reports the following exchange between the judge and Mr. Carafa:

> His body is covered in white-supremacist tattoos, including one on his forehead that reads "Rahowa," which is short for "racial holy war." The term is a battle cry for the Creativity Movement, whose leader, Matthew Hale, was sentenced last year to 40 years in prison for plotting to kill a Chicago federal judge.
>
> U.S. District Judge Robert B. Kugler asked Carafa yesterday whether he was a member of the Hated. Carafa said he was.
>
> "Is that what you have on your forehead?" Kugler asked.
>
> "Yes, sir."[46]

That a young man would tattoo his body in hate slogans vividly illustrates the extreme mentality of some White supremacists. And this hate ideology is exported as well. One fairly recent example of this is when the White Crusaders of the RaHoWa (a U.S.-based hate group) "set up a local website which lists a contact address as a suburban Adelaide post office box and an Australian business number."[47] While the Creativity Movement presents itself as a religion, it is, as previously mentioned, atheist and anti-Christian. Some might say the same thing about "Christian Identity"—that, in practice, it is antithetical to Christianity as well.

What is the role of religion in White nationalist ideology? Specifically, what is the role of Christianity in Christian Identity? One of the scholars who has addressed this question was Professor Betty Dobratz. After a disciplined inquiry, Dobratz concludes that the answer itself remains elusive, inconclusive: "The extent of the centrality of 'Identity' beliefs to this movement needs to be further examined in order to understand the unity and dissent within the movement and the development of collective conscious-ness." [48] The other two of the three major forms of religious belief among White supremacists—the Creativity Movement and Odinism—are openly critical of Christianity. White supremacists, to the extent that some of them profess a religious belief, will never agree on matters of religion. Religion is simply a means to a racialist end.

Consider "Pastor" Bertrand L. Comparet. A graduate of Stanford University, Comparet was admitted to the California Bar in 1926, and so was a lawyer by profession. Christian Identity groups revere "Pastor" Comparet as a great biblical scholar. In his sermon, "Man and Beast," Comparet uses biblical text as a pretext to justify White racialism: "Some races God classi-fies as *animals.* Their *nations are symbolized* as beasts in numerous proph-ecies." [49] In the same vein, in his sermon, "The Children of the Beast," Wesley Swift invokes a putative verse from the epistle of *Jude,* to wit: "I have separated and segregated you from all the people of the earth." [50] There is no such verse in *Jude.* But even if there were, the interpretive modality is still the same: drawing an equivalence between the word "beasts" in scripture and "pre-Adamic races." Many similar examples can be adduced. But the point remains the same.

Although the present writer cannot prove this, it seems that the animating vision of RaHoWa can be traced back to Wesley Swift himself, who, in 1966 wrote:

America will be delivered. God says: . . . "There is going to be a might[y] attack from the air. There will be great Hail Stones. There will be storms and strong winds will sweep the world. . . . War is going to save America. Battling in the streets of the cities is going to say [save] your civilization from mongrelization and this battling is going to save you from being absorbed forever. You say: . . . Oh, Dr. Swift, don't talk that way, they may find a way to silence us. Well, one thing they cannot stop and that is "Thus saith the Lord." With all the power they think they have in reserve, they can't stop that.[51]

Here, in saying that "War is going to save America" and then directly con-necting this "battling in the streets of the cities" with the goal of saving "civ-ilization from mongrelization," the elements of a racial holy war are present. This is no swords-into-plowshares vision of peace. It is an apocalyptic sce-nario with an idealized apartheid as its outcome. Therefore, it is not just the Creativity Movement that envisions a racial conflagration, but the great ideo-logue of Christian Identity itself, Wesley Swift.

It seems patent enough that the "missionary" outreach of Christian Identity is to recruit others for furthering a racial agenda. Identity therefore has only the *trappings* of Christianity. If mainstream Christianity's mission, generally, is to save sinners, then one may ask if Identity adherents have the same goal in mind as the established churches. The answer appears to be no. It is clear that Christian Identity, as well as similar supremacist enclaves, uses its "Christian" identity for fundamentally un-Christian and unholy purposes—ethnoviolence in the name of Christ. This ethnoviolence, if seriously prosecuted, can only lead to blood in the streets of America cities, where everyone's skin color will be tinged with the crimson of bloodshed.

CHAPTER 8

Black Muslim Myths and Visions of America

The Kingdom of God is an egalitarian kingdom structured on truth, where each of us will be treated with fairness and justice. America could become the basis for the Kingdom of God.

—Louis Farrakhan (1993)[1]

How is God going to destroy America? What instrument is He going to use? . . . The Honorable Elijah Muhammad told us of a giant Mother Plane that is made like the universe, spheres within spheres. White people call them unidentified flying objects (UFOs).

—Louis Farrakhan (1996)[2]

A black man with a white mother became a savior to us. . . . A black man with a white mother could turn out to be one who can lift America from her fall.

—Louis Farrakhan (2008)[3]

The Nation of Islam has an apocalyptic and frighteningly literal interpretation of Ezekiel Chapter 1 (considered by some to be the most mystical and recondite chapter in the Bible), in which the destruction of America is foretold. Black Muslims believe that Ezekiel saw and described a giant spaceship, referred to as the "Mother Wheel" or the "Mother Plane." To punish America for its evils of past slavery and current racism, the Mother Wheel will remove Blacks and then destroy White America.[4] A member of one of the branches of the Nation of Islam (the "Five Percent Nation of Islam") is a popular hip-hop artist, the rapper known as "Killah Priest" or simply as

"Priest." Priest was interviewed in 1997 with questions that probed his religious beliefs.[5] At that time, Priest was a Black Muslim. In the course of the interview, Priest was asked: "Why, then, do you rap so much about outer space?" To which Priest answered: "Because that's where we're from! Black people come from space. When you look at the sky, it's black." Priest then talked about UFOs (unidentified flying objects): "I'm talking about pure facts. . . . But space travel is real. . . . Ezekiel saw UFOs back then—only they were IFOs, because he identified them. . . . They were chariots of fire." Alluding to the destruction of America that will be inflicted by the Mother Wheel, Priest invoked Isaiah and connected it with the destruction of America (although Priest does not explicitly mention America): "Isaiah 66:15—'the Lord will come with fire, and his chariots like a whirlwind.' He's going to come and wreak vengeance." [6] In one of his rap songs, "Madness," Priest speaks of the apocalypse as foretold by the Nation of Islam:

> I see prophecies unfold that was told by the prophets of old
> Looked up, I saw the clouds in Heaven roll
> Back like a gigantic scroll
> UFO's came down to damage the globe.[7]

This is a transparent reference to the "baby planes," which are small spacecraft whose mission is to drop their payloads of "drill bombs" on White America in a literal Day of Judgment for the Babylon that America has become. This chapter will enlarge on some of the central Black Muslim myths and visions of America that Killah Priest has invoked.

Black nationalism is a response to White nationalism. For decades, the leading Black nationalist movement in contemporary America has been the Nation of Islam (NOI), whose followers are known as "Black Muslims." Indeed they are Black, but are they Muslims? But that was not the point at all. There was a special reason for calling this religion "Islam": since Christianity was perceived as the "White man's religion," Islam was presented as an alternative religion—the "Black man's religion." The Nation of Islam had therefore appropriated the name of "Islam" as this alternative religion. Yet the teachings of the NOI, at first, had very little to do with traditional Islam.

The Nation of Islam's core teachings would appear, to ordinary Muslims at least, to have both congruities and incongruities with traditional Islam. For instance, while Whites may convert to Islam, they have never been allowed to convert to the Nation of Islam. As Malcolm X said in his 1962 speech, "Black Man's History," a Black Muslim, by definition, is black, and "the only ticket you need to get into Muhammad's Mosque is to be black." [8] This racial exclusion—this self-segregation is in an already-segregated society—contributed enormously to the NOI's popular appeal among socially disenfranchised African Americans, who wanted liberation, since integration was not an option at that time.

During "America's apartheid" in the Jim Crow era, the Nation of Islam, adopting a prophetic voice with a shrill rhetoric to match, advocated a Black homeland, free of White oppression. Not surprisingly, the Nation preached (and still preaches) a Black gospel—a theology of Black liberation. Its prophets are "Master Fard Muhammad Allah" (God), Elijah Muhammad (the Messiah), and Louis Farrakhan (the Messiah's envoy), not to mention the stellar role played by Malcolm X. Today, despite its radical beginnings, the Nation of Islam's teachings have changed over time. Today, in fact, NOI doctrine and discourse may be described as moderate and somewhat egalitarian. This evolution is far more pronounced in the NOI's public rhetoric, but not so much in its private discourse. Nevertheless, the NOI has come a long way since Farrakhan's song, "A White Man's Heaven Is a Black Man's Hell."[9]

The "Lost-Found Nation of Islam" was founded by an itinerant peddler, Wallace D. Fard, also known as Fard Muhammad and, later on, as "Master W. Fard Muhammad." After being released from San Quentin Prison for having sold narcotics, he moved to Detroit in 1930. There, he peddled silk garments to Blacks, gained their confidence, and began to teach them their "lost" Afrocentric history. Fard was clearly influenced by the ideas of Noble Drew Ali (aka Timothy Drew), the Black founder of the Moorish Science Temple of America (MSTA), which introduced such Islam-esque precepts and praxis as the prohibition of pork, the use of Arabic personal names, and the emblematic display of the crescent-and-star motif. Drew, who was looked to by his followers as a prophet, foretold the apocalyptic annihilation of all Whites. Fard was, in fact, a member of the MSTA.

A figure shrouded in mystery, Fard either disappeared or died as of June 30, 1934. He was succeeded by Elijah Muhammad (originally, Elijah Poole, 1897–1975). The son of an ex-slave and Baptist preacher, Poole met W. D. Fard in 1931 at one of Fard's meetings on Hasting Street—the main thoroughfare in black Detroit—and believed he had found a savior for the Black race. Recounting that fateful encounter over 30 years later, Muhammad told *Ebony* magazine: "He [Fard] didn't have to tell me that he was Allah. I recognized him. And right there I told him that he was the one the world had been looking for to come [*sic*]."[10]

For a long time prior to this, Elijah himself had wanted to save his race. As a boy, Elijah witnessed a lynching. The victim had allegedly insulted a White woman. This was a horrible thing to witness firsthand, and young Elijah was deeply disturbed by it: "That event had impressed me so much that I cannot get over it; I did never [*sic*] forget it, not until this day."[11] As a youth, after listening to accounts of cruelty and suffering under slavery, Elijah used to say: "My grandmother, when I get to be a man, if the Lord helps me I will try to get my people out of the grip of this White man because I believe that we will not be able to get along with peace under his government." [12] Elijah Muhammad went on to lead the Nation of Islam from 1934 to 1975. In addition to its theology of a Black God and gospel of Black liberation, the Nation of Islam promoted self-reliance by encouraging the large-scale development of Black-owned businesses. In its heyday, the NOI was a successful and wealthy enterprise. Unfortunately, Muhammad's leadership was marred by moral contradictions in his own personal life. In January 1960, Elijah Muhammad's first out-of-wedlock child was born—the first of 13 illegitimate children whom he fathered over a seven-year period by seven different mistresses.

During his tenure as leader of the Nation of Islam, Elijah Muhammad attracted two converts who would become his most famous protégés: Malcolm X and Louis Farrakhan. While in prison, Malcolm X converted to the Nation of Islam in late 1948, and he went on to have a colorful and controversial career. From his parole from prison in 1952 until his break with the Nation in 1964, Malcolm X helped the ranks of the Nation swell from an estimated 500 members in 1952 to 30,000 strong in 1963.

One of the lesser-known incidents in his life involved negotiations with the Ku Klux Klan (KKK). In December 1960, Elijah Muhammad ordered Malcolm X to meet representatives of the KKK in Atlanta, to investigate their offer to Muhammad of a tract of land "so that his program of separation would sound more feasible to Negroes and therefore lessen the pressure that the integrationists were putting upon the white man." [13] Later, when he found out about Elijah Muhammad's sexual escapades, Malcolm X began to have serious doubts, not only about Muhammad's integrity in the wake of such moral turpitude, but about whether Muhammad was really a messenger of Allah, as he had claimed. On March 12, 1964, Malcolm X announced that he was leaving the Nation of Islam. He went on to found the Muslim Mosque, Inc. and later, on June 28, 1964, the Organization of Afro-American Unity. On April 19, 1964, Malcolm X completed his pilgrimage (*Hajj*) to Mecca and became El-Hajj Malik al-Shabazz, his new Muslim name. On February 21, 1965, Malcolm X was assassinated on the stage of the Audubon Ballroom in Harlem (with a strong suspicion that the NOI's paramilitary wing, the Fruit of Islam, was behind the assassination), thus ending a prophetic career as a social reformer.

Meanwhile, in 1955, Louis Eugene Wolcott, a former nightclub singer, joined the Nation of Islam. He was recruited by both Elijah Muhammad and Malcolm X. Wolcott first became known as Minister Louis X, and later as Abdul Haleem Farrakhan. When Elijah Muhammad died on February 25, 1975, many thought that Farrakhan would succeed him. But Elijah Muhammad had appointed his youngest son, Wallace Muhammad, as his successor instead. During his first three years as leader of the Nation of Islam, Wallace Muhammad (1933–2008), also known as Warith Deen Mohammed, gradually renounced the teachings of his late father and converted a great number of former members of the Nation into traditional Muslims. Having led the Nation of Islam into mainstream Islam, Wallace Muhammad changed the Nation's name to the "American Muslim Mission." In 1977, Farrakhan left the American Muslim Mission, and, having taken several thousand followers with him, reestablished the Nation of Islam under the name, the "Original Nation of Islam."

The Nation of Islam's rise to power and influence reached its peak in October 1995. The Million Man March, conceived and organized under NOI leader Louis Farrakhan, was the largest gathering of African Americans in U.S. history. The Million Man March was the crowning testimony to the power and influence of Louis Farrakhan as a Black leader and power broker. Yet, fairly recently, in fact, the Nation of Islam has come to embrace traditional Islam. Like the conversion of Malcolm X—from the Nation of Islam to traditional Islam—the NOI, in several major ways, has undergone a slow conversion to traditional Islam. Farrakhan finally led a transition of the NOI back to traditional Islam—culminating in his open espousal of classical Islam—when he ostensibly reconciled with Warith Deen Mohammed on "Saviour's Day" in February 1999. Yet, today, the Nation of Islam still maintains a distinct Black national identity, and has never disclaimed its Black nationalist myths, which are the subject of this chapter. The major religious myths of the Nation of Islam are the Yacub Myth, the Mother Plane Myth, and the Destruction of America Myth, which is where jeremiad and apocalyptic rhetoric ultimately intermix.

THE YACUB MYTH

Although this myth sprung from the fertile imagination of Elijah Muhammad, it was Malcolm X who gave definitive expression to this myth in short form, as Terrill observes generally about Malcolm X's repackaging of Elijah Muhammad's teachings: "While a minister in the Nation of Islam, Malcolm crafted from the rambling revelations of Elijah Muhammad a hermetically sealed prophetic rhetoric—it called upon its audience to realign their values and behaviors with a foundational set of truths presented in and through that very discourse." [14] Just before Christmas in December 1962, Malcolm X delivered his vociferously anti-White sermon, "Black Man's History," [15] at the Harlem's Nation of Islam's Mosque No. 7 in Harlem. On Malcolm's instructions, this speech was recorded by "Benjamin 2X" (now Benjamin Karim), one of Malcolm's most trusted and faithful lieutenants.

In "Black Man's History," Malcolm X restates Elijah Muhammad's esoteric teachings about the origin of races, beginning with the proposition: "The birth of the white race has always been a secret." [16] According to Malcolm X, Blacks came into existence 66 trillion years ago:

> The Honorable Elijah Muhammad teaches us that sixty-six trillion years ago our people were living on this planet: the black man was living on this planet. But in those days it was larger than it is now, and the planet Mars, that was off here beyond it, had an effect upon our planet then in the same manner that the moon affects us today. [17]

They were an advanced race. For eons, Blacks led a blissful existence. But their paradise suddenly ended 6,000 years ago when an evil Black scientist, Yacub, was bent on creating the White race. When he succeeded, the White race, evil by nature, would rule over Blacks for 6,000 years.

Malcolm goes on to retell the fantastic tale of the origins of the White race, at the hands of evil black scientist Yacub. Born in the year 8,400, Yacub discovered the law of magnetism at the age of six. As polar opposites attract, magnetism inspired Yacub to create a race that was the polar opposite of Blacks. By so doing, he would create a human magnetic force field. Yacub later discovered the secrets of genetics. This enabled Yacub to act on his wish to create a new race. When the book of Genesis says, "Let us make man," these were Yacub's words, not God's. Yacub accomplished this by means of a nefarious birth control law designed to favor light-skinned offspring over black-skinned infants. Yacub forbade Black couples to marry. But if one partner was brown in color, they could. If they gave birth to a black child, doctors were to "put a needle in its brain and feed it to a wild animal or give it to the cremator." [18] Within 200 years, no more Black babies were born.

After Yacub's death at age 150, this process of favoring lighter-skinned offspring continued. Thus the brown race emerged from the black, the yellow race from the brown, and the white race from the yellow. After 200 years, the brown race was destroyed, leaving only "a yellow or mulatto-looking civilization." [19] After a full 600 years had elapsed, "they had grafted away the black, grafted away the brown, grafted away the yellow, so that all they had left was a pale-skinned, blue-eyed, blonde-haired thing that you call a man." [20] But this was no man: "actually the Bible calls him the devil, ... old Lucifer, Satan, or the serpent." [21] Malcolm X concludes this segment of his speech in saying: "They had to murder off the black, brown, and yellow in order to get to the white. And right to this very day the white man by nature wants to murder off the black, brown, and yellow." [22] And further: "You're not using the right language when you say the white man. You call it the devil." [23] A further instance of the anti-White invectives of this remarkable (and equally disturbing) speech is the teaching that Whites cannot walk truly upright, since they evolved from cavemen who crawled on all fours.[24] Malcolm X goes on to deepen anti-White antipathy by exciting feelings of repulsion for the moral depravity of the White race. Here, Malcolm X suggests that White women mated with dogs:

> Oh yes, this was the white man, brother, up in the caves of Europe. He had a tail that long . . . The Honorable Elijah Muhammad says . . . what the white man would do, he'd dig a hole in the hill, that was his cave. And his mother and his daughter and his wife would all be in there with the dog. The only thing that made friends with the white man was the dog. . . . It was then that the dog and the white man amalgamated. The white woman went with the dog while they were living in the caves of Europe. And right to this very day the white woman will tell you there is nothing she loves better than a dog. They tell you that a dog is a man's best friend. They lived in that cave with those dogs and right now they got that dog smell.[25]

Yacub would then teach this man "tricknology"[26]—the science of deceit.

THE MOTHER PLANE MYTH

The Nation of Islam developed an apocalyptic scenario that promised racialized retribution. To vanquish evil, the world must be freed of the White Devil. The White race will be obliterated, as Elijah Muhammad has stated: "According to the history of the white race (devils) they are guilty of . . . causing war among the people and themselves ever since they have been on our planet Earth. So the God of the righteous . . . has decided to remove them from the face of the Earth."[27] Under this vision of the end, God would judge between the "white devil" and the black man. Justice would then prevail, not as equalization, but in annihilation of the white man. Armaggedon is thus to be a racial war[28]—an eschatology of reverse racism, if you will. (One may think about the NOI apocalypse as a functional counterpart to the "Racial Holy War" predicted by the Creativity Movement, as discussed in the previous chapter.)

How would all this take place? In one sense, the countdown to Armageddon began when the slave ship Jesus of Lubeck, captained by the white devil John Hawkins, came upon the shores of West Africa. "In effect, slavery brought the original people like a Trojan horse into the fortress of evil," Mattias Gardell observes, "giving the African American a key role in the approaching apocalypse."[29] Armageddon will be preceded by a kind of Black "rapture." Like faithful Christians being swept up into the air before Jesus comes on a mushroom cloud, Black Muslims will be transported by spacecraft to the Mother Wheel, their safe haven for the duration of the apocalyptic upheaval.[30] The White race, however, will be exterminated under a hail of bombs dropped by space warplanes that are sent out on missions of destruction by the Mother Plane.[31]

The "Mother Wheel" myth is based on Ezekiel's wheel of fire, originally derived from Elijah Muhammad's allegorization of passages from Ezekiel 10:2–11.[32] This is clear in Chapter 125 of *Message to the Blackman,* "Battle in the Sky Is Near." But the most extensive description is by Elijah Muhammad, in Chapter 58, "The Mother Plane," in his book, *The Fall of America,* available online, an excerpt of which will serve to illustrate this flight of imagination:

> The Mother Plane was made to destroy this world of evil and to show the wisdom and mighty power of the God Whom came to destroy an old world and set up a new world. . . . The same type of plane was used by the Original God to put mountains on His planets. . . . Allah (God) Who came in the Person of Master Fard Muhammad, . . . taught me that . . . He will raise these mountains to a height of one (1) mile over the United States of America.[33]

Elijah Muhammad says that the Mother Plane was taught by W. D. Fard himself. Be that as it may, this teaching is said to be grounded in Ezekiel's vision. This is Elijah Muhammad's exegesis of it, in brief:

> Ezekiel saw the Mother Plane in a vision. . . . According to the Bible, he looked up and saw this Plane (Ez. 1:16) and he called it a wheel because it was made like a wheel. A Plane that is wheel-shaped can turn in any direction, at any time. He admitted that the Plane was so high that it looked dreadful, and he cried out, "O wheel" (Ez. 10:13). Ezekiel saw great work going on in the wheel and four living creatures "and their work was as it were a wheel in the middle of a wheel." (Ez. 1:16). And when the living creatures went, the wheels went with them: and when the living creatures were lifted up from the earth, the wheels, were lifted up (Ez. 1:19).
>
> In Ezekiel's vision concerning the wheel, he said that he heard the voice of one tell the other to take coals of fire and to scatter it over the cities; this means bombs. . . . Allah (God) taught me that these bombs are not to be dropped into water. They are to be dropped only on the cities. . . . Allah (God) Whom came in the Person of Master Fard Muhammad, to Whom praises are due forever, taught me that the Mother plane is a little human-made planet.[34]

Elijah Muhammad goes on to explain that the "four creatures represents the four colors of the original people of the earth"—that is, "the four colors of the Black man (Black, brown, yellow and red)."[35] Excluded here is the evil White race, which will be destroyed. This fate of the White race is not, however, absolute. Claude Andrew Clegg makes this important observation: "As one of the few major changes that Elijah Muhammad introduced into the

Nation's overall belief system, over time white Muslims became eligible for salvation; however, their hereafter would supposedly be qualitatively inferior to that of blacks." [36] A "remnant" of the White race would be saved. This is hardly reassuring for Whites, as Clegg observes: "For the most part, the question of white redemption was academic insofar as so few would be able to contradict their wicked nature and save America by extending freedom, justice, and equality to the so-called Negro." [37] Those few Whites who would be saved, however, will only be converts to Islam.

The divine judgment executed by the Mother Wheel would pave the way for the promised golden age, a utopian vision that Black Muslims would dream of. This is the Millennium, which will be a Black paradise. The Black Nation will be raised upon the smouldering ashes of the vanquished Caucasian civilization. The remnant of humanity will number a little more than the 144,000 spoken of in the Book of Revelation. All vestiges of the old world will have been obliterated. In a mere 20 years' time, the very memory of American civilization will vanish from the minds of the saved. The new government will be "based upon truth, freedom, justice, and equality." [38] The Original People will be biologically enhanced, physically fitter. They will be "clothed in silk interwoven with gold." ... [39] Appearing as youthful 16-year-olds, Black people will have a life-span of a thousand years or longer.[40]

THE DESTRUCTION OF AMERICA MYTH

A further development of the Mother Plane Myth is the Destruction of America Myth. Again, this is the product of Elijah Muhammad's imaginative end-time scenario. However, the way in which Malcolm X relates it may be of more interest to readers. On December 4, 1963, Malcolm X would deliver his speech, "God's Judgment of America" [41]—later changed to "God's Judgment of White America." This was popularly known as "The Chickens Come Home to Roost" speech. The reason is this: shortly after making this speech, Malcolm was asked by the press for his opinion on the recent assassination of President John F. Kennedy. In response, Malcolm caustically remarked that Kennedy "never foresaw that the chickens would come home to roost so soon." This callous quip set off a firestorm, leading Elijah Muhammad to impose 90 days of silence on his leading spokesman. Remarkably, "God's Judgment of White America" incorporates hardly any of the elements of Elijah Muhammad's apocalyptic scenario, except to say that "the white world" would somehow come to an end, as this excerpt from the speech will serve to illustrate:

When The Honorable Elijah Muhammad says "end of the world," he does not mean the end of the earth; he is referring to the end of a race of "world of people," and their removal from this earth: the removal of their world. There are many "worlds" here on this earth: the Buddhist world, Hindu world, Jewish world, Christian world—Capitalist world, Communist world, Socialist world—Eastern world and Western world—Oriental world and Occidental world—dark world and white world. Which of these many worlds has come to the end of its rope, the end of its time? Look around you at all of the signs and you will agree that it is the end of time for the Western world, the European world, the Christian world, *the white world.*[42]

This was public discourse. The nitty-gritty detail of the Black Muslim apocalypse was, in fact, reserved for private discourse, which FBI surveillance tapes would later disclose:

LITTLE [Malcolm X] told this group that there was a space ship 40 miles up which was built by the wise men of the East and in this space ship there are a number of smaller space ships and each one is loaded with bombs. LITTLE stated that when ELIJAH MOHAMMED of Chicago, Illinois, gives the word these ships will descend on the United States, bomb it and destroy all the "white devils". According to LITTLE these bombs will destroy all the "devils" in the United States and that all the Muslims in good standing will be spared. LITTLE claimed that their Prophet ELIJAH MOHAMMED was sent to the United States 20 years ago to save the "Black people." [43]

The new information disclosed here is that Elijah Muhammad himself would give the order for the destruction to start. Note that Whites are not called "people," but instead are objectified—and demonized, quite literally —as "devils." The word "people" (with the connotation of "human") is reserved for "Black people" alone. This judgment, therefore, is not a judgment of individuals, but of races and religions. All good Muslims would be spared. The clear implication here is that Blacks who are not Black Muslims would not be spared. They would, however, be warned in advance of the impending doom. Not to be unjust, just how would all good Muslims be spared? In another FBI surveillance tape, Malcolm X is reported to have said:

First the planes would drop pamphlets written in Arabic and English explaining that they should get on to your own kind at once. He stated at this time the Muslims would have already left North America, and you would have to find a way out for yourself. He stated that next there would come a trumpet so piercing to your ears that it would drive men insane, pregnant women would have their babies, and some would drop dead. The last part of the destruction would be an airplane returning ALLAH to the Almighty God Himself. He would light a match that would cause a fire which no man could put out.[44]

America will literally be burned alive by divine conflagration.

It was only during his stellar rise as a minister of the Nation of Islam, from 1952 until late 1959, that Malcolm X talked about the Mother Plane. Thereafter, he appeared to abandon that topic altogether. "As the profile of the Nation grew in the national press," Wayne Taylor observes, "Malcolm eschewed his earlier musings on the mother ship and shifted his focus to more earthly matters."[45] This raises a question: did Malcolm X simply shift his focus to more practical matters, or did he actually reject the myth of the Mother Ship? If so, would this not have signaled a departure from the NOI norm, or mark a crisis in faith? Taylor seems to suggest that both answers are true: "In his struggle to bring African Americans closer to a paradise on earth, Malcolm turned away from the fantastic visions and began to concentrate on creating brotherhood in the African Diaspora through political and economic strategies."[46] Still, for the seven years that he would teach his fellow Black Muslims about the Mother Plane, the result was electric, for it had such great appeal for the rank-and-file Black Muslim: "Malcolm's racialized vision of the Armageddon captivated an audience desperate for deliverance."[47] Yet, despite Malcolm's eschewal of it, the myth persisted having, as it were, a life of its own.

In fact, the Mother Plane Myth was remarkably long-lived. Four decades after Malcolm's 1955 speech, Louis Farrakhan spoke at the Mosque Maryam in Chicago, on June 9, 1996, on the topic: "The Divine Destruction of America: Can She Avert It?" In no uncertain terms, Farrakhan said that God's "intention is the total destruction of America." Corrupt to the core, America is the Babylon whose destruction was foretold in the Book of Revelation, for "[n]o city or people answers the description of a mystery Babylon better than the cities and the people of America." After describing various cataclysms that would take place, Farrakhan described a giant spacecraft called the "Mother Plane" (or "Mother Wheel").[48] His description of it reveals how meticulously Farrakhan had followed Elijah Muhammad's teaching.

Literally made in Japan, the "giant Mother Plane"—which White people have sighted called unidentified flying objects (UFOs)—was foretold by the prophet Ezekiel, who described it as "a wheel that looked like a cloud by day but a pillar of fire by night." This was the creation of "some of the original [black] scientists" and "took 15 billion dollars in gold at that time to build it." This gargantuan warship, "made of the toughest steel," is "a half mile by a half mile," "is like a small human built planet," and is like a giant hangar, housing 1,500 smaller ships, each of which is equipped with three "drill bombs." "And the final act of destruction," Farrakhan warns, "will be that Allah will make a wall out of the atmosphere over and around North America." God will then "cut a shortage in gravity and a fire will start from 13-layers up and burn down, burning the atmosphere." America will then "burn for 310 years and take 690 years to cool off."[49]

All this might seem fanciful enough. Farrakhan, after all, was simply elaborating on what Elijah Muhammad and Malcolm X had previously said. But one gets the impression that Farrakhan may have completely bought into the myth. In 1985, Farrakhan had a vision, in which he was actually taken up in this heretofore imaginary spacecraft. Matthias Gardell describes Farrakhan's reported experience as follows:

> In the vision, Farrakhan walked up a mountain to an Aztec temple together with some companions. When he got to the top of the mountain, a UFO appeared. Farrakhan immediately realized the importance of the moment.... Farrakhan, feeling a bit afraid, asked his companions to go with him but was corrected from the spacecraft: "Just you, brother Farrakhan." He walked and was placed next to the pilot. The spacecraft took off with Farrakhan, who knew that the pilot was sent by God and was to take him to the Mother Wheel. After being inside, he heard the well-known voice of the Honorable Elijah Muhammad, which confirmed his being alive. Farrakhan was authorized to lead his God-fearing people through these latter days. The Messiah spoke many things and a scroll full of divine cursive writing was rolled down inside Farrakhan's head. The spaceship shot out of the tunnel and the pilot took the plane up to a terrific height and maneuvered the vehicle to allow Farrakhan to look down on the wheel. He saw a city, a magnificent city, the New Jerusalem, in the sky. Instead of going back to Mexico, the craft carried him with terrific speed to Washington, DC, and dropped him off outside of the city. He walked into the capital and delivered his announcement, the final warning to the United States government.[50]

Louis Farrakhan was certainly not the only one to believe in the actual existence of the Mother Wheel. Most Black Muslims, in fact, believed in the reality of this fantastic spacecraft after Farrakhan's verification of its existence. According to Dr. Vibert White, Jr., author of *Inside the Nation of Islam,* great excitement was generated in February 1984 on "Saviour's Day," an annual NOI event when, in his speech, Louis Farrakhan spoke of his personal experience of the Mother Plane. This ignited a wave of interest and expectation throughout the Nation of Islam, as Dr. White further relates:

> When the Nation's ministers started to follow the lead of Farrakhan in lecturing at length on the Mother Plane, members of the Nation became possessed with the Mother Plane story. For instance, in Fruit of Islam classes that were held in the basement of the Final Call building in Chicago, a week did not pass before several brothers reported that they had seen the Mother Plane. In fact, it was not unusual for members to stay up all night looking and pointing out the Mother Plane. Strangely, as it sounds now, I reported that not only did I see the Mother Plane but, also, had a vision of the craft before observing it.[51]

This testimony shows how effectively this "technological monstrosity" [52] had captured the imagination of Black Muslims. Note how Dr. White's "vision" of the Mother Plane preceded—and probably preconditioned—his reported sighting of it. After the 1995 Million Man March, however, Vibert White became increasingly disillusioned with Louis Farrakhan, and critical of the Nation of Islam. Eventually, Dr. White left the Nation in 1996,[53] having been a member for some 20 years. Two years later, in October 1998, Dr. White embraced the Bahá'í Faith, following a presentation by the present writer in the Bahá'í Center in Springfield, Illinois.

As for Farrakhan himself, he apparently began to follow much the same course as Warith Deen Mohammed, in finding his way to authentic Islam. It just took Farrakhan a lot longer to do so. First diagnosed in 1991 with prostate cancer, Farrakhan faced a crisis in his personal health that some say may have precipitated a crisis of faith with respect to the teachings of his preceptor and predecessor, Elijah Muhammad. Without actually renouncing Elijah Muhammad's teachings, Farrakhan took a decisive move in openly committing himself to mainstream Islam. How sincere this move was is still open to question.

Writing for the Religious News Service in 1999, Arthur J. Magida, author of *Prophet of Rage: A Life of Louis Farrakhan and His Nation,* reported that Farrakhan was rumored to have distanced himself away from Elijah Muhammad's teachings in favor of traditional Islam, and was steering the NOI leadership in that same direction:

> While there has been no public statement by Farrakhan that he is divorcing himself from these central tenets of the Nation of Islam, he reportedly told a closed-door meeting here of Nation of Islam ministers from around the country in late January or early February that they should disregard the "old teachings." [54]

The far more public rapprochement came one year later. On February 25, 2000, during a Jumu'ah prayer service held at the McCormick Center as part of the Nation of Islam's Saviours' Day 2000 celebration in Chicago, Farrakhan and Deen embraced in a symbolic show of reconciliation.[55] Notwithstanding Farrakhan's show of solidarity with traditional Islam, Warith Deen Mohammed remained critical of the Nation of Islam. After his August 10, 2007, lecture at the Clinton Presidential Library, W. D. Mohammed told the press: "The time for those leaders who had that hate rhetoric has come and passed and they know it." He added: "For the last 10 years or more, they've just been selling wolf tickets to the white race and having fun while they collect money and have fancy lifestyles." [56] Warith Deen Mohammed passed away on September 9, 2008.[57]

The Nation of Islam is significant in part because it gave so many African Americans, whether Black Muslims or not, a renewed identity, and fired them with new hope and resolve. Despite its inchoate racism and the internal corruption of the NOI itself, NOI rhetoric served as the voice of an oppressed people, as a theology of liberation, and even as the conscience of America itself. Before its recent reconciliation with traditional Islam, the original message of the Nation of Islam was one of Black superiority and White inferiority, a Black God in place of a White God, and Black Nation to be set apart from any White nation.[58] The Nation of Islam preached, and continues to preach, a gospel of Black nationalism. In the Yacub Myth, the NOI had formulated a negative theology of America, perhaps more aptly described as a *theodicy* (explanation of the origins of evil and of "God's justice"). Over time, the Yacub Myth had become an embarrassment for the Nation. If not sheer madness, the myth was a social liability. Its ideology of Black supremacy, which was once a bulwark against White supremacy, ultimately became a barrier to interracial harmony. Over the years, though, the social message of the NOI has softened considerably as the Nation of Islam began to embrace traditional Islam.

As recently as February 24, 2008, Farrakhan said of a non-Muslim candidate for the U.S. presidency, Senator Barack Obama: "A black man with a white mother became a savior to us. . . . A black man with a white mother could turn out to be one who can lift America from her fall." [59] This single statement implicitly marks the utter abrogation of the Yacub Myth, *for Obama cannot be a "savior" if his mother was a White "devil"!* The wider implications of Farrakhan's endorsement of Senator Obama are equally clear: The Nation of Islam has publicly abandoned, although not abnegated, its own religious myths of America, in favor of an egalitarian vision of America. However, as Chapter 12 will demonstrate, Farrakhan is still a firebrand of religious racism and anti-semitism, even in 2007 and 2008.

CHAPTER 9

Contemporary Muslim Myths and Visions of America

Let the entire world hear me. Our hostility to the Great Satan [America] is absolute. . . . I conclude my speech with the slogan that will continue to reverberate on all occasions so that nobody will think that we have weakened. Regardless of how the world has changed after 11 September, Death to America will remain our reverberating and powerful slogan: Death to America.

—Hassan Nasrallah (2002)[1]

A civil war is raging within the soul of Islam pitting radicals, along with their terrorist offspring, against moderate Muslims who wish to embrace modern democratic, social, and economic principles. The subjects of this dispute are encapsulated by America. In effect, then, America has become a party to that religious war.

—Hillel Fradkin (2004)[2]

In 2005, a young African American Muslim was asked what it was like living in post-9/11 America. "It's like being black," he replied, "Twice."[3] The terrorist attacks on the Twin Towers in New York on September 11, 2001, have cast a spotlight on the American Muslim community.[4] The pressures that American Muslims have come to experience are exacerbated by anti-American sentiments voiced abroad by Radical Islamists, who may be defined as "anyone who wants to govern a country in accordance with the *Shari'a,* Islamic law"[5] and who resorts to terror or force to reassert the *Shari'a.* As a result of such anti-Americanism overseas and as a consequence of Islamophobia (fear and loathing of Islam and Muslims) at home, many

American Muslims feel like they are on "trial" in both their public and their private lives. To create a framework of social significance within which to situate this entire discussion, consider the fact that the reciprocal demonization between the United States and Iran impacts American Muslims at home, who thereby experience the worst of two modes of prejudice: religious and racial.

The problem of anti-Americanism abroad by radical Islamists is largely one of religious nationalism. Nationalism and religion often combine to form religious nationalism, as stated in Chapter 1. "Religious nationalism is the fusion of nationalism and religion such that they are inseparable," according to Barbara-Ann J. Rieffer.[6] "It is a community of religious people or the political movement of a group of people heavily influenced by religious beliefs who aspire to be politically self-determining."[7] The Palestinians, Chechens, Filipino Moros, and Kashmiris are cases of religious nationalism that arise in conjunction with liberation movements.[8] Among such groups, it is the religious nationalism of the Islamic Republic of Iran that has generated the most salient and powerful religious myth of America within the contemporary Muslim world. On January 29, 2002, U.S. President George W. Bush responded with his "State of the Union Address" in which he vilified Iran as a cohort in the "Axis of Evil" that also includes Iraq (under Saddam Hossein) and North Korea. Here is a classic case of myth and counter-myth, in the context of reciprocal demonization. This mutually reinforcing demonization has greatly exacerbated the problem of Islamophobia in the United States, which perpetuates an unhealthy, even if understandable, state of affairs with respect to interfaith relations and the simple, everyday encounter of Muslims and non-Muslims in the streets of American cities.

THE "GREAT SATAN" MYTH

The first thing that comes to mind when the topics of "Islam" and "America" are brought together is the image of America as "the Great Satan" in the eyes of Iran and elsewhere. For nearly three decades, Revolutionary Iran has stigmatized the United States as "the Great Satan." As the name suggests, "Satan" is the archetypal principality of evil, both in Islam (where his Qur'anic name is Iblis) and in Christianity (known also as Lucifer) alike. Loathsome and odious, "the Great Satan" evokes contempt and outrage; use of this name is meant to rally Muslims around a common enemy—America.

It was Ayatollah Ruhollah Khomeini—supreme leader of Revolutionary Iran, credited as the first "Islamist" government in the twentieth century— who, on November 5, 1979, demonized America as "the Great Satan, the wounded snake."[9] Russia was named the "Other Satan" and Britain the "Little Satan." Other countries in the West have been variously branded as Little

Satans, as has Israel. "The use of the term Great Satan was in fact a brilliant rhetorical device used by Khomeini to great effect during the course of the hostage crisis," writes William O. Beeman, author of *The "Great Satan" vs. the "Mad Mullahs": How the United States and Iran Demonize Each Other.*[10] This is rhetorical essentialism at the height of its evocative power.

Here, the demonization is quite literal: America is vilified as the greatest of all demonic powers, Satan himself. "No image could be more deeply evocative than the characterization of the United States as the Great Satan by Iran," Beeman adds.[11] This inflammatory rhetoric articulated a powerful myth of America that has swept across the Middle East and beyond. And the image of America as "the Great Satan" is deeply embedded in anti-American rhetoric. One year after the September 11, 2001, terrorist attacks on the World Trade Center in New York City, Hezbollah Leader Nasrallah, on September 27, 2002, reignited the inflammatory rhetoric to keep the fires of hate ablaze:

> Let the entire world hear me. Our hostility to the Great Satan is absolute. . . . I conclude my speech with the slogan that will continue to reverberate on all occasions so that nobody will think that we have weakened. Regardless of how the world has changed after 11 September, "Death to America" will remain our reverberating and powerful slogan: "Death to America." [12]

The Great Satan myth is a national and transnational myth that gives meaning and moment to Iranian anti-imperialism and Islamic radicalism. It is important to situate the Great Satan myth in its historical context. In 1979, the Islamic Revolution of Iran overthrew Mohammad Reza Pahlavi, who had ruled over Iran for over 35 years. From the early 1940s forward, the Pahlavi regime attempted to reform Iranian society along Western lines. The Shah of Iran established a civil service. He also instituted a national bank based on the European model. This process of secularization and Westernization proceeded apace, the Shah eventually replaced Islamic and traditional courts with civil courts. In keeping with previous reforms, these courts followed canons of Western jurisprudence. At a distance, in the view of Western observers at least, these reforms were generally progressive, as they were intended by the Shah to be.

The Shah's progressive policies, however, were ultimately undone by his repressive policies. To make matters worse, he was also seen as a puppet of the West, since he was re-enthroned in August 1953 after the overthrow of Premier Mohammad Mossadeq in a military coup, instigated by the CIA under the code name "TP-AJAX" (or "Operation Ajax")—an operation that entailed considerable covert U.S. financial and political support.[13] The perception of the Shah as a stooge of the West was reinforced by his frequent diplomatic visits with Presidents Nixon and Carter. To make matters worse, the Shah was seen not only to be repressive, but corrupt, as oil revenues were diverted to the military, or directly to the Shah himself, and away from the vast majority of Iranians, who otherwise stood to benefit from oil revenues. For these and other reasons, the Shah's western-style reforms—particularly his programs promoting modernization and secularization—had largely become ineffective by the 1970s. Significant sectors of the Iranian population had already been alienated.[14] Animosity toward the Shah of Iran mounted, and that very discontent was a social resource that could be exploited to its fullest. Regime change was in the offing. It would prove inevitable.

Led by Ayatollah Khomeini, the 1979 Islamic Revolution of Iran was effectively directed by Shi'i clerics, who succeeded in mobilizing the masses in public demonstrations calling for the downfall of the Shah. This anti-Shah movement rejected the current regime's authoritarianism, corruption, maldistribution of wealth, and all-too-rapid westernization of Iran. The national, social, and economic themes of the Revolution, as defined by Khomeini himself, emphasized the importance of religious nationalism, of social justice, of political participation, and of a return to Persian culture. The grassroots religious national movement that Khomeini orchestrated (and oversaw from Paris) demanded an end to corruption, the removal of foreign influences, and respect for religious national identity. The massive street demonstrations were ultimately successful and, in February 1979, the Pahlavi dynasty collapsed. A popular referendum was held in March, mandating a change from monarchy to an Islamic republic. By the end of that year, a new constitution was drafted by a 75-member "Council of Experts," which was likewise ratified by a popular referendum.[15] Khomeini subsequently stigmatized America as "the Great Satan."

In Persian (Farsi) the native expression is "Shaytán-i Buzurg." [16] In Arabic, the Great Satan is "al-Shaytán al-Kabír." This is the same name as the stele popularly known as al-Shaytan al-Kabir, which is the buttress at Al-Muna, where Muslims, as a pilgrimage ritual, stone Satan. What follows is the celebrated 1855 account by Sir Richard Francis Burton (1821–1890) of this Muslim ritual:

We were now to mount for "the Throwing," as a preliminary to which we washed "with seven waters" the seven pebbles brought from Muzdalifah, and bound them in our Ihrams. Our first destination was the entrance to the western end of the long line which composes the Muna village. We found a swarming crowd in the narrow road opposite the "Jamrat al-Akabah," or, as it is vulgarly called, the *Shaytan al-Kabir*—the "Great Devil." ... The "Shaytan al-Kabir" is a dwarf buttress of rude masonry, about eight feet high by two and a half broad, placed against a rough wall of stones at the Meccan entrance to Muna. As the ceremony of "Ramy," or Lapidation, must be performed on the first day by all pilgrims between sunrise and sunset . . . .

The narrow space was crowded with pilgrims, all struggling like drowning men to approach as near as possible to the Devil; it would have been easy to run over the heads of the mass. . . . I had duly provided myself with a hidden dagger. The precaution was not useless. Scarcely had my donkey entered the crowd than he was overthrown by a dromedary, and I found myself under the stamping and roaring beast's stomach. Avoiding being trampled upon by a judicious use of the knife, I lost no time in escaping from a place so ignobly dangerous. . . .

Finding an opening, we approached within about five cubits of the place, and holding each stone between the thumb and the forefinger of the right hand, we cast it at the pillar, exclaiming, "In the name of Allah, and Allah is Almighty! (I do this) in Hatred of the Fiend [Satan] and to his Shame." [17]

Although Khomeini's likely allusion to the Muslim ritual of stoning Satan will be lost on most Americans, on closer examination, the implication is obvious: As *al-Shaytán al-Kabír* incarnate, America (and Americans) should be stoned. But what is the Islamic meaning of "stoning" here? While the phrase, the "stoning of Satan," resonates with Muslims generally, the stoning of Satan does not parallel the stoning of the adulterer. In other words, while the punishment for adultery in classical Islam is death by stoning (since adultery is considered a capital offense), there is no legal issue here. Rather, the stoning of Satan is a repudiation of Satan, not an attempt to kill him (especially since he cannot be killed anyway).[18] Thus, the force of the rhetoric behind "the great Satan" is repudiation, not punishment.

In classical Islam, the fallen angel (or jinn) is known by two names in the Qur'an, Iblís and Shaytán. Explaining the relationship between the two names, Canadian Islamicist Andrew Rippin comments:

It is notable that the two names, Iblís and al-Shaytán, are used within the same narrative (Q. 2:30-9; 7:11–25; 20:116–23) in such a manner as to discount a simple blending of separate myths related to these two names; rather, the narrative appears integrated and the change in name is best interpreted to suggest that Iblís gained the name al-Shaytán after his disobedience, which is how the Muslim tradition has frequently understood it.[19]

The connection between Satan and ritual stoning is suggested by the Qur'an itself. When the first man, Adam, was created, God commanded that all of the angels bow down before him. Adam, after all, was the pinnacle of God's creation—a marvel that should elicit the respect and admiration, indeed the veneration, of the heavenly host. The angels obeyed God's command—that is, all except Iblís. Iblís refused (Q. 2:34; 7:11; 15:31; 17:61; 18:50; 20:116; 38:74-5), on the logical, but defective grounds that Adam was a creation from mere clay and water (e.g., Q. 15:33: "I am not going to bow to man whom You have created from clay of moulded mud"). In consequence of this signal act of defiance, God then curses Iblís, calling him "accursed" (*rajím*). The word "accursed" literally means "stoned" (Q. 15:34; 38:77), being a transparent allusion to the rituals of the Islamic pilgrimage (*hájj*),[20] as explained above. God then cast Satan out of heaven, much as he did with Lucifer in Christian tradition. Thus, Lucifer and Iblís are Christian and Islamic horns on the same diabolical head.

According to Andrew Rippin, classical Islam downplayed the figure of Satan in favor of the fallen angel Iblís who, in some Sufi renditions, is the perfect Muslim because he refused to bow down before anything other than God. Iblís is an ambiguous figure but in making him so, classical Islam avoided the Manichean tendency of Satan. Islam in modern times, however, has moved towards the Satanic "other" in the face of the loss of Muslim communal identity, the challenges of the postcolonial times, the rise of the Wahhabi power with its emphasis on correct action. Thus, "the Great Satan" needs to be seen within the moral framework of modern Islam, not just the categories of conservatism.[21]

The genesis of "Great Satan" rhetoric can be traced back to Sayyid Qutb (1906–1966). John Zimmerman underscores this ideological pedigree: "The 11 September attacks cannot be understood fully without an understanding of the ideas of Sayyid Qutb, who is widely acknowledged as the intellectual godfather for the various modern radical Islamic movements."[22] As the principal voice for the Muslim Brotherhood in Egypt, Sayyid Qutb is the great ideologue for Radical Islamism in general. Early in life, Qutb had embraced Westernization, but reportedly grew disenchanted with it after Israel became a state in 1948, and after experiencing, firsthand, anti-Arab prejudice during his sojourn in the United States as a student in 1949–1951.[23] With his trademark emphasis on Islamic morality and society, Sayyid Qutb championed a return to "pure Islam," unadulterated by what he perceived to be the pernicious amorality of the West.

Qutb's writings would later form the theoretical basis and philosophical foundation for a number of Radical Islamist groups today. Indeed, Sayyid Qutb is considered to be the intellectual preceptor of Osama bin Laden, leader of al-Qaeda. In the case of al-Qaeda, in fact, the connection is direct: Sayyid Qutb's brother, Professor Muhammad Qutb, was a teacher and mentor to the young Osama bin Laden. Qutb's book, *Ma'álim 'ala Al-Tariq* (*Milestones* [or *Signposts*] *on the Road,* or *Landmarks along the Way,* 1964), was an instant best seller and is widely recognized as one of the most influential Islamist tracts ever written. In his book, *The America I Have Seen* (*Amrika allati Raaytu*), Qutb registers this concession regarding the role of America in the world today:

America has a principal role in this world, in the realm of practical matters and scientific research, and in the field of organization, improvement, production, and management. All that requires mind power and muscle are where American genius shines, and all that requires spirit and emotion are where American naiveté and primitiveness become apparent. For humanity to be able to benefit from American genius they must add great strength to the American strength. But humanity makes the gravest of errors and risks losing its account of morals, if it makes America its example in feelings and manners.[24]

Notwithstanding this positive assessment of America from a material standpoint, Sayyid Qutb found American society to be morally bankrupt. Qutb held that contemporary societies, including America, were in a state of Jahiliyyah. In classical Islam, Jahiliyyah (often translated as the "Age of Ignorance") referred to the pre-Islamic period prior to the advent of the Prophet Muhammad, founder of Islam, in the seventh century. Although Qutb was not the first ideologue to apply the term to contemporary society, the consequence of that pejorative view of the non-Muslim world is what makes Qutb's cultural critique of America and the West so radical, insofar as "Qutb's answer to the worldwide state of Jahiliyyah was *jihad*." [25]

Jihad (Arabic for "struggle") was primarily, although not exclusively, interpreted by Qutb as holy war, which was "necessary to 'establish God's authority on earth . . . to abolish all the Satanic forces and Satanic systems of life.' " [26] Note the rhetoric of Satan here, with reference to the West. The transfer of this stock diabolical imagery to America by Khomeini was as predictable as it was inevitable. Qutb further clarifies his position on Islamic jihad: "Those who recognize the nature of this religion . . . also recognize that the active movement for Islam would have to begin with jihad by the sword, in addition to jihad by teaching. They likewise recognize that this jihad was not a defensive movement." [27] As for Qutb's direct impact on al-Qaeda, John Zimmerman concludes:

> We may never know what the 19 Al-Qaeda hijackers of 11 September 2001 were thinking as they steered the airplanes toward the twin towers of the World Trade Center, the Pentagon and an open field in Pennsylvania. However, we can be certain that they were immersed in the ideas of Sayyid Qutb.[28]

The Great Satan myth is an official rather than a populist creation, although it enjoys widespread popular appeal. Notwithstanding, many Iranians continue to be enamored of America in various ways. Taking a wider perspective, the Great Satan myth, subsequent to Khomeini's coining of that invective, has been taken up by radical Islamists outside Iran as well as within. The myth now belongs to the discourse of "Islamic fundamentalism," also known as radical Islamism. Let us first define what is meant by "radical Islamism" vis-à-vis contemporary Islam.

Islam is not monolithic. In other words, there is a diversity in Islamic orientations. These orientations, in turn, have produced correspondingly diverse discourses. In approaching modern Islam, the present writer has refined a typology that accounts for the wide-ranging, often disparate, and even conflicting attitudes towards the West that find ideological and political expression throughout the Muslim world today. In this approach, the author has taught students (Muslim students included) to clearly differentiate among five Islamic "responses to modernity." From "right to left," so to speak, they are the following: (1) Radical Islamism, (2) Traditionalism, (3) Neo-Traditionalism, (4) Modernism, (5) Secularism, (6) Postmodernism, and (7) Post-Islamism. This typology is based on a fivefold schema developed by William Shepard.[29] However, the present writer will describe these terms in the ways in which they made most sense to students, with occasional reference to a more recent typology advanced by Haroro J. Ingram.[30] Wherever possible, relations back to the myth of the Great Satan will be made by way of additional commentary.

Briefly, what is meant by "modernity"? Andrew Rippin characterizes modernity cumulatively as "that which renders the past problematic."[31] Peter Berger's five "dilemmas of modernity" include Abstraction, Futurity, Individuation, Liberation, and Secularization. Similarly, Harvey Cox's "Five Pillars of Modernity" emphasize the roles of Nationalism, Technology, Bureaucracy, Profit Maximalization, and Secularization. The core values of modernity, now "global values," derive in part from the individual values of liberty, equality, and fraternity as espoused in the French Revolution, and social values of progress and science-based rationality characteristic of the Industrial Revolution.[32] However one looks at modernity, this much is true: as Rippin says, modernity poses a challenge to traditional religions generally. Their "responses to modernity" represent various coping strategies. In the case of modern Islam, certain patterns emerge that the following typology attempts for capture.

(1) *Radical Islamism:* Think of Islamist terrorists, principally al-Qaeda and its affiliates, like the Taleban. Jemaah Islamiyah (responsible for the Bali bombings of 2002), represents al-Qaeda's Southeastern Asian affiliate, not to mention the Moro Islamic Liberation Force. Among radical Islamists today, Osama bin Laden and Ayman al-Zawahiri are the most notorious. Also think of "Islamic fundamentalism." These terms are roughly equivalent. "Revolutionary radical Islamism," states Andrew Rippin, is "that fringe element which dominates the media picture of Islamic fundamentalism."[33] Radical Islamists are as peripheral as they are self-canonizing. They do not represent mainstream Islam. Yet their influence outstrips their relative

numbers. As Gabriel Weimann, professor of communication at the University of Haifa, Israel, has shown in his forthcoming book, *Terror on the Internet: The New Arena, the New Challenges,* some 4,800 terrorist Web sites, forums, and chat rooms operate on the Internet today.[34]

"Radicals believe that selectively literalist interpretations of Islamic doctrine should play a crucial role in both the personal and collective spheres as an all-encompassing framework for life," Ingram observes. "For radicals, Islam as a framework for life is incompatible with any secular ideology." [35] The radical Islamist goal is to establish *shariʿa*-ruled states—by force, if necessary. The means justifies the end in this holy quest to reassert the Islamic law code, or *shariʿa,* in order to bring about an Islamic theocracy.

Iranian support for radical Islamists is well-known. Besides Iranian funding of the Hesbollah, Iran's backing of the Iraqi cleric Muqtada al-Sadr is a known fact, despite Iran's denials to the contrary. During a June 2003 visit to Iran, for instance, al-Sadr met with Expediency Council Chairman Ayatollah ʿAli-Akbar Hashemi Rafsanjani. During a January 2006 visit to Iran, al-Sadr met with Iranian Foreign Minister Manuchehr Mottaki and Supreme National Security Council secretary, Ali Larijani.[36]

"Also notable is the tendency to view things as opposing spheres," Rippin further explains, "for example, the Government of God versus the Great Satan in Iranian propaganda." [37] Thus, "the Great Satan" myth of America properly belongs to radical Islamist discourse. The implication here is that the other Islamic responses to modernity are not as inclined—or may even be disinclined—to refer to America as the Great Satan.

(2) *Traditionalism:* Traditionalists are known as "the People of the Way of the Prophet and the Community [of Muslims]" (*Ahl al-Sunna wa al-Jamaʿa*). Think of the orthodox *ulama* (Muslim clerics). Their goal is to preserve the *status quo,* as Rippin points out:

> The Traditionalist group contains within it many of the learned scholars ("*ulama*") who might be thought to have a vested interest in maintaining the status quo, . . . and the vast majority of those who have not been exposed to modern education and thus to a great extent have not experienced the challenge of modernity to such a degree as to consider it a personal problem.[38]

Traditionalist Muslims believe that whatever does not conform to the Qurʾan and the traditions of the Prophet Muhammad is, by definition, false. Moreover, the Islamic precepts and praxis, as defined by the consensus of the early generations of Muslim scholars, is binding for all Muslims. The Qurʾan and Tradition (*hadīth*), moreover, cannot be challenged by rational reasoning. All Islamic laws are fixed and immutable.[39] Traditionalists may or may not sympathize with the radical Islamist view of America as the Great Satan, but they tend not to be vocal about it.

(3) *Neo-Traditionalism:* Neo-Traditionalists are conservative Muslims that can tolerate gradual change, while conserving the essentials of traditional Islam. Thus, they can accept the new with the old, but to a very limited degree. "One trend within Traditionalism can be termed 'Neo-traditionalism,'" Rippin writes. "This is a tendency which has been seen as a transitional position from Traditionalism to any of the other groups." [40] "It may be, however, that as a position it has its own inherent permanent protagonists," Rippin adds. "Such a position . . . urges a gradual change, seeing the advantage in certain elements of modern technology, for example, but wanting to withstand the rush of the acceptance of it all." [41]

(4) *Modernism:* Modernist Muslims see the need to adapt Islam to modernity, but not to alter Islam's basic character. Modernists allow for greater change than do Neo-traditionalists. "Islamic modernism wants Islam to be the basis for political life as well as the religious," Rippin explains, "but it perceives a need to reinterpret those structures in the light of contemporary needs, frequently with a clear and unapologetic adoption of Western notions." [42] This Islamic response to modernity sees itself as positive and progressive. Just as the rest of the modern world has been undergoing profound change, so also must Islam. Islam must keep pace with the social and scientific revolutions that have come to define modernity. This does not, however, entail a rejection of Islam, but simply an adaptation—a measured readjustment of it: "In formal contrast to secularism, Islamic modernism insists that Islam does provide an adequate ideological base for public life," writes Shepard.[43] Ingram usefully adds that

> modernists are defined not only by their belief that Islam does provide an adequate basis for life, but that it is also compatible with secular ideological perspectives. For example, modernists will characteristically claim that Islamic principles are compatible with secular philosophies of democracy and capitalism.[44]

Such proponents of Islamic modernism as Jamál al-Dín al-Afghání (1839–97), Muhammad 'Abduh (1849–1905), and Rashíd Ridá (1865–1935) in Egypt, and Sayyid Ahmad Khán (1817–1898) and Muhammad Iqbál (1876–1938) in India, were part of a movement that "displayed an affinity with the Enlightenment, daring criticisms of the orthodoxy, re-examinations of Islamic theology and its normative rules of conduct in light of the prevailing scientific standards, and an orientation towards social reforms and political moderation." [45] Islamic modernists are perhaps the most effective bulwark against radical Islamists. As Bernard Lewis commented over a decade before the September 11, 2001, terrorist attacks on the United States, the hope is that moderate Islamic values will, over time, discredit the radical

Islamist agenda: "The movement nowadays called fundamentalism is not the only Islamic tradition. There are others, more tolerant, more open, that helped to inspire the great achievements of Islamic civilization in the past, and we may hope that these other traditions will in time prevail." [46] The tendency of Islamic Modernists is not to demonize America as the Great Satan, even though they may still be very critical of America's support for Israel when the Palestinian question continues to be unresolved and the Palestinian people continue to suffer as a consequence. "Modernism, then, differs from secularism by the efforts it makes to find support in the Qur'an and the *sunna*," Rippin observes. "From the critic's point of view, this method is only 'a cover for what secularists do more openly'." [47]

(5) *Secularism:* Think of the Republic of Turkey. As Rippin implied, secularists in Turkey did openly what some modernists might only contemplate or do covertly. Ingram provides this simple definition: "Secularists believe that there should be a separation between the realm of religion and politics. In other words, Islam should not act as a framework for shaping the political sphere. For secularists the role of Islam should remain purely personal." [48] The Republic of Turkey, in its current bid to become a member of the European Union, would never dare to call America "the Great Satan." With its secular values, Turkey would never be so inclined, anyway, as Turkey and the United States have far more in common than whatever might be a source of contention.

(6) *Postmodernism:* Think of radical Islamic feminism and Marxism. "Post-modernism entails confrontation with the social issues of the day," Rippin states, "here conceived within a religious framework: feminism, peace and war, minority expressions of theology, political stances, economics and so forth." [49] To the extent that a Muslim views reality from any of these frameworks apart from Islam, and does not accept an Islamic worldview as primary, such a Muslim may be characterized as postmodernist. Admittedly, this is a controversial category. Although this might seem to be an oxymoron, a Muslim with a Marxist orientation would be a postmodernist Muslim, by this definition. The term "the Great Satan" would therefore have no real meaning.

(7) *Post-Islamism:* Think of the Bahá'í Faith. Just as America is the great ideological "other" from the perspective of radical Islamism, the Bahá'í Faith represents the great religious "other" from the perspective of orthodox Islam, which classically views itself as the last "revealed" religion. This is primarily because, as the "daughter religion of Islam," the Bahá'í Faith is post-Islamic: "The Bahá'í Faith has been described as a derivative ('secondary') monotheism in the sense that it is the daughter religion of Islam." [50] As previously mentioned in the Preface, the religious precursor to the Bahá'í Faith was the

Bábí religion, which had already effected a clear break from Islam. The Bahá'í Faith is now the youngest independent world religion.

The great flaw in most instances of religious nationalism is its tendency to exclude and alienate others: "The exclusionary nature of religious nationalism often leads to violent conflict between religious groups," comments Barbara-Ann J. Rieffer. "Often, in the development of the religious national identity, an 'alien other' is created or identified." [51] Nowhere has this been truer than in the case of the Bahá'ís of Iran, who have been systematically stigmatized and persecuted in their objectified role as the excluded "other." (The Bahá'ís will be discussed in Chapter 11, *infra*.) The case of the Bahá'ís has lent considerable weight to Rieffer's theory "that religious nationalism frequently leads to discrimination, violence, human rights violations and intolerant polities." [52] Iranian religious nationalism tends to exclude American Muslims as well.

These diverse Islamic orientations have generated a discursive pluralism in the contemporary Muslim world. Today, the Islamic world lacks a central authority. It was Kemal Ataturk who, in 1924, abolished the Caliphate, which, for centuries, had operated as the supreme authority of Sunni Islam. This is why there is no such thing as "the" Islamic myth of America. Even so, while no definitive Islamic myth of America exists, what persists is the radical Islamist myth of America as the Great Satan. Although the sevenfold typology of Muslim responses to modernity, outlined above, is a scholarly framework of analysis, it immediately demonstrates to the reader that there is a spectrum of perspectives within the contemporary Muslim world. The myth of America as the Great Satan is to be primarily located in the Radical Islamist group.

There are disquieting indications that this demonization of the United States will not go away soon. So long as the roots of the problem remain, the Great Satan myth will perdure. In 2006, for instance, Iranian President Mahmoud Ahmadinejad launched his own weblog, www.ahmadinejad.ir. There, in the course of criticizing America, he spoke of the "Great Satan USA." [53] A visit to that site and a quick search verify the BBC report. In his post of August 8, 2006, Ahmadinejad writes:

> Although, right at the beginning of the movement of Imam Khomeini, the type of Government Imam was seeking to establish was known to everybody, however, Imam repeatedly laid great emphasis that everyone's opinion should be taken into consideration (by holding a referendum) for the establishment of the type of new government in Iran. . . . This action of Imam and vehement participation and positive reply to the establishment of Islamic Republic by the Iranian nation, caused disappointment of some of the political groups that were affiliated to great world powers. . . . Although these terrorist groups are still under the

protection and shameful support of *Great Satan USA,* however, the slap that these groups have received from the brave nation of Iran will never be forgotten by them.[54]

Evidently, President Ahmadinejad was careful to avoid that inflammatory rhetoric in his subsequent blogs. Today, it is al-Qaeda that has perpetuated the rhetoric of "the Great Satan." On the pro-al-Qaeda Web site, www.wwod.com (WWOD stands for, "What Would Osama Do?"), al-Qaeda's senior vice president of Asset Management and Shawarma Supply, Abu Ali Baqliyya, posted this comment:

> The great Satan was very sly in sending his infidel troops to Iraq and waging war. What were we supposed to do? Sit here in the hills and watch the poppies grow? No! We had to send our own children of God to Iraq to introduce our innocent brothers to the ways of terror. The same goes for the other fronts where the lying Satan says there are terrorists. We are now spread too thin and need the assistance of Blackwater so that our great Jihad may continue.[55]

Founded in 1997 by a former Navy SEAL, Blackwater USA is a private military security firm. Now a multibillion dollar corporation, according to one news report, Blackwater had been hired by al-Qaeda to protect many of al-Qaeda's bases, caves, and training camps.[56] The author has been unable to determine whether this report is truth or fiction. But that is beside the point. It is al-Qaeda's continuing "Great Satan" rhetoric that is in evidence here.

There is hope for the Great Satan—maybe. In 1993, the incumbent president of Iran was Ali-Akbar Hashemi Rafsanjani. When asked, "Should the situation vis-a-vis the U.S. improve, will the descriptive 'Great Satan' disappear?" Rafsanjani replied: "If the U.S. does good, then it cannot be considered to be Satan." [57] But then, in 2005, Iranian President Mahmoud Ahmadinejad predicted that Britain, Israel, and the United States would, in time, vanish from the face of the earth, like the Egyptian pharaonic kings: "The oppressive powers will disappear while the Iranian people will stay. Any power that is close to God will survive while the powers who are far from God will disappear like the pharaohs." To which he added, for emphasis: "It is a divine promise." [58]

Other Iranian leaders, bent on maintaining some semblance of productive diplomacy with the United States, try to press a distinction between American foreign policy and the American people. When, in 2006, *Time* magazine asked Iran's former president, Mohammad Khatami, "This is your first visit to Washington. What do you think of the country that has been called the Great Satan?", Khatami's response was "I never say 'Great Satan.' But I get really upset when Iran is called part of the 'Axis of Evil.' Even [Ayatollah] Khomeini [who coined the phrase] was referring only to U.S. policies—not to the American people or America itself, which is a great and big country." [59] Khatami is not the only one to get upset by Iran being branded as part of the "Axis of Evil"—a slur that may be analyzed, partly, as America's response to the Radical Islamist myth of America as the Great Satan.

THE "AXIS OF EVIL" COUNTER-MYTH

This process of demonization is reciprocal in that it engenders a reactionary discourse. On January 29, 2002, President George W. Bush delivered his "State of the Union Address." The most poignant moment in that speech is when Bush named Iran, Iraq, and North Korea as the "Axis of Evil": "States like these, and their terrorist allies, constitute an Axis of Evil, arming to threaten the peace of the world." [60] One observer notes: "'Axis' evokes 'our' enemies of the Second World War, and it is a metonymy for Nazism and fascism." [61] The original Axis was between Hitler's Germany and Mussolini's Italy—such that Germany and Italy became "the Axis Powers"—with Japan added later on. [62] This rhetoric may be a faint echo of Ronald Reagan's formulation of "Evil Empire" to demonize the Soviet Union. [63] This signature phrase—this demonization by the world's champion of freedom, America— is a stigmatization that attaches as much to the citizens of the country from which it originated (the United States) as to the citizens of the country at which it is targeted (Iran, as well as Iraq and North Korea). It is interesting to note that "Axis of Evil" was not President Bush's creation alone. It was, as it were, the product of the team effort, as explained by the following:

> The phrase itself was constructed by David Frum, a White House speech writer, who came up with "axis of hatred" to describe the linkage between Iraq and terrorism. Frum's boss, Michael Gerson, a self-described evangelical Christian, changed the phrase to "Axis of Evil" to make it sound "more sinister, even wicked." Later Condoleezza Rice, President Bush's National Security Advisor, and Stephen Hadley, Deputy National Security Advisor, suggested adding North Korea and Iran as part of the axis. Hadley had second thoughts about adding Iran, because it had a democratically elected president, but Bush liked the idea of including Iran. "No, the president said, "I want it in." ...
>
> In the end, President Bush's senior advisors thought that the "Axis of Evil" was a signature phrase, "a declaration ... that the country now would have a great mission. It was big, new, and different." Although some doubted whether it would make sense to link the three countries, the metaphor was regarded by the President's advisors as a "watershed" that would define the problem in "graphic, biblical terms without publicly committing to a particular solution." [64]

Thus, it will come as some surprise to many Americans that it was actually Condoleezza Rice who first suggested adding Iran to the "Axis of Evil" phrase. One would hardly have expected a former provost of Stanford

University to have offered such a suggestion, which is quintessentially at odds with the canons of academic discourse. The point here is neither to criticize President Bush or Condoleezza Rice, but rather to focus on the "Axis of Evil" rhetoric and its social impact. The reader should also know that the present writer disclaims any intent here to implicate partisan politics, much less to take a partisan stance. Rather, later in this chapter, the writer will look at efforts by the U.S. government to counter its own demonization of Iran in order to demonstrate sympathy, rather than antipathy, towards the religion of Islam in general.

In any event, President Bush's arrow quickly flew back at the archer. Bush's demonization of Iran foreclosed any remaining possibilities of productive diplomacy for years to come, and diplomatic relations between the two countries have yet to normalize. The "Axis of Evil" was rhetorically effective, but served only to deepen the gulf that has separated America and Iran and have generally made matters worse. In the three words of that singular metaphor, Bush burned the diplomatic bridge, with the result that Iran's encounters with the United States (and with the West generally) continue to be conflicted.

What is the effect on American Muslims of the "Axis of Evil" rhetoric? In other words, what is its social impact domestically? In 2001, after pointing out that Iranian anti-Americanism is politically orchestrated, while the populace remains widely enamored of American popular culture, H. E. Chehabi of Boston University observes that negative stereotypes of Iranians persist in American popular thinking:

> In America, by contrast, anti-Iranism is not government-sponsored and is more diffuse, as many average Americans see Iranians as somehow genetically programmed to burn the American flag and shout "Death to America", images indelibly burned into American minds and perceptions by the television pictures of the hostage crisis.[65]

While the type of Islam practiced in Iran is that of the minority "Shi'a" Islam (as opposed to the mainstream "Sunni" Islam), Iran's institutionalization and expression of Shi'a Islam has come to represent Islam as a whole in the popular imagination of Americans.

The "Axis of Evil" rhetoric may have resonated with some evangelical Christians, who characteristically (with significant exceptions, of course) view the world in such polarities—a world enchanted by principalities of good and evil. That is the "Evil" prong of the metaphor. Religiously speaking, the idea of "evil" tends to cut more deeply. To call someone or to label something as "evil," in an Iranian context at least, cuts to the quick of religious sensibilities. Arguably, this renders the rhetoric all the more effective, but sometimes in unexpected or in undesirable ways, as G. Matthew Bonham and Daniel Heradstveit conclude:

> The main mistake of this metaphor is that it targets entire countries, not their leaders. It does not differentiate between the evil leaders and the others who live in the country. The reformers, for example, did not want to be viewed as evil, but the metaphor painted them with the same brush of evil. This must be resisted by joining with the conservatives and rallying around the government. In other words, the metaphor mobilized the entire country.[66]

In other words, the "Axis of Evil" metaphor further radicalized Iran, arguably reversing the former gains made by Iranian moderates and reformers, thereby exacerbating destabilization in the region. The future can only tell whether the force of such rhetoric will soon spend its force, or whether it will pave the way for drastic, unilateral measures to come. Bonham and Heradstveit characterize the "Axis of Evil" metaphor as pretextual for legitimizing, *carte blanche,* all policy options: "As a rhetorical device, the 'Axis of Evil' exploits both the history of the Second World War (as a metonym for fascism, involving memories of disastrous appeasement) and religious eschatology (with its implication that We are on the side of Good and so can do anything we like)." [67] The difference here is that "the Great Satan" is not a principality, but rather a country, that is, America. Conversely, the reciprocal difference inheres in the fact that the "Axis of Evil," while targeted at three nations rather than at three principalities, taints Iranians (and, by extension, Muslims generally), as a consequence of Iran's inclusion as one of the three of adamantine tines of this rhetorical trident. To its credit, however, the U.S. government has gone to great lengths to reverse this unfortunate outcome by reaching out to Muslims.

EFFORTS TO DISPEL THE "GREAT SATAN" MYTH AND TO MINIMIZE THE FALLOUT FROM THE "AXIS OF EVIL" MYTH

Islam is now America's third-largest religion and, within a decade from now, may surpass the number of American Jews. American Muslims are here to stay, and are part and parcel of the American social fabric. Can the perspectives of American Muslims on America be determined? Ingrid Mattson's study, "How Muslims Use Islamic Paradigms to Define America," is suggestive for Islamic myths of America in general: "Muslims need to define not only Islam but also America. Muslims need to place America in its proper theological and legal category so they can determine what kind of relationship is possible and desirable for them to have with this country." [68] As the Council on American-Islamic Relations observes, "American Muslims have deep appreciation and love for America just as they have empathy and understanding of the Muslim world." [69] American Muslims should therefore be seen as an asset to America, and may even, if called upon to do so, play a critical role in diplomatic relations between America and Muslim countries abroad: "Thus American Muslims can serve as the perfect bridge between America and the Muslim world. To enable this aspiration, American policy makers need to constructively engage American Muslims." [70] Was the U.S. Department of State perhaps deaf to this sage advice? How many American Muslims were not recruited for such diplomatic missions?

The U.S. Department of State has, in fact, experimented with reaching out to Muslims to dispel the myth of America as anti-Muslim and as the Great Satan. On February 14, 2002, U.S. Secretary of State Colin Powell appeared on MTV. MTV held an international forum, entitled, "Be Heard: An MTV Global Discussion with Colin Powell." Young people from the United States, India, the Middle East, Italy, the United Kingdom, Ireland, Brazil, and Russia were given the opportunity to ask provocative questions, live via satellite. One forum participant, from a studio in London, asked Powell how he felt "about representing a country commonly perceived as the Satan of contemporary politics." [71] Secretary Powell replied: "So, far from being the Great Satan, I would say that we are the Great Protector. We have sent men and women from the armed forces of the United States to other parts of the world throughout the past century to put down oppression." [72]

American public diplomacy, with a large budget from the public treasury, targeted the Middle East and the wider Muslim world beginning in 2002. On October 31, 2002, Charles Dolan, vice chairman of the bipartisan U.S. Advisory Commission on Public Diplomacy, told the Public Relations Society of America in Washington, D.C., that a wide-scale public relations effort was underway to dispel the Muslim myth of America as the Great Satan through initiating a "dialogue with the press and public" in order "to dispel the negative myth of America as anti-Muslim." [73] This American outreach to the wider Muslim world was orchestrated by the Broadcasting Board of Governors (BBG), an organization of U.S. international broadcasters. Pursuant to the 1998 Foreign Affairs Reform and Restructuring Act (Public Law 105-277), on October 1, 1999, the BBG became the independent federal agency responsible for all federally sponsored, nonmilitary, international broadcasting. [74] The BBG oversees the Voice of America (VOA), Radio Free Europe/Radio Liberty (RFE/RL), Radio Free Asia (RFA), Radio and TV Marti (OCB), and Middle East Broadcasting Networks (MBN), with the assistance of the International Broadcasting Bureau (IBB). This public relations campaign operated under a five-year plan, from 2002 through 2007, at which time the following assessment was made:

Under the 2002–2007 strategic plan, the BBG took significant steps toward this goal. We launched, among many other smaller initiatives, 24/7 broadcasting valued at more than $100 million annually for Iran (expanded VOA TV and Radio Farda), the Middle East (Al-Hurra TV and Radio Sawa), and Afghanistan (RFE/RL's Dari and Pashto, then meshed with VOA's Dari and Pashto in a coordinated programming stream), and Pakistan (Aap ki Dunyaa and BTH). These initiatives have gained us some 40 million additional weekly listeners and viewers, boosting the BBG's global audience from 100 to 140 million weekly.[75]

Despite continued jamming by Iranian authorities, Radio Farda is said to be reaching its target audience of younger listeners in Iran. In 2008, the campaign continues.

Four years earlier, on February 14, 2004, the BBG launched Al-Hurra (Arabic for "the free one") Television, covering 22 countries in the Middle East via the same satellites used by major indigenous Arabic channels. The official Web site of Al-Hurra Television is http://www.alhurra.com. Another part of America's public relations outreach to the Muslim world is Radio Sawa, a 24/7 network of stations targeting a large segment of the Arabic-speaking population under the age of 35. Radio Sawa went on the air in March 2002. Today, Radio Sawa broadcasts on medium wave to Egypt, Yemen, Saudi Arabia, and Sudan, and on FM in Iraq (Baghdad, Nasiriya, Basra, Mosul, Kirkuk, Sulimaniya, and Erbil), the Palestinian Territories (Ramallah and Jenin), Lebanon (Beirut, North Lebanon, South Lebanon, and Bekaa Valley), Morocco (Rabat, Casablanca, Tangier, Meknes, Marrakesh, Agadir, and Fes), Jordan (Amman and Ajlun), Kuwait (Kuwait City), Bahrain (Manama), Qatar (Doha), U.A.E. (Abu Dhabi and Dubai), and Djibouti.[76] Radio Sawa's Web site may be accessed at http://www.radiosawa.com, with the English version at http://www.radiosawa.com/english.aspx.

With the exception of one failed program, called the "Shared Values Initiative," the present writer has not been able to find an independent assessment of the relative effectiveness of this public relations outreach to Muslims abroad. In 2003, Christopher Ross, special coordinator for Public Diplomacy, commented on the challenge that the U.S. government faced: "The gap between who we are and how we wish to be seen, and how we are in fact seen, is frighteningly wide." [77] (This quote is usually attributed to Charlotte Beers, under secretary of state for Public Diplomacy and Public Affairs, who testified before the Senate Foreign Relations Committee on February 27, 2003.) The United States continues to face this daunting challenge. The American government's intellectual weapons in the war of ideas, entailing considerable U.S. public diplomacy expenditures, may be a valiant battle that, so far, has yet to win any significant victories. Yet public diplomacy continues apace.

The two concepts—"the Great Satan" and the "Axis of Evil"—are symbiotic in that they feed each other. This reinforcing of mutual demonization demonstrates the grim reality that religious symbols play in modern political rhetoric. While the "Axis of Evil" is not of Iran (and, by extension, of Islam) alone, it does show how effectively this demonization of the "other" is part and parcel of the larger religious myth of Islam as played out in America—that is, Muslims have been, and continue to be, defined by being part of the Axis of Evil. It is the myth that they ineluctably inhabit, even if it is not their own creation. The "Axis of Evil" metaphor had the result, even if unintended, of aggravating Islamophobia within the United States.[78]

The stirring up of this hornet's nest invites a broader comment regarding the problem of Islamophobia in general. Islamophobia is a neologism for anything and everything anti-Islamic or anti-Muslim. The branding of America as "the Great Satan" and the reciprocal stigmatizing of Iran in particular, and of Islam in general, as the "Axis of Evil" has had a synergizing effect. The two metaphors, in fact, are parasitic.

It is clear that the Great Satan myth of America had a considerable impact in international relations. But what impact did the Great Satan myth have at home? What was the impact of that myth on American Muslims? Imagine: how would it feel to be a Muslim living in America and to be tarred by that same brush? Fachrizal Halim has characterized the impact as the escalation of hatred towards Muslims:

> Indeed, the terrorist attacks on September 11, 2001 have pushed Muslims into a more difficult situation, as hatred toward them has intensified. Although the events of the terrorist attacks made a significant change in how non-Muslims differentiate between actual Muslims and those groups which use Islam as a political symbol, the same event has had an unpredictable effect on Muslim communities in America. Muslims in this situation have made the difficult choice to be more mature in this unprecedented situation.[79]

An equally penetrating question is one that has been raised by Americans who are not Muslim: Why was there no outright denial of the Great Satan myth, no distancing from it, no rousing patriotic reaffirmation of American values, no significant social commentary or high-profile editorial by those who speak for American Muslims, as a collective American Muslim response to Khomeini's evil epithet? Was the relative silence by American Muslims to be understood as tacit acknowledgement that what Khomeini said might have had some appreciable truth to it? The answer is that American Muslim leaders did, in fact, go out of their way to register their loyalty to both Islam and America. One recent example of this is a commentary by Imam Luqman Ahmad, a free-lance writer, a lecturer, an African American Muslim, and an

Imam of Masjid Ibrahim Islamic Center, a *masjid* (mosque) in Sacramento, California. In a thought-provoking piece entitled, "Islam American Style," Sheikh Luqman writes:

> Since the tragic events of September 11th, Muslims in America have been expressing their patriotism and Americanism to more varying degrees than in the past. Virtually every Muslim organization and community has not failed to make others aware of or to tout their Americanness. And rightfully so . . . We've been told that America is the great Satan. Well I've got news for you. The Shaitaan (Devil) is an equal opportunity deceiver; he respects no borders, color, nationality or even religion. Yes, it is true that *Shaitaan* [Satan] is busy in America but he's busy elsewhere as well. Yet, all of the forces of the devil did not stop the *athaan* (Muslim call to prayer) from being called from Sarasota Florida, to Sacramento California. That's America. When the *hijab* [head scarf for Muslim women] was banned in France, Turkey and on Public Television news in Egypt, it still prevailed in America. That alone deserves a hearty "*Allahu Akbar*" (God is Great). The truth is that we as Muslims have decided to make this great nation our home despite her flaws. Obviously our Islam should be first, and we are obligated to practice it, and share it with whoever wants it. Americanism and Islam are not mutually incompatible. The relationship between the two just has to be tweaked a little.[80]

Even though Satan is alive and well, according to Sheikh Luqman, and sinisterly operates in America and abroad, America is not Satan incarnate.

American Muslim communities have generally decried terrorism. While, from their perspectives, American culture may be corrupt and morally bankrupt among large segments of the population, there is much to commend America. The very fact that American Muslims are free to practice Islam in their own way speaks volumes about how America actually protects the religious rights of Muslims in America. These very sentiments are echoed elsewhere. Imam Al-Hajj Talib Abdur-Rashid, prayer leader of the Mosque of the Islamic Brotherhood on the corner of 113th Street and St. Nicholas Avenue in Harlem, had this to say in a 2005 *Seattle Times* interview: "We who have served in the armies of America as Muslim African-Americans since the American Revolution are not at odds with the West. We are the West." [81]

In fine, the "Great Satan" myth of America was met with the "Axis of Evil" counter-myth tilted at Iran. Both pejorative epithets are roughly equivalent and are functionally comparable. The obvious rhetorical intent is to demonize the other. However productive such discourse may be deemed to be domestically in rallying public opinion behind a given foreign policy, the net effect of the opposing rhetoric is to render any attempt at diplomacy incapable of progress. In finding, in each, a common enemy, all common ground has been forfeited. The rhetoric has a life of its own, independent of any groundswell of support which, in any case, may be expected to diminish over time. These myths, which are powerful when first bruited, are, after all, myths. One observer of U.S.-Iran relations notes that those who demonized America now seek an opportunity for dialogue: "Ironically, the very clerics who demonized the United States now want to gain domestic support by interacting with the former 'Great Satan.' " [82] On the part of the United States, the same observer recommends: "We should try to get to a place where we can define Iran not only in terms of its negatives, which are formidable, but also its promise and its potential." [83] In other words, the Great Satan (America) and the Axis of Evil (here, Iran) would do well to abandon name-calling and engage in dialogue. If and when that happens, the myth of America as the Great Satan will fade into memory, having lost whatever credibility it once may have enjoyed. If and when that happens, the myth of Iran (and Islam) as the third pivot of the Axis of Evil will also recede into historical memory. However, if "the reality" is "that myth is just as important to US policy making as it is to revolutionary Iran," [84] then the cessation of reciprocal "mything" will not likely occur very soon.

What about the continuing role of the Great Satan myth of America in the wider Islamic world? In "Love and Hate: Anti-Americanism in the Islamic World," [85] Giacomo Chiozza, post-doctoral fellow in national security, Olin Institute for Strategic Studies, Harvard University, inventoried the perceptions of the United States in the mass publics in eight predominantly Islamic countries—Egypt, Indonesia, Iran, Kuwait, Lebanon, Pakistan, Saudi Arabia, and United Arab Emirates. Based on his statistical survey, Chiozza finds that "ambivalence is a prominent feature of people's attitude towards America in the Islamic world. The general public *loves* America, when America means democracy, movies, education, people, and science, but *hates* America, when America means foreign policies towards Arab nations, the Palestinians, and Iraq." [86] While this generalization holds true to a certain extent, "differences still exist" among the eight Islamic countries surveyed, such that "popular opposition to America is greater in Iran and Egypt, and lower in Pakistan, Lebanon, and Indonesia." [87] The greater opposition to America in Iran comes as no surprise. Its type of antipathy to the United States has been termed, "legacy anti-Americanism," which "stems from resentment of past wrongs committed by the United States to another society," [88] combined with "Radical Muslim Anti-Americanism" generally.[89]

As for American Muslim myths and visions of America, within America itself, there is no single, dominant paradigm. However, there is a dynamic relationship between what American does overseas and how America is viewed by Muslims at home in the United States. Ingrid Mattson describes this dynamic relationship between foreign policy and domestic attitudes among American Muslims:

> In many cases, those Muslims who begin from a position of "selective embrace" of America move eventually to a position of "full embrace." When their efforts to effect positive change in society bear fruit, they may come to see advantages in the American political system that they did not see before. At this point, they may abandon former paradigm they used to define America in favor of one is more positive and comprehensive. The shift, however is not inevitable. . . . No matter what happens within America, the deep connections between American Muslims and their brothers and sisters overseas means that American foreign-policy will always have a profound effect on the way Muslims in this country. . . . Perhaps, then, the most powerful paradigm underlying all Muslim definitions America is the dominant Islamic theological belief in that one's true convictions will inevitably it made manifest by one's actions.[90]

In light of this insight, a new paradigm of Islamic society and culture appears to be developing within America. It may be, of course, too soon to tell. But from all indications, some distinctive patterns are emerging. For instance, second-generation Muslims, generally speaking, are far less inclined to be swayed by anti-Americanism overseas than their parents, whose homeland ties tend to remain perpetual and strong—unless, of course, they themselves were victims of their own home country. The American Muslim community, which is diverse and heterogeneous, is far from monolithic. This means that a comprehensive and coherent domestic position on America, held by the majority of American Muslims, is not yet possible. Over time, with each succeeding generation, a more native and authentic consensus may emerge. At such time as the American Muslim community surpasses, in population, the size of the American Jewish community, one can expect that the voice of American Muslims will begin to be heard, with greater clarity and rhetorical force, in the public sphere. Not only will calls for certain changes in both American foreign and domestic policy be expected, but also calls for change (that is, reform) in the contemporary Muslim world may be raised. One obvious call for reform, by American Muslim leaders, has already been voiced: viz., that offensive *jihad* is fundamentally un-Islamic. Moreover, that same call may be aimed at Muslim leaders abroad—at the clerical leadership in Iran, for instance—to ensure that Islam, as practiced and as enforced by law, respects the human rights of all citizens. In Iran, the most egregious of such human rights violation have been, and continue to be, experienced by Iran's largest religious minority, the Bahá'ís, who have suffered persecution in their native country for well over a century and a half.[91] That same American Muslim voice may also demand that the draconian anti-Ahmadi laws in

Pakistan be revoked.[92] Expected also may be calls for greater rights for women in Islamicate states.

In other words, from the United States of America, a voice of moderate Islam may emerge that speaks to fellow Muslims across the chasm of West and East, calling for change. That same call for change will also have an American component, as American Muslim leaders take part in consultation on pressing social concerns at home, and, finding common cause with the leaders of other faiths, thereby engendering greater respect for Islamic values, and perhaps even for the Islamic holy book itself, the Qur'an.[93] If and when that sea change takes place, then the myth of "the Great Satan" will become increasingly difficult for Iran, for Radical Islamists generally, and for sympathizers across the Islamic world, to sustain. Reciprocally, if and when the voice and influence of moderates in the Islamic world are ascendant, then Iran (and the ideological transferral to Muslims generally) will no longer be part and parcel of the "Axis of Evil." In time, "the Great Satan" will die a natural death, and the "Axis of Evil" will rust, if not break.

CHAPTER 10

Buddhist Myths and Visions of America

So in this respect, our entire humanity has a responsibility, particularly this nation. Among others, you have economic power, but the most important thing you have is the opportunity to utilize your human creativity. This is something very good. Therefore, I think America has the potential to make this world straight. . . . I think this nation is the only superpower. Therefore, I think you have the opportunity or ability to change it.

—Dalai Lama (1991)[1]

At once ancient and modern, Buddhism is a highly adaptive, missionary religion. In America, as elsewhere, Buddhism is a "transplanted" religion that is now accepted as mainstream. "Buddhism" is a universal message with a number of disparate sects serving as its exponents. In other words, as a transcultural phenomenon, Buddhism is not a single lotus blossom of enlightenment teachings, but a garden of lotuses of varying hues. Two Buddhist groups, Soka Gakkai and Tibetan Buddhism, have spoken to Americans about America's world role, both spiritually and politically. While Soka Gakkai is "missionary" in the more traditional sense—of actively seeking converts—Tibetan Buddhism is "missionary" in the promotion of its positive ideals across religious boundaries. The Dalai Lama, now "informal head of Tibetan Buddhists and formal head of the Tibetan government in exile"[2] tells "those who are not Buddhists *not* to convert to Buddhism."[3]

The first of the Buddhist myths and visions of America to be examined is Soka Gakkai's myth and vision of the "Second American Renaissance," followed by the Tibetan Buddhist perspective of Robert Thurman—the first American to be ordained as a Tibetan Buddhist monk—and his myth and vision of America's "Second Renaissance." Finally, the Dalai Lama's "Buddhist democracy" myth and his vision of America's world role will be presented. The Dalai Lama—one should hasten to add—may well be the world's most influential spiritual teacher today, next to the current leader of the Catholic church, Pope Benedict XVI.

SOKA GAKKAI'S MYTH OF "AMERICA'S SECOND RENAISSANCE"

America's world role is seen as a specifically Buddhist mission in the Japanese sect of Soka Gakkai, which has been transplanted to the United States and has achieved a certain measure of popularity. Soka Gakkai ("Value Creation Society") equates faith with spiritual and material benefits (or "inconspicuous and conspicuous benefits") that derive from such faith. Soka Gakkai has more than 12 million adherents in 190 countries and territories worldwide. Probably the most well-known practitioner of Soka Gakkai is actor Orlando Bloom, of *Pirates of the Caribbean* and *Lord of the Rings* fame. Vocalist Tina Turner is also a practitioner. Both individually and communally, Soka Gakkai International (SGI) Buddhists chant *Nam-myoho-renge-kyo* before the *Gohonzon,* which is a mandala ascribed to Nichiren (1222–1282), "a fiery prophet who insisted that the *Lotus Sutra,* one of the great Mahayana texts, is the supreme expression of the Buddha's teaching and the one and only version of Buddhism for our day." [4] This is the core practice of SGI. Faith in the efficacy of chanting *Nam-myoho-renge-kyo* is at the heart of a movement that promises the world and enlightenment as well, if the practitioner has the requisite faith.

Antonio Gualtieri, senior colleague of the present writer when teaching in the Department of Religion at Carleton University in Ottawa (1994–1996), argued that the original teachings of Jesus and the Buddha were too difficult for their followers to practice. [5] In examining "the discrepancies between the spiritual and moral demands of the founders of great religious traditions and the actual outlook and practice of their followers," [6] and in raising the question: "Why do the rigorous soteriological and moral messages of the Buddha and the Christ continue within their respective traditions if they embody a way of life to which the vast majority of their communities do not subscribe?," [7] Gualtieri found that Buddhists and Christians (whom Gualtieri characterizes as "apostates" in deviating from the strict moral and mental demands of the Buddha and Christ) were "reading and hearing the founders' teachings differently than they intended." [8] This accommodating process, where rigors of the Noble Eightfold Path prescribed by the historical Buddha are satisfied by the substitute of faith and devotional practice, is perfectly exemplified by Soka Gakkai. Yet, with "earnest resolve," SGI Buddhists chant in order to reveal the innate Buddhahood each human being may potentially realize.

In America, SGI Buddhists formerly chanted for worldly desires but are now chanting for world peace. In the 1970s, SGI practitioners had the reputation of being self-centered and materialistic. At Buddhist meetings—several of which the present writer had attended—adherents would give personal testimonies as to how chanting *Nam-myoho-renge-kyo* would gain for them the wine, sex, and money they were seeking. However, Daisaku Ikeda—as third president of the Soka Gakkai and founder of the Soka Gakkai International—has transformed the materialistic promises of SGI practices into social premises that all can respect. Ikeda has almost single-handedly matured SGI.

Among SGI's stated "Purposes and Principles" today is "the ideal of global citizenship" with its concomitant adjuncts of "fundamental human rights" and "freedom of religion and religious expression" and eschews any and all discrimination. Global prosperity, respect for education (and the "development of scholarship"), and environmentalism are among its noble goals. These sacralized secular values are characteristic of progressive internationalism. They also resonate with American values.

In his small volume of poems, *Songs for America,*[9] which are essentially directed to his Buddhist followers in the form of personal meditations in free verse form, Ikeda reveals a deep admiration for America in his vision of America's role in the spiritual transformation of the world. In so doing, President Ikeda echoes and amplifies the perspectives of his predecessors—presidents Makiguchi and Toda—on America's potential for the spread of Buddhism and its expected influence in bringing about world peace. Ikeda notes that, in early years of the twentieth century, Tsunesaburo Makiguchi, founder of Soka Gakkai,

saw in America
the land where future civilizations
would encounter and unite.

This vaticinatory vision of America, while not a Buddhist tenet, paved the way and justified an intense missionary effort to spread Soka Gakkai's message to America. In the same vein, Ikeda further remarks that Josei Toda, Makiguchi's successor,

often recalled that it was
America that brought
freedom of religion to post-war Japan,
opening the way

for a peace movement based
on this Buddhism to unfold.[10]

Here, "this" Buddhist peace movement obviously refers to Soka Gakkai.
Once transplanted to the United States, it is only natural that further reflections on America's world role would emerge out of the visions of SGI's
founding presidents.

President Ikeda, in Whitman-esque fashion, praises America as a "republic
of ideals" in which freedom and equality have served as "uniting principles"[11] Here, Ikeda celebrates the cosmopolitan social fabric of America,
which is a demographic microcosm of the world. Despite Ikeda's high regard
for America's ideals, a disparity exists between America's noble professions
of freedom and equality and its sobering social reality. A prime example of
this dissonance between the ideal and the real is the sociomoral disease of racism, in which "the soul of your idealism" is in peril. America's idealism is in
jeopardy, and "grieves at the stark realities of racial strife."[12]

Here, America is not alone. Ikeda strikes a warning note in saying that
the world is now in serious trouble. It is sick and "ailing." Pathologically,
America is

about to succumb
to the same illness.[13]

Sickness requires a cure, and the panacea inheres in the spread of those pallia-
tive ideals and practices that SGI Buddhism incarnates. America is in an ideal
position to promote those socially curative precepts and practices. This is precisely what attracted SGI leaders to the prospects and promises of America as
a Buddhist mission field.

As the grand social experiment that it is, American society should be
imbued "with the love of humanity."[14] There are signs that this is already
happening, as Ikeda sees it:

This rich spiritual soil,
this great earth alive with the diversity
of peoples and traditions—
giving rise to a new culture,
a new humanity.[15]

By implication, what America achieves at home should be promoted abroad.
America's mission, therefore, is to export and internationalize its internal values of freedom and respect for human rights, which vast sectors of the planet
sadly lack.

With this global mission comes America's destiny in that this "multiracial nation, America" holds such great promise that it "represents humanity's future." America "holds secret stores" of "unbounded possibility." The engine of this social transformation is powered by

> transforming
> the energy of different cultures
> into the unity of construction" and converting "the flames of conflict
> into the light of solidarity.[16]

Just how is this going to happen, the reader may well ask? How will this transformation occur? With what engines of social change will America become an exemplary social order for the rest of the world to admire and emulate?

Domestic peace can promote world peace. Ikeda recognizes that, for America to gain the moral authenticity and authority it needs to fulfill its potential for catalyzing world peace, it should do everything in its power to harmonize its own society. America is a land that can potentially unite nations since America itself is "a miniature of the entire world." Ikeda sees "unity and solidarity" of America's diversity to be the "principle and formula" for "global peace." [17] The Buddhist leader calls this social awakening a social renewal: "Our goal—the Second American Renaissance" in which American society will "advance" from conflict, divisiveness, and hatred to "union," "coexistence," and "fraternity." [18] Without saying so explicitly, Ikeda clearly has his audience in view in speaking of "our goal"—which is the goal of Buddhists in exerting their leavening influence in helping America realize its own high ideals. Ikeda envisions America as "the protagonist and producer" of the "drama of world history." America's "powerful vigor" will determine the "destiny of our precious oasis"—that is, "Our spaceship Earth." [19] What Ikeda says in poetry is more explicitly spelled out in prose.

In *My Dear Friends in America* (2001),[20] Ikeda states that progress in America contributes to progress abroad directly and exponentially: "The advance of America is the advance of the world. An inch of growth for America is an inch of growth for the rest of the world. I am convinced that, in the future, America will of necessity become the central stage for the SGI movement." [21] Given the extraordinary magnitude of America's influence, the Buddhist community within America has its own special mission, which is to promote what SGI characterizes as its "new humanism":

> Today, too, the renewal of the United States is linked to the renewal of the world, and the revitalization of the American people, awakened to a new humanism, must become the basis for the revitalization of the country. The SGI's movement of human revolution is the most fundamental contribution we can make to the renewal of the United States and the world.[22]

This is an important statement, and certainly reflects the maturity of SGI, which is due, for the most part, to Ikeda's leadership.

While SGI sees the United States of America (and the United Nations) as potent agents of social change, this special Buddhist vision of America, while clearly and publicly articulated by its three presidents, has not quite achieved the status of a religious doctrine. Although SGI leaders have made some exceptional statements about America's actual and ideal role in Buddhist terms, lay Buddhists are not particularly focused on their leaders' statements with regard to America's world role in terms of international peace and in the spread of Buddhism. In the SGI-USA *Buddhist Learning Review: 2007 Study Guide,* the words "America" and the "United States"—beyond the copyright page itself—are nowhere mentioned.

Nor does Ikeda's appreciation of America enjoy any status whatsoever as a doctrine. It is a sentiment expressed by Ikeda and often seemingly not entirely shared by the majority of SGI-USA members. This is a case where the leader speaks, the practitioners listen with respect, yet no real doctrinal or programmatic development flows from the leader's presentiments in this regard. SGI's vision of America is a vehicle of socially progressive ideals that, if translated in social reality within the SGI community and without, will no doubt contribute to the advancement of its Buddhist vision, with its message and modality of personal and communal empowerment.

Notwithstanding the fact that *Songs for America* is available to all Soka Gakkai adherents, there appears to be no universally held religious appreciation of America among its grassroots practitioners. There may be wisdom in this, since SGI has adherents in 190 other countries and territories. A universal outreach can scarcely afford to be compromised by too great a focus on one single country, even if it is the world's only superpower. Moreover, the kind of enthusiasm that Ikeda expresses in *Songs for America* can be found elsewhere, as he praises other places and other peoples. Such effusion is part of his style. President Ikeda's *Songs for America,* therefore, is an unfinished symphony.

ROBERT THURMAN'S MYTH OF AMERICA'S "SECOND RENAISSANCE"

One of the foremost popularizers of Buddhism in America today is Robert Thurman. Like actor Richard Gere, Robert Thurman is something of a national celebrity when it comes to Buddhism. After the traumatic loss of an eye while at Harvard, in 1961 Thurman embarked on a spiritual quest that took him to Turkey, Iran, and India. Prior to this, Thurman's first wife, Christophe de Menil, divorced him as she did not want to travel to India with Thurman to seek enlightenment. In India, Thurman met and befriended the Dalai Lama in 1962, and became his steadfast disciple. In 1964, the Dalai Lama ordained Thurman as a Tibetan Buddhist monk, marking him with the distinction of being the first Westerner ever to do so. Several years later, Thurman returned to America. He exchanged his Buddhist robes for those of a professor, and promulgated his newfound knowledge, particularly as a "Dharmic" writer. He remarried and had five children, including Uma Thurman, who went on to become a famous Hollywood actress. In 1997, Thurman was named one of *Time* magazine's 25 most influential persons of that year. Today, Thurman is the Jey Tsong Khapa Professor of Indo-Tibetan Buddhist Studies at Columbia University, is co-founder (with Richard Gere) and president (of the board of trustees) of Tibet House U.S., and is also president of the American Institute of Buddhist Studies. As a scholar, Thurman has translated major Buddhist treatises from the Tibetan *Tanjur*. (In the Tibetan Buddhist canon, the *Kanjur* is the collection of discourses of the Buddha, and the *Tanjur* is the collection of 225 books of commentary on the Buddha's teachings.)

In 1998, Thurman published his Buddhist manifesto, *Inner Revolution: Life, Liberty, and the Pursuit of Real Happiness,*[23] with a foreword by the Dalai Lama himself. The title's resonance with the Declaration of Independence shows that Thurman was writing to an American audience. In *Inner Revolution,* Thurman argues that America is uniquely poised to realize Buddhist values of individual enlightenment and social harmony. Thurman describes how the ideals of America's Founding Fathers—life, liberty, and the pursuit of happiness—and the founding principles of American democracy—equality, individual rights, due process, and economic well-being—resonate with the Buddha's teachings, endowing America with the potential to become the next great civilization: "To finish building the free society dreamed of by Washington, Franklin and Jefferson, we must draw upon the resources of the enlightened imagination, which can be systematically developed by the spiritual sciences of India and Tibet." [24]

Thurman's concept of an "inner revolution" is a psychosocial transformation that individuals and societies achieve when they seek and practice enlightenment, which includes what is described as a quasi-scientific "elucidation of causation." This "inner revolution" comes about through a profound insight into the nature of reality, of the cause of and cure for human suffering, and a resolved compassion for all suffering beings—for wisdom and compassion.

At the end of *Inner Revolution,* Thurman offers ten planks for a political platform based on enlightenment ideals and 30 axioms for a politics of enlightenment. In rapid fire, they are, in brief, as follows:

First: "Democracy's quintessential universalism must be re-revoked as an ideal goal for the entire planet." [25]

Second: "Acknowledging the very grave injustices there still inflicted on billions of beings, we proclaim everyone's right to equality of opportunity in all respects, regardless of racial, sexual, religious, national, ethnic, or economic group membership." [26]

Third: "We pledge to adopt a fully consensual tax system that will allow individual taxpayers to earmark their contributions for programs they choose." [27] "We should increase the graduated income tax." [28]

Fourth: "We deplore capital punishment and resolve to eradicate it in our aspiring-to-be-civilized society." [29]

Fifth: "We affirm each woman's right to choose for herself whether she will offer residence in her body to a new life, and therefore we pledge to deploy all forms of sex education and contraception to give women maximum control." [30]

Sixth: "We affirm each individual's right to freedom of choice of lifestyles and medical therapies, free conscience in matters of religion, freedom of speech, and freedom of sexual preference—as long as these freedoms are not harmful to others." [31]

Seventh: "Aware of our complicity in a catastrophic mis-direction of efforts and resources over this last century of militarism, we pledge to cut our defense budgets by two-thirds, reappropriating $200 billion a year in America alone and . . . to build enlightened, disarmed democracies" in Tibet and elsewhere.[32]

Eighth: "We pledge to make lifelong education for all citizens the nation's top priority." [33]

Ninth: "We reaffirm the enlightenment principle of altruistic support for all, implementing rights to a job, education, shelter, sustenance, a healthy environment, a universal health-care system along Canadian or European lines, which would encompass a competitive plurality of health systems, including Chinese, Tibetan, Indian, and others." [34]

Tenth: "At the heart of our system, and in this hour of its crisis, we affirm the need for strong executive leadership all democracies." [35]

The reader gets the picture: this is a highly idiosyncratic political platform and does not represent a collective Buddhist vision of America. However, Thurman urges Westerners to adopt five political principles that are said to derive from the spiritual precepts of Tibetan Buddhism: "transcendent individualism, nonviolent pacifism, educational evolutionism, ecosocial altruism, and universal democratism." [36]

Thurman also advocates a "Second Renaissance," which is the discovery and application of the advanced "inner science" of ancient Tibetan Buddhist precepts and practices. As the Robert Thurman Web site represents these ideas, Thurman is still promoting his enlightenment agenda for noble purposes:

Professor Thurman's scholarly and popular writings focus on the "inner revolution" that individuals and societies successfully negotiate when they achieve
enlightenment. He defines this inner revolution as accurate insight into the true
nature of reality and determined compassion for the suffering beings. He also
works toward what he terms a "Second Renaissance," which he sees currently
taking place as Western culture goes beyond the 14th-century European discovery of the natural sciences of the ancient Greeks that catalyzed the "first
renaissance" to discover and apply in practice the advanced "inner science" of
ancient Indian culture.[37]

In effect, Robert Thurman has offered a "vision quest for the creation
of a mandala of an enlightened America," [38] from his Tibetan Buddhist
perspective:

> Most of the teachers from various enlightenment movements seem to agree on
> one thing: If there is to be a renaissance and enlightenment science in our times,
> it will have to begin in America. . . . The enlightenment movement can bring a
> full range of identity-analysis tools as well as self-esteem-building disciplines
> and arts so that Americans can realize individual king- and queenship.[39]

Thurman is hopeful for America's prospects of evolving into an enlightened society, adding that: "There is much to build on in American modernity
and American spirit." [40] To be sure, Robert Thurman does not have the
authority, as the Dalai Lama certainly does, to promulgate his ten "planks"
and five principles for an enlightened America—as official Buddhist doctrine.
However, Thurman exercises considerable influence as a popularizer of
Tibetan Buddhism in America today. For this, one must credit Thurman with
having imparted a Buddhist-inspired mission of an enlightened America,
founded on spiritual principles that incarnate compassion for all sentient
beings, with justice and opportunity for all people, beginning in America.

THE DALAI LAMA'S "BUDDHIST DEMOCRACY" MYTH AND VISION OF AMERICA'S WORLD ROLE

What is a "Dalai Lama"? In Tibetan belief, the Dalai Lamas are manifesta-
tions of Avalokitesvara, the Buddha of Compassion, called *Chenrezig* in
Tibetan. As enlightened beings who can see the past, present, and future
within multiple realms of existence, the Dalai Lamas are uniquely gifted in
the art of good governance. Unlike ordinary beings, the Dalai Lamas can
choose where to be reborn. In an unbroken succession over time, the position
of the Dalai Lama is passed from incarnation to incarnation to ensure that the
same enlightened being remains in power. When a Dalai Lama passes away, a
search task force is convened to locate his new reincarnation. Once found, the

child is brought to Lhasa, the capital of Tibet. That child is then educated within the Tibetan Buddhist tradition, steeped in enlightenment ideals, and trained to govern.[41] This tradition was dramatized in the Hollywood film, *Kundun* (1997), directed by Martin Scorsese (1997).

This is what happened with the current Dalai Lama. Born on July 6, 1935, to a peasant family in a small village called Taktser in northeastern Tibet, Lhamo Dhondrub, as the child was named, was, in accordance with Tibetan tradition, recognized at the age of two as the reincarnation of his predecessor the thirteenth Dalai Lama, and thus an incarnation of Avalokitesvara. Lhamo Dhondrub then became His Holiness, the fourteenth Dalai Lama, Tenzin Gyatso. The new Dalai Lama was enthroned on February 22, 1940, in Lhasa, capital of Tibet.

At the age of six, the young Dalai Lama began his intensive Buddhist education. At 25, he received his Doctorate of Buddhist Philosophy in 1959. After some 80,000 Peoples Liberation Army soldiers invaded and captured Tibet, the Dalai Lama assumed full political power as head of state on November 17, 1950. In 1959, after a massive demonstration demanding that China leave Tibet and recognize Tibet's independence, the "Tibetan National Uprising" was brutally crushed by the Chinese military. Disguised as a soldier, the Dalai Lama escaped, on horseback, to India, where he was granted political asylum. He was followed into exile by some 80,000 Tibetan refugees. Today, more than 120,000 Tibetans are living in exile. Since 1960, the Dalai Lama has resided in Dharamsala, known as "Little Lhasa," seat of the Tibetan government-in-exile.

In 1963, the Dalai Lama drafted and promulgated a proposed constitution for a future Tibet, promulgated on March 10, 1963. The preamble of the constitution, while clearly modeled on the U.S. Constitution, invokes Buddhist principles:

> Whereas it is deemed desirable and necessary that the principles of justice, equality and democracy laid down by the Lord Buddha should be reinforced and strengthened in the government of Tibet . . . now, therefore, His Holiness the Dalai Lama has been pleased to ordain [this constitution] as follows . . .[42]

Similarly, the foreword of the Tibetan Constitution states:

> This [Constitution] takes into consideration the doctrines enunciated by the Lord Buddha, the spiritual and temporal heritage of Tibet and the ideas and ideals of the modern world. It is thus intended to secure for the people of Tibet a system of democracy based on justice and equality and ensure their cultural, religious and economic advancement.[43]

To advance the Tibetan cause of independence, the Dalai Lama has fashioned a model constitution that adroitly embodies Buddhist ideals, democratic principles of good governance, and progressive economic reforms. A longtime advocate of democracy, the Dalai Lama, while drafting this constitution, thoughtfully reflected:

> Even prior to my departure from Tibet . . . I had come to the conclusion that in the changing circumstances of the modern world the system of governance in Tibet must be so modified and amended as to allow the elected representatives of the people to play a more effective role in guiding and shaping the social and economic policies of the State. I also firmly believed that this could only be done through democratic institutions based on social and economic justice.[44]

With the Dalai Lama represented as head of state, leaders of the National Democratic Party for Tibet, a political party founded by Tibetan exiles in India in 1994, have commented on its uniqueness: "Tibetan democracy is unique in many ways. Its principal characteristic is that it has been gifted by His Holiness the Dalai Lama himself even at the open reluctance or sheer indifference of the Tibetan public. It is, therefore, immensely sacred and precious."[45] After his many years of efforts to regain the independence of Tibet, on December 11, 1989, the Dalai Lama was awarded the Nobel Peace Prize.[46] On that memorable day, the Dalai Lama spoke on his proposed "Five Point Peace Plan," entailing a broader understanding of what peace entails:

> Peace, in the sense of the absence of war, is of little value to someone who is dying of hunger or cold. It will not remove the pain of torture inflicted on a prisoner of conscience. It does not comfort those who have lost their loved ones in floods caused by senseless deforestation in a neighboring country. Peace can only last where human rights are respected, where the people are fed, and where individuals and nations are free. True peace with one's self and with the world around us can only be achieved through the development of mental peace.[47]

"Mental peace" is where spiritual orientation and discipline come in. Buddhism provides an instrumentality for developing this internal equanimity and composure from which peaceful actions and reactions flow: "Inner peace is the key: If you have inner peace, the external problems do not affect your deep sense of peace and tranquillity. In that state of mind you can deal with situations with calmness and reason, while keeping your inner happiness."[48] (This connection with Buddhism is only implied, however, as the Dalai Lama's only reference to Buddhism in this speech was to "Tibet's historic role as a peaceful Buddhist nation.") That much may work for inner peace. But what about international peace? As the world's superpower, what is America's role in the world today, from the Dalai Lama's perspective?

The Dalai Lama has made forthright—albeit diplomatically measured—statements about America's mission and destiny that repay study. Two years after he was awarded the Nobel Peace Prize in 1989, the Dalai Lama spoke of America's role in the world today:

> So in this respect, our entire humanity has a responsibility, particularly this nation. Among others, you have economic power, but the most important thing you have is the opportunity to utilize your human creativity. This is something very good. Therefore, I think America has the potential to make this world straight. Certain activities or certain atmospheres are unhealthy and seem to be very crooked. I think in order to make them straight and more honest, with more human feeling, this nation has the real potential and the ability to correct those smaller nations trying to change the world, but the existing pattern may face some immediate consequences which they cannot face. I think this nation is the only superpower. Therefore, I think you have the opportunity or ability to change it.[49]

The Dalai Lama's statement—"America has the potential to make this world straight"—is a clear recognition of America's world role both economically and spiritually. But there is a political dimension as well. In a 1995 discourse, the Tibetan Buddhist leader stated:

> The United States must not underestimate its role in the world today. As Americans you should be proud of your heritage, proud of the values upon which your Constitution is based. Accordingly, you should not shirk from your responsibility to bring those same fundamental rights and freedoms to people living under totalitarian regimes.[50]

While made by a religious leader, neither of these statements is inherently religious. In fact, they are covertly if not overtly political. In speaking of "people living under totalitarian regimes" generally, he surely has in mind the people of Tibet particularly.

The Dalai Lama clearly links democracy and Buddhism, seeing the former in terms of the latter: "While it is true that no system of government is perfect, democracy is the closest to our essential human nature and allows us the greatest opportunity to cultivate a sense of universal responsibility."[51] This is as overt a Buddhist endorsement of democracy as possible. The Dalai Lama, throughout his discourse, strikes linkages between Buddhist beliefs and democratic concepts, such as First Amendment freedoms and consensus building. In so doing, the Dalai Lama goes beyond drawing parallels to suggest that bringing a Buddhist influence to bear on democracy would be a good thing: "As a Buddhist, I strongly believe in a humane approach to democracy, an approach that recognizes the importance of the individual without sacrificing a sense of responsibility toward all humanity." [52]

In conclusion, one finds that Buddhism in America variously sees America either as a mission field for the propagation of Buddhism (Soka Gakkai) or sees America as having the potential for developing an enlightened society (Robert Thurman), which, in turn, will empower America to pursue its world role in furthering universal democracy, human rights, prosperity, education, freedom, and compassion (Dalai Lama), in an enlightened self-interest that can ultimately potentialize the self, through acts of selflessness. What is the Buddhist vision of America in a nutshell?: Through the first principles of Buddhist enlightenment, America can achieve a "Second Renaissance."

CHAPTER 11

Bahá'í Myths and Visions of America

The American people are indeed worthy of being the first to build the Tabernacle of the Great Peace, and proclaim the oneness of mankind.... For America hath developed powers and capacities greater and more wonderful than other nations.... Its future is even more promising, for its influence and illumination are far-reaching. It will lead all nations spiritually.

—'Abdu'l-Bahá (1912)[1]

Exert yourselves; your mission is unspeakably glorious. Should success crown your enterprise, America will assuredly evolve into a center from which waves of spiritual power will emanate, and the throne of the Kingdom of God will, in the plentitude of its majesty and glory, be firmly established.

—'Abdu'l-Bahá (1917)[2]

As the religious landscape of America continues to diversify, there is one new religion that seeks to unify: the Bahá'í Faith, which historically dates back to 1844.[3] "The Bahá'í Faith is the youngest of the world's independent religions," states the official Web site of the Bahá'î World Centre, located on Mount Carmel in Haifa, Israel.[4] Established in 189 independent countries and 46 territories, the Bahá'í community today numbers around 5.5 million members, who hail from across the world's races, religions, and nations, including over 2,100 different ethnicities.[5] The Bahá'î Faith preaches a gospel of unity, and it has a global community to match and to model the potentialities of its grander vision. The distinctive nature of the Bahá'í Faith is its emphasis on promoting the oneness of humankind and bringing about world unity. "In every Dispensation, the light of Divine Guidance has been focused upon one central theme," proclaims 'Abdu'l-Bahá (1844–1921), son of and successor to Bahá'u'lláh (1817–1892), prophet-founder of the Bahá'í Faith. "In this wondrous Revelation, this glorious century, the foundation of the Faith of God and the distinguishing feature of His Law is the consciousness of the Oneness of Mankind." [6] This is the hallmark, the salient leitmotiv, the organizing principle, the moral basis, and the grand vision of the Bahá'í Faith as a whole. As such, Bahá'ís, whether in America or abroad, are described as the "bearers of a new-born Gospel." [7] A previously little-known religion, the Bahá'í Faith is emerging from obscurity, as the following newsworthy items will demonstrate.

On July 8, 2008, the UNESCO World Heritage Committee determined that two Bahá'í shrines in Israel—the Shrine of the Báb on Mount Carmel in Haifa, Israel, and the Shrine of Bahá'u'lláh, located near Old Acre on Israel's northern coast, possess "outstanding universal value" and should be considered as part of the cultural heritage of humanity.[8] Joining such other internationally recognized sites like the Great Wall of China, the Pyramids, the Taj Mahal, Stonehenge, the Vatican, the Old City of Jerusalem, and the remains of the recently destroyed Bamiyan Buddhist statues in Afghanistan, the Bahá'í shrines are the first sites associated with a religious tradition born in modern times to be added to the list. Similarly, in 2007 the State of Illinois announced that the Bahá'í House of Worship in Wilmette (north of Chicago) had been voted one of the "Seven Wonders" of Illinois.[9]

Ideologically, the Bahá'í perspective on the destiny of America should be contextualized within the Bahá'í paradigm of unity, and, more specifically, within the Bahá'í view of "sacred history" (or as systematic theologians of Christian doctrine would term it, "salvation history"). That is to say, America will fulfill a world-unifying purpose consonant with a larger civilizational purpose for which the Bahá'í religion sees its own instrumental role. Briefly, the Bahá'í Faith is a world religion whose purpose is to unite all the races, religions, and nations into one common homeland. Bahá'ís are the followers of Bahá'u'lláh, who essentially claimed to be a world messiah, fulfilling what are believed to be convergent prophecies from historically prior world religions.[10] In his epistle to Queen Victoria, written from his prison cell in 'Akká, Palestine around 1870, Bahá'u'lláh proclaims: "That which the Lord hath ordained as the sovereign remedy and mightiest instrument for the healing of all the world is the union of all its peoples in one universal Cause, one common Faith." [11] This, in part, is a statement about how it is now time for the peoples of the world, as a whole, to recognize the essential oneness humanity—and of the world religions as well—as the collective consciousness needed to bring about world peace, and that this process will ultimately validate all faiths.

The Bahá'í vision of the destiny of America is part of a grander vision of social evolution, affecting the planet as a whole, which, in the course of human events, will lead to *a Golden Age* of world unity—a unity character- ized not by regimented uniformity, but by spectacular diversity within a morally and technically advanced global civilization. The unity that the Bahá'í Faith promotes is a guarantor of diversity by fostering social environ- ments where diversity can flourish, thereby enriching the human experience. As the epigraph above suggests, America "will lead all nations spiritually." What is the logic behind this claim? An even more basic question is this: What is the character of this new religion that makes such an auspicious claim regarding America?

A BRIEF INTRODUCTION TO THE BAHÁ'Í FAITH[12]

Before "social justice" served as the secular philosophy of modern democ- racies, the great world religions had established ethical principles and social laws for the ennobling of individuals and the ordering of societies. The Bahá'í Faith claims to be "endowed with a system of law, precept, and institutions capable of bringing into existence a global commonwealth ordered by princi- ples of social justice."[13] In the Bahá'i hierarchy of values, social justice is a cardinal principle. As a collective ethical orientation, the Bahá'í concept of social justice is intimately linked with the principle of unity. "The purpose of justice," declared Bahá'u'lláh, "is the appearance of unity among men."[14] Unity, which is predicated on social justice, is thus the organizing principle of the Bahá'í system of values. As such, a Bahá'í theory of social justice can be articulated from the Bahá'í sacred writings themselves, and amplified by offi- cial Bahá'í statements at the diplomatic level. A brief historical sketch of the religion will render a phenomenology of its social justice/unity orientation more meaningful.

The Bahá'í Faith developed from its roots in the Bábí religion, a messianic movement originating within Shí'a Islam, yet bearing all of the earmarks of a new and independent religion.[15] Bahá'í history dates back to the evening of May 22, 1844, in the city of Shíráz in Persia (now Iran), when a young merchant, Sayyid 'Alí-Muhammad, declared himself to be the Báb (1819– 1850), or "Gate"—that is, a messenger from God sent to proclaim the immi- nent advent of one greater than himself. Religious and state persecution fell upon him and his followers, leading to the torture and religious martyrdom of many. After the Báb was executed by a firing squad of 750 soldiers in the barracks square of Tabriz on July 9, 1850, the majority of his correligionists, the Bábís, turned to Mirzá Husayn-'Alí Núrí—known as Bahá'u'lláh (a spiri- tual title, meaning the "Glory of God")—as the messianic figure whose immi- nent advent was the central religious message of the Báb.

Born to a high-ranking minister of the Sháh in 1817 Tehran, Bahá'u'lláh was incarcerated in a subterranean dungeon in 1852—because he was a leader of the proscribed Bábí religion—then was exiled to Baghdad in 1853, where he remained until his subsequent exile to Istanbul (Constantinople) and Edirne (Adrianople) in 1863, and from thence to the fortress prison of 'Akká (Palestine, now Israel), where he arrived in August 1868. One of the signal events of Bahá'u'lláh's ministry was the public proclamation of his mission, the purpose of which was to unify the world through advanced social principles and new institutions. This proclamation may also be regarded as one of the first international peace missions of modern times. Beginning in September 1867, Bahá'u'lláh addressed individual and collective epistles to world leaders—including Queen Victoria, Kaiser Wilhelm I, Czar Alexander Nicholas II of Russia, Emperor Napoleon III, Pope Pius IX, Emperor Franz Joseph, Sultan 'Abdu'l-Aziz, Nasiri'd-Din Sháh, the presidents of the Americas collectively, among others—summoning them to disarmament, reconciliation, justice, and the "Most Great Peace." Bahá'u'lláh also addressed the leaders of the Zoroastrian, Jewish, Christian, and Muslim faiths, calling them to religious reconciliation and recognition of Bahá'u'lláh as the promised messiah of all religions.

Upon his death in 1892, Bahá'u'lláh was succeeded, under the terms of his will and testament, by his eldest son, 'Abdu'l-Bahá, who further developed the Bahá'í community in gradual application of the laws and precepts that Bahá'u'lláh had laid down in his Most Holy Book (Arab, *al-Kitáb al-Aqdas*; Persian, *Kitáb-i Aqdas*). When he was liberated by the Young Turks Revolution in 1908, 'Abdu'l-Bahá traveled to Europe, North Africa, and North America to promulgate his father's principles of social justice and unity. A frequent theme of his public addresses was interracial harmony, interrreligious reconciliation, and ideal international relations. He also promoted gender equality and the establishment of adjudicative organs to resolve international disputes. 'Abdu'l-Bahá lent great impetus to the spread of the Bahá'í Faith in America and abroad when he revealed his *Tablets of the Divine Plan* in 1916. After his passing in 1921, and in accordance with the terms of his will and testament, 'Abdu'l-Bahá's eldest grandson, Shoghi Effendi (who was studying at Oxford University at the time), assumed leadership of the Bahá'í world until his death in 1957. Based on the *Tablets of the Divine Plan* as a model for fostering systematic growth, Shoghi Effendi (1897–1957) promulgated a series of expansive "Plans" for systematically establishing Bahá'í communities in a greater number of countries, territories, and locales—and had the charisma to inspire their successful completion.

In his most important work (*Kitáb-i Aqdas*), Bahá'u'lláh had called for the establishment of a local House of Justice in every community. To distinguish these from institutions with an agenda for political power, 'Abdu'l-Bahá gave them the temporary title of "Spiritual Assemblies." Each nine-member local and National Spiritual Assembly, elected annually by all of the adult Bahá'ís in the respective local or national community, oversees the growth and welfare of the Bahá'í community within its jurisdiction, fosters unity among the various elements of society, and furthers the work of social and economic development.

In 1963, the Bahá'í world had become sufficiently internationalized to elect the first Universal House of Justice (the world Bahá'í governing body) in the Royal Albert Hall in London. With its Seat located in the Bahá'í World Centre on Mt. Carmel in Haifa, Israel, the Universal House of Justice— elected every five years by the members of all of the National Spiritual Assemblies from around the world—administers the affairs of the Bahá'í world and promotes Bahá'í principles of justice and unity worldwide. As publicly declared in its *Constitution,* the stated mission of the Universal House of Justice is, *inter alia:* "to do its utmost for the realization of greater cordiality and comity amongst the nations and for the attainment of universal peace"; "to safeguard the personal rights, freedom and initiative of individuals"; "to give attention to the preservation of human honour, to the development of countries and the stability of states"; "to provide for the arbitration and settlement of disputes arising between peoples"; "to foster that which is conducive to the enlightenment and illumination of the souls of men and the advancement and betterment of the world." [16] These are some of the duties of the Universal House of Justice that are mandated in its charter document. In fine, the Universal House of Justice works to promote ideal international relations through the application of Bahá'í principles and practices at local, national, and international levels.

The diplomatic work of the Bahá'í Faith is carried out by the Universal House of Justice, the Bahá'i International Community (BIC), and external affairs representatives appointed by their respective National Spiritual Assemblies. Ethics-based and religious nongovernmental organizations (RNGOs) are playing increasingly significant roles in their consultative collaborations with the United Nations. As an RNGO, the BIC represents a network of 182 democratically elected National Spiritual Assemblies that act on behalf of Bahá'ís worldwide. The BIC is the voice of the Bahá'í community in international affairs. The BIC focuses on four core areas, each of which encompass social justice issues: (1) promotion of a universal standard for human rights (2) advancement of women; (3) promotion of just and equitable global prosperity and (4) development of moral capabilities. The BIC also defends the rights of Bahá'ís in countries where they are persecuted, such as in Iran and Egypt.

As previously stated, Bahá'í communities are established in 235 countries and dependent territories, representing more than 2,100 different tribal, racial, and ethnic groups. At present, the country with the greatest number of Bahá'ís is India, where its magnificent "Lotus Temple" just outside of New Delhi is now said to be the most visited religious edifice in the world. Although its adherents number only 5.5 million, the Bahá'í Faith is now the second most widespread of the world's independent religions, according to the *World Christian Encyclopedia*[17] and *Encyclopedia Britannica Book of the Year* (1992). The statistical distribution of Bahá'ís worldwide may be studied by consulting the *Britannica* yearbooks in their annual reports on religion.

Social justice is relative to prevailing social values. Yet out of this relativity, consensus may be reached by identifying common denominators. "Justice ... is a universal quality," 'Abdu'l-Bahá stated in Paris on November 17, 1912. He added that "justice must be sacred, and the rights of all the people must be considered."[18] The Bahá'í ethical commitment to social justice is paramount. "The best beloved of all things in My sight is Justice," Bahá'u'lláh writes, "turn not away therefrom if thou desirest Me, and neglect it not that I may confide in thee." "By its aid thou shalt see with thine own eyes and not through the eyes of others, and shalt know of thine own knowledge and not through the knowledge of thy neighbor," Bahá'u'lláh goes on to say. "Ponder this in thy heart; how it behooveth thee to be. Verily justice is My gift to thee and the sign of My loving-kindness. Set it then before thine eyes."[19] The challenge for Bahá'ís, then, is to more systematically develop Bahá'í principles of social justice, to apply them within their own faith-communities, and then to offer these practiced precepts as a model for wider adoption. In his epistle to Queen Victoria (c. 1869), Bahá'u'lláh endorsed parliamentary democracy as an ideal form of governance:

> We have also heard that thou hast entrusted the reins of counsel into the hands of the representatives of the people. Thou, indeed, hast done well. . . . O ye the elected representatives of the people in every land! Take ye counsel together, and let your concern be only for that which profiteth mankind and bettereth the condition thereof, if ye be of them that scan heedfully.[20]

Referring to his own mission as that of a "World Reformer,"[21] Bahá'u'lláh promulgated social principles that are wider in scope than the process of electing governments. Democracy is more than the election of governments; it is the refinement of governments as well.

The Bahá'í community, in a measured participation in political democracy, eschews partisan politics as polarizing and divisive. While exercising their civic obligation in voting, individual Bahá'ís distance themselves from the political theatre of party politics. Embracing many aspects of democracy, they shun campaigning. Instead, Bahá'ís work within the body politic, applying Bahá'í principles to better society. These principles include, among others:

(1) human unity; (2) social justice; (3) racial harmony; (4) interfaith co-operation; (5) gender equality; (6) wealth equity (economic justice); (7) social and economic development; (8) international law; (9) human rights; (10) freedom of conscience; (11) individual responsibility; (12) harmony of science and religion; (13) international scientific cooperation; (14) international standards/world intercommunication; (15) international language; (16) universal education; (17) environmentalism; (18) world commonwealth; (19) world tribunal; (20) world peace; (21) search after truth; (22) oneness of religion; (23) love of God; (24) nobility of character (acquiring virtues); (25) advancing civilization (individual purpose); (26) work as worship; (27) ideal marriage; (28) family values; (29) model communities; (30) religious teleology (Progressive Revelation); (31) Bahá'í doctrinal integrity; (32) Bahá'í institutional support (the "Covenant"); (33) promoting Bahá'í values. These principles and practices work synergistically in concert to refine moral character, advance civilization, inspire new approaches to conflict resolution, and endow human consciousness with a vibrant vision of social harmony.

In its June 4, 1992, presentation to the Plenary of the United Nations Conference on Environment and Development (UNCED, Earth Summit '92, Rio de Janiero), the BIC has epitomized the foundation of social justice from a Bahá'í perspective: "The fundamental spiritual truth of our age is the oneness of humanity." [22] (In Bahá'í terminology, "oneness" means "unity.") It follows that "universal acceptance of this principle—with its implications for social and economic justice, universal participation in non-adversarial decision making, peace and collective security, equality of the sexes, and universal education—will make possible the reorganization and administration of the world as one country, the home of humankind." [23] Note the linkage that such Bahá'í statements strike between social justice and world unity. These principles are comprehensive and perhaps may best be studied within a framework suggested by 'Abdu'l-Bahá himself: "The teachings of Bahá'u'lláh are the light of this age and the spirit of this century. Expound each of them at every gathering:

The first is investigation of truth,
The second, the oneness of mankind,
The third, universal peace,
The fourth, conformity between science and divine revelation,
The fifth, abandonment of racial, religious, worldly and political prejudices,
    prejudices which destroy the foundation of mankind,
The sixth is righteousness and justice,
The seventh, the betterment of morals and heavenly education,
The eighth, the equality of the two sexes,
The ninth, the diffusion of knowledge and education,
The tenth, economic questions, and so on and so forth." [24]

While space does not permit elaboration of these (and other) Bahá'í principles of unity, many are fairly self-evident. They provide a necessary context
for understanding what lies behind the Bahá'í vision of the destiny of
America. By Bahá'í standards, America will be measured by its ability to further unity at home and abroad, through developing an exemplary society
while instrumentally promoting world order.

BAHÁ'Í MYTHS AS A "SACRED HISTORY" OF AMERICA

There are actually a number of passages in Bahá'í texts concerning the destiny of America. They are too numerous to treat here. While many, these
statements reiterate salient themes. Throughout the remainder of this chapter,
some of these themes will be highlighted. First, the term "America," as found
in Bahá'í texts, needs to be contextualized geopolitically.

Various configurations of the term "America" have rather self-evident geographical distinctions, such as "the Americas," "the Continent of America,"
"North America," and then, "America," which by itself most often is a metonymy (or synonym) for the "United States of America." Similarly, the meaning
of "America" in Bahá'í texts is context dependent, in that "America" variously represents: (1) the United States (including Alaska); (2) the United
States and Canada; (3) North America; and (4) the Americas. In a talk delivered on September 5, 1912, at the St. James Methodist Church in Montreal,
Canada, 'Abdu'l-Bahá indicates that Canada shares much the same destiny
as the United States:

> Praise be to God! I find these two great American nations highly capable and
> advanced in all that appertains to progress and civilization. These governments
> are fair and equitable. The motives and purposes of these people are lofty and
> inspiring. Therefore, it is my hope that these revered nations may become promi-
> nent factors in the establishment of international peace and the oneness of the
> world of humanity; that they may lay the foundations of equality and spiritual
> brotherhood among mankind.[25]

This is a mission and mandate to both the United States and Canada alike,
indicating that "international peace and the oneness of the world of humanity" and laying the "foundations of equality and spiritual brotherhood among
mankind" is not the province of any one country alone, but—to varying
degrees according to the respective capacity of each—of all countries.
Returning to the meaning of "America" in Bahá'í texts, one passage that
offers a prime example of a range of meanings that "America" adumbrates
(i.e., the United States, Canada, North America, and the Americas) is as
follows:

The Báb had in His *Qayyúmu'l-Asmá,* almost a hundred years previously, sounded His specific summons to the "peoples of the West" to "issue forth" from their "cities" and aid His Cause. Bahá'u'lláh, in His *Kitáb-i-Aqdas,* had collectively addressed the Presidents of the Republics of the entire Americas, bidding them arise and "bind with the hands of justice the broken," and "crush the oppressor" with the "rod of the commandments" of their Lord, and had, moreover, anticipated in His writings the appearance "in the West" of the "signs of His Dominion." 'Abdu'l-Bahá had, on His part, declared that the "illumination" shed by His Father's Revelation upon the West would acquire an "extraordinary brilliancy," and that the "light of the Kingdom" would "shed a still greater illumination upon the West" than upon the East. He had extolled the American continent in particular as "the land wherein the splendors of His Light shall be revealed, where the mysteries of His Faith shall be unveiled," and affirmed that "it will lead all nations spiritually." More specifically still, He had singled out the Great Republic of the West, the leading nation of that continent, declaring that its people were "indeed worthy of being the first to build the Tabernacle of the Most Great Peace and proclaim the oneness of mankind," that it was "equipped and empowered to accomplish that which will adorn the pages of history, to become the envy of the world, and be blest in both the East and the West." [26]

In this chapter, "America" will be understood to mean the United States of America. In a word, the place of America in the grand scheme of things is intimately bound up with the purpose of the existence of the Bahá'í Faith itself: world unity. It should be added that "world unity" is an outcome of an integrated approach to social and economic development, equitable management of world resources, the potentializing of human resources through advanced educational strategies, effective conflict resolution, and the spiritual awakening of societies as a whole. The earliest mention of "America" in the Bahá'í Writings occurs in a passage, the context of which indicates that "America" stands for what today would be commonly referred to as "the Americas," or the Western Hemisphere. In 1873, Bahá'u'lláh addressed the rulers and leaders of the Americas in the single most important Bahá'í text, the Most Holy Book (*Kitáb-i Aqdas*):

Hearken ye, O Rulers of America and the Presidents of the Republics therein, unto that which the Dove is warbling on the Branch of Eternity: "There is none other God but Me, the Ever-Abiding, the Forgiving, the All-Bountiful." Adorn ye the temple of dominion with the ornament of justice and of the fear of God, and its head with the crown of the remembrance of your Lord, the Creator of the heavens. Thus counselleth you He Who is the Dayspring of Names, as bidden by Him Who is the All-Knowing, the All-Wise. The Promised One hath appeared in this glorified Station, whereat all beings, both seen and unseen, have rejoiced. ... Bind ye the broken with the hands of justice, and crush the oppressor who flourisheth with the rod of the commandments of your Lord, the Ordainer, the All-Wise.[27]

This passage was written in 1873 or shortly prior to that. Serving as presidents (or as prime minister, as in the case of Canada) of the countries of the Americas in 1872 were the following (with nations listed alphabetically): Domingo Faustino Sarmiento, president of Argentina; John A. Macdonald, prime minister of Canada; Federico Errázuriz Zanartu, president of Chile; Eustorgio Salgar and Manuel Murillo Toro, presidents of Colombia; Tomás Guardia Gutiérrez, president of Costa Rica; Buenaventura Báez, president of the Dominican Republic; Gabriel García Moreno, president of Ecuador; Justo Rufino Barrios, president of Guatemala; Nissage Saget, president of Haiti; Benito Juárez and Sebastián Lerdo de Tejada, presidents of Mexico; José Vicente Cuadra, president of Nicaragua; Francisco Solano López, president of Paraguay; Manuel Pardo, president of Peru; Ulysses S. Grant, president of the United States of America; Lorenzo Batlle y Grau and Tomás Gomensoro, presidents of Uruguay; and Antonio Guzmán Blanco, president of Venezuela.[28] Here, the admonition to "bind ye the broken with the hands of justice, and crush the oppressor" would naturally devolve upon the United States of America, of which Ulysses S. Grant was president, as well as the other countries of the Western Hemisphere, as every nation has this obligation to safeguard and to promote the commonweal of its own citizens.

According to Shoghi Effendi, not only were "the Rulers of America" significantly "spared the ominous and emphatic warnings" that Bahá'u'lláh had "uttered against the crowned heads of the world," but "upon the sovereign rulers of the Western Hemisphere" was conferred the "distinction" of exhorting them to "bring their corrective and healing influence to bear upon the injustices perpetrated by the tyrannical and the ungodly."[29] "Had this Cause been revealed in the West," Bahá'u'lláh is reported to have said in the untranslated portion of Nabíl's Narrative (an authoritative account of Bábí and early Bahá'í history), "had Our verses been sent from the West to Persia and other countries of the East, it would have become evident how the people of the Occident would have embraced Our Cause."[30] It is clear that Bahá'u'lláh saw greater capacity and receptivity to his sociomoral principles in the West than in the East. Above and beyond those passages that clearly foreshadow the "signs of His dominion" in the West, Shoghi Effendi points to the "no less significant verbal affirmations" in which Bahá'u'lláh, "according to reliable eyewitnesses," had "more than once made in regard to the glorious destiny which America was to attain in the days to come."[31] So, while no direct writing by Bahá'u'lláh regarding the destiny of America is extant, reliable sources provide sufficient attestation of Bahá'u'lláh's oral statements regarding America's promise and future preeminence.

Subsequent to Bahá'u'lláh was 'Abdu'l-Bahá, who, after his father, Bahá'u'lláh, had passed away in 1892, led the Bahá'í world until he himself left this mortal world in 1921, when he was succeeded by his grandson, the Oxford-educated Shoghi Effendi. Both 'Abdu'l-Bahá and Shoghi Effendi had some profound thoughts about the destiny of America. In the course of their respective pronouncements on America, certain characterizations of American history and America's world role were articulated in order to register particular points, as the rhetoric and rationale of those comments occasionally dictated. Such glosses on America gave rise to sometimes idealized representations and, at time, generalized critiques of America as well—all of which, taken together, comprise what may well be described, for the purposes of this book at least, as the Bahá'í myths and visions of America.

According to historian Robert Stockman, American Bahá'ís, on the basis of these various pronouncements, have articulated a grand myth of America, which incorporates Bahá'í ideals: "The American Bahá'ís utilized the historic events and basic principles of their new religion to define a new myth of America, one that contained much of the confidence and optimism of the traditional Protestant view of America as a 'redeemer nation.'"[32] Stockman elaborates further:

> Like any religious group, the American Bahá'ís have constructed a sacred history, or myth, about their country. This sacred history is primarily based on the values found in Bahá'í scripture and does not appear to be borrowed from American Protestantism or secular culture to a significant degree. However, the Bahá'í myth's concept of America's uniqueness, its view of the possible future greatness of America, and its consequent critique of current American social conditions bear some remarkable parallels to the Protestant myth.[33]

Here, by religious "myth," Stockman means a "sacred history." No one should misconstrue the meaning of the term, "myth." Stockman is careful to explain that the terms "sacred history" and "myth" are, here at least, used "synonymously." These terms denote a "theologically based understanding of the importance of the events of history." Since history cannot possibly record every single fact, consequently "historians must sift through facts and select only those that are most relevant to their studies." This selection process necessarily includes "a strong element of judgment and bias based on one's methods, ideological assumptions, and interests." A sacred history is no exception, for "it is distinguished by the use of theological beliefs as the primary selection criteria for the inclusion of facts." In Stockman's and the present writer's use of these more or less interchangeable terms, a caveat is in order: the "use of the word myth is not meant to suggest that a sacred history is untrue," but simply a way "to give religious meaning to mundane events."[34]

The specific parallel with the Protestant myth of America that Robert Stockman adduces is with America's world role as "redeemer nation." Earlier in the present book, the Protestant "master myth" of America has been described several times as a mandate "to colonize, Christianize, and civilize" and is closely associated with the doctrine of Manifest Destiny. This would seem to be very different from the "redeemer nation" vision alluded to in the passages above from Stockman's work. It is important not to associate the Bahá'í view with the superiority and prejudice inherent in "colonize, Christianize, and civilize." Rather, the emphasis here is on America's redemptive role: Stockman particularly alludes to a classic work in American studies, Ernest Lee Tuveson's *Redeemer Nation: The Idea of America's Millennial Role*,[35] in which the idea of redemptive mission—which has motivated so much of American foreign policy—is as old as the Republic itself. Tuveson traces the development of this aspect of the American heritage from its Puritan origins, and tracks the idea of America's mission and the millenarian ideal through successive stages of American history.

Americanist Deborah Madsen, succinctly recapitulates this notion of America as a "redeemer nation." America began as an experiment in theocracy (the reign of God). Puritans of the Massachusetts Bay Colony believed that God intervened in human history to effect the salvation not only of individuals but also entire nations. Thus, the Puritans believed that the New World, and the Puritans themselves, had been singled out by God and were charged with a special destiny—to establish model Christian community for the rest of the world to emulate. Madsen explains that

> this idea of ecclesiastical perfection combined with millennial expectations and gave rise to the theory that here in the New World the purified church would create the conditions for Christ's return to earth. The mission that inspired the Massachusetts Bay colonists was then charged with exceptional importance and urgency.[36]

The New World is thus the last and best hope for a fallen humanity that has only to look to the sanctified church in America for redemption. Consequently,

> America and Americans are special, exceptional, because they are charged with saving the world from itself and, at the same time, America and Americans must sustain a high level of spiritual, political and moral commitment to this exceptional destiny—America must be as "a city upon a hill" exposed to the eyes of the world.[37]

In Madsen's view, exceptionalism is an integral and distinctive feature of the American experience: "This concept has generated a self-consciousness and degree of introspection that is unique to American culture." [38] The doctrine of America as a redeemer nation later developed into "an unquestioning belief in the doctrine of Manifest Destiny, a profound commitment to the inevitability of American expansion and an uncompromising vision of America as the redeemer nation committed to extending the domain of freedom and America's control over it" [39] as well as a "racialised interpretation of national destiny" (i.e., American Anglo-Saxonism).[40] Under this analysis, Stockman's parallel is valid insofar as the Puritan ethic is concerned, but must be distanced from its pejorative transmogrification into the doctrine of Manifest Destiny. Indeed, a Bahá'í view of America as a "redeemer nation" could only come about if America first redeems itself from the materialism and moral laxity that represents the very antithesis of the Puritan vision.

America is not the only country that is the subject of a Bahá'í sacred history. Stockman points out that there are Bahá'í sacred histories about other countries as well:

> The American Bahá'í sacred history is not a unique phenomenon; Bahá'í sacred histories of Germany, Russia, China, India, Japan, Iran, Canada, and other countries undoubtedly have been created by the Bahá'ís of those countries, based on statements about those nations in the Bahá'í scriptures. A folk tradition is inevitable whenever the Bahá'í religion is introduced to a new culture or nation.[41]

As for the Bahá'í myth of America, Stockman further notes that "the creation of an American Bahá'í sacred history inevitably represents an act of social criticism as well, for some events in American history are negatively valued, such as America's persistent streak of racism, its materialism, and its excessive and isolationist nationalism." [42] This is an important observation, because, as will be discussed below, there are certain American social problems that have drawn recurrent criticism in Bahá'í texts. For instance, the problem of racism in the United States is termed, in the Bahá'í Writings, as "the most challenging issue." In an official position statement issued in 1991 by the National Spiritual Assembly of the Bahá'ís of the United States[43]—entitled, *The Vision of Race Unity: America's Most Challenging Issue*—the problem of racism in America is framed so:

> Racism is the most challenging issue confronting America. A nation whose ancestry includes every people on earth, whose motto is *E pluribus unum,* whose ideals of freedom under law have inspired millions throughout the world, cannot continue to harbor prejudice against any racial or ethnic group without betraying itself. Racism is an affront to human dignity, a cause of hatred and division, a disease that devastates society. Notwithstanding the efforts already expended for its elimination, racism continues to work its evil upon this nation.

The American audience is in full view here, where racism is characterized as fundamentally un-American, facially contradicting America's celebrated motto, which translates, "Out of many, One." Therefore, unity is faithful to the America ideal, whereas racism tears at America's social fabric. America has no spiritual destiny so long as rampant racism remains. The persistence of racism, even in its most subtle forms (what sociologists have termed, "polite racism"), retards America's social advancement, and vitiates its moral authority under the close watch of the community of nations. Further in this statement, the National Spiritual Assembly connects the fostering of racial harmony—seen as the divinely ordained antidote to racism—with the destiny of America:

> Aware of the magnitude and the urgency of the issue, we, the National Spiritual Assembly of the Bahá'ís of the United States, speaking for the entire U.S. Bahá'í community, appeal to all people of goodwill to arise without further delay to resolve the fundamental social problem of this country. We do so because of our feeling of shared responsibility, because of the global experience of the Bahá'í community in affecting racial harmony within itself, and because of the vision that the sacred scriptures of our Faith convey of the destiny of America.

America's prospective leadership in international affairs must be grounded in domestic social policy that other nations may regard as exemplary and as a model to follow. Of course, this cannot happen unless and until America succeeds in eradicating racism and promoting interracial harmony. Stockman registers one more point: "In this way the sacred history becomes a spur to Bahá'í efforts to reform society. It also helps American Bahá'ís to form an American identity that is congruent with the Bahá'í scriptures." [44] In other words, if America solves its racial crisis at home, it will then gain the moral authority to promote similar social cohesion abroad.

THE BAHÁ'Í EMANCIPATION/CIVIL WAR MYTH

The year 1912 was the year that 'Abdu'l-Bahá came to America. On just his tenth day in America—Saturday, April 20—'Abdu'l-Bahá arrived in Washington, D.C., and stayed until Sunday, April 28. On Tuesday morning, April 23, 'Abdu'l-Bahá spoke in Rankin Chapel at Howard University. Well over a thousand faculty, administrators, students, and guests [45] crowded the relatively small space of this modest chapel to hear him speak. In this historic speech, 'Abdu'l-Bahá draws on American history (or a certain view of it) in order to promote unity between the races: "The first proclamation of emancipation [the Emancipation Proclamation] for the blacks was made by the whites of America. How they fought and sacrificed until they freed the blacks! Then it spread to other places." 'Abdu'l-Bahá further states that the Emancipation Proclamation was followed by the Europeans, and had a liberating impact on Africans as well, such that "Emancipation Proclamation became universal." [46]

In this general statement, 'Abdu'l-Bahá evidently points to some of the political and social effects of the Emancipation Proclamation (and its later developments) as a reflex of American exemplarism abroad, as well as at home. To idealize the Civil War is to mythologize it. Here, 'Abdu'l-Bahá mythologizes the Civil War by essentializing it. This Civil War myth, like most myths, serves as a vehicle of a social and moral truth: the need for interracial unity. 'Abdu'l-Bahá's observations, as quoted above, had their basis in later developments in the Civil War and beyond.

On January 1, 1863, President Abraham Lincoln's Emancipation Proclamation was promulgated—although Lincoln arguably had no constitutional authority to actually free slaves. (By dint of his authority as commander in chief, the Proclamation was technically a military order.) Its reach was not universal, as it legally freed slaves only in the Southern states. The Emancipation Proclamation was the precursor of the Thirteenth Amendment. On December 18, 1865, Congress's Thirteenth Amendment freed slaves nationally. The Thirteenth Amendment abolished slavery, and thus radically altered the U.S. Constitution, as part of what some legal scholars call the "Second Constitution." Ironically, ratification of the Thirteenth Amendment marks the first time that the word "slavery" appeared in the Constitution, even though the Constitution had explicitly protected slavery. 'Abdu'l-Bahá's statement, therefore, would presumably adumbrate the Thirteenth Amendment as an extension of Lincoln's Emancipation Proclamation.

Originally known as the "Abolition Amendment," the intent of the Thirteenth Amendment was to give practical effect to the Declaration of Independence's self-evident truths "that all men are created equal; that they are endowed by their creator with certain unalienable rights; that among these, are life, liberty, and the pursuit of happiness." Of course, such unalienable rights did not extend to aliens (noncitizens), which is why the Fourteenth Amendment (1868) had, perforce, to precede the Fifteenth, by granting citizenship to anyone born or naturalized in the United States.

Under Section 2, which legal scholars call the Enforcement Clause, the Thirteenth Amendment was also supposed to eradicate any vestiges of forced labor ("badges and incidents of servitude"). Thus, to enforce the Thirteenth Amendment, Congress quickly passed the Civil Rights Act of 1866 (over President Andrew Johnson's veto), the Slave Kidnapping Act of 1866, the Peonage Act of 1867, and the Judiciary Act of 1867. But a series of Supreme Court decisions during Reconstruction effectively emasculated the Amendment, through crabbed interpretation and curtailed application. With the splendid exception of peonage cases, the Thirteenth Amendment remained a dead letter under segregationist Supreme Court rulings like *Plessy v. Ferguson,* which used color as a badge for discrimination while professing an "equal but separate" doctrine. One reason for this is that the Thirteenth Amendment was deficient in that it lacked any formal recognition of equality under the law. This defect would later be cured by enactment of the Equal Protection Clause under the Fourteenth Amendment.

The Thirteenth Amendment is far more than an emancipation law. Through its enforcement power, it is also a civil rights instrument, although rarely used. The social transformation that the framers of the Thirteenth Amendment had envisioned could only be achieved where the federal government could enforce freedom. Sadly, it took over a century for the Supreme Court to discover in the Thirteenth Amendment a fresh constitutional source of power for enforcing certain civil rights. The landmark decision of *Jones v. Alfred H. Mayer Co.,* 392 U.S. 409 (1968), restored the civil rights value of the Amendment and transformed it into a potentially potent civil rights instrument. *Jones* established Congress's power to enact legislation against private racial discrimination. Today, the Thirteenth Amendment arguably remains a little-used, but potentially important, federal power for enforcing civil rights against all vestiges of slavery that reincarnate as racial discrimination. Alexander Tsesis, who may be today's leading authority on the Thirteenth Amendment, observes that each new generation must reexamine the nation's past, its core documents, and its moral progress as a constitutional democracy.

Such legislation, alone, cannot solve the racial crisis that continues to affect America, even though such discrimination has taken on subtle forms—what sociologists generally term, "polite racism." Abolition of slavery, after all, is not freedom from all oppression. Slavery's roots are deep in American history, and are not yet fully extirpated. Racism is a ghost of the slaver's psyche, and legislation alone cannot humanify the heart. Bahá'í texts are fully alive to this problem, which is why, according to 'Abdu'l-Bahá, Whites should "endeavor to promote your advancement and enhance your honor," referring to African Americans. "Differences between black and white will be completely obliterated; indeed, ethnic and national differences will all disappear." [47] There is an element of prophecy in 'Abdu'l-Bahá's prediction that racial, ethnic, and national differences would, in the future, vanish as socially repugnant. Just about any prophecy requires mechanisms for its fulfillment. Accordingly, 'Abdu'l-Bahá invites his audience to build on history by making history, in commencing a new era of racial harmony.

On Wednesday, April 24, 1912—the day after speaking in Rankin Chapel at Howard University—'Abdu'l-Bahá said, at a Bahá'í-sponsored interracial meeting: "A meeting such as this seems like a beautiful cluster of precious jewels—pearls, rubies, diamonds, sapphires. It is a source of joy and delight. In the clustered jewels of the races may the blacks be as sapphires and rubies and the whites as diamonds and pearls. How glorious the spectacle of real unity among mankind! This is the sign of the Most Great Peace; this is the star of the oneness of the human world." Throughout his travels and speaking engagements in the United States and Canada, 'Abdu'l-Bahá continued to stress the vital importance of race unity for America and for the world.

THE BAHÁ'Í WILSONIAN MYTH

In the Bahá'í vision of America, America's world role is to foster ideal international relations. Such world diplomacy and international cooperation will, in turn, prove hugely instrumental in unifying the world (which, after all, is the principal purpose of the Bahá'í Faith). In its religious myth (or, sacred history) of America, several Bahá'í texts single out, for distinction, an American president who tried to do exactly that: Woodrow Wilson. Indeed, President Wilson was a "statesman whose vision both 'Abdu'l-Bahá and Shoghi Effendi have praised." [48] These passages lionize President Woodrow Wilson by focusing exclusively on his legacy as an internationalist. Such praise is both deserved and controversial. Wilson is immortalized in history as an internationalist who championed the formation of the League of Nations (precursor of the United Nations). Historians generally agree that Woodrow Wilson, in so doing, was the first U.S. president to define America's world role. This largely explains why Bahá'í sources attach considerable religious significance to President Wilson. Yet Wilson was also a racist, which fact finds no purchase in the Wilsonian idealism given such prominence in Bahá'í texts.

Shoghi Effendi states that Wilson holds a special place as the most honored statesman in the Bahá'í writings:

> To her President, the immortal Woodrow Wilson, must be ascribed the unique honor, among the statesmen of any nation, whether of the East or of the West, of having voiced sentiments so akin to the principles animating the Cause of Bahá'u'lláh, and of having more than any other world leader, contributed to the creation of the League of Nations—achievements which the pen of the Center of God's Covenant ['Abdu'l-Bahá] acclaimed as signalizing the dawn of the Most Great Peace. [49]

Note that the passage distinguishes this American president as "the immortal Woodrow Wilson," notwithstanding the fact that Wilson was an erstwhile racist. While racism is absolutely antithetical to Bahá'í principles of unity, the Bahá'í Woodrow Wilson myth is consistent with the function of myth-making in general, which is to confer meaning and inspire action. Myths, after all, are about storytelling in order to moralize and incentivize, not to memorialize the naked facts for their own sake. Here, the purpose of idealizing the past is to inspire an ideal future.

In a word, Wilsonian idealism is internationalism.[50] A comparison of Wilsonian idealism and Bahá'í principles shows a powerful resonance that is nothing short of resounding harmonics. Stephen Skowronek condenses and characterizes Wilsonian idealism as effectively as any of his predecessors have done, if not more so:

"Peace without victory"; self-determination; the equality of states; renunciation of indemnities and annexations; rejection of the balance of power; promotion of the community of powers, of collective security under a league of nations, of a world safe for democracy—these were the principles Wilson enunciated in 1917, and these were the principles that catapulted him into the top ranks of democratic visionaries in world history.[51]

On these resonances between Wilsonian internationalism and Bahá'í principles of ideal international relations leading to world unity, 'Abdu'l-Bahá, observed: "As to President Wilson, the fourteen principles which he hath enunciated are mostly found in the teachings of Bahá'u'lláh and I therefore hope that he will be confirmed and assisted." [52] In 'Abdu'l-Bahá's estimation, Wilson's enlightened internationalism attracted divine favor:

The President of the Republic, Dr. Wilson, is indeed serving the Kingdom of God for he is restless and strives day and night that the rights of all men may be preserved safe and secure, that even small nations, like greater ones, may dwell in peace and comfort, under the protection of Righteousness and Justice. This purpose is indeed a lofty one. I trust that the incomparable Providence will assist and confirm such souls under all conditions.[53]

Thus, in the Bahá'í view, President Wilson's principles of internationalism were providentially inspired. According to Shoghi Effendi, the "ideals that fired the imagination of America's tragically unappreciated President" were "acclaimed as signalizing the dawn of the Most Great Peace" by "'Abdu'l-Bahá, through His own pen." [54]

Such is the Wilsonian Myth. Yet the Bahá'í writings do not idealize Wilson so much as they champion Wilsonian idealism.[55] In lionizing Wilson the statesman, and in overlooking Wilson the racist, the Bahá'í Wilsonian myth lives up to the purpose of a religious myth of America, as *idealized or sacralized history exemplifying key precepts and practices.*

THE BAHÁ'Í VISION OF THE DESTINY OF AMERICA

In 2001, there came a moment in time when the National Spiritual Assembly of the Bahá'ís of the United States (elected governing council of the American Bahá'í community) decided to offer *a perspective on the destiny of America as the promoter of world peace.* At a time of national crisis following the terrorist attacks of September 11, 2001, the National Spiritual Assembly published a full-page display ad, "The Destiny of America and the Promise of World Peace," which appeared on page A29 in the *New York Times* on December 23, 2001.[56] This 645-word document highlights six prerequisites for world peace: (1) promoting "universal acceptance" of the oneness of humanity to realize world peace; (2) eradicating racism ("a major barrier to peace") to achieve racial harmony; (3) fostering "the emancipation of women" to achieve "full equality of the sexes"; (4) greatly reducing the "inordinate disparity between rich and poor"; (5) transcending "unbridled nationalism" and inculcating "a wider loyalty" to "humanity as a whole"; (6) overcoming "religious strife" to enjoy harmony among religions.[57] The full-page display ad was later reprinted in dozens of newspapers around the country.

While the September 11, 2001, terrorist attacks are not explicitly mentioned in the proclamation, they are implied in the words, "At this time of world turmoil."[58] How true this statement was. Americans, particularly, were still in a state of shock. America, under direct attack, was understandably alarmed. Thus "9/11" was, and remains, a deeply disturbing experience for the American nation. If the American Bahá'ís had anything to say, this was the time to say it: "The United States Bahá'í community," the ad goes on to say, "offers a perspective on the destiny of America as the promoter of world peace."[59]

This Bahá'í proclamation introduces the American public to "Bahá'u'lláh, the founder of the Bahá'í Faith," who, "addressing heads of state, proclaimed that the age of maturity for the entire human race had come." This refers to what the present writer calls *the first international peace mission in modern history.* The proclamation of Bahá'u'lláh took place primarily in the years 1867–1870. During this time, Bahá'u'lláh addressed epistles to, *inter alia,* Kaiser Wilhelm I, Tsar Alexander II, Emperor Napoleon III, Pope Pius IX, Queen Victoria, Emperor Franz Joseph, Sultan Abdul-Aziz, and the king of Iran, Nasiri'd-Dín Sháh. Speaking of the peace proposals and principles of ideal international relations that Bahá'u'lláh communicated to the reigning pontiff and potentates, 'Abdu'l-Bahá (Bahá'u'lláh's eldest son, successor, and interpreter), commented: "These precepts were proclaimed by Bahá'u'lláh many years ago. He was the first to create them in the hearts as moral laws. Writing to the sovereigns of the world, he summoned them to universal brotherhood, proclaiming that the hour for unity had struck—unity between countries, unity between religions."[60] The Bahá'í Faith promotes peace as a direct extension of the fact that its founder, Bahá'u'lláh, dedicated his life to the cause of world peace and promulgated the principles necessary to achieve it.

The *Times* display ad places Bahá'u'lláh's messages to the kings and rulers of the world in this perspective: "The unity of humankind was now to be established as the foundation of the great peace that would mark the highest stage in humanity's spiritual and social evolution. Revolutionary and world-shaking changes were therefore inevitable." "The Destiny of America and the Promise of World Peace" goes on to quote the following passage from the Bahá'í Writings:

> The world is moving on. Its events are unfolding ominously and with bewilder-ing rapidity. The whirlwind of its passions is swift and alarmingly violent. The New World is insensibly drawn into its vortex. . . . Dangers, undreamt of and unpredictable, threaten it both from within and from without. Its governments and peoples are being gradually enmeshed in the coils of the world's recurrent crises and fierce controversies. . . . The world is contracting into a neighborhood. America, willingly or unwillingly, must face and grapple with this new situation. For purposes of national security, let alone any humanitarian motive, she must assume the obligations imposed by this newly created neighborhood. Paradoxi-cal as it may seem, her only hope of extricating herself from the perils gathering around her is to become entangled in that very web of international association which the Hand of an inscrutable Providence is weaving.[61]

This passage in *The Advent of Divine Justice,* by Shoghi Effendi, who, as "Guardian" of the Bahá'í Faith, led the Bahá'í world from 1921 to 1957, is part of a lengthy letter written December 25, 1938, to the Bahá'ís of the United States and Canada.[62] Here, the Guardian states that America will be so inextricably drawn into the vortex of international relations that she will be forced to assume a leadership role in the international community, not out of any humanitarian motives per se, but purely out of enlightened political self-interest. Notwithstanding, that enlightened self-interest will, in time, develop into an enlightened global interest.

The National Spiritual Assembly goes on to forecast the destiny of America as a future leader and catalyst of world peace:

> The American nation, Bahá'ís believe, will evolve, through tests and trials to become a land of spiritual distinction and leadership, a champion of justice and unity among all peoples and nations, and a powerful servant of the cause of ever-lasting peace. This is the peace promised by God in the sacred texts of the world's religions.[63]

However, the six prerequisites to world peace, mentioned above, must first be met.

This public message from the American Bahá'í leadership to the American people was a significant public gesture. The message goes on to quote from a

Bahá'í prayer for America: "May this American Democracy be the first nation to establish the foundation of international agreement. May it be the first nation to proclaim the unity of mankind. May it be the first to unfurl the standard of the Most Great Peace." The proclamation closes on an optimistic note, with this heartening word of encouragement: "During this hour of crisis," the National Spiritual Assembly of the Bahá'ís of the United States concludes, "we affirm our abiding faith in the destiny of America. We know that the road to its destiny is long, thorny and tortuous, but we are confident that America will emerge from her trials undivided and undefeatable." With this message of hope and inspiration, the National Spiritual Assembly offers a fresh perspective on America that charts its destiny, prioritizes its social agenda, and conveys a forward-looking sense of purpose and resolve.

As previously stated, a number of passages in Baha'i texts address the destiny of America. One of these statements, apart from its exhortative tenor, contains a significant allusion to an earlier moment in Bahá'í history:

> This nation so signally blest, occupying so eminent and responsible a position in a continent so wonderfully endowed, was the first among the nations of the West to be warmed and illuminated by the rays of the Revelation of Bahá'u'lláh, soon after the proclamation of His Covenant on the morrow of His ascension.[64]

The allusion to what took place "soon after" may be a reference to the first public mention of the Bahá'í Faith in America, which took place during the World's First Parliament of Religions, held in Chicago in connection with the Columbian Exposition of 1893, commemorating the four-hundredth anniversary of the discovery of America.[65] The paper, entitled "The Religious Mission of the English Speaking Nations," was presented on September 23, 1893.[66] While the paper was written by the Reverend Henry Harris Jessup, D.D. (1832–1910), Director of Presbyterian Missionary Operations in North Syria, it was George A. Ford, a longtime missionary to Sidon (in Syria), who read the paper on Jessup's behalf. The paper was part of a full day of addresses on the theme "Criticism and Discussion of Missionary Method." [67] This historic public reference to the fledgling Bahá'í religion is as follows:

> In the palace of Behjeh, or Delight, just outside the fortress of Acre, on the Syrian coast, there died a few months since a famous Persian sage, the Babi Saint, named Behâ Allah—the "Glory of God"—the head of a vast reform party of Persian Moslems, who accept the New Testament as the Word of God and Christ as the deliverer of men, who regard all nations as one, and all men as brothers. Three years ago he was visited by a Cambridge scholar and gave utterances to sentiments so noble, so Christ-like, that we repeat them as our closing words:

"That all nations should become one in faith and all men as brothers; that the bonds of affection and unity between the sons of men should be strengthened; that diversity of religion should cease and differences of race be annulled; what harm is there in this? Yet so it shall be. These fruitless strifes, these ruinous wars shall pass away, and the 'Most Great Peace' shall come. Do not you in Europe need this also? Let not a man glory in this, that he loves his country; let him rather glory in this, that he loves his kind." [68]

America's future destiny was presaged by its finest moments in the past. Shoghi Effendi credits America with having played a preponderant role in both World Wars:

This nation, moreover, may well claim to have, as a result of its effective participation in both the first and second world wars, redressed the balance, saved mankind the horrors of devastation and bloodshed involved in the prolongation of hostilities, and decisively contributed, in the course of the latter conflict, to the overthrow of the exponents of ideologies fundamentally at variance with the universal tenets of our Faith. [69]

As favorable an estimate as this is, Shoghi Effendi elsewhere portends a fire by ordeal:

The American nation . . . will find itself purged of its anachronistic conceptions, and prepared to play a preponderating role, as foretold by 'Abdu'l-Bahá, in the hoisting of the standard of the Lesser Peace, in the unification of mankind, and in the establishment of a world federal government on this planet. These same fiery tribulations will not only firmly weld the American nation to its sister nations in both hemispheres, but will through their cleansing effect, purge it thoroughly of the accumulated dross which ingrained racial prejudice, rampant materialism, widespread ungodliness and moral laxity have combined, in the course of successive generations, to produce, and which have prevented her thus far from assuming the role of world spiritual leadership forecast by 'Abdu'l-Bahá's unerring pen—a role which she is bound to fulfill through travail and sorrow. [70]

Note that this "world spiritual leadership forecast by 'Abdu'l-Bahá's unerring pen" will only come about after America experiences upheaval and consequent social transformation. It will not come easily. It has to be earned. America has to learn the hard way. What has prevented America from assuming a spiritual leadership role is its "ingrained racial prejudice, rampant materialism, widespread ungodliness and moral laxity." Elsewhere, Shoghi Effendi revoices these same criticisms of America, which was "immersed in a sea of materialism, a prey to one of the most virulent and long-standing forms of racial prejudice, and notorious for its political corruption, lawlessness and laxity in moral standards." [71] These are retardant conditions that must first be palliated by equal and opposite conditions of racial harmony, spirituality, godliness, and moral rectitude. This is where religion in general, including the Bahá'í Faith, can and should act as a catalyst in the moral and spiritual regeneration of America as a precondition to its ability to live up to its destiny, in the Bahá'í view of it, described by Shoghi Effendi in this signal passage:

> Then, and only then, will the American nation ... be in a position to raise its voice in the councils of the nations, itself lay the cornerstone of a universal and enduring peace, proclaim the solidarity, the unity, and maturity of mankind, and assist in the establishment of the promised reign of righteousness on earth. Then, and only then, will the American nation, while the community of the American believers within its heart is consummating its divinely appointed mission, be able to fulfill the unspeakably glorious destiny ordained for it by the Almighty, and immortally enshrined in the writings of 'Abdu'l-Bahá. Then, and only then, will the American nation accomplish "that which will adorn the pages of history," "become the envy of the world and be blest in both the East and the West."[72]

While the destiny of America is well established in Bahá'í texts, one extended analysis of it is that of John Huddleston. As the International Monetary Fund's former chief of the Budget and Planning Division, British economist John Huddleston has contributed an analysis of the Destiny of America theme that runs through selected Bahá'í texts, such as those cited above.[73] According to Huddleston, "The Bahá'í view of the spiritual destiny of America is a logical development of the traditional American dream. It foresees a leadership role for America in the achievement of both the Lesser Peace and the Most Great Peace."[74]

The "Lesser Peace" and the "Most Great Peace" are Bahá'í terms that envision stages in the process of world peace, leading from the first efforts to covenant and codify international law to the full-blown emergence of world commonwealth of nations. The establishment of world peace will "be a gradual process" leading "at first to the establishment of that Lesser Peace which the nations of the earth, as yet unconscious of His Revelation and yet unwittingly enforcing the general principles which He has enunciated, will themselves establish."[75] The next stage is "the spiritualization of the masses, consequent to the recognition of the character, and the acknowledgement of the claims, of the Faith of Bahá'u'lláh."[76] This is "the essential condition" that will serve as the foundation for the "ultimate fusion of all races, creeds, classes, and nations."[77] On this foundation will the "Most Great Peace" be established. The Most Great Peace may be described as a future golden age in which "a world civilization be born, flourish, and perpetuate itself, a civilization with a fullness of life such as the world has never seen nor can as yet conceive." [78]

The Most Great Peace is not only about establishing a world common-wealth but is associated with establishing the Kingdom of God on earth, meaning the realization of Bahá'í principles and ideals throughout the world, and the emergence of the Bahá'í Faith as the world religion of the future. In so saying, a fundamental premise of the Faith is the "oneness of religion." This means that all of the major world religions (and others lost to history) are iter-ations of the one Faith of God—that is, all revealed religions, in their pristine forms, are reflections of eternal spiritual reality as suited to the needs of humanity from age to age. Under the corollary doctrine of "Progressive Revelation," the principles and teachings of the Bahá'í Faith are held to be ideally suited to this day and age, as well as into the foreseeable future. Fea-tures of the Most Great Peace will be highlighted at the end of this chapter.

In a cablegram dated April 26, 1942, Shoghi Effendi presaged America's lion's share in helping establish the Lesser Peace: "The great Republic of the West is inescapably swept into the swelling tide of the world tribulations, presaging the assumption of a preponderating share in the establishment of the anticipated Lesser Peace." [79] Exactly how this will come about is not clear: "The distance that the American nation has traveled since its formal and categoric repudiation of the Wilsonian ideal," writes Shoghi Effendi, alluding to Congress's refusal to join the League of Nations, is

> to every Bahá'í observer, viewing the developments in the international situa-tion, in the light of the prophecies of both Bahá'u'lláh and 'Abdu'l-Bahá, most significant, and highly instructive and encouraging. To trace the exact course which, in these troubled times and pregnant years, this nation will follow would be impossible.[80]

Yet there is a shared understanding among Bahá'ís as to America's capacity to assume a "preponderating share" in bringing the Lesser Peace into being.

America will also have a central role in bringing about the Most Great Peace, according to the Bahá'í view of the future. "Whatever the Hand of a beneficent and inscrutable Destiny has reserved for this youthful, this virile, this idealistic, this spiritually blessed and enviable nation ... ," Shoghi Effendi asserts, "we may, confident in the words uttered by 'Abdu'l-Bahá, feel assured that that great republic ... will continue to evolve, undivided and undefeatable, until the sum total of its contributions to the birth, the rise and the fruition of that world civilization, the child of the Most Great Peace and hallmark of the Golden Age of the Dispensation of Bahá'u'lláh, will have been made, and its last task discharged." [81]

These words are far more than prediction: they are spoken with religious conviction and with absolute confidence in their fruition.

"Indeed, the most important quality America brings to the world scene," Huddleston observes, "is its sheer capacity to get things done." [82] Even more significant than "American know-how" and its "can-do" capabilities is the historic quality of the American experience itself, and its moral impact on other countries. Huddleston notes the worldwide influence of the Civil Rights movement ("the spark that illumined the world") and how it has further prepared America for its world role: "In short, beyond the model of the US Constitution is an inheritance in the American political experience of an immense struggle to implement its true spirit through application of a systematic approach to human rights—an experience that is surely not matched in intensity by any other nation." [83] Shoghi Effendi articulates those distinctively American qualities that endow it with the capacity to realize its spiritual destiny:

> To the matchless position achieved by so preeminent a president [Woodrow Wilson] of the American Union, in a former period, at so critical a juncture in international affairs, must now be added the splendid initiative taken, in recent years by the American government, culminating in the birth of the successor of that League [the United Nations] in San Francisco, and the establishment of its permanent seat in the city of New York. Nor can the preponderating influence exerted by this nation in the councils of the world, the prodigious economic and political power that it wields, the prestige it enjoys, the wealth of which it disposes, the idealism that animates its people, her magnificent contribution, as a result of her unparalleled productive power, for the relief of human suffering and the rehabilitation of peoples and nations, be overlooked in a survey of the position which she holds, and which distinguishes her from her sister nations in both the new and old worlds.[84]

Note here the outspoken recognition of the outstanding qualities and capacities that America possesses: international influence, economic and political power, prestige, wealth, idealism, productivity, and altruism. And so, given these recognized qualities, capacities, and potentialities, the Bahá'í writings are remarkably clear in their vision of America's mission and destiny. There are, however, great challenges facing the American nation that Bahá'í texts directly address. These are social deficits the solution of which will directly impact America's moral authority in terms of its world role. Among these social ills is racism, which is as persistent and pervasive as it is historic. "Racism is the most challenging issue confronting America" is the opening sentence in *The Vision of Race Unity,* an official Bahá'í statement published in 1991. Racism, in Bahá'í analysis, is the original sin of America.

(Many historians would agree.) Race unity is therefore a key to America's social salvation.

The Vision of Race Unity statement integrates racial harmony with America's destiny, as the two are coefficient with each other:

> Aware of the magnitude and the urgency of the issue, we, the National Spiritual Assembly of the Bahá'ís of the United States, speaking for the entire U.S. Bahá'í community, appeal to all people of goodwill to arise without further delay to resolve the fundamental social problem of this country. We do so because of our feeling of shared responsibility, because of the global experience of the Bahá'í community in effecting racial harmony within itself, and because of the vision that the sacred scriptures of our Faith convey of the destiny of America.

Thus, throughout the United States, Bahá'ís actively promote a message of race unity, equality of women and men, and other teachings that can help make America a better place.

Religious communities are proper objects of scientific study, where their professions may literally be measured against their actual practices. Like other faith-communities, Bahá'ís have faith that an ideal can become real. The efficacy of these Bahá'í endeavors have been documented in several sociological studies, such as in the 2006 monograph, *The Equality of Women and Men: The Experience of the Bahá'í Community of Canada,* by Deborah K. van den Hoonaard, Canada Research Chair in Qualitative Research and Analysis at St. Thomas University, Fredericton, New Brunswick, and Will C. van den Hoonaard, Professor at the University of New Brunswick and author of *Walking the Tightrope: Ethical Issues for Qualitative Researchers.*[85] On the race relations front, doctoral research on the Bahá'í community of Atlanta, Georgia, revealed that "nearly one-fourth were black or African American," which is a significant demographic finding given the problem of self-segregation in American religious settings. The author of that study, a social scientist, observed that Bahá'í efforts to promote race unity in Atlanta "inform African American Bahá'ís in a way that Martin Luther King, Jr. or Malcolm X cannot."[86]

In fine, the destiny of America is to play a preponderating role in the political process of establishing the Lesser Peace, as well as to lead all nations spiritually in an evolutionary process culminating in the Most Great Peace and a great world civilization. This future golden age is spoken of in glorious terms by Shoghi Effendi, whose vision of it reads, in condensed part, as follows:

- The unity of the human race, as envisaged by Bahá'u'lláh, implies the establishment of a world commonwealth in which all nations, races, creeds and classes are closely and permanently united . . .

- This commonwealth must . . . consist of a world legislature . . .
- A world executive, backed by an international Force, will . . . apply the laws enacted by this world legislature . . .
- A world tribunal will adjudicate and deliver its compulsory and final verdict in all and any disputes that may arise . . .
- A mechanism of world inter-communication will be devised . . .
- A world metropolis will act as the nerve center of a world civilization . . .
- A world language . . . will be taught in the schools of all the federated nations as an auxiliary to their mother tongue.
- A world script, a world literature, a uniform and universal system of currency, of weights and measures . . . will simplify and facilitate intercourse and understanding among the nations . . .
- Science and religion, the two most potent forces in human life, will be reconciled, will cöoperate, and will harmoniously develop . . .
- The press will . . . cease to be mischievously manipulated by vested interests, whether private or public . . .
- The economic resources of the world will be organized . . . and the distribution of its products will be equitably regulated . . .
- Racial animosity and prejudice will be replaced by racial amity, understanding and cöoperation . . .
- The causes of religious strife will be permanently removed . . .
- The inordinate distinction between classes will be obliterated . . .
- Universal recognition of one God and . . . allegiance to one common Revelation —such is the goal towards which humanity, impelled by the unifying forces of life, is moving.[87]

One cannot be but struck by the sheer scope, grandeur, and maturity of this vision. It would appear that America—once successful in its mission to taking a leading role in bringing about world unity, which will develop in stages and progress as a gradual process—will gracefully become part of the framework of the world federation of nations that it has helped shape. A great catalyst in this process will be the burgeoning influence of Bahá'í principles that will further animate the progressive outlook of world leaders.

Obviously none of this will happen by magic. One might well ask: How will this noble vision ultimately be realized in the realm of the mundane? How will all this be expected to come about? The short, but not simple, answer is this: Beyond its emphasis on egalitarian social principles, the Bahá'í Faith's grand vision of world unity necessarily requires a human spiritual transformation at the levels of the individual and community is needed in order to put those principles into practice, involving "the spiritualization of human consciousness and the emergence of the global civilization." [88]

Overcoming racism and other social evils clearly requires both policy and personal change. Here, precept and praxis go hand-in-hand. Bahá'í principles of unity will be effective only to the degree that they are put into practice, both individually and collectively. The role of Bahá'ís in America is to purify the inward life of their own community, to assail the racism and other social evils in the American nation at large, and to offer in practice and principle the Bahá'í vision of world unity.[89] This is concurrent with the international relations role of America in establishing the Lesser Peace, a process that has little to do with Bahá'í efforts.

In the full-page display ad, "The Destiny of America and the Promise of World Peace," which appeared on page A29 in the *New York Times* on December 23, 2001,[90] the National Spiritual Assembly of the Bahá'ís of the United States quotes from a Bahá'í prayer for America, revealed by 'Abdu'l-Bahá, the full text of which is as follows:

O Thou kind Lord! This gathering is turning to Thee. These hearts are radiant with Thy love. These minds and spirits are exhilarated by the message of Thy glad-tidings. O God! Let this American democracy become glorious in spiritual degrees even as it has aspired to material degrees, and render this just government victorious. Confirm this revered nation to upraise the standard of the oneness of humanity, to promulgate the Most Great Peace, to become thereby most glorious and praiseworthy among all the nations of the world. O God! This American nation is worthy of Thy favors and is deserving of Thy mercy. Make it precious and near to Thee through Thy bounty and bestowal.[91]

Here, this Bahá'í "Prayer for America" envisions America's world role, which is "to upraise the standard of the oneness of humanity, to promulgate the Most Great Peace." In their complementary role as a spiritualizing and socially leavening influence, the American Bahá'ís—individually and collectively—strive to do their part in realizing this noble vision. As Bahá'í philosopher Alain Locke (1895–1954) has said:

America's democracy must begin at home with a spiritual fusion of all her constituent peoples in brotherhood, and in an actual mutuality of life. Until democracy is worked out in the vital small scale of practical human relations, it can never, except as an empty formula, prevail on the national or international basis. Until it establishes itself in human hearts, it can never institutionally flourish. Moreover, America's reputation and moral influence in the world depends on the successful achievement of this vital spiritual democracy within the lifetime of the present generation. (Material civilization alone does not safeguard the progress of a nation.) Bahá'í Principles and the leavening of our national life with their power, is to be regarded as the *salvation of democracy*. In this way only can the fine professions of American ideals be realized.[92]

CHAPTER 12

Conclusion: How Minority Faiths Redefined America's World Role

Religious institutions play only a modest, indirect role in the development and implementation of foreign policy. But as moral teachers and the bearers of ethical traditions, religious communities can help to structure debate and illuminate relevant moral norms. They can help to develop and sustain political morality by promoting moral reasoning and by exemplifying values and behaviors that are conducive to human dignity.

—Mark R. Amstutz (2001)[1]

The very notion that America has a world role has its roots in American exceptionalism. Journalist Michael Barone captured the logic of U.S. exceptionalism when he opened his article in the *U.S. News and World Report's* June 2004 special issue, *Defining America: Why the U.S. Is Unique,* with this oft-quoted line: "Every nation is unique, but America is the most unique."[2] Throughout American history and in recent world affairs, American exceptionalism—"the perception that the United States differs qualitatively from other developed nations, because of its unique origins, national credo, historical evolution, and distinctive political and religious institutions"[3]—has been a powerful myth indeed. It has functioned as a national creed. How that myth arose in the first place has much to do with the religious origins of America, beginning with the Puritans. How the myth of American exceptionalism has been defined—and will continue to be *redefined*—must also include the role of religious influences on competing social myths of American nationalism and nationhood. Not until the twentieth century, however, was the myth of American exceptionalism sufficient to define a world role for America beyond exemplarism and "democracy promotion."

It was President Woodrow Wilson—awarded the Nobel Peace Prize in 1919—who is almost universally recognized as having first defined America's world role geopolitically. "Woodrow Wilson . . . can be credited with having been the first to transform American exceptionalism into a universal public good," writes Edward Kolodziej, "to be enjoyed by all peoples as an outright gift of the American public and to harness American military and economic power to these global objectives of American-dictated world order." [4] On January 8, 1918, before a joint session of Congress, President Wilson formulated his celebrated "Fourteen Points" for a post–World War I settlement and the establishment of a stable world order. The fourteenth point of Wilson's visionary proposal called for the formation of a League of Nations: "A general association of nations must be formed under specific covenants for the purpose of affording mutual guarantees of political independence and territorial integrity to great and small states alike." [5] In 1919, however, Congress refused to ratify the Treaty of Versailles, despite an impassioned plea by President Wilson who invoked "the hand of God" at work in the creation of a League of Nations:

> It is thus that a new role and a new responsibility have come to this great Nation that we honor and which we would all wish to lift to yet higher levels of service and achievement. The stage is set, the destiny disclosed. It has come about by no plan of our conceiving, but by the hand of God, who led us into this way. It was of this that we dreamed at our birth. America shall in truth show the way. The light streams upon the path ahead, and nowhere else. [6]

Of the Treaty's 440 articles, the first 26 set forth the Covenant of the League of Nations. Wilson's plea for the United States to join the League of Nations, however, simply could not overcome the isolationism and narrowing nationalism of his day. Although Wilsonian internationalism has been seen as essentially nationalist by at least one major Wilson biographer,[7] President Wilson was arguably ahead of his time. In 1919, there was little by way of *religious* consensus in support of Wilson's personal vision. Later in the twentieth century, however, religious influence in favor of America's world role began to be felt.

As the twentieth century progressed, there was increasing receptivity to the idea that America ought to play a greater role in international affairs—indeed, that America was destined for it, as the global spread of fundamental American values could be instrumental in shaping an emerging world order. In this sense, American internationalism could be thought of as *American exceptionalism universalized.* The time was right. Indeed, the twentieth century was famously described as the "American Century" in 1941 by *Time* magazine publisher Henry Luce, who wrote:

AMERICA'S VISION OF OUR WORLD

What can we say and foresee about an American Century? . . . [W]hat internationalism have we Americans to offer? . . . It must be a sharing with all peoples of our Bill of Rights, our Declaration of Independence, our Constitution, our magnificent industrial products, our technical skills. It must be an internationalism of the people, by the people and for the people.[8]

There is no religious rhetoric here. But the vision of America's world role is expressed with religious conviction.

While religious influences have not had a direct impact on U.S. foreign policy subsequent to the doctrine of Manifest Destiny,[9] religious perspectives have played a part in what Donald White calls "consensus beliefs" and the American "consensus perception of world affairs." White notes the transformative power of a public sense of American national identity: "The origin of the American role in the world was dependent not only on material elements *but also on intangibles.*"[10] White credits the emergence of a belief in America's world role to the power of public consensus: "The United States began its world role because of a consensus in the society over internationalism."[11] White further explains:

The emergence of the world role of the United States in the twentieth century depended on the will of the people. The conversion to an international outlook among the leaders of government and society became accepted by the mass of people of different occupations, home towns, political parties, religions, ethnic groups, and races, who, though divided by their separate interests, adopted *unifying concepts* to bring them together in a collective worldview.[12]

What about the twenty-first century? Can minority faiths collectively provide intangible yet persuasive "consensus beliefs" regarding America's world role? To address this question, a review of the dynamics of religious visions —favored truths animated by the power of religious myths—is instructive. Religious myths and visions of America are essentially *unifying concepts* among the adherents of their respective faith-communities. As such, one can say that the essence of this book can be summed up in three words: *Religions remythologize America.* This summation would be more complete with these three additional words: *Religions re-envision America.* Put together, this book demonstrates that *religions remythologize and re-envision America.*

Here, the *way* in which religions remythologize and re-envision America requires further explanation. First, the reader will recall that "America" is a figment of the nationalistic imagination in that America is, at once, *nation and notion, country and creed, entity and ideology.* Thus the "idea of America," when religiously inspired, can give rise to a progressive religious nationalism that enriches American civil religion. To oversimplify, this is *Puritanism pluralized.*

However, all is not so bright and rosy in the mythic realm, insofar as America is concerned. Because of this historical and long-standing racial injustice, there are starkly pejorative visions of America as well. In the Nation of Islam, for instance, religious myths and visions of America are dark and foreboding, even catastrophic in outlook. Elijah Muhammad's and Louis Farrakhan's visions of the destruction of America—in an apocalyptic attack by the "Mother Wheel"—are menacing and chilling, not so much for their content as in the fact that people actually believe in the reality of these myths. Surprisingly, these scenarios have taken grip of the minds of not a few Black Muslims, who honestly *believe* these myths. (The present writer has personally met such individuals in Decatur and Springfield, Illinois, from 1997 to 2000.) In other words, these myths have imaginative reality. As a "true lie," the Mother Wheel myth may be understood and appreciated as a clarion call for America to make a renewed effort to promote racial justice and reconciliation in order to avert the further decay of American society.

This process of remythologizing is in evidence when racial and ethnic notions are brought into play. This study has shown that myths and visions of America can have a decidedly ethnic and racially referenced dimension. For instance, in Chapter 3, American exceptionalism was shown to have largely been the product of Anglo-Saxon ethnogenesis.[13] In other words, the greatness of America, expressed universally—under its nineteenth-century Protestant formulation—was a coded expression of Anglo-Saxon hubris, which, by virtue of the vaunted superiority of the White race, was decidedly exclusive. This overweening ethnonationalism represented a nativist expression of the dominant ethnicity.[14] This should come as no surprise really, for it is quite natural (although, by today's standards, not desirable) when one considers the relationship between ethnicities and nations, as Eric Kaufmann observes: "The nations of the world, almost without exception, were formed from ethnic cores, whose pre-modern myth–symbol complex furnished the material for the construction of the modern nation's boundary symbols and civil religion."[15] If nations—or, more precisely, nationalisms—were originally ethnic *constructions,* then it stands to reason that the *reconstruction* of nationalisms can be a function of subsequent multiethnic social realities.

From a certain perspective, racism in America can be seen as a historical consequence of privileging the Anglo-Saxon or White race as divinely destined to prosecute the Protestant mission to *conquer, colonize, and Christianize* the entire continent of North America, under the imperialist doctrine of

Manifest Destiny. While Manifest Destiny was, at one time, the prevailing vision of America as far as domestic and foreign policy was concerned, Manifest Destiny has since been discredited and is of historical interest only.

The subsequent history of the religious idea of America, therefore, can be analyzed, in part, as an evolution—protracted and painful—in the idea of the place of race and ethnicity in American life, *as religiously valued.* The evolution of American thought, with respect to the idea of America itself, is roughly a progression from religious—and often racial—particularism to universal inclusivism. That is to say, the religious idea of America represents a transformation of Protestant ethnoreligious homogeneity to multiethnic and multireligious plurality, reflecting a direct, albeit delayed and long-overdue, response to America's changing demography and religious landscape. Religious myths of America—true to changed historical circumstances and social dynamics—eventually give way to new myths and visions of America. The process of remythologizing therefore reflects progress in the social evolution of America.

This social evolution, in terms of the broadening mind-set it directionally represents, remains as incomplete as it is perhaps inevitable. To the extent that America succeeds, in time, in overcoming racial limitations will America's world role become a morally authentic enterprise. In that world microcosm and social laboratory known as "America," such a transformation of the American ideal is arguably a major consequence of the influence of minority faiths. The end result is the deconstruction of the Puritan and Anglo-Saxon sense of divine election, but without devaluing the essential mission of America to become a "city upon a hill"—that is, as an exemplary society that may serve as a social model for other societies to emulate.

Religions remythologize America to the degree that the old myths are rendered obsolete when new myths of America take their place. Generally speaking, one can say that, over time, religious myths and visions of America are largely products of their respective times and places. Within a given religious tradition, there will be change over time, in what Americanists regard as the evolution of American thought. These new myths, therefore, conform to new modes of thinking and valuation as a function of the evolution of American thought.

RELIGIOUS MYTHS AND VISIONS OF AMERICA RECAPITULATED

If lessons are to be drawn from American history and thought, then what significance, it may be asked, do religious myths and visions of America have for Americans today? Recall that historian James Moorhead had suggested that the Protestant myth of America—America's master myth—has been reshaped by minority faiths: "But the point is that minority faiths themselves played no small part in the weakening of white Protestant hegemony. Their creativity in adapting and reinterpreting the symbols of American destiny broadened the framework of discourse within which citizens explained national identity." [16] Within this wider framework of discourse, new religious voices are heard and fresh perspectives are gained. In one sense, the wider framework of discourse of which Moorhead speaks implicates the end result: a universalizing of America's founding principles of equality and egalitarianism, as applied to all of America's constituents.

Of primary interest in this book has been America's "world role." By "world role," as previously stated, is simply meant *the part that America should play in world affairs.* It is time to bring America's world role, from the perspective of minority faiths, into sharper focus, and, perhaps, to take the "latest and greatest" expressions of those perspectives as exemplary. As the times change, so do religions. Therefore, this concluding chapter will recapitulate the more recent visions of America's world role, as respectively held by the minority faiths treated in the preceding pages, with reference also to contemporary Protestant visions of America.

Native American Myths and Visions of America

The original myths and visions of America were from Native Americans themselves, as exemplified by the Iroquois version of the Turtle Island Myth and by the pan-Indian Myth of "Mother Earth." Thus it is clear that religious myths and visions of America have existed ever since the colonial period and, in the case of the Iroquois myth of "Turtle Island," in the precontact period as well. The pan-Native American myth of Mother Earth, in fact, is a somewhat later development, and there is a very real sense in which the Mother Earth myth actually remythologizes the Turtle Island myth by transforming it from a nature-referenced narrative into a more environmentally value-laden perspective. Both myths are nature-based, to be sure, but the Mother Earth myth is more ecologically conscious because it was promoted and popularized as such in the course of its development.

As we are now in the "age of ecology," the "Turtle Island" myth itself is currently one of the great cultural symbols of nature-conscious environmentalism, as is the myth of "Mother Earth." These symbols have been absorbed by American popular culture quite apart from the original Native American context. Both "Turtle Island" and "Mother Earth" are ways of sacralizing (making sacred) the physical environment, or promoting a nature-inclusive spirituality. Because these nature myths have been so successfully and ubiquitously popularized, they now play a conceptual and symbolic role in "greening" other religions in order to promote respect for the environment and inculcate environmentally beneficent behaviors among their adherents.

This process has been called the "greening-of-religions phenomenon"[17] and the infusing of "environmental ethics" into traditional religious worldviews.[18] As one illustrative example of the renewed cross-cultural identification of "Turtle Island" with North America, consider poet Gary Snyder's reworking of the America's "Pledge of Allegiance":

> I pledge allegiance to the soil of Turtle Island, and to the beings who thereon dwell one ecosystem in diversity under the sun With joyful interpenetration for all.[19]

In 1975, Snyder's 1974 collection of poems, *Turtle Island,* won the Pulitzer Prize for Poetry in 1975. The assimilation of the myth (or at least the concept) of Turtle Island (as well as Mother Earth) is a testament to the revitalization and contemporary relevance of a Native American religious myth. Extrapolating from this myth, one can say that, from a Native American religious perspective, America's world role is to promote environmental ethics and ecological sustainability.

The Iroquois Confederacy is generally acknowledged as the first New World democracy. Given this priority in time, the Iroquois myth (or, because of its acknowledged historicity, the "legend") of Deganawidah may have had some influence on the shaping of the American republic, although this remains controversial, as the Iroquois Influence Thesis continues to be debated. Is it myth or history? The answers, either way, continue to be hotly contested. Notwithstanding, the reader will recall that, on October 4, 1988, the U.S. House of Representatives passed H.Con.Res. 331—*A concurrent resolution to acknowledge the contribution of the Iroquois Confederacy of Nations to the development of the United States Constitution and to reaffirm the continuing government-to-government relationship between Indian tribes and the United States established in the Constitution*—by a vote of 408–8. By voice vote, the Senate agreed to H.Con.Res. 331 on October 21, 1988. That Congressional resolution reads, in part:

> Whereas the original framers of the Constitution, including, most notably, George Washington and Benjamin Franklin, are known to have greatly admired the concepts of the six Nations of the Iroquois Confederacy; Whereas, the Confederation of the original Thirteen Colonies into one republic was influenced by the political system developed by the Iroquois Confederacy as were many of the democratic principles which were incorporated into the Constitution itself; . . . *Resolved by the House of Representatives (the Senate concurring)*, That—(1) the Congress, on the occasion of the two hundredth anniversary of the signing of the United States Constitution, acknowledges contribution made by the Iroquois Confederacy and other Indian Nations to the formation and development of the United States.[20]

The reader will also recall that, in 2007, U.S. Representative Joe Baca and U.S. Senator Daniel Inouye, respectively, introduced H.R. 3585 and S. 1852 to the House and Senate, to wit: *Native American Heritage Day Act of 2007,* "A bill to designate the Friday after Thanksgiving of each year as 'Native American Heritage Day' in honor of the achievements and contributions of Native Americans to the United States." This proposed legislation, in its current draft, acknowledges the contribution of the Iroquois League of Nations. This draft resolution reads, in part: "Congress finds that . . . the Founding Fathers based the provisions of the Constitution on the unique system of democracy of the six Nations of the Iroquois Confederacy, which divided powers among the branches of government and provided for a system of checks and balances." [21] Here, it can definitely be said that "the mystique of Iroquois unity and power had taken on a life of its own." [22] That the Iroquois influence myth has indeed taken on a life of its own, as the Congressional resolution clearly illustrates, is noted by one scholar so: "Despite the highly speculative nature of the evidence, this misconception has become a shibboleth, one which has been given even the official imprimatur of the United States Senate (United States Congress, Senate Resolution No. 76 [Washington, D.C.: U.S.G.P.O., 1988])." [23] From this, it can be extrapolated that the Iroquois vision of America is the promotion of the democratic way of life worldwide, in the interests of peace.

Protestant Myths and Visions of America

Today, there are largely liberal expressions of Protestant Christianity that seek to apply Christian principles to the social problems of the day. The idea that Protestant ethics, as it were, can be usefully implemented to improve social conditions can certainly be traced back to the Puritan origins of present-day America. As presented in Chapter 3, the Puritans established what has come to be regarded as the foundational myth of America. Their vision generated the greater—and perhaps grander—Protestant master myth of America: "The Puritans provided the scriptural basis for what we have come to call the myth of America." [24] Mimicking the style of the prologue of the Gospel of John, the famed Americanist Sacvan Bercovitch characterizes the Puritan myth of America so: "*In the beginning was the word, 'America,' and the word was in the Bible, and the word was made flesh in the Americans, this new breed of humans, destined to build a shining city upon a hill.*" [25] Here, Bercovitch's reference to "city upon a hill" alludes to the first definitive Puritan discourse on America, "A Modell of Christian Charity" (1630), which is John Winthrop's speech to his fellow Puritans aboard the *Arbella,* on its voyage across the Atlantic to the Massachusetts coast. This homily was destined to become one of the most powerful, pervasive, and persistent visions of America—the doctrine of American exceptionalism.

Generally, American exceptionalism sees America as a favored nation with a world mission. The Puritans were the first exponents of American exceptionalism. This Puritan myth has five key ideographs: liberty, egalitarianism, individualism, populism, and laissez-faire.[26] These are *civic* American values. There are also *religious* American values, as expressed in ideographs that represent myths. Perhaps the best example of this is John Winthrop's celebrated ideograph: "Wee shall be as a Citty upon a Hill, the Eies of all people are uppon us."[27] Thus, in 1630, the Puritans constructed a national identity out of their own sense of uniqueness—that is, the Puritans aspired to establish a model society that would serve as a moral exemplar for the world to emulate. Thus, with respect to the Puritan Myth of America, it can be inferred that America's "world role" (although not expressed in those terms), was to be an exemplar society for all the world to behold, admire, and emulate.

For the vanquished, at least, the "Manifest Destiny" Myth was a perversion of the Puritan Myth of America. While some may say that Manifest Destiny is now disguised as hegemonic interests by the world's only superpower, it has long since been discredited. And while the legacy of "Jim Crow" racism persists in socially subtler forms, the "Curse of Ham" Myth has fallen by the wayside as a discarded myth as well. America's social sea change from Protestantism to pluralism and from racialism to interracialism, although demographically uneven and institutionally incomplete, was greatly catalyzed by the civil rights movement, which had social implications not only for America but also for the world. The social significance of the civil rights movement for the world at large was best articulated by Dr. Martin Luther King, Jr. in his prophetic vision of "The World House":

> This is the great new problem of mankind. We have inherited a large house, a great "world house" in which we have to live together—black and white, Easterner and Westerner, Gentile and Jew, Catholic and Protestant, Moslem and Hindu—a family unduly separated in ideas, culture and interest, who, because we can never again live apart, must learn somehow to live with each other in peace. . . . The large house in which we live demands that we transform this world-wide neighborhood into a world-wide brotherhood.[28]

While Dr. King's promotion of a "world-wide brotherhood" within the "World House" is not representative, much less central, to Protestantism in America generally, it remains as arguably the most prophetic Protestant vision of America. Complementing this world-encompassing vision is America's mission at home: "King believed that the mission of American Protestantism was not merely to make Christians of all Americans, but to

Christianize America." [29] Perhaps this reading of King is too narrow, in that King's metaphor of the "World House" is a panoramic vision of interfaith ecumenism.

One of the latest reformulations of Puritan providentialism is Stephen H. Webb's 2004 book, *American Providence: A Nation with a Mission*.[30] *American Providence* is arguably the finest "theology of America" published in recent years. Webb, professor of religion and philosophy at Wabash College, argues that all of history—and the history of each and every nation—should be interpreted providentially. Regarding America itself, Webb holds that God has chosen America, above and beyond all other nations, for a special mission: to complete the Great Commission (spread of the message of Christ throughout the world) by promoting political freedom (that is, the freedom of religion whereby people can freely become Christians) and evangelical Christianity. It is not America *per se* that is intrinsically significant, but its capacity to incarnate Christian virtues within a social order: "The significance of America has to do with what it believes in, not what it is. America is the dream that faith and freedom can be mutually reinforcing within a given social order." [31] Although America has a providential mission and destiny, it is Webb's conviction that Christianity has an even greater destiny in that it will emerge as the world religion of the future: "The destiny of Christianity, however, is much greater than the destiny of America. . . . Christians believe only one globalism will triumph in the end—and that it will be a globalism of the one true God." [32]

Catholic Myths and Visions of America

Although the Americanist Myth of America was put to an abrupt end by Pope Leo XIII, its legacy continues—not as infallible Catholic doctrine promulgated *ex cathedra*—but as edifying papal *dicta*. Recall that, on April 17, 2008, Pope Benedict XVI said to America:

> Today, in classrooms throughout the country, young Christians, Jews, Muslims, Hindus, Buddhists, and indeed children of all religions sit side-by-side, learning with one another and from one another. This diversity gives rise to new challenges that spark a deeper reflection on the core principles of a democratic society. May others take heart from your experience, realizing that a united society can indeed arise from a plurality of peoples—"*E pluribus unum*": "out of many, one"—provided that all recognize religious liberty as a basic civil right.[33]

Here, Pope Benedict XVI has charged America with the task of promoting "religious liberty as a basic civil right," in the hope that other nations will be inspired by the American model and establish freedom of religion in their own respective societies.

The reader will also recall how, on January 27, 2004, Pope John Paul II received Vice President Dick Cheney, who represented President George W. Bush, and said to him:

> Mr. Vice President, . . . I encourage you and your fellow-citizens to work, at home and abroad, *for the growth of international cooperation and solidarity in the service of that peace which is the deepest aspiration of all men and women.* Upon you and all the American people I cordially invoke the abundant blessings of Almighty God.[34]

No more explicit mandate could be given to America. In a word, America's world role is to promote Catholic values and principles of social justice, at home and abroad.

Jewish Myths and Visions of America

One of the significant findings of this book is that American Judaism, generally speaking, has fully embraced American values. What Jonathan Sarna calls the "cult of synthesis" might be more positively characterized as a "grand synthesis" of American Judaism and Americanism. Having reviewed the Jewish myth of America as "The Promised Land" and the Jewish "Myth of Columbus" as well, the reader will appreciate how Orthodox, Conservative, Reform, and Reconstructionist Judaism's respective myths and visions of America express elements of "Jewish Americanism" as part of a social phenomenon that Jonathan Sarna calls the "Cult of Synthesis." [35] In a very real and practical sense, Jewish Americanism functioned as an ideal survival strategy. Adoption of American values and the enjoyment of protection under the American system of fundamental rights and civil liberties had its advantages, not only for American Judaism at large, but for distinct communities within American Judaism. The American tradition of religious freedom operates to safeguard religious pluralism within American Judaism itself.

Take Reform Judaism, for instance. Founded in 1889, the Central Conference of American Rabbis (CCAR) is the organized rabbinate (body of rabbis) for Reform Jews in America. In a December 1988 *responsa,* the CCAR declared: "We must now deal with this new state of affairs and support unity and pluralism." [36] While this is in reference to the divisions within Judaism itself, the principle doubtless generalizes to society as a whole. The reader will recall that the term, "cultural pluralism"—which, of course, adumbrates religious pluralism—was coined by Jewish philosopher Horace Kallen, in conversation with Alain Locke (first African American Rhodes Scholar, "Dean of the Harlem Renaissance," and "Bahá'í philosopher") at Oxford

University in 1907. Pluralism maintains the continued viability of Orthodox, Conservative, Reform, and Reconstructionist Judaism within America, and has been offered as a model for the State of Israel to emulate.

As for America's world role, this is perhaps best expressed in the Jewish prayer for America, composed by Louis Ginzberg:

> May this land, under your providence, be an influence for good throughout the world, uniting all people in peace and freedom—helping them to fulfill the vision of your prophet: "Nation shall not lift up sword against nation, neither shall they experience war any more" (Isaiah 2:4). And let us say: Amen.[37]

Here is a call for America and its people to promote "peace and freedom" throughout the world, in order to make Isaiah's future vision a present reality.

Mormon Myths and Visions of America

Of the minority faiths treated in this book, Mormonism arguably has the richest array of America-centered myths. Chapter 6 treated the Mormon Garden of Eden Myth, the Lost Tribes Myth, the Columbus Myth, the Constitution Myth, the Founding Fathers Myth, the Theodemocracy Myth, the America as Zion Myth, and the Mark of Cain Myth. The Garden of Eden was not in the Euphrates Valley of the Old World, but rather in the Mississippi Valley of the New World. From prehistory to modern history, Mormon scriptures present an exalted vision of America. "And for this purpose have I established the Constitution of this land," states the Book of Mormon, "by the hands of wise men whom I raised up unto this very purpose," [38] in reference to America's Founding Fathers. This short prayer for America is scriptural: "Have mercy, O Lord, upon all the nations of the earth; have mercy upon the rulers of our land; may those principles, which were so honorably and nobly defended, namely, the Constitution of our land, by our fathers, be established forever." [39] Of these, the Theodemocracy Myth is the one most directly concerned with good governance. Taken together, these Mormon myths synthesize and mythologize distinctively American values, within a complex of equally distinctive Mormon values. These myths are not relics; they are alive and well. The Mark of Cain Myth, however, has been abandoned, although not officially repudiated.

America remains an exalted place, a chosen nation, in the Mormon worldview. As "the land of promise," [40] America has been "lifted up by the power of God above all other nations, upon the face of the land which is choice above all other lands." [41] Indeed, Brigham Young envisioned America's place in the future golden age to come: "When the day comes in which the Kingdom of God will bear rule, the flag of the United States will proudly flutter unsullied on the flagstaff of liberty and equal rights, without a spot to sully its fair surface."[42] This, generally, may be seen as America's world role, in Brigham Young's conception of it, to promote "liberty and equal rights."

Christian Identity Myths and Visions of America

The Christian Identity movement is the name attached to what may be described as White nationalism's collective theology, as promoted by a loosely organized network of white supremacist groups whose presence is primarily maintained in cyberspace on various Internet sites. In Chapter 7, the Two-Seed Myth, the Mud Races Myth, the Lost Tribes Myth, the White Homeland Myth, and the Racial Holy War Myth were presented. In "The Role of Religion in the Collective Identity of the White Racialist Movement," Iowa State University sociologist Betty A. Dobratz observes that, because the White supremacist movement actually has three competing religions—Christian Identity, the World Church of the Creator (anti-Christian), and neo-pagan Odinism—there is no definitive religious expression of that movement. "Religion could be a crucial ingredient in a group's identity when the group shares a distinctive religion," Dobratz writes. "However, in this movement, various religious beliefs are competing, and no one common belief has emerged."[43] In other words, Christian Identity myths, while distinctive, are not necessarily definitive. To the extent that the Christian Identity movement can be said to have a unified vision of America, it follows that America's "world role," if any, is to preserve the purity of the White race and to establish a Whites-only homeland. In its failure to dissociate Whiteness from Christianity, Christian Identity represents the extreme of religio-racial mythologizing, in the very antithesis of Christian universalism.

Black Muslim Myths and Visions of America

Like the Mark of Cain Myth in Mormonism, the Yacub Myth, the Mother Plane Myth, and the Destruction of America Myth have largely been abandoned, although not repudiated. The Nation of Islam, predicated on Black nationalism, formerly entailed what is fair to characterize as "religious racism." But times are changing, and, over the course of the past three and a half decades, Louis Farrakhan has changed considerably himself.

In his 1993 chapter, "A Vision for America," Louis Farrakhan proclaimed that America, although not the land of promise for African Americans, had the potential to become so: "The Kingdom of God is an egalitarian kingdom structured on truth, where each of us will be treated with fairness and justice. America could become the basis for the Kingdom of God."[44] America, although a professedly Christian country, has "missed the message of Christ, or has yet to receive His true message." [45] This can be achieved, according to Farrakhan, by "righteousness, justice and peace," which, when practiced, can "form the basis of the Kingdom of God on earth." [46] However "egalitarian" this message may sound, however, there is a catch. In 2007, in an interview with *The Final Call* newspaper (an official Nation of Islam publication), Farrakhan was asked:

> After Saviours' Day 2007, you delivered a series of spiritual messages under the general title of "One Nation Under God," culminating with your message "Come Out of Her, My People" delivered at the 12th Anniversary Commemoration of the Million Man March on Oct. 16, 2007 in Atlanta, Ga. What is your statement to Black America about the significance and prophetic meaning of these messages for our survival?

Farrakhan's answer, although surprising at first to outsiders, should ultimately come as no surprise, given his long-standing patterns of thinking:

> Allah (God) knows that we need prayer, but if we don't separate from an enemy bent on our destruction, prayer alone will not help us to survive. The Honorable Elijah Muhammad points out to us in the scriptures of Bible and Qur'an that the day has arrived for our separation, and the enemy has used integration as a hypocritical trick to make those of us who have been under his foot for 400 years think that our 400-year-old enemy has all of a sudden become our friend. We must wake up to the time and what must be done in such a time. *It is not a time for integration; it is a time for us to separate from our former slave-masters* and their children and go for self, do for self, and build a Nation under the Guidance of Almighty God.[47]

Farrakhan maintains "there can be no peace between us and our former slave masters and their children as long as we do not go along with the status quo. When we demand Justice, Freedom and Equity, we excite the worst in our slave masters and their children." [48] Speaking of recent hate crimes committed in 2007 "throughout America by evil White people bent on teaching us a lesson," Farrakhan warns: "We must unite or suffer the consequences, for these events are going to multiply at such a pace that every Black person in America will see the face of a beast that has been masquerading as a friend." [49] To make matters worse, Farrakhan still adheres to a Jewish conspiracy theory. In the same 2007 interview, Farrakhan said that "the Zionists have worked their way into control in America, Britain, France, Germany and other countries of the world." [50] As for America itself, in 2007 Farrakhan predicted, in his "absence" (presumably after his death) "you see the horrors of the fall of this Great Mystery Babylon—the United States of America." [51] Farrakhan, and therefore the Nation of Islam that is still under his shadow, holds a deeply conflicted vision of America, inauthentically promulgated in the name of the religion of Islam—to the extent that religious racism devalues the polished rhetoric of faith-based egalitarianism.

Contemporary Muslim Myths and Visions of America

Before all else, it is important to point out that there is no single Muslim perspective on America. Notwithstanding this fact, America receives considerable criticism from abroad, as the "Great Satan" Myth amply demonstrates. That myth was answered by the opposite and equal "Axis of Evil" counter-myth. In other words, the arrow quickly flew back at the archer, so to speak. The result is reciprocal demonization. Quite expectedly, the Great Satan Myth has created problems for Muslims in America. Is an American Muslim somehow "satanic" by virtue of being a citizen of the "Great Satan"? Reciprocally, are Americans to understand that Islam, as understood in the contemporary Muslim world, intrinsically anti-America? The answer to both rhetorical questions is obviously negative. However, largely as a consequence of American foreign policy considerations, American Muslims are as conflicted about America as they are diverse with respect to their range of "responses to modernity," as discussed in Chapter 9. By no stretch of the imagination does Radical Islamism represent mainstream Islam. Yet one would hardly reach this conclusion if based on what the popular media represents.

As the "Great Satan," America has no positive world role from the Radical Islamist perspective. While the "Axis of Evil" counter-myth does imbue America with a world role in promoting democracy and freedom in the Middle East and around the world, this vision arises out of a context completely foreign to the Muslim world. Efforts to dispel the "Great Satan" Myth and to minimize the fallout from the "Axis of Evil" Myth are focused primarily on the issue of whether America is anti-Islamic or pro-Islamic. As such, America has no positive role even from a moderate Islamic perspective. Might America have a world role from the perspective of "Progressive Islam"?

The most vocal proponent of Progressive Islam is Omid Safi, associate professor of Islamic Studies and Director of Middle East and Islamic Studies at Colgate University, in Hamilton, New York. Co-chair for the Study of Islam Section at the American Academy of Religion, Dr. Safi has edited the 2003 multiauthor work, *Progressive Muslims: On Justice, Gender, and Pluralism.*[52] Progressive Islam is defined, in part, as follows:

> Progressive Muslims espouse a critical and non-apologetic "multiple critique" with respect to both Islam and modernity. They are undoubtedly postmodern in

the sense of their critical approach to modernity. That double engagement with the varieties of Islam and modernity, plus an emphasis on concrete social action and transformation, is the defining characteristic of progressive Islam today.[53]

As for Safi and the Progressive Muslim movement, there has been some debate about the group in its blurring the line between academic and confessional.[54] Does Safi represent the voices of academics or of "Progressive Muslims" themselves?

"Progressive *ijtihád* (reasoning)" is the hallmark of the movement. As a "global phenomenon," Shafi distances himself and the movement from any explicit association with America, as it "would be a clear mistake to somehow reduce the emergence of progressive Islam to being a new 'American Islam.' "[55] Shafi points to the fact that "Progressive Muslims are found everywhere in the global Muslim *umma* [community]."[56] Because "almost all progressive Muslims are profoundly skeptical of nationalism," they "instinctively and deliberately reject" and attempt to "transform it into an 'American Islam' commodity to be exported all over the world."[57] They also studiously avoid "appropriation by the United States' administration, which has used the language of reforming Islam to justify its invasion of Muslim countries such as Iraq."[58] Proponents of Progressive Islam "promise of ushering in a real paradigm shift in the relationship of Muslims to both Islam and modernity."[59] Even so, Progressive Islam has not defined a world role for America. To do so would be to defeat the universal outlook and scope of Progressive Islam as a reform movement within the contemporary Muslim world itself.

Buddhist Myths and Visions of America

Apart from Robert Thurman's "ten planks" as presented in an appendix in his Buddhist manifesto, *Inner Revolution,* and beyond Daisaku Ikeda's vision of the "Second American Renaissance" as heralded in *Songs for America,* what unifies the visions of the Dalai Lama, Robert Thurman, and Ikeda is the goal of establishing democracy on the order of enlightenment principles. According to one commentator, "Buddhist Democracy refers to a parliamentary democracy in which every individual has been awakened to the Principles of Buddhism."[60] While there is a great difference between Soka Gakkai and Tibetan Buddhism, both are agreed that democracy, enlightened by Buddhist precepts and praxis, combine to form the most potentially ideal form of governance for the world.

In 1991, the Dalai Lama, who has promoted the concept of a "Buddhist Democracy" among his fellow Tibetans, said that "America has the potential to make this world straight."[61] By this, he meant America's world role—

primarily economically and politically. In 1995, the Dalai Lama further elaborated:

> The United States must not underestimate its role in the world today. As Americans you should be proud of your heritage, proud of the values upon which your Constitution is based. Accordingly, you should not shirk from your responsibility to bring those same fundamental rights and freedoms to people living under totalitarian regimes.[62]

America's world role, therefore, is to promote enlightened democracy.

Bahá'í Myths and Visions of America

The Bahá'í Emancipation/Civil War Myth and the Bahá'í Wilsonian Myth are retrospective perspectives within the Bahá'í vision of the destiny of America—which vision is primarily prospective in that it is forward-looking, focusing on America's world role in promoting world unity. The Bahá'í Faith defines a world role for America, which is to play a leadership role in creating an emancipatory future for societies globally. However, the Bahá'í religion studiously eschews any involvement in partisan politics, which is seen as fundamentally divisive. Bahá'ís are therefore apolitical, while working with "the body politic" in trying to broaden and heighten "the consciousness of the oneness of mankind": "In every Dispensation, the light of Divine Guidance has been focused upon one central theme," writes 'Abdu'l-Bahá. "In this wondrous Revelation, this glorious century, the foundation of the Faith of God and the distinguishing feature of His Law is the consciousness of the Oneness of Mankind."[63] One particular Bahá'í text develops specific reasons for the spiritual leadership that America has the opportunity and, in a sense, the moral obligation to exercise:

> On the other hand is a nation that has achieved undisputed ascendancy in the entire Western Hemisphere, whose rulers have been uniquely honored by being collectively addressed by the Author of the Bahá'í Revelation in His Kitáb-i-Aqdas; which has been acclaimed by 'Abdu'l-Bahá as the "home of the righteous and the gathering-place of the free,"[64] where the "splendors of His light shall be revealed, where the mysteries of His Faith shall be unveiled"[65] and belonging to a continent which, as recorded by that same pen, "giveth signs and evidences of very great advancement,"[66] whose "future is even more promising,"[67] whose "influence and illumination are far-reaching,"[68] and which "will lead all nations spiritually."[69] Moreover, it is to this great republic of the West that the Center of the Covenant of Bahá'u'lláh has referred as the nation that has "developed powers and capacities greater and more wonderful than other nations,"[70] and which "is equipped and empowered to accomplish that

which will adorn the pages of history, to become the envy of the world, and be blest in both the East and the West for the triumph of its people." [71] It is for this same American democracy that He expressed His fervent hope that it might be "the first nation to establish the foundation of international agreement," "to proclaim the unity of mankind," and "to unfurl the Standard of the Most Great Peace," [72] that it might become "the distributing center of spiritual enlightenment, and all the world receive this heavenly blessing," [73] and that its inhabitants might "rise from their present material attainments to such a height that heavenly illumination may stream from this center to all the peoples of the world." [74] It is in connection with its people that He has affirmed that they are "indeed worthy of being the first to build the Tabernacle of the Great Peace and proclaim the oneness of mankind." [75]

This is a remarkably visionary statement. Observe how Shoghi Effendi's vision of America goes far beyond a nationalistic civil religion. This vision transcends national boundaries, overleaps vested national interests, and addresses the interests of the widest "body politic"—the planet Earth itself.[76] In addition to the Bahá'í Faith's emphasis on egalitarian social principles, a human spiritual transformation at the levels of the individual and community is needed in order to put those principles into practice. Overcoming racism and other social evils clearly requires both policy and personal change. Here, precept and praxis go hand-in-hand. Bahá'í principles of unity will be effective only to the degree that they are put into practice, both individually and collectively.

Among the American Bahá'ís, it may be said that the Bahá'í community has its counterpart of Dr. Martin Luther King, Jr. in Bahá'í philosopher Dr. Alain Leroy Locke (1885–1954). Of Locke, Martin Luther King himself said: "We're going to let our children know that the only philosophers that lived were not Plato and Aristotle, but W. E. B. Du Bois and Alain Locke came through the universe." [77] Interestingly, Locke developed a philosophy of democracy in nine dimensions. Locke's grand (though not systematic) theory of democracy sequenced local, moral, political, economic, and cultural stages of democracy as they arced through history, with racial, social, spiritual, and world democracy completing the trajectory. Adjunct notions of natural, practical, progressive, creative, intellectual, equalitarian democracy crystallized the paradigm. Seeing America as "a unique social experiment," Locke's larger goal was to "Americanize Americans" [78] and to further democratize democracy itself with the simple yet profound message that equality is the bedrock of democracy: "Eventually, however, just as world-mindedness must dominate and remould [sic] nation-mindedness, so we must transform eventually race-mindedness into human-mindedness." [79]

The Bahá'í perspective on the destiny of America is a singular example of how minority religions, as James Moorhead rightly observed, have contributed and can presently consecrate their own religious myths of and visions of America for the social benefit of America as a whole.

AN OVERVIEW OF AMERICA'S WORLD ROLE

In the chart below, America's world role—as defined by Protestantism and as redefined by the minority faiths treated in this book—presents a convenient, albeit oversimplified, representation of the results of the investigation conducted over the course of this book. The reader will note points of convergence among the more progressive minority faiths, where America, ideally, would serve as a particular instrument of a universal purpose. Here, the very notion of Manifest Destiny (the right of America to *conquer, colonize, and Christianize* the continent of North America) is replaced by a concept of what might be thought of as a "common destiny"—an overarching, cosmopolitan worldview. This is perhaps best seen in a conspectus of the various visions of America's world role as recapitulated in Table 12.1.

FINAL REFLECTIONS: A WORLD CIVIL RELIGION?

Is there some larger significance to the existence of these myths and visions of America? Without wishing to state the obvious, the religious myths and visions surveyed here deal with some of the perennial problematics in the American experience. They operate as social commentaries on the realities of American life, especially as measured against the ideals of American civil religion—which is where these myths intersect in the public sphere and in civil discourse. These religious myths and visions of America present a full range of mythic and ideological possibilities. To the extent that myths are vehicles of social truths (and thus function as "true lies" [80]), the myths themselves may be compared. From this comparison, certain salient characteristics will fall into focus, which will be briefly touched on here.

Taking an inventory of the ten religions covered in this book, two negative themes stand out: *racial prejudice and religious prejudice.* The obvious examples of these are the religions presented back-to-back in Chapters 7 and 8, that is, Christian Identity and the Nation of Islam. Christian Identity has always been considered radical, and it can never become mainstream. Its proposed homeland (the Northwest Imperative) is, in a sense, the logical outcome of Identity's Two-Seed Myth, the Mud Races Myth, the Lost Tribes Myth, and the Racial Holy War Myth.

In somewhat the same way as Identity represents an extreme form of white nationalism, the Nation of Islam is a species of Black nationalism, as the Black Muslim Yacub Myth, Mother Plane Myth, and the Destruction of America Myth bear out. However, their functional parallelism is a case of

Table 12.1   America's World Role as Defined by Protestantism and Minority Faiths

MINORITY FAITH	AMERICA'S WORLD ROLE
Native American Religion	To promote environmental ethics and ecological sustainability throughout "Turtle Island" and beyond. In the heritage of Deganawidah, to advance global democracy in the interests of world peace.
Protestantism	To promote originally Puritan values of liberty, egalitarianism, individualism, populism, and laissez-faire. To promote global democracy. To promote "worldwide brotherhood," as expressed by Dr. Martin Luther King's vision of "the World House."
Catholicism	To promote "religious liberty as a basic civil right." To foster "the growth of international cooperation and solidarity in the service of that peace."
Judaism	To promote unity and pluralism "uniting all people in peace and freedom."
Mormon	To promote liberty and equal rights. To strengthen the foundation of society by fostering family values.
Christian Identity	To preserve the purity of the White race. To establish a Whites-only homeland.
Nation of Islam	To realize America's potential to become the "Kingdom of God on earth"—"an egalitarian kingdom structured on truth, where each . . . will be treated with fairness and justice." However: "It is not a time for integration; it is a time for us to separate from our former slave-masters." (2008)
Contemporary Islam	Radical Islamism: No positive world role for America. (Progressive Islam: No definitive world role for America.)
Buddhism	To "bring those same fundamental rights and freedoms to people living under totalitarian regimes" and "to make this world straight." (Dalai Lama) To cultivate "a renaissance and enlightenment science [of] our times." (Robert Thurman) To promote a "Buddhist Democracy." (Dalai Lama, Thurman, Ikeda)
Bahá'í Faith	To "lead all nations spiritually" in order to "unify the world."

two lines diverging. Although they may have functionally intersected in the past, their current directions are increasingly divergent. This is because of the Nation of Islam's relatively recent reconciliation with mainstream Islam. Black Muslims are still Black nationalists, but they have quietly put Elijah Muhammad's racist myths (shared by Malcolm X in "Black Man's History") behind them. The dramatic change that took place when Malcolm X—after his pilgrimage to Mecca, where he personally witnessed a brotherhood of peoples of all races united by their common identity as Muslims—came to a realization that all whites were not "devils" as Elijah Muhammad had maintained. This is the Malcolm X that America has come to know and honor. The earlier Malcolm X would brook no tolerance in American mainstream society today.

The Protestants, collectively speaking, forged the "master myth" of America. Under its secularized corollary (albeit with much Christian support), the Manifest Destiny Myth, when translated into Congressional policy and duly executed, amounted to wholesale genocide of entire populations of the American Indian, and generally had a devastating impact on all things Indian. As racial prejudice sought religious sanction in the "Curse of Ham" Myth, it was effectively challenged by the African American Exodus Counter-Myth, which functioned to insulate African American Christians from the further impact of what may be described as essentially White forms of "Christianity," and to produce an African American theology of liberation in its wake. The Latter-day Saints' Mark of Cain Myth and, to a lesser extent, the Lost Tribes Myth are vestiges of racist beginnings that have effectively been renounced by the Latter-day Saints, but without overt repudiation. It would take something similar to the 1978 revelation received by LDS president Spencer Kimball to overturn some of the entrenched racial attitudes that overtly persist in Christian Identity and that covertly persist in the Nation of Islam, although it is expected that such vestiges of anti-White sentiment will subside within a more racially egalitarian America.

Religious prejudice, the other pervasively negative theme, has run its course as well, although plenty of religious prejudice remains. Not only was Christian Identity motivated by racial hate, but by religious prejudice as well, particularly with respect to Jews. The irony is that Jewish source material— primarily, what Christians have traditionally referred to as the "Old Testament"—was taken up and reworked to serve the purposes of White nationalism. Adam became the progenitor and patriarch of Whites, while Satan had intercourse with Eve and spawned the reptilian non-White races. The same was true in Identity's appropriation of the Jewish Lost Tribes Myth. While Mormons were not anti-semitic, they also wrested the Lost Tribes Myth out of its originally Jewish context and made them American Indians, whose skin was originally white, but was later cursed with dark skin as a consequence of their unrighteousness. World unity—championed especially by the Dalai Lama's reformulation of Tibetan Buddhism and by the Bahá'í Faith—reconciles and resolves such racial and religious prejudices into a progressive and constructive agenda for the reconstruction of the world globally.

The alternative visions of America, presented by minority faiths, may be seen as responses to the challenges of pluralism and race, in which minority faiths—America's alternative religions—implicitly seek to transcend the legacy of Puritanism in shaping American self-image. Wherever they embody egalitarian and progressive ideals, these minority faiths may be said to share important points of convergence. If visions of America's role in promoting an egalitarian, justice-based world are translated into reality, then, in effect, they operate as projects of universal emancipation. Progressive visions of America's world role, as held by some of the minority faiths presented in this book, have the potential and power to contribute to what White calls "consensus beliefs" and the American "consensus perception of world affairs."

Whatever the merits and demerits of these myths and visions of America, they serve to stimulate reflection on social policy at a national level, and on purpose at an individual level. "What does it mean to be an American?" is a venerable, yet surprisingly fresh question. The question itself, not to mention its possible answers, invites renewed thinking on the purpose for which, under various religious views, people were created and for which America is now the world's superpower. As presented in this book, these myths and visions of America serve as a mirror in which individual and national reflection may take place. True, the mirror may be distorted, but the mirror may also be refined such that it may one day reflect, not the world as it has been, but the world as it may become. America is something to be "religious" about, especially if one has the conviction that America—if it is to live up to its founding and quintessential values—is all about making the world a better place.

Recall that, in *Myths America Lives By,* author Richard Hughes had presented five foundational myths of America. Again, these are the following: (1) the Myth of the Chosen Nation; (2) the Myth of Nature's Nation; (3) the Myth of the Christian Nation; (4) the Myth of the Millennial Nation; and (5) the Myth of the Innocent Nation.[81] Perhaps—and this is tentative at best —the title should now, or in good time, be revised to reflect the past tense— *Myths America Lived By.* If this title is to be kept in its present tense, however, here is how these same myths might have been reshaped by America's minority faiths: (1) the Myth of the *Multilateral* Nation; (2) the Myth of the *Environmental* Nation; (3) the Myth of the *Multifaith* Nation; (4) the Myth of the *Ethical* Nation; and (5) the Myth of the *Cosmopolitan* Nation. This revisioning of the mission and destiny of America is actually the third of three basic types of American civil religion.

In Chapter 1, the reader will recall that Dean Hoge, sociologist at Catholic University of America, has outlined three types of civil visions of America, the first two of which clearly have American Protestant origins. The present writer will simply term these three visions of America as (1) Exemplarism; (2) Vindicationism; and (3) Cosmopolitanism.[82] In the first two instances, Henry Kissinger has characterized America's world role as both beacon and crusader.[83] These may be briefly recapitulated as follows.

(1) *Exemplarism:* The first vision of America is the Puritan vision, as first articulated by John Winthrop: "*Wee shall be as a Citty upon a Hill, the Eies of all people are uppon us.*" [84] According to Hoge, the Puritan vision "focused on making America an example to the world, a model society to show all the world what a godly and free nation can be." [85]

(2) *Vindicationism:* From the vision of America as a model nation for other nations to follow led to a more proactive program of action, in which America's mission was to influence (or coerce) other nations to incorporate American principles of religion and good governance. This second vision, Hoge notes, "saw America as a chosen people with an obligation to work actively in the world to win others to American principles and to safeguard those principles everywhere." [86] Although weak at first, this vision was the direct precursor of the doctrine of Manifest Destiny: "It was clearly stated in the doctrine of Manifest Destiny, that America's destiny was to settle the whole continent—and later, to bring freedom and civilization to all peoples." [87] This "activistic vision" of America "was a motivating source of the world Christian mission movement and of American expansionism in the late nineteenth century" in that "America would save the world for Christ or for democracy." [88]

The problem with Manifest Destiny is that the means justified the end, and great evils were perpetrated on Native Americans (i.e., the "First Nations," to invoke a Canadian term) not to mention pretextual territorial gains at the expense of other nations, of which the U.S.–Mexican War of 1846–1848 offers a prime instance in American history. This was America's first major conflict driven by the policy of "Manifest Destiny"—the doctrine that America, by dint of its divine destiny, had a God-given right to expand the nation's borders from sea to shining sea.[89] As a result of the U.S.–Mexican War, America acquired the northern half of Mexico—a vast territory that later became the states of California, Nevada, Arizona, New Mexico, and Utah.

(3) *Cosmopolitanism:* "A third vision of America's mission," Hoge goes on to say, "calls for internationalism based not on messianic ideas but on a posture of openness and cooperation, assuming that others have legitimate interests and identities and equally valid perceptions of truth." [90] Hoge connects this third ideal with Robert Bellah's ideal of a "world civil religion." [91] If America is to be reshaped as a multilateral, environmental, multifaith, ethical, and cosmopolitan nation, it may, in large part, be due to the collective influence of progressive minority faiths. This convergent influence may well be mediated through the instrumentality of commonly held "civil religion," which may be described as a "vehicle of national religious self-understanding." [92]

First described by Robert N. Bellah (professor emeritus of sociology and comparative studies at the University of California, Berkeley), American civil religion is itself in flux. In the conclusion of his seminal essay, "Civil Religion in America," Bellah foresees the emergence of a "world civil religion" coefficient with "the emergence of a genuine transnational sovereignty." [93] This world civil religion would necessarily incorporate "vital international symbolism into our civil religion" whereby "American civil religion" would become "simply one part of a new civil religion of the world." [94] Obviously it would "draw on religious traditions beyond the sphere of biblical religion alone." [95] In other words, while American civil religion has Protestant origins and is a decidedly American phenomenon, a world civil religion would be international in scope and interfaith in nature.

Bellah's vision of a world civil religion has attracted genuine and widespread criticism. In his defense, Paul Nathanson, author of *Over the Rainbow: The Wizard of Oz as a Secular Myth of America,* notes that "Bellah believed that this process" of promoting a world civil religion "need not disrupt the continuity of American civil religion." [96] This is because the notion of a world civil religion is "based not on worship of the nation itself, but on an understanding of American history in the light of an ultimate and universal reality." [97] The emergence of a world civil religion would, in the American context, represent a shift from a *national* to a *global* perspective. These two perspectives need not be at odds with one another. A reconciliation is possible. This would necessarily entail an aligning of the two perspectives. "A world civil religion," Bellah concludes in "Civil Religion in America," is a world-embracing vision that "could be accepted as a fulfillment and not as a denial of American civil religion"—as "the eschatological hope of American civil religion from the beginning." [98] Bellah wrote this statement in 1967. Forty years later, in 2007, Bellah revisited his notion of a world civil religion, reflecting on the role that world religions may play in promoting such a common vision:

> But for the creation of a viable and coherent world order a world civil society is surely an essential precondition, and, dare I say it, any actual civil society will have a religious dimension, will need not only a legal and an ethical framework, but some notion that it conforms to the nature of ultimate reality. The biggest immediate problem is the strengthening of global civil society. As I will elaborate in my next post, I would suggest that perhaps the *religious communities of the world may have something to contribute to that global civil society,* and, indeed, that *their participation may be essential for its success.* [99]

Is there a harmonic convergence of the visions of America as held by Protestantism and as redefined by America's minority faiths? If so, it would look something like this: In the Native American vision of America's world role, America should promote environmental ethics and ecological sustainability throughout "Turtle Island" and beyond. In the heritage of Deganawidah, America should advance global democracy in the interests of world peace abroad and at home, beginning with healing and repairing the injustices of the past and mitigating their continuing social and economic effects upon America's indigenous peoples in the present.

In the Protestant vision of America, America should foster the originally Puritan values of liberty, egalitarianism, individualism, populism, and laissez-faire, and promote democracy globally as well, through enlightened exemplarism, vindicationism, and cosmopolitanism. The quality of that democracy will be greatly enhanced when America uses her influence to realize and bring into reality a "worldwide brotherhood," as foreseen in Dr. Martin Luther King's vision of "the World House." While the subtitle of this book is "How Minority Faiths Transformed America's World Role," it should be noted that it took the prophetic voice of a vocal minority—primarily African American civil rights leaders—to influence (although not wholly transform) the Protestant vision of America's world role.

Briefly, America fulfills its Catholic mandate by promoting "religious liberty as a basic civil right," and fostering "the growth of international cooperation and solidarity in the service of that peace." [100] Judaism's vision of America is that it promote unity and pluralism "uniting all people in peace and freedom." [101] The Mormon vision of America, *inter alia,* is to promote liberty and equal rights, and to strengthen the foundation of society by fostering family values.[102] (Joseph Smith's 1844 political platform of "theodemocracy," however, appears to have no real place in Mormon doctrine.)

America should brook no tolerance for Christian Identity's goal of establishing a Whites-only homeland. While eschewing, if possible, the self-segregation that Louis Farrakhan continues to advocate as of December 2007—"*It is not a time for integration; it is a time for us to separate from our former slave-masters*" [103]—America can take cognizance of the Nation of Islam's vision that America may realize its potential to become the "Kingdom of God on earth"—"an egalitarian kingdom structured on truth, where each ... will be treated with fairness and justice." [104] Since contemporary Radical Islamism has no positive world role for America, and since progressive Islam has no definitive world role for America either, the Islamic mandate for America has not reached anything closely resembling a true consensus. Tibetan Buddhism's vision of America is to "bring those same fundamental rights and freedoms to people living under totalitarian regimes," "to make this world straight" (Dalai Lama), and to cultivate "a renaissance and enlightenment science our times" (Robert Thurman), as well as to promote a "Buddhist Democracy" (Dalai Lama, Thurman, Ikeda).

America will fulfill the Bahá'í Faith's vision of its great destiny when it arises to "lead all nations spiritually" in order to "unify the world." America will then be "prepared to play a preponderating role, as foretold by 'Abdu'l-Bahá, in the hoisting of the standard of the Lesser Peace, in the unification of mankind, and in the establishment of a world federal government on this planet." [105] Only then will

> that great republic . . . continue to evolve, undivided and undefeatable, until the sum total of its contributions to the birth, the rise and the fruition of that world civilization, the child of the Most Great Peace and hallmark of the Golden Age of the Dispensation of Bahá'u'lláh, will have been made, and its last task discharged.[106]

Civil religion can be the common ground of progressive religious values, which have the potential to exert a positive influence in the civic sphere. To the extent that civil religion incorporates the myth of America's spiritual destiny, that very myth will itself be subject to change and modifications, in accordance with the requirements of the times in which people live. "Part of the myth's resilience is due to the ability of Americans to adjust their religious sense of the nation's destiny to changed circumstances and altered expectations," Conrad Cherry observes. "It is reasonable to conclude that the same resilience will be evident in the future." [107] As social commentator John O'Sullivan puts it, America's "sense of itself" has always had to adjust to new historical circumstances and changed historical realities:

> America's sense of itself always had a self-conscious, even ideological, side. First, the United States, founded by a rebellion against legitimate authority, had to explain and justify that rebellion to mankind. Then, the growing nation had to justify taking over a continent from its previous owners. Finally, it had to persuade the immigrants arriving on that continent that, in assimilating to the American nation, they were not being false to themselves, that Americanism was in some sense a universal creed to which all could be admitted.[108]

The changed circumstances of today may be summed up in one word: *globalization*. Globalization refers to "both the compression of the world and intensification of consciousness of the world as a whole" and as "both concrete global interdependence and consciousness of the global whole." [109] It is further defined as "the intensification of worldwide social relations which link distant localities in such a way that local happenings are shaped by events occurring many miles away and vice versa." [110] Ethical responses to globalization, which are essentially world order issues,[111] have given rise to a search for values of egalitarianism, equity, and sustainability—a worldview that some have called "globalism." As a response to globalization, globalism may be viewed as a reflex or extension of Kantian cosmopolitanism and as the "moral universalism of international relations." [112] Globalism, as a form of international ethics, may be considered to be the equivalent of a renewed cosmopolitanism that, today, views the world as an organic whole and advocates a global ethic commensurate with the needs of the twenty-first century.

Religions in America can and should translate their shared ideals into an American civil religion—and a corresponding ethic—that can help form a basis for the world civil religion that Robert Bellah envisions. To refine the point, religions ideally will remythologize and revision America in increasingly convergent and harmonic ways, offering an informal consensus on what may be called *proactive American cosmopolitanism,* where national interests are integrated with supranational interests, linking American foreign policy and the requirements of world order. If attuned to the needs of this day and age, these thought-orienting myths and action-incentive visions have every potential to serve as a spiritual mandate for America. Under the gaze of their ideals, universally minded religions can set the stage for the next quantum leap in the world's social evolution—transitioning from war to peace, from nationalism to internationalism, from religious particularism to spiritual universalism, from racial animosity to racial amity, from gender repression to gender equality, and from resource exploitation to environmental renewal. Universal values actually devalue uniformity and promote diversity. Where there is a common ground of universal values, unity can therefore be the *effect* of diversity.

Myths and visions of American have attracted the theoretical interests of scholars for generations. The late Canadian Americanist Sacvan Bercovitch was among the foremost of these scholars. Bercovitch wrote of "transformations in the symbolic construction of America." [113] What would happen if the three paradigmatic visions of America—exemplarism, vindicationism, and cosmopolitanism—were interwoven and transformed to meet the needs of the world of today and tomorrow? Telescoping these into the future, perhaps America can, one day, draw on the power of its moral authority (exemplarism)—if and when America resolves its race, class, and gender issues—to benignly and effectively exert its considerable political influence (vindicationism) for the promotion of global peace through world unity (cosmopolitanism).

For this ever to happen, the adoption of universal principles of good governance, of individual and group rights, of the equitable distribution of the world's wealth and resources, of environmental sustainability, and of an emergent cosmopolitan order, will stand as a set of self-evident moral imperatives. In all this, America's leadership in bringing about enlightened internationalism may be paradoxically characterized as a *unilateral multilateralism* —in which America *unilaterally* takes the initiative to foster the conditions whereby the community of nations works in *multilateral* concert, in an orchestration of sovereign powers for the global good. Whether this entails endorsing arbitration treaties, lending more authority to the Hague courts, or encouraging qualified disarmament, national interest and world order can be guided by the ethical principles offered by universally oriented religious worldviews.

Consider the example of President Theodore Roosevelt (1858–1919), 1906 Nobel Peace Prize laureate, who, in 1902, took the initiative in opening the international Court of Arbitration at The Hague. Although founded in 1899, the Court of Arbitration had not been called upon by any power in its first three years of existence. When the United States and Mexico agreed to arbitrate, before the Hague Tribunal, their differences over the Pious Foundations of California, this example was followed by other powers, thus rendering the formerly inert arbitration machinery operational. Roosevelt played a prominent role in extending the use of arbitration to international problems in the Western Hemisphere as well.[114] Such leadership in international affairs was guided by religious principle. Writing that American leadership must exemplify the "ideals of democracy, of liberty under law, of social progress through peaceful industry, of education and commerce, and of uncorrupted Christianity," Roosevelt was steered by the moral compass of Micah 6:8: "He has told you, O moral, what is good; and what does the Lord require of you but to do justice, and to love kindness, and to walk humbly with your God."[115] As President Roosevelt prophetically said: "Upon the success of our experiment much depends, not only as regards our own welfare, but as regards the welfare of mankind."[116] In fine, America's political, economic, and scientific power can also serve as a reflex of *moral power*. Will America—taking Theodore Roosevelt and Woodrow Wilson as moral exemplars of American cosmopolitanism—*unilaterally* take a leading role in initiating the *multilateral* process of bringing about the following event, as presaged by one of the minority faiths, the Bahá'í Faith?

> True civilization will unfurl its banner in the midmost heart of the world whenever a certain number of its distinguished and high-minded sovereigns—the shining exemplars of devotion and determination—shall, for the good and happiness of all mankind, arise, with firm resolve and clear vision, to establish the Cause of Universal Peace. They must make the Cause of Peace the object of general consultation, and seek by every means in their power to establish a Union of the nations of the world. They must conclude a binding treaty and establish a covenant, the provisions of which shall be sound, inviolable and definite. They must proclaim it to all the world and obtain for it the sanction of all the human race. This supreme and noble undertaking—the real source of the peace and well-being of all the world—should be regarded as sacred by all that dwell on earth. All the forces of humanity must be mobilized to ensure the stability and permanence of this Most Great Covenant. In this all-embracing Pact the limits and frontiers of each and every nation should be clearly fixed, the principles underlying the relations of governments towards one another definitely laid down, and all international agreements and obligations ascertained.[117]

In this remarkable religious text, written by 'Abdu'l-Bahá in 1875, the cause of universal peace—the product of a stable and enlightened world order—should be regarded as a "sacred" undertaking by peoples of all nations and faiths. In 1963—88 years later—Pope John XXIII opened his magisterial *Pacem in Terris* with these words: "Peace on Earth—which man throughout the ages has so longed for and sought after—can never be established, never guaranteed, except by the diligent observance of the divinely established order." [118] In other words, world order—that is, the state of ideal international relations described by 'Abdu'l-Bahá as "true civilization" and Pope John XXIII as "peace on earth"—is essentially a sacred task best served when based on the principles of justice and reciprocity advocated by the religions of the world, whether in America or abroad. Indeed, according to the Universal House of Justice (internationally elected Bahá'í governing council) in a message addressed "To the Peoples of the World" in 1985, "World peace is not only possible but inevitable." [119] In this document, the role of religion is made clear: "No serious attempt to set human affairs aright, to achieve world peace, can ignore religion." [120] America, in protecting *freedom* of religion while proscribing the *establishment* of religion, would do well to heed the enlightened cosmopolitanism of the minority faiths that promote it.

As a grand synthesis of the ideals held by America's progressive Protestant and minority faiths, American civil religion can play a preponderating role in inspiring a world civil religion that, in turn, universalizes these egalitarian values for all nations. As Pope John Paul II said to President Ronald Reagan in 1987, America has a great responsibility in the world today:

> The more powerful a nation is, the greater becomes its international responsibility, the greater also must be its commitment to the betterment of the lot of those whose very humanity is constantly being threatened by want and need. . . . America needs freedom to be herself and to fulfill her mission in the world.[121]

If America arises to accomplish this mission, then America will fulfill its world role and realize its prophetic destiny—*whether imagined or real*. America will have lived up to the grand destiny envisioned by the more optimistic religions surveyed in these pages. Then will the noblest myths of America have become reality and their grandest visions realized—in the new American cosmopolitanism of world unity which, in the immortal words of Dr. Martin Luther King, Jr., will "transform this world-wide neighborhood into a world-wide brotherhood" [122] and by which, according to one Bahá'í text, "the oneness of the whole body of nations will be made the ruling principle of international life." [123]

Notes

CHAPTER 1: AMERICA: NATION AND NOTION

1. Lauren Gail Berlant, *The Anatomy of National Fantasy: Hawthorne, Utopia, and Everyday Life* (Chicago: University of Chicago Press, 1991), 1.

2. Kevin Lewis, "Nathanael West and American Apocalyptic." *Tradition and Postmodernity: English and American Studies and the Challenge of the Future.* Proceedings of the Eighth International Conference on English and American Literature and Language. Ed. Teresa Bela and Zygmunt Mazur (Krakow, Poland: Jagiellonian University, 1999), 435–443 [435].

3. Conrad Cherry, "Preface to the Revised and Updated Edition." *God's New Israel: Religious Interpretations of American Destiny.* Ed. idem. Rev. ed. (Chapel Hill: University of North Carolina Press, 1998), x.

4. Donald W. White, *The American Century: The Rise and Decline of the United States as a World Power* (New Haven and London: Yale University Press, 1996), 1.

5. Jonathan Sarna, "The Cult of Synthesis in American Jewish Culture." *Jewish Social Studies* 5, 1–2 (1999): 52–79.

6. Malcolm Bull and Keith Lockhart, *Seeking a Sanctuary: Seventh-day Adventism and the American Dream* (Bloomington, IN: Indiana University Press, 2006), 254. The author thanks Andrew Rippin for this reference. Rippin to author, e-mail dated August 13, 2008.

7. J. N. Andrews, qtd. in Bull and Lockhart, *Seeking a Sanctuary: Seventh-day Adventism and the American Dream,* 57.

8. Dawn L. Hutchinson, "Antiquity and Social Reform: Religious Experience in the Unification Church, Feminist Wicca and the Nation of Yahweh" (Ph.D. dissertation: Florida State University, 2007). Available at http://etd.lib.fsu.edu/theses/available/etd-04092007-153203/unrestricted/hutchinson_dis.pdf. Accessed September 28, 2008.

9. Ibid., 4.

10. Ibid., 54.

11. Ibid., 4.

12. Ibid., 160–161.

13. Richard T. Hughes, *Myths America Lives By.* Foreword by Robert N. Bellah (Champaign: University of Illinois Press, 2004).

14. Robert N. Bellah, "Foreword." Hughes, *Myths America Lives By,* xii.

15. Michael Angrosino, "Civil Religion Redux." *Anthropological Quarterly* 75.2 (2002): 239–267 [241].

16. Peter D. Salins, *Assimilation, American Style* (New York: Basic Books, 1997), 102.

17. James H. Moorhead, "The American Israel: Protestant Tribalism and Universal Mission." *Many Are Chosen: Divine Election and Western Nationalism.* Ed. William R. Hutchison and Hartmut Lehmann (Philadelphia: Fortress Press, 1994), 145–166.

18. John O'Sullivan, "America's Identity Crisis." *National Review* 46 (November 21, 1994): 36–45 [36]; Robert J. Scholnick, "Extermination and Democracy: O'Sullivan, the *Democratic Review,* and Empire, 1837–1840." *American Periodicals: A Journal of History, Criticism, and Bibliography* 15.2 (2005): 123–141.

19. Dean R. Hoge, "Theological Views of America among Protestants." *Sociological Analysis* 37.2 (1976): 127–139 [127].

20. Ibid., 127.

21. White, *The American Century: The Rise and Decline of the United States as a World Power,* 13; Bruce Kuklick, "Myth and Symbol in American Studies." *American Quarterly* 24 (October 1972): 435–450.

22. Susan-Mary Grant, "Making History: Myth and the Construction of American Nationhood." *Myths and Nationhood.* Ed. Geoffrey Hosking and George Schöpflin (New York: Routledge, 1997), 88–106.

23. Sacvan Bercovitch, *The Rites of Assent: Transformations in the Symbolic Construction of America* (New York: Routledge, 1993).

24. Barbara-Ann J. Rieffer, "Religion and Nationalism: Understanding the Consequences of a Complex Relationship." *Ethnicities* 3.2 (2003): 215–242 [225].

25. Ibid., 225.

26. Richard Slotkin, "Myth and the Production of History." *Ideology and Classic American Literature.* Ed. Sacvan Bercovitch and Myra Jehlen (Cambridge: Cambridge University Press, 1986), 70–90 [70].

27. George Schöpflin. "The Functions of Myth and a Taxonomy of Myths." *Myths and Nationhood.* Ed. Geoffrey Hosking and George Schöpflin (New York: Routledge, 1997), 19–35.

28. Ibid., 35.

29. Mary Fulbrook, "Myth-making and National Identity: The Case of the G.D.R." *Myths and Nationhood,* 72–87 [73].

30. Anthony D. Smith, "Ethnic Election and National Destiny: Some Religious Origins of Nationalist Ideals." *Nations and Nationalism* 5.3 (1999): 331–355 [332].

31. William Doty, *Mythography: The Study of Myths and Rituals* (Tuscaloosa: University of Alabama Press, 2000), 132.

32. Anthony D. Smith, "The 'Sacred' Dimension of Nationalism." *Millennium: Journal of International Studies* 29.3 (2000): 791–814.

33. Smith, "Ethnic Election and National Destiny," 332.

34. Susan-Mary Grant, "Making History: Myth and the Construction of American Nationhood." *Myths and Nationhood,* 88–106.

35. See Sacvan Bercovitch, "The Myth of America." *Puritan Origins of the American Self* (New Haven: Yale University Press, 1986), 136–186; Moorhead, "The American Israel."

36. Robert N. Bellah, "Civil Religion in America." Special Issue: Religion in America. *Dædalus: Journal of the American Academy of Arts and Sciences* 96.1 (Winter 1967): 1–21; reprinted in idem, *Beyond Belief: Essays on Religion in a Post-Traditionalist World* (Berkeley: University of California Press, 1991).

37. Dean Hoge, "Theological Views of America among Protestants." *Sociological Analysis* 37.2 (1976): 127–139 [128].

38. Ibid., 128.

39. Ibid., 128.

40. Ibid., 128.

41. Ibid., 128.

42. Ibid., 128.

43. John L. O'Sullivan coined "Manifest Destiny" in "The Great Nation of Futurity." *The United States Democratic Review* 6.23 (November 1839): 426–430.

44. James H. Moorhead, " 'God's Right Arm'?: Minority Faiths and Protestant Visions of America." *Minority Faiths and the American Protestant Mainstream.* Ed. Jonathan D. Sarna (Urbana/Chicago: University of Illinois Press, 1998), 335–361 [356].

45. David W. Wills, "The Central Themes of American Religious History: Pluralism, Puritanism, and the Encounter of Black and White." *Religion and Intellectual Life* 5 (1987): 30–41.

46. Paul Harvey, " 'A Servant of Servants Shall He Be': The Construction of Race in American Religious Mythologies." *Religion and the Creation of Race and Ethnicity: An Introduction* (New York: New York University Press, 2003), 13–27 [14]. Emphasis in original.

CHAPTER 2: NATIVE AMERICAN MYTHS AND VISIONS OF AMERICA

1. Benjamin Franklin, "To James Parker" (Philadelphia, March 20, 1750). *The Writings of Benjamin Franklin. Vol. III, 1750–1759.* Ed. Albert Henry Smyth (New York: Macmillan, 1905), 40–45 [42].

2. Bruce E. Johansen, "Dating the Iroquois Confederacy." *Akwesasne Notes* 1.3/4 (Fall 1995): 62–63.

3. The Haudenosaunee ("People of the Longhouse") were called "Iroquois" by the French.

4. Qtd. Donald A. Grinde, Jr. and Bruce E. Johansen, *Exemplar of Liberty: Native America and the Evolution of Democracy* (Los Angeles: American Indian Studies Center, University of California, 1991).

5. Gladys A. Reichard, "Literary Types and Dissemination of Myths." *Journal of American Folklore* 34, no. 133 (July–September 1921): 269–307 [274–277].

6. William Nelson Fenton, Chapter 2: "This Island, the World On the Turtle's Back." *The Great Law and the Longhouse: A Political History of the Iroquois Confederacy* (Norman: University of Oklahoma Press, 1998), 35.

7. Barbara Alice Mann, "Spirits of Sky, Spirits of Earth: The Spirituality of Chingachgook." *James Fenimore Cooper Society Miscellaneous Papers* No. 17 (September 2002): 1–5.

8. Bruce Elliott Johansen and Barbara Alice Mann, eds., *Encyclopedia of the Haudenosaunee (Iroquois Confederacy)* (Westport, CT: Greenwood Publishing, 2000), s.v. "The First Epic of Time: Creation Keepings," 85.

9 Fenton, *The Great Law and the Longhouse,* 34.

10. Sam D. Gill, *Mother Earth: An American Story* (Chicago: University of Chicago Press, 1987), 129.

11. Sam D. Gill, "The Academic Study of Religion." *Journal of the American Academy of Religion* 62 (Winter 1994): 965–975.

12. Cornstalk, June 1, 1776. Qtd. Richard White, *The Middle Ground: Indians, Empires, and Republics in the Great Lakes Region* (Cambridge: Cambridge University Press, 1991), 366.

13. Morgan Letterbook, *American Commissioners for Indian Affairs to Delawares, Senecas, Munsees, and Mingos* (Pittsburgh, 1776). Qtd. Richard White, *The Middle Ground,* 366.

14. Deganawidah, qtd. William Nelson Fenton, *Parker on the Iroquois, Book III: The Constitution of the Five Nations.* Ed. W. Fenton (Syracuse, NY: Syracuse University Press, 1968), 3:33.

15. Christopher Vecsey, *Imagine Ourselves Richly: Mythic Narratives of North American Indians* (New York: Crossroad, 1988), 96.

16. Famed philologist, Horatio E. Hale, wrote in 1883: "The Tuscaroras were admitted in 1714; the two other nations were received about the year 1753." Horatio E. Hale, *The Iroquois Book of Rites.* 2nd ed. (Toronto: University of Toronto Press, 1963 [1883]), 79.

17. Jay Hansford C. Vest, "An Odyssey among the Iroquois: A History of Tutelo Relations in New York." *American Indian Quarterly* 29.1–2 (Winter–Spring 2005): 124–155 [136].

18. See Alice B. Kehoe, *North American Indians: A Comprehensive Account.* 3rd ed. (Upper Saddle River, NJ: Prentice Hall, 2006), 227.

19. Deganawidah, qtd. John Arthur Gibson, *Concerning the League: The Iroquois League Tradition as Dictated in Onondaga by John Arthur Gibson. Newly Elicited, Edited and Translated by Hanni Woodbury in Collaboration with Reg Henry and Harry Webster on the Basis of A. A. Goldenweiser's Manuscript* (Winnipeg, Manitoba: Algonquian and Iroquoian Linguistics, 1992), 36–41.

20. Emphasis added. Paul A. W. Wallace, "Dekanahwideh," in *Dictionary of Canadian Biography Online.* Based on the *Dictionary of Canadian Biography/Dictionnaire biographique du Canada.* Ed. John English (Toronto and Montreal: University of Toronto and Université Laval, 1959).

21. Bruce E. Johansen, *Forgotten Founders: Benjamin Franklin, the Iroquois, and the Rationale for the American Revolution* (Ipswich, MA: Gambit, 1982); Donald A. Grinde, Jr. and Bruce E. Johansen, *Exemplar of Liberty: Native America and the Evolution of Democracy* (Los Angeles: UCLA American Indian Studies Center, 1991).

22. Benjamin Franklin, ed., *Indian Treaties Printed by Benjamin Franklin, 1736–1762*. Ed. Carl Van Doren and Julian P. Boyd (Philadelphia, PA: The Historical Society of Pennsylvania, 1938), 41–79 [78].

23. Qtd. Timothy J. Shannon, *Indians and Colonists at the Crossroads of Empire: The Albany Congress of 1754* (Ithaca/Cooperstown: Cornell University Press and New York State Historical Association, 2000), 103.

24. Benjamin Franklin, *Not Your Usual Founding Father: Selected Readings from Benjamin Franklin*. Ed. Edmund S. Morgan (New Haven: Yale University Press, 2006), 175.

25. Benjamin Franklin, "Remarks Concerning the Savages of North America" (1783). In Franklin, *Not Your Usual Founding Father*, 52–53.

26. See Richard B. Morris, "Benjamin Franklin's Grand Design: The Albany Plan of Union Might Have Made the Revolution Unnecessary." *American Heritage Magazine* 7.2 (February 1956).

27. Benjamin Franklin, "Albany Plan of Union" (1784). In Franklin, *Not Your Usual Founding Father*, 5.

28. Randall G. Holcombe, "Constitutional Theory and the Constitutional History of Colonial America." *The Independent Review* 3.1 (Summer 1998): 21–36. (See 27–32.)

29. See http://www.Senate.gov/reference/resources/pdf/hconres331.pdf.

30. Text available. See http://www.govtrack.us/congress/billtext.xpd?bill=h1 10-3585.

31. Michael N. McConnell, *A Country Between: The Upper Ohio Valley and Its Peoples, 1724–1774* (Lincoln/London: University of Nebraska Press, 1992), 56.

32. Laurence M. Hauptman, Chapter Three, "Speculations on the Constitution." *Tribes and Tribulations: Misconceptions about American Indians and their Histories* (Albuquerque: University of New Mexico Press), 27.

33. Shannon, *Indians and Colonists at the Crossroads of Empire*, 7.

CHAPTER 3: PROTESTANT MYTHS AND VISIONS OF AMERICA

1. John Winthrop, "A Model of Christian Charity." *God's New Israel: Religious Interpretations of American Destiny* (Chapel Hill: University of North Carolina Press, 1998), 41.

2. Sacvan Bercovitch, "Rhetoric as Authority: Puritanism, the Bible, and the Myth of America." *Social Science Information* 21.1 (January 1982): 5–17 [14].

3. Eric Kaufmann, "American Exceptionalism Reconsidered: Anglo-Saxon Ethnogenesis in the 'Universal' Nation, 1776–1850." *Journal of American Studies* 33.3 (1999): 437–457 [439]. Emphasis added.

4. Bercovitch, "Rhetoric as Authority," 5.

5. Ibid., 5–6.

6. Ibid., 14.

7. Robert Charles Winthrop, ed., *Life and Letters of John Winthrop* (Boston: Ticknor and Fields, 1864–1867), 18–20.

8. Matthew 5:14 (KJV).

9. Gary Gerstle, "American Freedom, American Coercion: Immigrant Journeys in the 'Promised Land.'" *Social Compass* 47.1 (2000): 63–76 [72].

10. Conrad Cherry, *God's New Israel: Religious Interpretations of American Destiny*. Ed. idem. Rev. ed. (Chapel Hill: University of North Carolina Press, 1998).

11. Gerstle, "American Freedom, American Coercion," 64–65.

12. Szilvia Csábi, "The Concept of America in the Puritan Mind." *Language and Literature* 10.3 (2001): 195–209 [198].

13. Ibid., 198.

14. Ibid., 198.

15. Kaufmann, "American Exceptionalism Reconsidered," 441–442.

16. Cian O'Driscoll, "Jean Bethke Elshtain's Just War Against Terror: A Tale of Two Cities." *International Relations* 21.4 (2007): 485–492 [489].

17. Lori Merish, *Sentimental Materialism: Gender, Commodity Culture, and Nineteenth-Century American Literature* (Durham, NC: Duke University Press, 2000), 318.

18. Kaufmann, "American Exceptionalism Reconsidered," 442.

19. John L. O'Sullivan, "Annexation." *The United States Magazine and Democratic Review* 17 (July–August 1845): 5–10 [5] (emphasis added); John L. O'Sullivan, "The Great Nation of Futurity," *The United States Democratic Review* 6.23 (November 1839): 426–430.

20. Robert J. Scholnick, "Extermination and Democracy: O'Sullivan, the Democratic Review, and Empire, 1837–1840." *American Periodicals: A Journal of History, Criticism, and Bibliography* 15.2 (2005): 123–141 [124].

21. Glenn Wallach, *Obedient Sons: The Discourse of Youth and Generations in American Culture, 1630–1860* (Amherst: University of Massachusetts Press, 1997), 209.

22. "The True Title." *New York Morning News* (December 27, 1845). Qtd. Julius W. Pratt, "The Origin of 'Manifest Destiny.'" *American Historical Review* 32.4 (July 1927): 795–798 [796].

23. Mostafa Rejai, *Political Ideologies: A Comparative Approach*. 2nd ed. (Armonk, NY/London: M. E. Sharpe, 1995), 36–37.

24. Anders Stephanson, *Manifest Destiny: American Expansionism and the Empire of Right* (New York: Hill and Wang, 1995).

25. Ibid., xiv.

26. Ibid., xii.

27. Ibid., xiii.

28. Ibid., xiii.

29. Ibid., xiv.

30. Ibid., 20.

31. Ibid., 5.

32. Ibid., 5.

33. Ibid., 21.

34. Ibid., 21.

35. Ibid., 112.

36. John Christopher Pinheiro, *Crusade and Conquest: Anti-Catholicism, Manifest Destiny, and the United States-Mexican War of 1846–1848* (Ph.D. dissertation: University of Tennessee, 2001). (Abstract.)

37. Maria del Rosario Rodriguez Diaz, "Mexico's Vision of Manifest Destiny During the 1847 War." *Journal of Popular Culture* 35.2 (Fall 2001): 41–50 [44–45]; Gene Brack, *The Diplomacy of Racism: Manifest Destiny and Mexico, 1821–1848* (St. Charles, MO: Forum Press, 1974).

38. Reginald Horsman, *Race and Manifest Destiny: The Origins of American Racial Anglo-Saxonism* (Cambridge, MA: Harvard University Press, 1981), 20.

39. Colossians 4:1 (KJV).

40. David H. Aaron, "Early Rabbinic Exegesis on Noah's Son Ham and the So-Called 'Hamitic Myth.' " *Journal of the American Academy of Religion* 63 (1995): 721–759.

41. Christopher A. Luse, "Slavery's Champions Stood at Odds: Polygenesis and the Defense of Slavery." *Civil War History* 53.4 (December 2007): 379–412.

42. Stephen G. Ray, Jr., "Review of the Myth of Ham in Nineteenth-Century American Christianity: Race, Heathens, and the People of God." *Conversations in Religion and Theology* 4.1 (2006): 36–38 [36].

43. David M. Goldenberg, *The Curse of Ham: Race and Slavery in Early Judaism, Christianity, and Islam* (Princeton: Princeton University Press, 2003).

44. Genesis 9:18–25 (RSV).

45. Goldenberg, *The Curse of Ham,* 1.

46. Ibid., Chapter Seven, "The Colors of Mankind."

47. Ibid., 142.

48. Ibid., 142.

49. Ibid., 143.

50. Ibid., 176.

51. Robert Oscar Lopez, "The Colors of Double Exceptionalism: The Founders and African America." *Literature Compass* 5.1 (2008): 20–41.

52. Eddie S. Glaude, "Myth and African American Self-Identity." *Religion and the Creation of Race and Ethnicity: An Introduction.* Ed. Craig R. Prentiss (New York: New York University Press, 2003), 28–42 [39].

53. Ibid., 35.

54. Rhondda Robinson Thomas, "Exodus: Literary Migrations of Afro-Atlantic Authors, 1760–1903" (Ph.D. dissertation: University of Maryland, 2007).

55. Albert J. Raboteau, "African-Americans, Exodus, and the American Israel." *African-American Christianity: Essays in History.* Ed. Paul E. Johnson (Berkeley: University of California Press, 1994), 1–17 [13].

56. Raboteau, "African-Americans, Exodus, and the American Israel." In idem, *A Fire in the Bones* (Boston: Beacon Press, 1996), 17–36 [28].

57. Paul Laurence Dunbar, "An Ante-Bellum Sermon" (1895).

58. David T. Shannon, " 'An Ante-Bellum Sermon': A Resource for an African American Hermeneutic." *Stony the Road We Trod: African American Biblical Interpretation.* Ed. Cain Hope Felder (New York: Fortress Press, 1991), 98–123 [119].

59. David W. Wills, "The Central Themes of American Religious History: Pluralism, Puritanism, and the Encounter of Black and White." *Religion and Intellectual Life* 5 (1987): 30–41. Reprinted in Timothy E. Fulop and Albert J. Raboteau, eds., *African-American Religion: Interpretive Essays in History and Culture* (New York/ London: Routledge, 1997), 7–20 [20].

CHAPTER 4: CATHOLIC MYTHS AND VISIONS OF AMERICA

1. John Paul II, "Meeting with the President of the United States of America, Mr. Ronald Reagan. Address of John Paul II." Vizcaya Museum, Miami. Thursday, September 10, 1987.

2. "Fissiparous [divisive, tending to split up] Protestantism" is an expression ascribed to Kenneth Scott Latourette.

3. William L. Portier, "Heartfelt Grief and Repentance in Imperial Times" (Balthasar Conference, April 17, 2005), 3–4.

4. Pope Leo XIII, "Concerning New Opinions, Virtue, Nature and Grace, with Regard to Americanism. *Testem Benevolentiae Nostrae.*" Encyclical of Pope Leo XIII promulgated on January 22, 1899.

5. Pope Benedict XVI, "Address of His Holiness Benedict XVI, 'Rotunda' Hall of the Pope John Paul II Cultural Center of Washington, D.C." Thursday, April 17, 2008.

6. Pope John Paul II, "Address of John Paul II to Hon. Richard B. Cheney, Vice President of the United States of America." Tuesday, January 27, 2004.

7. Pope John Paul II, "Welcome Address of His Holiness John Paul II." International Airport of Miami. Thursday, September 10, 1987."

8. John Paul II, "Meeting with the President of the United States of America, Mr. Ronald Reagan. Address of John Paul II." Vizcaya Museum, Miami. Thursday, September 10, 1987.

9. Mark S. Burrows, "The Catholic Revision of an American Myth: The Eschatology of Orestes Brownson as an Apology of American Catholicism." *Catholic Historical Review* 76 (1990): 18–43; Carl Krummel, "Catholicism, Americanism, Democracy, and Orestes Brownson." *American Quarterly* 6.1 (Spring 1954): 19–31.

10. Robert Herrera, "Orestes Brownson's Vision of America." *Modern Age* 43.2 (Spring 2001): 133–145 [133].

11. Robert A. Herrera, *Orestes Brownson: Sign of Contradiction* (Wilmington, DE: ISI Books, 1999), 74. Qtd. Eric J. Scheske, "Orestes Brownson: His Life, His Catholicism." *Logos: A Journal of Catholic Thought and Culture* 7.2 (2004): 137–164 [150].

12. Orestes Brownson, "Mission of America." *The Works of Orestes A. Brownson.* Ed. Henry F. Brownson (Detroit: T. Nourse, 1884), vol. 11: 551–584 [567]. Qtd. James Emmett Ryan, "Orestes Brownson in Young America: Popular Books and the Fate of Catholic Criticism." *American Literary History* 15.3 (2003): 443–470 [450].

13. See especially Patrick W. Carey, *Orestes A. Brownson: American Religious Weathervane* (Grand Rapids, MI: Wm. B. Eerdmans, 2004); and idem, ed., *Orestes A. Brownson: Selected Writings*. Sources of American Spirituality (Mahwah, NJ: Paulist Press, 1991).

14. O. A. Brownson, LL.D., *The American Republic: Its Constitution, Tendencies, and Destiny* (New York: P. O'Shea, 1866).

15. Ibid., "Chapter XV. Destiny—Political and Religious."

16. Ibid., "Chapter XI. The Constitution, Concluded."

17. Ibid., "Chapter XV. Destiny—Political and Religious."

18. Dennis Joseph Dease, *The Theological Influence of Orestes Brownson and Isaac Hecker on John Ireland's Americanist Ecclesiology* (Ph.D. dissertation: The Catholic University of America, 1978).

19. Translation: "Mayest thou [America] endure forever!" John Ireland, "The Church and Modern Society." In idem, *The Church and Modern Society: Lectures and Addresses* (New York: D. H. McBride, 1903), 27–65 [64–65]; Marvin O'Connell, *John Ireland and the American Catholic Church* (St. Paul: Minnesota Historical Society, 1988), 192–195; Neil T. Storch, "John Ireland's Americanism After 1899: The Argument from History." *Church History* 51.4 (1982): 434–444.

20. John Ireland, "The Church in America," *Lecture and Addresses*. Vol. II (St. Paul, MN: Pioneer Press, 1905), 240–241.

21. Pope Leo XIII, "Concerning New Opinions, Virtue, Nature and Grace, with Regard to Americanism. *Testem Benevolentiae Nostrae*." Encyclical of Pope Leo XIII promulgated on January 22, 1899.

22. Qtd. Monsignor John Tracy Ellis, ed., *Documents of American Catholic History* (Milwaukee, WI: Bruce Publishing, 1956), 533.

23. See Gerald P. Fogarty, "The Vatican and the Americanist Crisis: Denis J. O'Connell, American Agent in Rome, 1885–1903." *Miscellanea Historiae Pontificiae,* 36 (Rome Università Gregoriana Editrice, 1974); and idem, "Americanism." *The New Dictionary of Catholic Social Thought*. Ed. Judith A. Dwyer (Collegeville, MN: The Liturgical Press, 1994), 39–42.

24. John Paul II, "John Paul II on the American Experiment." *First Things* 82 (April 1998): 36–37.

25. Joseph Cardinal Bernardin, *A Moral Vision of America*. Ed. John P. Langan (Washington, DC: Georgetown University Press, 1998).

26. John Courtney Murray, *We Hold These Truths: Catholic Reflections on the American Proposition* (Lanham, MD: Rowman and Littlefield, 2005 [1960]).

27. See the "Foreword" by Walter J. Burghardt, S.J. (Georgetown University) to Murray, *We Hold These Truths,* vii–x [vii]. The author of the *Time* cover story on Father Murray was Protestant writer Douglas Auchincloss.

28. Peter Lawler, "Critical Introduction," in Murray, *We Hold These Truths,* 2.

29. Murray, *We Hold These Truths,* xv.

30. Ibid., xv.

31. Joseph A. Varacalli, *Bright Promise, Failed Community: Catholics and the American Public Order* (Lanham, MD: Lexington Books, 2000).

32. Ibid., 113.

33. Joseph A. Varacalli, "On Being Catholic American." *Homiletic and Pastoral Review* (August–September 2004).

CHAPTER 5: JEWISH MYTHS AND VISIONS OF AMERICA

1. Lecture delivered before the Theological and Religious Library Association of Cincinnati, January 7, 1869. See Isaac Mayer Wise, "Our Country's Place in History." *God's New Israel: Religious Interpretations of American Destiny,* 224–234 [224, 226, 231, 234].

2. Qtd. Beth S. Wenger, "Making American Civilization Jewish: Mordecai Kaplan's Civil Religion." *Jewish Social Studies* 12.2 (2006): 56–63 [61].

3. Eli Lederhendler, "America: A Vision in a Jewish Mirror." *Jewish Responses to Modernity: New Voices in America and Eastern Europe* (New York: New York University Press, 1994), 104–139 [113].

4. James H. Moorhead, " 'God's Right Arm'? Minority Faiths and Protestant Visions of America." *Minority Faiths and the American Protestant Mainstream.* Ed. Jonathan D. Sarna (Urbana/Chicago: University of Illinois Press, 1998), 335–361 [356].

5. Sam B. Girgus, "The New Covenant: The Jews and the Myth of America." *The American Self: Myth, Ideology, and Popular Culture.* Ed. idem (Albuquerque: University of New Mexico Press, 1981), 105–123; Girgus, *The New Covenant: Jewish Writers and the American Idea* (Chapel Hill, NC: University of North Carolina Press, 1984).

6. Jonathan Sarna, "Free-Market Judaism."

7. Jonathan S. Woocher, "Spirituality and the Civil Religion." *Secularism, Spirituality, and the Future of American Jewry.* Ed. Elliott Abrams and David G. Dalin (Washington, DC: Ethics and Public Policy Center, 1999), 19–25 [22]; idem, " 'Sacred Survival' Revisited: American Jewish Civil Religion in the New Millennium." *The Cambridge Companion to American Judaism.* Ed. Dana Evan Kaplan (Cambridge: Cambridge University Press, 2005), 283–298; idem, *Sacred Survival: The Civil Religion of American Jews* (Bloomington and Indianapolis: Indiana University Press, 1986).

8. See "Treaty of Peace and Friendship between The United States and the Bey and Subjects of Tripoli of Barbary, 1796–1797." *Treaties and Other International Acts of the United States of America.* Ed. Hunter Miller. Vol. 2. 1776–1818 (Washington, DC: U.S. Government Printing Office, 1931), 383; and *The Journal of the Senate, including The Journal of the Executive Proceedings of the Senate, John Adams Administration, 1797–1801, Volume 1: Fifth Congress, First Session; March–July, 1797.* Ed. Martin P. Claussen (Wilmington, DE: Michael Glazier, Inc., 1977).

9. Jonathan Sarna, "Church-State Dilemmas of Jewish Americans." *Jews and the American Public Square: Debating Religion.* Ed. Alan Mittleman, Robert Licht, and Jonathan D. Sarna ((Lanham, MD: Rowman and Littlefield, 2002), 47.

10. See, e.g., Michael A. Meyer, "America: The Reform Movement's Land of Promise." *The American Jewish Experience.* Ed. Jonathan D. Sarna (New York: Holmes and Meier, 1997), 60–81; Alvin H. Rosenfeld, "Promised Land(s): Zion, America, and American Jewish Writers." *Jewish Social Studies* 3.3 (Spring–Summer 1997): 111–131.

11. Myer Moses, *An Oration Delivered Before the Hebrew Orphan Society on the 15th of October, 1806* (Charleston, SC, 1807), 6, 18, 19. Qtd. James William Hagy, *This Happy Land: The Jews of Colonial and Antebellum Charleston.* Judaic Studies Series (Unnumbered) (Tuscaloosa: University of Alabama Press, 1993), 55.

12. "The Hebrews of America; The Union of Congregations in Session at Richmond Discusses the Zionistic Movement." *New York Times* (December 8, 1898). Qtd. "Delegates Arrive for Hebrew Council; Representatives of 187 Congregations Gathering for the 22d Convention of the Union." *New York Times* (January 16, 1911).

13. Jacob Neusner, "Is America the Promised Land for Jews?" *The Washington Post* (1987). Reprinted in *Zionism: The Sequel.* Ed. Carol Diament (New York: Hadassah, 1998): 121–128.

14. Jacob Neusner, "Stranger at Home: 'The Holocaust.'" *Zionism, and American Judaism* (Chicago: University of Chicago Press, 1981), 1 (emphasis added).

15. Michael Alexander, "The Meaning of American Jewish History." *Jewish Quarterly Review* 96.3 (2006): 423–432. (See p. 427, where Alexander comments: "Exile is a powerful hermeneutic prism for the reading of history, and Sarna takes the view of his subjects as his own; exiles and returns, awakenings and declensions, these are different nomenclature for the same interpretive principle.")

16. Seymour Martin Lipset, "A Unique People in an Exceptional Country." *American Pluralism and the Jewish Community* (New Brunswick, NJ: Transaction, 1990), 3–29.

17. Jonathan Sarna, "Columbus and the Jews." *Commentary* 94:5 (November 1992): 38–41. Revised and expanded in idem, "The Mythical Jewish Columbus and the History of America's Jews." *Religion in the Age of Exploration.* Ed. Bryan F. Le Beau and Menaham Mor (Omaha: Creighton University Press, 1996), 81–95.

18. Jonathan Sarna, *Jacksonian Jew: The Two Worlds of Mordecai Noah* (New York: Holmes and Meier, 1981), 205, n. 46.

19. Gordon M. Freeman, "The Conservative Movement and the Public Square." *Jewish Polity and American Civil Society: Communal Agencies and Religious Movements in the American Public Square.* Ed. Alan Mittleman, Robert A. Licht, and Jonathan D. Sarna (New York: Rowman and Littlefield, 2002), 235–260 [236].

20. Rabbi Elliot L. Stevens, "The Prayer Books, They Are A'Changin'." *Reform Judaism* (Summer 2006). Emphasis added.

21. Jonathan Sarna, "Jewish Prayers for the United States Government: A Study in the Liturgy of Politics and the Politics of Liturgy." *Moral Problems in American History: Essays in Honor of David Brion Davis.* Ed. Karen Halttunen and Perry Lewis (Ithaca: Cornell University Press, 1998), 200–221 [201–202]. Reprinted in *Liturgy in the Life of the Synagogue: Studies in the History of Jewish Prayer.* Ed. Ruth Langer and Steven Fine. Duke Judaic Studies 2 (Winona Lake, IN: Eisenbrauns, 2005).

22. For the complete text of the prayer, see "Items Related to New York Congregation." *Publications of the American Jewish Historical Society* 27 (1920): 34–37.

23. Michael Feldberg, Karla Goldman, Scott-Martin Kosofsky, Pamela S. Nadell, Jonathan D. Sarna, and Gary P. Zola, *Three Hundred Fifty Years: An Album of American Jewish Memory* (New York: American Jewish Historical Society and the American Jewish Archives, 2005), 43.

24. [Tefilot Yisra'el]. *Prayers of Israel, with an English Translation.* 5th ed. (New York: Henry Frank, 1856), 198–199 [198]. See Jonathan Sarna, "A Forgotten 19th-Century Prayer for the United States Government: Its Meaning, Significance, and Surprising Author." *Hesed Ve-Emet: Studies in Honor of Ernest S. Frerichs.* Ed. Jodi Magness and Seymour Gitin (Atlanta, GA: Scholars Press, 1998), 431–440 [432–433]. The present writer thanks the author, Jonathan Sarna, for providing a copy of this excellent book article.

25. Sarna, "A Forgotten 19th-Century Prayer for the United States Government: Its Meaning, Significance, and Surprising Author," 435.

26. Jonathan Sarna, "Early Prayers for the United States Government." *Prayer in America: Community Outreach Guide* (PBS), 111–124 [119].

27. Ruth Langer, "Theologies of Self and Other in American Jewish Liturgies." *CCAR Journal: A Reform Jewish Quarterly* (Winter 2005): 3–41 [17].

28. Louis Jacobs, *The Jewish Religion: A Companion* (Oxford: Oxford University Press, 1995), 370.

29. Ibid., 370.

30. Ibid., 371.

31. Ibid., 372.

32. "Prayer for the Government," *Daily Prayer Book (Ha-Siddur Ha-Shalem).* Translated and annotated with an Introduction by Philip Birnbaum (New York: Hebrew Publishing Company, 1977), 380.

33. Michael Walzer, "Who Is an American Jew?" *Occasional Papers on Jewish Civilization, Jewish Thought and Philosophy* (Washington, DC: Program for Jewish Civilization, Georgetown University, 2007), 8–15 [11].

34. Sarna, "Jewish Prayers," 220.

35. Ibid., 220.

36. Ibid., 220.

37. Jacobs, *The Jewish Religion,* 92.

38. Israel Friedlaender, "The Problem of Judaism in America." *Past and Present: A Collection of Jewish Essays* (Cincinnati: Ark Publishing Co., 1919), 273, who adds: "America is fast becoming the center of the Jewish people of the Diaspora. . . . America is already the center of the Jews."

39. David Golinkin, "Prayers for the Government and the State of Israel Yom Haatzmaut 5766." *Insight Israel: The View from Schechter.* Second Series (Jerusalem: The Schechter Institute of Jewish Studies, 2006), 114–125 [121].

40. Sarna, "Jewish Prayers," 217.

41. Ibid., 217, n. 49.

42. Rabbi Morris Silverman, "A Prayer for Our Country." *High Holiday Prayer Book.* Compiled and arranged by Rabbi Morris Silverman (Hartford, CT: Prayer Book Press of Media Judaica, 1951, 1962, 1979), 115.

43. *Siddur Sim Shalom: A Prayer Book for Shabbat, Festivals, and Weekdays.* Edited, with translations, by Rabbi Jules Harlow (New York: The Rabbinical Assembly, The United Synagogue of America, 1985), 415; David Golinkin, ed., *The Responsa of Professor Louis Ginzberg* (New York, 1906), 54–55; *Festival Prayer Book* (New York, 1927), 201; *Sabbath and Festival Prayer Book* (New York, 1946), 130.

44. Langer, "Theologies of Self and Other in American Jewish Liturgies," 41.

45. Sarna, "Jewish Prayers," 217.

46. Ibid., 217.

47. James William Hagy, *This Happy Land: The Jews of Colonial and Antebellum Charleston.* Judaic Studies Series (Unnumbered) (Tuscaloosa: University of Alabama Press, 1993), 155.

48. Jonathan Sarna, "Early Prayers for the United States Government." *Prayer in America: Community Outreach Guide* (Public Broadcasting System, 2007), 111–124 [117].

49. Michael A. Meyer, "America: The Reform Movement's Land of Promise." *Response to Modernity: A History of the Reform Movement in Judaism* (Oxford: Oxford University Press, 1988; Detroit: Wayne State University Press, 1995).

50. Jacobs, *The Jewish Religion,* 416.

51. Central Conference of American Rabbis, "A Statement of Principles for Reform Judaism."

52. Jacobs, *The Jewish Religion,* 416.

53. Michael A. Meyer, "America: The Reform Movement's Land of Promise." *Response to Modernity: A History of the Reform Movement in Judaism* (Oxford: Oxford University Press, 1988; Detroit: Wayne State University Press, 1995).

54. Lecture delivered before the Theological and Religious Library Association of Cincinnati, January 7, 1869. See Isaac Mayer Wise, "Our Country's Place in History." *God's New Israel: Religious Interpretations of American Destiny,* 224–234 [224, 226, 231, 234]. For similar messianic views of America, see Gershon Greenberg, "The Significance of America in David Einhorn's Conception of History." *American Jewish Historical Quarterly* 63 (December 1973): 160–184.

55. Chaim Stern, ed. *Gates of Prayer: The New Union Prayer Book* (New York: Central Conference of American Rabbis, 1975).

56. Sarna, "Jewish Prayers," 220.

57. Abraham J. Karp, *Jewish Continuity in America: Creative Survival in a Free Society.* Judaic Studies Series (Unnumbered) (Tuscaloosa: University of Alabama Press, 1998), 27.

58. Sarna, "Jewish Prayers," 220.

59. Provided courtesy of Dr. Jay Liebowitz, Duquesne University, sent June 6, 2008.

60. Arnold M. Eisen, *The Chosen People in America: A Study in Jewish Religious Ideology* (Bloomington, IN: Indiana University Press, 1995), 52.

61. Jacobs, *The Jewish Religion,* 413.

62. Ibid., 414.

63. See Eric Caplan, *From Ideology to Liturgy: Reconstructionist Worship and American Liberal Judaism.* Monographs of the Hebrew Union College Series, no. 26. (Cincinnati: Hebrew Union College Press, 2002).

64. Jacobs, *The Jewish Religion,* 298.

65. Steven T. Katz, "Mordecai Kaplan's Theology and the Problem of Evil." *Jewish Social Studies* 12.2 (2006): 115–126 [115].

66. Mordecai M. Kaplan, *Judaism as a Civilization: Toward a Reconstruction of American-Jewish Life* (1934; reprint, Philadelphia, 1994).

67. Noam Pianko, "Reconstructing Judaism, Reconstructing America: The Sources and Functions of Mordecai Kaplan's 'Civilization.' " *Jewish Social Studies: History, Culture, and Society* 12.2 (Winter 2006): 39–55 [53].

68. Mordecai M. Kaplan, *Judaism as a Civilization* (1934; reprint, Philadelphia, 1994), 79. Qtd. Noam Pianko, "Reconstructing Judaism, Reconstructing America: The Sources and Functions of Mordecai Kaplan's 'Civilization.' " *Jewish Social Studies: History, Culture, and Society* 12.2 (Winter 2006): 39–55 [50].

69. Beth S. Wenger, "Making American Civilization Jewish: Mordecai Kaplan's Civil Religion." *Jewish Social Studies* 12.2 (2006): 56–63 [56–57].

70. Pianko, "Reconstructing Judaism, Reconstructing America," 40.

71. Mordecai Kaplan, J. Paul Williams, and Eugene Kohn, eds., *The Faith of America: Readings, Songs and Prayers for the Celebration of American Holidays* (New York: Reconstructionist Press, 1951; reprint, New York, 1963).

72. Qtd. Wenger, "Making American Civilization Jewish," 58.

73. Mordecai Kaplan, *The Greater Judaism in the Making* (New York, 1960), 477–478. Qtd. Mordecai Menahem Kaplan, *Dynamic Judaism: The Essential Writings of Mordecai M. Kaplan.* Ed. Emanuel S. Goldsmith and Mel Scult (New York: Fordham University Press, 1991), 170.

74. Wenger, "Making American Civilization Jewish," 61.

75. Wenger, "Making American Civilization Jewish," 62; Kaplan, Williams, and Kohn, eds., *The Faith of America,* 305–328.

76. *Sabbath Prayer Book: With a Supplement Containing Prayers, Readings and Hymns and with a New Translation* (New York: The Jewish Reconstructionist Foundation, Inc., 1945).

77. Abraham Lincoln, "First Inaugural Address" (Monday, March 4, 1861), paragraph 31.

78. Abraham Lincoln, "The Gettysburg Address" (November 19, 1863).

79. Ibid.

80. *Sabbath Prayer Book,* 539. Qtd. Wenger, "Making American Civilization Jewish," 61; Eric Caplan, *From Ideology to Liturgy: Reconstructionist Worship and American Liberal Judaism.* Monographs of the Hebrew Union College Series, no. 26 (Cincinnati: Hebrew Union College Press, 2002), 101.

81. Mordecai M. Kaplan, Ira Eisenstein, and Eugene Kohn, eds., *The New Haggadah for the Pesah Seder.* Illus. Leonard Weisgard (New York: Behrman House, Inc., 1941; Newly Revised Edition, 1978), 51. Qtd. Deborah Dash Moore, "Judaism as a Gendered Civilization: The Legacy of Mordecai Kaplan's Magnum Opus." *Jewish Social Studies* 12.2 (2006): 172–186 [176].

82. "The Old and the New," *Time* magazine, Monday, June 25, 1945.

83. Jeffrey S. Gurock and Jacob J. Schachter, *A Modern Heretic and a Traditional Community: Mordecai M. Kaplan, Orthodoxy and American Judaism* (New York: Columbia University Press, 1997).

84. Arthur Green, "Response to Paper by David Novak" (unpublished address, Association of Jewish Studies, 1990), 3–5 (condensed). Qtd. Nancy Fuchs-Kreimer,

"Seventy Years After Judaism as a Civilization: Mordecai Kaplan's Theology and the Reconstructionist Movement." *Jewish Social Studies* 12.2 (2006): 127–142 [129].

85. "Tefilah Lememshalah/Prayer for the Country." *Kol Hanesshamah: Shabbat Vehagim* (Wyncote, PA: Reconstructionist Press, 1994), 418 [Hebrew, 419]. (Prayer from Rabindranath Tagore [Adapted] on p. 419.)

86. "Torah Service (*Siddur Sim Shalom,* page 139)."

87. Langer, "Theologies of Self and Other in American Jewish Liturgies," 3.

88. Rabbi Elliot L. Stevens, "The Prayer Books, They Are A'Changin'." *Reform Judaism* (Summer 2006) (emphasis added).

89. Freeman, "The Conservative Movement and the Public Square," 235.

90. Jonathan Sarna, "The Cult of Synthesis in American Jewish Culture." *Jewish Social Studies* 5.1–2 (1999): 52–79.

91. Qtd. Sarna, "Cult of Synthesis," 53 (internal citation omitted).

92. Qtd. Sarna, "Cult of Synthesis," 52 (internal citation omitted).

93. Ibid., 57.

94. Qtd. Sarna, "Cult of Synthesis," 57 (internal citation omitted).

95. Ibid., 57.

96. See Christopher Buck, "Melting Pot." *Encyclopedia of Race, Ethnicity, and Society.* Ed. Richard T. Schaefer (Thousand Oaks, CA: Sage Publications, 2008), 885–888 [886], and the references cited.

97. Charles Liebman, "Reconstructionism in American Jewish Life." *American Jewish Year Book* 71 (1970): 68. Qtd. Sarna, "Cult of Synthesis," 53.

98. Sarna, "Cult of Synthesis," 56.

99. Ibid., 56.

100. Ibid., 72.

CHAPTER 6: MORMON MYTHS AND VISIONS OF AMERICA

1. *The Doctrine and Covenants of the Church of Jesus Christ of Latter-day Saints* (D&C) 101:80.

2. Joseph Smith, letter to N. C. Saxton, Kirtland, Ohio (January 4, 1833). *History of the Church* 1:315. Mr. Saxton's name is incorrectly given as "N. E. Seaton."

3. Newsroom (The Church of Jesus Christ of Latter-day Saints), "Statistical Information: Official 2007 Statistics about the Church of Jesus Christ of Latter-day Saints." See http://newsroom.lds.org/ldsnewsroom/eng/statistical-information.

4. See "Top Ten LDS News Stories of 2007." *Deseret News.*

5. See National Council of Churches, *The Yearbook of American and Canadian Churches* (2008).

6. Article 6, *The Articles of Faith of the Church of Jesus Christ of Latter-day Saints.*

7. Article 10, *The Articles of Faith of the Church of Jesus Christ of Latter-day Saints.*

8. D&C 76:58 (emphasis added).

9. D&C 88:107 (emphasis added).

10. Jan Shipps, "The Reality of the Restoration and the Restoration Ideal in the Mormon Tradition." *The American Quest for the Primitive Church.* Ed. Richard T.

Hughes (Urbana/Chicago: University of Illinois Press, 1988): 181–195; idem, "Difference and Otherness: Mormonism and the American Religious Mainstream." *Minority Faiths and the American Protestant Mainstream.* Ed. Jonathan D. Sarna (Urbana/Chicago: University of Illinois Press, 1998): 81–109.

11. Grant Underwood. "Mormons and the Millennial World View." *Mormon Identities in Transition.* Ed. Douglas J. Davies (London: Cassell, 1996): 135–142; idem, *The Millenarian World of Early Mormonism* (Urbana/Chicago: University of Illinois, 1993); idem, "Early Mormon Perceptions of Contemporary America: 1830–1846." *Brigham Young University Studies* 26 (Summer 1986): 49–61.

12. John L. Brooke, *The Refiner's Fire: The Making of Mormon Cosmology, 1644–1844* (New York: Cambridge University Press, 1994), 34–36.

13. James Talmage, *A Study of the Articles of Faith: Being a Consideration of the Principal Doctrines of The Church of Jesus Christ of Latter-day Saints (Salt Lake City: Church of Jesus Christ of Latter-day Saints,* (1976), 204. Originally published in 1890.

14. "Latter-day Saints." *The HarperCollins Dictionary of Religion.* Ed. Jonathan Z. Smith (San Francisco: HarperSanFrancisco, 1995).

15. Joseph Smith, Jr., *The Papers of Joseph Smith. Vol. 1, The Autobiographical and Historical Writings.* Ed. Dean C. Jessee (Salt Lake City: Church of Jesus Christ of Latter-day Saints, 1989), 1: 6–7. Cited by Richard N. Ostling and Joan K. Ostling, *Mormon America: The Power and the Promise* (San Francisco: HarperSanFrancisco, 1999), 403.

16. James B. Allen, "The Significance of Joseph Smith's 'First Vision' in Mormon Thought." *Dialogue: A Journal of Mormon Thought* 1.3 (Autumn 1966): 29–44 [29].

17. *The HarperCollins Dictionary of Religion,* 652.

18. Jan Shipps, *Mormonism: The Story of A New Religious Tradition* (Urbana/Chicago: University of Illinois Press, 1985), 82–84.

19. Talmage, *Study of the Articles of Faith,* 204.

20. See D&C 132: 18–19.

21. See D&C 13.

22. See D&C 27.

23. Talmage, *Study of the Articles of Faith,* 204.

24. Joseph Fielding Smith, ed., *Teachings of the Prophet Joseph Smith* (Salt Lake City: Deseret, 1993), 374.

25. Brooke, *Refiner's Fire,* vii.

26. Ibid., xvi.

27. D&C 130:22.

28. "The King Follett Discourse." See Stan Larson, "The King Follett Discourse: A Newly Amalgamated Text." *Brigham Young University Studies* 18.2 (Winter 1978): 193–208.

29. Lorenzo Snow, *The Teachings of Lorenzo Snow, Fifth President of the Church of Jesus Christ of Latter-day Saints.* Ed. Clyde J. Williams (Salt Lake City: Bookcraft, 1984), 1.

30. Brooke, *Refiner's Fire,* 203.

31. Ibid., 199.

32. D&C 132:17.

33. See Numbers 27:21; I Samuel 23:10–12; Ezra 2:63.

34. *Book of Mormon,* "Introduction."

35. Joseph Fielding Smith, *Essentials in Church History* (Salt Lake City: Deseret, 1972), 70.

36. E. Douglas Clark, *The Grand Design: America from Columbus to Zion* (Salt Lake City: Deseret, 1992). The present writer thanks the author for kindly sending a copy of his book.

37. Richard L. Bushman, *Joseph Smith and the Beginnings of Mormonism* (Urbana: University of Illinois Press, 1984), 139.

38. Ibid., 140.

39. William Hosking Oliver, *Prophets and Millennialists: The Uses of Biblical Prophecy in England from the 1790s to the 1840s* (Auckland: Auckland University Press, 1978), 238.

40. Brigham Young, *Discourses of Brigham Young: Second President of the Church of Jesus Christ of Latter-day Saints.* Ed. John A. Widtsoe (Salt Lake City, UT: Deseret Book Co., 1954 [1925]), 157.

41. Brooke, *Refiner's Fire,* 198–199; cf. 232.

42. *Journal of Discourses,* 10:235.

43. Bushman, *Joseph Smith and the Beginnings of Mormonism,* 133, 134.

44. Brooke, *Refiner's Fire,* 198–199; cf. 232.

45. 2 Kings 17:6; 18:11

46. Ethan Smith, *View of the Hebrews: Or, the Tribes of Israel in America* (Poultney, VT: Smith and Shute, 1823).

47. Grant Underwood, *The Millenarian World of Early Mormonism* (Urbana/Chicago: University of Illinois, 1993), 66–67.

48. D&C 133:26f.

49. Cf. Judges 15:9.

50. Ether 3:1.

51. 1 Nephi 18:23.

52. 3 Nephi 20:22.

53. Ether 6:6.

54. Ether 1:2.

55. Ether 13:4.

56. 1 Nephi 18:23.

57. 1 Nephi 12:23.

58. 3 Nephi 20:22.

59. Ether 13:4.

60. Talmage, *Study of the Articles of Faith,* 289–290.

61. Ibid., 260.

62. Smith, *Essentials in Church History,* 53.

63. 1 Nephi 13:14.

64. Ether 7:27.

65. 3 Nephi 20:22.

66. 1 Nephi 13:15.

67. 3 Nephi 21:24.

68. D&C 32.

69. Smith, *Essentials in Church History,* 99.

70. Bushman, *Joseph Smith and the Beginnings of Mormonism,* 136.

71. 1 Nephi 13:12. See Arnold K. Garr, *Christopher Columbus: A Latter-day Saint Perspective* (Provo, UT: Religious Studies Center, Brigham Young University, 1992).

72. See Louise G. Hanson, "Columbus, Christopher." *Encyclopedia of Mormonism* (New York: Macmillan, 1992), 294–296.

73. D&C 101:80.

74. D&C 98: 5–6.

75. *Journal of Discourses,* 19:230. Qtd. by Clark, *The Grand Design: America from Columbus to Zion,* 129.

76. Wilford Woodruff, *Conference Report* (April 1898): 89–90. See Wilford Woodruff, *The Discourses of Wilford Woodruff.* Ed. G. Homer Durham (Salt Lake City: Bookcraft, 1946), 160–161. This passage qtd. by Ezra Taft Benson, "God's Hand in Our Nation's History," fireside address was given at Brigham Young University on March 28, 1976.

77. Ray C. Williams, ed., *"By the Hands of Wise Men": Essays on the U.S. Constitution* (Provo: Brigham Young University Press, 1979).

78. Some of the more notable of these include: 1 Nephi 2:20, 1 Nephi 13:15–19, 2 Nephi 1:6–7, 2 Nephi 10:10–14, Ether 2:9–10, 12, and Ether 13:3.

79. Kenneth H. Winn, *Exiles in a Land of Liberty: Mormons in America, 1830–1846.* Studies in Religion (Chapel Hill, NC: University of North Carolina Press, 1989), 198.

80. Joseph Smith, *Times and Seasons* 5.8 (April 15, 1844): 510.

81. Winn, *Exiles in a Land of Liberty,* 205.

82. Ibid., 199.

83. Article 10, *The Articles of Faith of the Church of Jesus Christ of Latter-day Saints.*

84. Moses 7:19, 21. See also D&C 36:8, 42:36.

85. Moses 7:18.

86. Bushman, *Joseph Smith and the Beginnings of Mormonism,* 186 (citing Moses 6:35, 38; 7).

87. *Journal of Discourses* 9:138. Cited by Clark, *The Grand Design: America from Columbus to Zion,* 215.

88. Joseph Smith, letter to N. C. Saxton, Kirtland, Ohio (January 4, 1833). *History of the Church* 1:315.

89. D&C 133:12–13. In Mormon apocalyptic premillennialism, Zion is to be a place of refuge before the great Tribulation, a seven-year period prior to Jesus's second Coming. In popular evangelical thought today, this concept of Zion is the functional equivalent of the Rapture.

90. Ether 13:4–8.

91. Underwood, *Millenarian World,* 31.

92. D&C 57:1–4.

93. Bushman, *Joseph Smith and the Beginnings of Mormonism,* 186–187.

94. Talmage, *Study of the Articles of Faith,* 353; 515–16.

95. Thomas G. Alexander, *Things in Earth and Heaven: The Life and Times of Wilford Woodruff, a Mormon Prophet* (Salt Lake City: Signature Books, 1991), 26 and 346, n. 13.

96. Richard N. Ostling and Joan K. Ostling, *Mormon America: The Power and the Promise* (San Francisco: HarperSanFrancisco, 1999), xviii.

97. Talmage, *Study of the Articles of Faith,* 346.

98. Joseph Smith, letter to N. C. Saxton, Kirtland, Ohio (January 4, 1833). *History of the Church* 1:315; Underwood, *Millenarian World,* 68.

99. W. H. Oliver, *Prophets and Millennialists: The Uses of Biblical Prophecy in England from the 1790s to the 1840s* (Auckland: Auckland University Press, 1978), 238.

100. Underwood, *Millenarian World,* 39.

101. Full statement of "Articles of Faith," no. 10: "We believe in the literal gathering of Israel and in the restoration of the Ten Tribes; that Zion (the New Jerusalem) will be built upon the American continent; that Christ will reign personally upon the earth; and, that the earth will be renewed and receive its paradisiacal glory." The original text reads as follows: "We believe in the literal gathering of Israel and in the restoration of the Ten Tribes. That Zion will be built upon this continent. That Christ will reign personally upon the earth, and that the earth will be renewed and receive its paradasaic glory." Joseph Smith, "Truth will Prevail" [popularly known as "The Wentworth Letter"], *Times and Seasons* 3.9 (Nauvoo, IL: March 1, 1842), 706–710. Republished as idem, Reprinted in Joseph Smith, "The Articles of Faith of the Church of Jesus Christ of Latter-day Saints," *The Pearl of Great Price* (Salt Lake City, UT: The Church of Jesus Christ of Latter-day Saints, 1989), 61.

102. Craig R. Prentiss, " 'Loathsome unto Thy People': The Latter-day Saints and Racial Categorization." *Religion and the Creation of Race and Ethnicity: An Introduction.* Ed. Craig R. Prentiss (New York/London: New York University Press, 2003), 124–139.

103. Lester E. Bush, Jr., "Mormonism's Negro Doctrine: An Historical Overview." *Dialogue* 8 (Spring 1973): 11–68.

104. Newell G. Bringhurst, *Saints, Slaves and Blacks: The Changing Place of Black People within Mormonism* (Westport, CT: Greenwood Press, 1981); Chester Lee Hawkins, "Selective Bibliography on African-Americans and Mormons, 1830–1990." *Dialogue* 25 (Winter 1992): 113–31.

105. Brooke, *Refiner's Fire,* 216.

106. Moses 7:8.

107. Moses 7:22.

108. Brooke, *Refiner's Fire,* 211.

109. Abraham 1:27. See also 3:1–28, 4:1–31.

110. Abraham 1:21–27.

111. D&C, Official Declaration 2. See E. Dale Le Baron, "Mormonism in Black Africa." *Mormon Identities in Transition.* Ed. Douglas Davies (London and New York: Cassell, 1996): 80–86 [83].

112. Le Baron, "Mormonism in Black Africa," 83.

113. Ibid., 83.

114. Ostling and Ostling, *Mormon America,* 102–103.

115. Ibid., 106.

116. Underwood, *Millenarian World,* 39.

117. *Pearl of Great Price* (1989 ed.), 61

118. Harold Bloom, *The American Religion: The Emergence of the Post-Christian Nation* (New York: Simon and Schuster, 1992), 82.

119. Ibid., 84.

120. Norman Douglas, "The Sons of Lehi and the Seed of Cain: Racial Myths in Mormon Scripture and Their Relevance to the Pacific Islands." *Journal of Religious History* 8 (1974): 90–104.

121. Ostling and Ostling, *Mormon America,* xix.

122. Brooke, *Refiner's Fire,* 156.

CHAPTER 7: CHRISTIAN IDENTITY MYTHS AND VISIONS OF AMERICA

1. Dr. Wesley A. Swift, "The Coming Liberation of America" (January 30, 1966).

2. Betty A. Dobratz, "The Role of Religion in the Collective Identity of the White Racialist Movement." *Journal for the Scientific Study of Religion* 40.2 (June 2001): 287–302 [289].

3. "CREATIVITY: Creed and Program" (emphasis added).

4. Ben Klassen, *White Man's Bible* (1992), 121.

5. Stanislav Vysotsky, "Understanding the Racist Right in the Twenty First Century: A Typology of Modern White Supremacist Organizations" (n.p.: Northeastern University, 2004), 9.

6. Stephen Shaw, "Harassment, Hate, and Human Rights in Idaho." *Politics in the Postwar American West.* Ed. Richard Lowitt (Norman: University of Oklahoma Press, 1995), 94–105 [98].

7. Betty A. Dobratz and Stephanie L. Shanks, *The White Separatist Movement in the United States: White Power, White Pride!* (Boston: Johns Hopkins University Press, 2001), 136.

8. Swift's sermons are posted online by the "Church of True Israel."

9. See "Kingdom Identity Ministries."

10. See "Kingdom Identity Ministries Doctrinal Statement of Beliefs."

11. "Kingdom Identity Ministries."

12. See "Herald of Truth" archived broadcasts.

13. Rev. David Ostendorf, "Christian Identity: An American Heresy." *Journal of Hate Studies* 1.1 (2001/2002): 23–55 [29].

14. Rev. William P. Gale, *Racial and National Identity: A Sermon.*

15. See official "Aryan Nations Church of Jesus Christ Christian" Web site.

16. See "Aryan Nations" Web site.

17. "Aryans Without a Nation." *Intelligence Report* (Fall 2000).

18. "Kingdom Identity Ministries Doctrinal Statement of Beliefs."

19. Douglas E. Cowan, "Theologizing Race: The Construction of 'Christian Identity.' " *Religion and the Creation of Race and Ethnicity: An Introduction.* Ed. Craig Prentiss (New York: New York University Press, 2003), 112–123 [122].

20. Craig R. Prentiss, "Coloring Jesus: Racial Calculus and the Search for Identity in Twentieth-century America." *Nova Religio* 11.3 (February 2008): 64–82.

21. Abby Ferber, "Of Mongrels and Jews: The Deconstruction of Racialised Identities in White Supremacist Discourse." *Social Identities* 3 (1997): 193–208.

22. "Kingdom Identity Ministries Doctrinal Statement of Beliefs."

23. King James Version (KJV).

24. Swift, "What Really Happened in the Garden of Eden?"

25. Michael Barkun, *Religion and the Racist Right: The Origins of the Christian Identity Movement* (Chapel Hill, NC: University of North Carolina Press, 1997), x–xi.

26. Dobratz, "The Role of Religion in the Collective Identity of the White Racialist Movement," 3.

27. Mitch Berbrier, "Impression Management for the Thinking Racist: A Case Study of Intellectualization as Stigma Transformation in Contemporary White Supremacist Discourse." *Sociological Quarterly* 40.3 (1999): 411–433.

28. "Kingdom Identity Ministries Doctrinal Statement of Beliefs."

29. "Kingdom Identity Ministries Doctrinal Statement of Beliefs."

30. Ostendorf, "Christian Identity," 28.

31. Ibid., 30.

32. "Kingdom Identity Ministries Doctrinal Statement of Beliefs."

33. Cited Ostendorf, "Christian Identity: An American Heresy," 31.

34. Southern Poverty Law Center, "Elder Statesman: A Life of Hate, and the Future in the Balance." *Intelligence Report* (Summer 1998): 2.

35. Southern Poverty Law Center, "Elder Statesman," 2.

36. James Ridgeway, *Blood in the Face: The Ku Klux Klan, Aryan Nations, Nazi Skinheads, and the Rise of a New White Culture* (New York: Thunder's Mouth Press, 1999), 148.

37. Wilmot Robertson, *The Ethnostate: An Unblinkered Prospectus for an Advanced Statecraft* (Cape Canaveral, FL: Howard Allen Enterprises, 1992).

38. *Time* 156.10 (September 4, 2000): 32–33.

39. "Aryans Without a Nation." *Intelligence Report* (Fall 2000).

40. See Michael F. Leavitt (student casenote), "*Keenan v. Aryan Nations,* No. CV-99-441 (Idaho 2000)." *Idaho Law Review* 37.3 (2001): 603–639.

41. Kathleen Stewart, "Bad Endings: American Apocalypsis." *Annual Review of Anthropology* 28 (1999): 285–310 [286].

42. "Kingdom Identity Ministries Doctrinal Statement of Beliefs."

43. "Kingdom Identity Ministries Doctrinal Statement of Beliefs."

44. Creativity Movement, *Little White Book.*

45. Ibid., 33.

46. Troy Graham, "Supremacist Pleads to Sale of Stolen Guns." *Philadelphia Inquirer* (May 5, 2006), 1.

47. "SA: Racist Group Bases Website Activity in SA." *AAP General News Wire* (Sydney: January 31, 2006), 1.

48. Dobratz, "The Role of Religion," 299.

49. "Pastor" Bertrand L. Comparet, "Man and Beast."

50. Wesley A. Swift, "The Children of the Beast."

51. Dr. Wesley A. Swift, "The Coming Liberation of America" (January 30, 1966).

CHAPTER 8: BLACK MUSLIM MYTHS AND VISIONS OF AMERICA

1. Louis Farrakhan, "A Vision for America" (reprinted from Farrakhan's book, *A Torchlight for America,* published in 1993).

2. Louis Farrakhan, "The Divine Destruction of America: Can She Avert It?" Speech delivered by the Honorable Louis Farrakhan, June 9, 1996, at Mosque Maryam in Chicago. *Final Call News* (1996). Available at http://www.finalcall.com /MLFspeaks/destruction.html.

3. Sophia Tareen, "A Spry Farrakhan Sings Obama's Praises." Associated Press, February 24, 2008.

4. Michael Lieb, " 'Above Top Secret': The Nation of Islam and the Advent of the 'Mother Plane.' " *Criterion* 43.1 (2004): 2–11, 38.

5. Kelefa Sanneh, "The Secret Doctrine: A Conversation with Killah Priest." *Transition* 74 (1997): 162–182.

6. Ibid., 173–174.

7. Killah Priest, "Madness." From the album, *Priesthood* (Babygrande Records, 2005).

8. Malcolm X, "Black Man's History." *The End of White-World Supremacy: Four Speeches by Malcolm X.* Ed. Benjamin Karim (New York: Little, Brown, 1971), 24.

9. Farrakhan's recording of "A White Man's Heaven Is a Black Man's Hell" is available online as a You Tube video. A rap by the same title was recorded by the musical group, Public Enemy, on their CD, *Muse Sick N Hour Mess Age,* but is not Farrakhan's song.

10. Qtd. Louis A. DeCaro, *Malcolm and the Cross: The Nation of Islam, Malcolm X, and Christianity* (New York/London New York University Press, 1998), 29.

11. Qtd. Louis A. DeCaro, *Malcolm and the Cross,* 25.

12. Qtd. Louis A. DeCaro, *Malcolm and the Cross,* 26.

13. Malcolm X, "There's a Worldwide Revolution Going On." *Malcolm X: The Last Speeches.* Ed. Bruce Perry (New York: Pathfinder Press, 1989), 123.

14. Terrill, Robert E. "Protest, Prophecy, and Prudence in the Rhetoric of Malcolm X." *Rhetoric and Public Affairs* 4.1 (2001): 25–53 [41].

15. Malcolm X, "Black Man's History." *The End of White-World Supremacy: Four Speeches by Malcolm X.* Ed. Benjamin Karim (New York: Little, Brown, 1971).

16. Ibid., 42.

17. Ibid., 44.

18. Ibid., 55.

19. Ibid., 56.

20. Ibid., 56.

21. Ibid., 56.

22. Ibid., 57.

23. Ibid., 57.

24. Ibid., 61.

25. Ibid., 63.

26. Ibid., 51.

27. Elijah Muhammad, Chapter 127: "The Battle in the Sky." *Message to the Blackman in America* (Bensenville, IL: Lushena Books, 2000 [1965]), 294.

28. Michael Lieb, "Armageddon and the Final Call." *Children of Ezekiel: Aliens, UFOs, the Crisis of Race, and the Advent of End Time* (Durham/London: Duke University Press, 1998), 198–229; 293–298.

29. Mattias Gardell, *In the Name of Elijah Muhammad: Louis Farrakhan and the Nation of Islam* (Durham, NC: Duke University Press, 1996), 153.

30. Ibid., 164.

31. Ibid., 164.

32. Claude Andrew Clegg III, *An Original Man: The Life and Times of Elijah Muhammad* (New York: St. Martin's Press, 1997), 66.

33. Elijah Muhammad, "The Mother Plane."

34. Ibid.

35. Ibid.

36. Clegg, *An Original Man,* 64.

37. Ibid., 64.

38. Ibid., 66.

39. Ibid., 67.

40. Ibid., 67.

41. Malcolm X, "God's Judgement of America." *The End of White World Supremacy.* Ed. Imam B. Karim (New York: Seaver Books, 1971): 121–148; Mattias Gardell, "Countdown to Armageddon: Minister Farrakhan and the Nation of Islam in the Latter Days." *Temenos* 31 (1995): 253–262.

42. Ibid. (emphasis added).

43. FBI Surveillance file, March 16, 1954. Qtd. by Wayne Taylor, "Premillennium Tension: Malcolm X and the Eschatology of the Nation of Islam." *Souls* 7.1 (Winter 2005): 52–65 [63].

44. FBI Surveillance file, May 23, 1955. Qtd. by Taylor, "Premillennium Tension," 64.

45. Taylor, "Premillennium Tension," 64.

46. Ibid., 64.

47. Ibid., 64.

48. Lieb, "The Eschatology of the Mother Plane." *Children of Ezekiel,* 155–177; 280–283.

49. Louis Farrakhan, "The Divine Destruction of America: Can She Avert It?" Speech delivered at Mosque Maryam, Chicago, June 9, 1996 (Chicago: *Final Call Online* Edition).

50. Gardell, *In the Name of Elijah Muhammad,* 132–133.

51. Vibert L. White, *Inside the Nation of Islam: A Historical and Personal Testimony by a Black Muslim* (University Press of Florida, 2000).

52. Clegg, *An Original Man,* 65.

53. Tom Teague, "From Farrakhan to New Philadelphia: Vibert White Embraces History at Every Crossroad." *Illinois Heritage* 5.2 (March/April 2002): 6–10 [10].

54. Ron Carter, "Winds of Change Blowing Through the Nation of Islam." *Vantage Point* (April 1999).

55. Warith Deen Mohammed, "A Message From: Imam Warith Deen Mohammed" (February 25, 2000). *The Final Call Online.*

56. Anti-Defamation League, "Warith Deen Mohammed Condemns the Nation of Islam" (August 14, 2007).

57. Associated Press, "Former Nation of Islam Leader Dies." *USA Today* (September 9, 2008).

58. Michael Lieb, "Heralding the Messenger." *Children of Ezekiel: Aliens, UFOs, the Crisis of Race, and the Advent of End Time* (Durham/London: Duke University Press, 1998), 129–154; 270–280.

59. Sophia Tareen, "A Spry Farrakhan Sings Obama's Praises." Associated Press, February 24, 2008.

CHAPTER 9: CONTEMPORARY MUSLIM MYTHS AND VISIONS OF AMERICA

1. Hassan Nasrallah (leader of Lebanon's Hezbollah, or "Party of God"), BBC Monitoring: Al-Manar (September 27, 2002).

2. Hillel Fradkin, "America in Islam." *The Public Interest* no. 155 (Spring 2004): 37–55 [51].

3. Qtd. Carol Eisenberg, "Black Muslims Seek Acceptance from Fellow Americans, Adherents." *Seattle Times* (January 22, 2005).

4. Eisenberg, "Black Muslims Seek Acceptance from Fellow Americans, Adherents."

5. John Zimmerman, "Sayyid Qutb's Influence on the 11 September Attacks." *Terrorism and Political Violence* 16.2 (April–June 2004): 222–252 [223].

6. Barbara-Ann J. Rieffer, "Religion and Nationalism: Understanding the Consequences of a Complex Relationship." *Ethnicities* 3.2 (2003): 215–242 [225].

7. Ibid., 225.

8. Ibid., 227.

9. William O. Beeman, "Images of the Great Satan: Representations of the United States in the Iranian Revolution." *Religion and Politics in Iran: Shi'ism from Quietism to Revolution.* Ed. Nikki R. Keddie (New Haven, CT: Yale University Press, 1983): 191–217.

10. William O. Beeman, *The "Great Satan" vs. the "Mad Mullahs": How the United States and Iran Demonize Each Other* (Westport, CT: Praeger, 2005), 119.

11. Ibid., 119.

12. "Hezbollah Leader Nasrallah Supports Intifadah, Vows 'Death to America' " (September 27, 2002). Qtd. "In Their Own Words: What the Terrorists Believe, What They Hope to Accomplish, and How They Intend to Accomplish It." Office of the Press Secretary. White House press release, dated September 5, 2006.

13. See the CIA document, Dr. Donald N. Wilber, "Overthrow of Premier Mossadeq of Iran" (Washington, DC: Central Intelligence Agency, March 1954). First published in an article written by James Risen of *The New York Times* in its editions of April 16 and June 18, 2000.

14. Rieffer, "Religion and Nationalism," 228.

15. Ibid., 228.

16. Ayatollah Khomeini, *Imam's Will* (Tehran: Ministry of Islamic Guidance, 1989), 4. Qtd. Enayatollah Yazdani and Rizwan Hussain, "United States' Policy towards Iran after the Islamic Revolution: An Iranian Perspective." *International Studies* 43 (2006): 267–289 [269].

17. Richard Burton, *Pilgrimage to Al-Madinah and Meccah* (1855), Chapter 30.

18. The present writer owes this distinction to Andrew Rippin, personal e-mail communication, July 12, 2008.

19. Andrew Rippin, "Iblís." *Encyclopaedia of the Qur'an.* Ed. Jane Dammen McAuliffe. Vol. II. (Leiden: E. J. Brill, 2002).

20. Ibid.

21. Rippin, personal e-mail communication, July 12, 2008.

22. Zimmerman, "Sayyid Qutb's Influence on the 11 September Attacks," 222.

23. Andrew Rippin, *Muslims: Their Religious Beliefs and Practices.* 3rd ed. (London: Routledge, 2005), 238.

24. Sayyid Qutb, " 'The America I Have Seen': In the Scale of Human Values (1951). Trans. Tarek Masoud and Ammar Fakeeh. *America in an Arab Mirror: Images of America in Arabic Travel Literature: An Anthology.* Ed. Kamal Abdel-Malek (New York: Palgrave Macmillan, 2000), 9–28 [26]; Ussama Makdisi, "'Anti-Americanism' in the Arab World: An Interpretation of a Brief History." *Journal of American History* 89.2 (September 2002). Reprinted in *History and September 11th.* Ed. Joanne Jay Meyerowitz (Philadelphia: Temple University Press, 2003), 131–156 [138].

25. Zimmerman, "Sayyid Qutb's Influence on the 11 September Attacks," 235.

26. Sayyid Qutb, qtd. Zimmerman, "Sayyid Qutb's Influence on the 11 September Attacks," 235 (internal citations omitted).

27. Ibid.

28. Zimmerman, "Sayyid Qutb's Influence on the 11 September Attacks," 242.

29. William E. Shepard, "Islam and Ideology: Towards a Typology." *International Journal of Middle East Studies* 19.3 (August 1987): 307–335. For a critique of Shepard's typology (and others), see Jeff Kenney, "The Politics of Sects and Typologies." *Nova Religio* 6.1 (October 2002): 137–146.

30. Haroro J. Ingram, "The Transformative Charisma Phenomenon in Islamic Radicalism and Militancy: Tracing the Evolutionary Roots of Islamic Terrorism." *Proceedings of Social Change in the 21st Century Conference 2006.*

31. Rippin, *Muslims,* 178.

32. Peter Beyer, *Religion and Globalization* (London: Sage, 1994), 99–101.

33. Rippin, *Muslims,* 193.

34. David Talbot, "Terrorists Increasingly Turn to the Internet." M.I.T.

35. Ingram, "The Transformative Charisma Phenomenon," 5. Ingram proposes a separate category, will he calls "Militant" (6), reflecting the openly terrorist agenda of *jihádí* radicalists.

36. Islamic Republic News Agency (IRNA), June 8, 2003. Iranian Students News Agency (ISNA) and IRNA, January 22, 2006.

37. Rippin, *Muslims,* 198.

38. Ibid., 192.

39. Mansoor Moaddel, "Discursive Pluralism and Islamic Modernism in Egypt." *Arab Studies Quarterly* 24.1 (Winter 2002): 1–29 [4].

40. Rippin, *Muslims,* 192.

41. Ibid., 192.

42. Ibid., 198.

43. Shepard, "Islam and Ideology," 311.

44. Ingram, "The Transformative Charisma Phenomenon," 5.

45. Moaddel, "Discursive Pluralism," 1.

46. Bernard Lewis, "The Roots of Muslim Rage: Why so many Muslims deeply resent the West, and why their bitterness will not easily be mollified." *The Atlantic Monthly* (September 1990): 1–10 [9].

47. Rippin, *Muslims,* 198 (internal citation omitted).

48. Ingram, "The Transformative Charisma Phenomenon," 5.

49. Rippin, *Muslims,* 190.

50. Christopher Buck, *Paradise and Paradigm: Key Symbols in Persian Christianity and the Bahá'í Faith* (Albany: State University of New York Press, 1999), 3.

51. Rieffer, "Religion and Nationalism," 234.

52. Ibid., 237.

53. BBC News, "Iran's President Launches Weblog" (August 14, 2006).

54. Mahmoud Ahmadinejad, "Autobiography." *Mahmoud Ahmadinejad's Personal Memos* (August 8, 2006). [Blog.] Available at http://www.ahmadinejad.ir/en/ . Select link "Autobiography."

55. Raoul Thibodeaux, "Al-Qaeda Hires Blackwater." *Avant News* (October 30, 2007).

56. Ibid.

57. James R. Gaines and Karsten Prager, "Rafsanjani's Advice to the 'Great Satan.'" *Time* (May 31, 1993).

58. "Ahmadinejad: Britain, Israel, US to 'vanish like the pharaohs.'" American Foreign Press (December 20, 2005).

59. Adam Zagorin, "Khatami: American 'Conceit and Pride' Led to Iraq Mess." *Time* (September 8, 2006).

60. "President Delivers State of the Union Address." Office of the Press Secretary. White House press release, dated January 29, 2002.

61. G. Matthew Bonham and Daniel Heradstveit, "The 'Axis of Evil' Metaphor and the Restructuring of Iranian Views Toward the US." *Vaseteh–Journal of the European Society for Iranian Studies* 1.1 (2005): 89–106 [92].

62. Ibid., 92.

63. Ibid., 91.

64. Ibid., 89 (internal citations omitted).

65. Chehabi, H. E. "Sport Diplomacy between the United States and Iran." *Diplomacy and Statecraft* 12.1 (2005): 89–106 [94].

66. Bonham and Heradstveit, "The 'Axis of Evil' Metaphor," 103.

67. Ibid., 102.

68. Ingrid Mattson, "How Muslims Use Islamic Paradigms to Define America." *Religion and Immigration: Christian, Jewish, and Muslim Experiences in the United States.* Ed. Yvonne Yazbeck Haddad, Jane Smith, and John Esposito (Walnut Creek, CA: Altamira Press, 2003), 198–215 [201].

69. Council on American-Islamic Relations (CAIR), "Islamophobia and Anti-Americanism Book Excerpts: Islamophobia" (2008).

70. Ibid.

71. Charisse L'Pree Corsbie-Massay, "International MTV and Globalization."

72. Charlotte Beers, Under Secretary for Public Diplomacy and Public Affairs, "Remarks at the National Defense University" (September 18, 2002). U.S. Department of State.

73. Charles Dolan, "America's Global Communications Efforts." Remarks to Public Relations Society of America, National Press Club, Washington, DC, October 31, 2002. Office of Electronic Information, Bureau of Public Affairs, U.S. Department of State.

74. "An Organization of U.S. International Broadcasters."

75. "Testimony of Joaquin Blaya, Broadcasting Board of Governors, Before the Subcommittee on the Middle East and South Asia Committee on Foreign Affairs" (May 16, 2007).

76. Ibid.

77. Christopher Ross, "American Public Diplomacy and Islam." *Ambassadors Review* (Spring 2003).

78. The present writer is indebted to Andrew Rippin for these insights. Personal communication, e-mail dated July 12, 2008.

79. Fachrizal Halim, "Pluralism of American Muslims and the Challenge of Assimilation." *Journal of Muslim Minority Affairs* 26.2 (August 2006): 235–244 [240].

80. Imam Abu Laith Luqman Ahmad, "Islam American Style" (2004).

81. Qtd. Carol Eisenberg, "Black Muslims Seek Acceptance from Fellow Americans, Adherents." *Seattle Times* (January 22, 2005).

82. Ellen Laipson, "The Absence of a U.S. Policy towards Iran and its Consequences." *The American Academy of Diplomacy Issues Brief* (September 21, 2004): 5.

83. Ibid., 6.

84. Ali M. Ansari, "Iran and the US in the Shadow of 9/11: Persia and the Persian Question Revisited." *Iranian Studies* 39.2 (June 2006): 155–170 [170].

85. Giacomo Chiozza, "Love and Hate: Anti-Americanism in the Islamic World." Paper prepared for presentation in the Department of Politics, New York University, November 22, 2004, 1–58.

86. Ibid., 2–3.

87. Ibid., 3.

88. Peter J. Katzenstein and Robert O. Keohane, "Varieties of Anti-Americanism: A Framework for Analysis." *Anti-Americanism in World Politics.* Ed. Peter J. Katzenstein and Robert O. Keohane (Ithaca, NY: Cornell University Press, 2007), 37 and 144.

89. Sophie Menuier, "The Distinctiveness of French Anti-Americanism." *Anti-Americanism in World Politics,* 144.

90. Mattson, "How Muslims Use Islamic Paradigms," 213.

91. Christopher Buck, "Islam and Minorities: The Case of the Bahá'ís." *Studies in Contemporary Islam* 5.1–2 (Spring/Fall 2003): 83–106; "Closed Doors: Iran's Campaign to Deny Higher Education to Bahá'ís."

92. Christopher Buck, "Minority Rights." *The Islamic World.* Edited by Andrew Rippin (London/New York: Routledge, 2008 [forthcoming]).

93. Christopher Buck, "Discovering." [the Qur'an]. *The Blackwell Companion to the Qur'an.* Edited by Andrew Rippin (Oxford: Blackwell, 2006), 18–35.

CHAPTER 10: BUDDHIST MYTHS AND VISIONS OF AMERICA

1. Dalai Lama, "Remarks by His Holiness the Dalai Lama to the Members of the United States Congress in the Rotunda of the Capitol Hill in Washington, D.C., 18 April 1991." Matthew E. Bunson, ed., *The Wisdom Teachings of the Dalai Lama* (New York: Plume, 1997), 226.

2. Robert Thurman, "Christian Experiences with Buddhist Spirituality: A Response." *Buddhist-Christian Studies* 21.1 (2001): 69–72 [69].

3. Ibid., 69.

4. Robert S. Ellwood, "East Asian Religions in Today's America." *World Religions in America.* Ed. Jacob Neusner (Louisville, KY: Westminster John Knox Press, 2000), 154–171 [166].

5. Antonio R. Gualtieri, "Founders and Apostates." *Journal of the American Academy of Religion* 1993, 61.1 (Spring 1993): 101–122.

6. Ibid., 101.

7. Ibid., 119.

8. Ibid., 119.

9. Daisaki Ikeda, *Songs for America: Poems* (Mount Rainier, MD: World Tribune Press, 2000).

10. Ibid., 14–15.

11. Ibid., 37.

12. Ibid., 37.

13. Ibid., 63.

14. Ibid., 65.

15. Ibid., 33.

16. Ibid., 37.

17. Ibid., 67.

18. Ibid., 43.

19. Ibid., 49.

20. Daisaku Ikeda, *My Dear Friends in America: Collected U.S. Speeches* (Mount Rainier, MD: World Tribune Press, 2001).

21. Ibid., 158.

22. Ibid., 215.

23. Robert Thurman, *Inner Revolution: Life, Liberty, and the Pursuit of Real Happiness* (New York: Putnam/Riverhead Books, 1998), 18.

24. Ibid., 221.
25. Ibid., 306.
26. Ibid., 307.
27. Ibid., 308.
28. Ibid., 309.
29. Ibid., 310.
30. Ibid., 311.
31. Ibid., 312.
32. Ibid., 313.
33. Ibid., 315.
34. Ibid., 317.
35. Ibid., 319.
36. Ibid., 301.
37. "Robert A. F. Thurman" Web site.
38. Thurman, *Inner Revolution,* 221.
39. Ibid., 280.
40. Ibid., 282.
41. Dalai Lama, qtd. Ann Frechette, "Democracy and Democratization among Tibetans in Exile." *Journal of Asian Studies* 66.1 (February 2007): 97–127 [107].
42. Dalai Lama, *Constitution of Tibet* (Delhi: Bureau of His Holiness the Dalai Lama, 1963). Qtd. Frechette, "Democracy and Democratization," 108.
43. Dalai Lama, *Constitution of Tibet.* Qtd. Frechette, "Democracy and Democratization," 108–109.
44. Frechette, "Democracy and Democratization," 105.
45. Qtd. Frechette, "Democracy and Democratization," 116.
46. Biographical facts based on Dalai Lama's official biographical sketch, "The Dalai Lama's Biography."
47. Dalai Lama, "His Holiness the Dalai Lama's Nobel Lecture, University Aula, Oslo, December 11th, 1989."
48. Ibid.
49. Dalai Lama, "Remarks by His Holiness the Dalai Lama to the Members of the United States Congress in the Rotunda of the Capitol Hill in Washington, D.C., 18 April 1991." Bunson, *Wisdom Teachings of the Dalai Lama,* 226.
50. Dalai Lama, "Statement by His Holiness the XIV Dalai Lama on His Visit to the United States, September 1995." Bunson, *Wisdom Teachings of the Dalai Lama,* 224.
51. Dalai Lama, "Buddhism, Asian Values and Democracy." *Journal of Democracy* 10.1 (January 1999): 3–7 [4].
52. Ibid., 4.

CHAPTER 11: BAHÁ'Í MYTHS AND VISIONS OF AMERICA

1. Qtd. Shoghi Effendi, *The Advent of Divine Justice* (Wilmette, IL: U.S. Bahá'í Publishing Trust, 1990 [1938]), 87–88. See also 'Abdu'l-Bahá, "Talk at Sanatorium of Dr. C. M. Swingle, Cleveland, Ohio, 6 May 1912. Notes by Sigel T. Brooks." *Promulgation of Universal Peace* (Wilmette, IL: U.S. Bahá'í Publishing Trust,

1982), 104. ("All the cities of America seem to be large and beautiful, and the people appear prosperous. The American continent gives signs and evidences of very great advancement; its future is even more promising, for its influence and illumination are far-reaching, *and it will lead all nations spiritually.* The flag of freedom and banner of liberty have been unfurled here, but the prosperity and advancement of a city, the happiness and greatness of a country depend upon its hearing and obeying the call of God." [Emphasis added.])

2. 'Abdu'l-Bahá, "Tablet to the Bahá'ís of the Central States." *Tablets of the Divine Plan* (Wilmette, IL: U.S. Bahá'í Publishing Trust, 1993), 79.

3. This claim excludes what historians and phenomenologists of religion call "new religious movements" (NRMs), which properly belong to larger religious categories, such as the Church of Jesus Christ of Latter-day Saints (presented in Chapter 6), which is part of Christianity (marginally so by orthodox standards), or like the Nation of Islam (treated in Chapter 8), which is an Islamic movement based in the United States.

4. Bahá'í International Community, "The Bahá'í Faith."

5. Bahá'í International Community, "The Bahá'í World Community."

6. Qtd. and trans. by Shoghi Effendi, *The World Order of Bahá'u'lláh* (Wilmette, IL: U.S. Bahá'í Publishing Trust, 1991 [1936]), 36.

7. Shoghi Effendi, "America and the Most Great Peace." *The World Order of Bahá'u'lláh,* 81.

8. See official announcement, "World Heritage Site: Bahá'i Holy Places." See also Bahá'í International Community, "Baha'i shrines chosen as World Heritage sites."

9. Vince Gerasole (CBS), "Rare Wilmette Temple Makes Cut in '7 Wonders' List" (April 30, 2007).

10. Christopher Buck, "The Eschatology of Globalization: Bahá'u'lláh's Multiple-Messiahship Revisited." *Studies in Modern Religions, Religious Movements and the Babi-Bahá'í Faiths.* Ed. Moshe Sharon. *Numen* Book Series: *Studies in the History of Religions,* 104 (Leiden: Brill Academic Publishers, 2004), 143–178; idem, "A Unique Eschatological Interface: Bahá'u'lláh and Cross-Cultural Messianism." *In Iran.* Ed. Peter Smith (Los Angeles: Kalimát Press, 1986), 157–179.

11. Bahá'u'lláh, "Queen Victoria." *The Summons of the Lord of Hosts* (Haifa: Bahá'í World Centre, 2002), 91.

12. This section is primarily based on a prior publication by the author: Christopher Buck, "Baha'i Faith and Social Action." *Encyclopedia of Activism and Social Justice.* Ed. Gary L. Anderson and Kathryn G. Herr (Thousand Oaks, CA: Sage Publications, 2007), vol. 1, 208–213.

13. Bahá'í World Centre. "The *Kitáb-i-Aqdas:* Its Place in Bahá'í Literature." *The Bahá'í World* (Haifa: Bahá'í World Centre, 1993), 107.

14. Bahá'u'lláh. *Tablets of Bahá'u'lláh Revealed after the Kitáb-i-Aqdas* (Wilmette, IL: Bahá'í Publishing Trust, 1978), 67.

15. See Armin Eschragi, " 'Undermining the Foundations of Orthodoxy': Some Notes on the Báb's Sharí'ah (Sacred Law)." *A Most Noble Pattern: Essays in*

the Study of the Writings of the Báb. Ed. Todd Lawson (Oxford: George Ronald, forthcoming).

16. Universal House of Justice, *The Constitution of the Universal House of Justice* (Haifa: Bahá'í World Centre, 1973), 5.

17. David B. Barrett, ed., *World Christian Encyclopedia: A Comparative Study of Churches and Religions in the Modern World, A.D. 1900–2000* (Oxford and New York: Oxford University Press, 1982).

18. 'Abdu'l-Bahá, *Paris Talks: Addresses given by 'Abdu'l-Bahá in Paris in 1911–1912*. 11th ed. (London: Bahá'í Publishing Trust, 1969), 159.

19. Bahá'u'lláh, *The Hidden Words of Bahá'u'lláh* (Wilmette, IL: Bahá'í Publishing Trust, 1985), 3–4.

20. Bahá'u'lláh, "Queen Victoria." *The Summons of the Lord of Hosts* (Haifa: Bahá'í World Centre, 2002), 90.

21. Ibid., 92.

22. Bahá'í International Community, "Sustainable Development and the Human Spirit." Based on the statement, "The Most Vital Challenge," presented to the Plenary of the United Nations Conference on Environment and Development (UNCED, Earth Summit '92).

23. Ibid.

24. 'Abdu'l-Bahá, *Selections from the Writings of 'Abdu'l-Bahá*. Compiled by the Research Department of the Universal House of Justice. Translated by Marzieh Gail et al. (Haifa: Bahá'í World Centre, 1978), 104.

25. 'Abdu'l-Bahá, "5 September 1912. Talk at St. James Methodist Church, Montreal, Canada," *Promulgation of Universal Peace*, 318.

26. Shoghi Effendi, *God Passes By* (Wilmette, IL: U.S. Bahá'í Publishing Trust, 1979 [1944]), 396–397.

27. Bahá'u'lláh, *The Kitáb-i-Aqdas: The Most Holy Book* (Haifa: Bahá'í World Centre, 1992), 52.

28. The author is indebted to Bahá'í scholar Peter Terry for compiling this list of heads of state of the Americas, who were contemporary with Bahá'u'lláh in 1872–1873. E-mail dated September 19, 2008. (Posting on the "Tarikh" listserve.)

29. Shoghi Effendi, *This Decisive Hour: Messages from Shoghi Effendi to the North American Bahá'ís, 1932–1946* (Wilmette, IL: U.S. Bahá'í Publishing Trust, 2002), paragraph 158.3.

30. Reported by the Bahá'í historian Nabíl-i-Zarandí, qtd. Shoghi Effendi, *God Passes By*, 263.

31. Shoghi Effendi, *This Decisive Hour: Messages from Shoghi Effendi to the North American Bahá'ís, 1932–1946*, paragraph 158.3.

32. Robert Stockman, *The Bahá'í Faith and American Protestantism* (Th.D.: Harvard University, 1990). Abstract.

33. Robert Stockman, "Redeemer Nation Revisited: The American Bahá'í Sacred History of America." Chapter 7. *The Bahá'í Faith and American Protestantism* (Th.D.: Harvard University, 1990), 1. The present writer is grateful to Dr. Stockman for his permission to draw from this chapter in his dissertation. Credit goes to David

Merrick, of Edinburgh, Scotland, for providing this chapter by e-mail, with Dr. Stockman's permission. The page numbering used here, however, does not correspond with the completed dissertation.

34. Stockman, "Redeemer Nation Revisited," 1, n. 1.

35. Ernest Lee Tuveson, *Redeemer Nation: The Idea of America's Millennial Role* (Chicago: University of Chicago Press, 1968).

36. Deborah L. Madsen, *American Exceptionalism* (Edinburgh: Edinburgh University Press, 1998), 3.

37. Ibid., 2.

38. Ibid., 2.

39. Ibid., 165.

40. Ibid., 165.

41. Stockman, "Redeemer Nation Revisited," 7.

42. Ibid., 17.

43. The National Spiritual Assembly of the Bahá'ís of the United States is the annually elected governing council of the American Bahá'í community.

44. Stockman, "Redeemer Nation Revisited," 17.

45. Allan L. Ward, *239 Days: 'Abdu'l-Bahá's Journey in America* (Wilmette, IL: U.S. Bahá'í Publishing Trust, 1979), 40.

46. 'Abdu'l-Bahá, "Talk at Howard University, Washington, D.C. (23 April 1912)." Translated by Amin Banani. 'Abdu'l-Bahá, *Promulgation of Universal Peace.* 2nd ed. (Wilmette, IL: U.S. Bahá'í Publishing Trust, 1982), 45–46.

47. 'Abdu'l-Bahá, *Promulgation of Universal Peace,* 46.

48. Louis Auchincloss, *Woodrow Wilson* (New York: Viking Penguin, 2000); A. Clements Kendrick, *Woodrow Wilson: World Statesman* (Lawrence: University Press of Kansas, 1987); Thomas J. Knock, *To End All Wars: Woodrow Wilson and the Quest for a New World Order* (Oxford: Oxford University Press, 1992).

49. Shoghi Effendi, *Citadel of Faith.* Third printing (Wilmette, IL: U.S. Bahá'í Publishing Trust, 1980), 36.

50. David Steigerwald, *Wilsonian Idealism in America* (Ithaca, NY: Cornell University Press, 1994).

51. Stephen Skowronek, "The Reassociation of Ideas and Purposes: Racism, Liberalism, and the American Political Tradition." *American Political Science Review* 100 (2006): 385–401 [396].

52. 'Abdu'l-Bahá, *Selections from the Writings of 'Abdu'l-Bahá* (Haifa: Bahá'í World Centre, 1982), 311–312.

53. Ibid., 109.

54. Shoghi Effendi, *The Advent of Divine Justice,* 88.

55. Gregory S. Butler, "Visions of a Nation Transformed: Modernity and Ideology in Wilson's Political Thought." *Journal of Church and State* 39.1 (Winter 1997): 37–51

56. National Spiritual Assembly (NSA) of the Bahá'ís of the United States, "The Destiny of America and the Promise of World Peace." *New York Times* (December 23, 2001): A29.

57. Ibid.

58. Ibid.

59. Ibid.

60. Abdu'l-Bahá, *'Abdu'l-Bahá on Divine Philosophy.* Ed. Isabel Fraser Chamberlain (Boston: The Tudor Press, 1917), 85. While no Persian or Arabic original exists to authenticate this statement recorded in English, its purport is accepted.

61. Qtd. National Spiritual Assembly of the Bahá'ís of the United States, "The Destiny of America and the Promise of World Peace" (December 23, 2001).

62. Shoghi Effendi, *The Advent of Divine Justice* (Wilmette, IL: U.S. Bahá'í Publishing Trust, 1990 [1938]), 87–88.

63. NSA, "Destiny of America."

64. Shoghi Effendi, *Citadel of Faith* (Wilmette, IL: U.S. Bahá'í Publishing Trust, 1980), 36–37.

65. Thanks to Steve Cooney of New Zealand for this suggestion. E-mail dated July 26, 2008. (Posting on the "Tarikh" listserve.)

66. Shoghi Effendi, *God Passes By,* 256.

67. Henry H. Jessup, "The Religious Mission of the English Speaking Nations." *The World's Parliament of Religions: An illustrated and popular story of the world's first Parliament of Religions, held in Chicago in connection with the Columbian Exposition of 1893.* Vol. 2. Ed. John H. Barrows. Chicago: Parliament Pub. Co., 1893), 1122–1126. Thanks to Reed Breneman for this reference, and also for pointing out that it was George A. Ford who read the paper on Jessup's behalf. E-mail dated July 26, 2008. (Posting on the "Tarikh" listserve.) See review by Eric J. Ziolkowsk, *Journal of the American Academy of Religion* 64.3 (Autumn 1996): 662–664, who notes that the editor of this collection had compared the two variant versions of Jessup's paper to produce a definitive text (663).

68. Jessup, "The Religious Mission of the English Speaking Nations," 1125–1126. These subsequently celebrated words of Bahá'u'lláh come from Edward G. Browne, "Introduction," in 'Abdu'l-Bahá, A Traveler's Narrative Written to Illustrate the Episode of the Báb. Trans. Edward G. Browne, 2 vols. (Cambridge: Cambridge University Press, 1891), 2: xxxix–xl. Robert Stockman points out that "Jessup did not reproduce the quotation exactly as Browne gave it." See idem, *Thornton Chase: The First American Bahá'í* (Wilmette, IL: Bahá'í Publishing Trust, 2001), Chapter 11.

69. Shoghi Effendi, *Citadel of Faith,* 37.

70. Ibid., 126–127.

71. Shoghi Effendi, *The Advent of Divine Justice,* 19.

72. Ibid., 90–91.

73. John Huddleston, "The Spiritual Destiny of America and World Peace." *Processes of the Lesser Peace.* Ed. Babak Bahador and Nazila Ghanea (Oxford: George Ronald, 2002), 107–161.

74. Ibid., 111.

75. Shoghi Effendi, *The Promised Day Is Come.* Rev. ed. (Wilmette, IL: U.S. Bahá'í Publishing Trust, 1980 [1941]), 123.

76. Ibid., 123.

77. Ibid., 123.

78. Ibid., 123.

79. Shoghi Effendi, *Citadel of Faith,* 55.

80. Shoghi Effendi, *The Advent of Divine Justice* (Wilmette, IL: U.S. Bahá'í Publishing Trust, 1990), 89.

81. Shoghi Effendi, *Citadel of Faith,* 38.

82. Huddleston, "The Spiritual Destiny of America and World Peace," 117.

83. Ibid., 132.

84. Shoghi Effendi, *Citadel of Faith,* 36.

85. Deborah K. van den Hoonaard and Will C. van den Hoonaard, *The Equality of Women and Men: The Experience of the Bahá'í Community of Canada* (Winnipeg, MB: Art Bookbindery, 2006).

86. Michael McMullen, "The Religious Construction of a Global Identity: An Ethnographic Look at the Atlanta Bahá'í Community." *Contemporary American Religion: An Ethnographic Reader.* Ed. Penny Edgell Becker and Nancy L. Eiesland (Walnut Creek, London, New Delhi: Altamira Press, 1997), 236–237 and 227.

87. Shoghi Effendi, *The World Order of Bahá'u'lláh* (Wilmette, IL: U.S. Bahá'í Publishing Trust, 1991 [1936]), 203–204 (formatting added).

88. *Century of Light.* Prepared under the direction of the Universal House of Justice (Wilmette, IL: U.S. Bahá'í Publishing Trust, 2001 [2003 printing]), 138.

89. Shoghi Effendi, *The Advent of Divine Justice,* 34.

90. National Spiritual Assembly of the Bahá'ís of the United States, "The Destiny of America and the Promise of World Peace." *New York Times* (December 23, 2001): A29.

91. 'Abdu'l-Bahá, "Prayer for America." *Bahá'í Prayers: A Selection of Prayers Revealed by Bahá'u'lláh, the Báb, and 'Abdu'l-Bahá* (Wilmette, IL: US Bahá'í Publishing Trust, 1991), 25.

92. Alain Locke, "America's Part in World Peace" (1925). Qtd. Christopher Buck, *Alain Locke: Faith and Philosophy* (Los Angeles: Kalimát Press, 2005), 241 (emphasis added). Under the auspices of the National Spiritual Assembly of the Bahá'ís of the United States, *World Order* magazine has published two special issues on Alain Locke. See Christopher Buck, "Alain Locke: Race Leader, Social Philosopher, Bahá'í Pluralist." Special Issue: Alain Locke: Dean of the Harlem Renaissance and Baha'i Race-Amity Leader. *World Order* 36.3 (2005): 7–36; Alain Locke, "Alain Locke in His Own Words: Three Essays" ("The Gospel for the Twentieth Century" [39–42]; "Peace Between Black and White in the United States" [42–45]; "Five Phases of Democracy" [45–48]; Alain Locke, "The Moon Maiden" [37]) *World Order* 36.3 (2005): 37–48 (previously unpublished essays, introduced by Christopher Buck and co-edited with *World Order* editor Dr. Betty J. Fisher); and (2) Christopher Buck and Betty J. Fisher, ed. and intro., "Alain Locke: Four Talks Redefining Democracy, Education, and World Citizenship." *World Order* 38.3 (2006/2007): 21–41. (Alain Locke, "The Preservation of the American Ideal"; "Stretching Our Social Mind"; "On Becoming World Citizens"; "Creative Democracy.")

CHAPTER 12: CONCLUSION: HOW MINORITY FAITHS REDEFINED AMERICA'S WORLD ROLE

1. Mark R. Amstutz, "Faith-Based NGOs and U.S. Foreign Policy." *The Influence of Faith: Religious Groups and U.S. Foreign Policy.* Ed. Eliott Abrams (Lanham: Rowman and Littlefield, 2001), 175–187 [175–176].

2. Michael Barone, "A Place Like No Other." Special issue: *Defining America: Why the U.S. Is Unique. U.S. News and World Report* (June 28, 2004): 38.

3. Harold Hongju Koh, "Foreword: On American Exceptionalism," 1481, n. 4.

4. Edward A. Kolodziej, "American Power and Global Order." *From Superpower to Besieged Global Power: Restoring World Order After the Failure of the Bush Doctrine.* Ed. Edward A. Kolodziej and Roger E. Kanet (Atlanta: University of Georgia Press, 2008), 3–30 [16–17].

5. Woodrow Wilson, "Wilson's Fourteen Points, January 8, 1918." PBS, "Woodrow Wilson." Primary Sources.

6. Woodrow Wilson, "Presenting the Treaty for Ratification Address to the Senate of the United States. July 19, 1919." *God's New Israel: Religious Interpretations of American Destiny,* 279–288 [288].

7. John A. Thompson, *Woodrow Wilson* (London: Longman, 2002).

8. *Reprinted:* Henry R. Luce, "The American Century." *Diplomatic History* 23.2 (2002): 159–171 [168].

9. Fareed Zakaria, *From Wealth to Power: The Unusual Origins of America's World Role* (Princeton: Princeton University Press, 1998).

10. Donald Wallace White, *The American Century: The Rise and Decline of the United States as a World Power* (New Haven and London: Yale University Press, 1996), 65 (emphasis added).

11. Ibid., 429.

12. Ibid., 78 (emphasis added).

13. Eric Kaufmann, "American Exceptionalism Reconsidered: Anglo-Saxon Ethnogenesis in the 'Universal' Nation, 1776–1850." *Journal of American Studies* 33.3 (1999): 437–457.

14. Ibid., 438.

15. Ibid., 439.

16. James H. Moorhead, " 'God's Right Arm'? Minority Faiths and Protestant Visions of America." *Minority Faiths and the American Protestant Mainstream.* Ed. Jonathan D. Sarna (Urbana/Chicago: University of Illinois Press, 1998), 335–361 [356].

17. J. Baird Callicott, "Natural History as Natural Religion." *Encyclopedia of Religion and Nature.* Ed. Bron Taylor and Jeffrey Kaplan (London/New York Continuum, 2005), 2: 1164–1169.

18. Bron Taylor, "Environmental Ethics." *Encyclopedia of Religion and Nature,* 1:597–608.

19. Gary Snyder, "For All." *Deep Ecology for the Twenty-First Century.* Ed. George Sessions (Berkeley: Shambhala, 1995), 462. See Gary Snyder, "For All." *The Gary Snyder Reader: Prose, Poetry, and Translations* (Washington, DC: Counterpoint, 2000), 504.

20. See http://www.Senate.gov/reference/resources/pdf/hconres331.pdf.

21. See http://www.govtrack.us/congress/billtext.xpd?bill=h110-3585.

22. Michael N. McConnell, *A Country Between: The Upper Ohio Valley and Its Peoples, 1724–1774* (Lincoln/London: University of Nebraska Press, 1992), 56.

23. Laurence M. Hauptman, Chapter Three, "Speculations on the Constitution." *Tribes and Tribulations: Misconceptions about American Indians and Their Histories* (Albuquerque: University of New Mexico Press), 27.

24. Sacvan Bercovitch, "Rhetoric as Authority: Puritanism, the Bible, and the Myth of America." *Social Science Information* 21.1 (January 1982): 5–1 [5].

25. Ibid., 14.

26. Seymour Martin Lipset, *American Exceptionalism: A Double-Edged Sword* (New York: Norton, 1996), 19.

27. John Winthrop, "A Model of Christian Charity." *God's New Israel: Religious Interpretations of American Destiny* (Chapel Hill: University of North Carolina Press, 1998), 41.

28. Martin Luther King, Jr., "The World House." *Where Do We Go from Here: Chaos or Community?* (Boston: Beacon Press, 1968).

29. Qtd. Gary Dorrien, *The Making of American Liberal Theology: Idealism, Realism, and Modernity, 1900–1950* (Louisville, KY: Westminster John Knox Press, 2003), 62.

30. Stephen H. Webb, *American Providence: A Nation with a Mission* (New York: Continuum, 2004).

31. Ibid., 168.

32. Ibid., 145.

33. "Address of His Holiness Benedict XVI, 'Rotunda' Hall of the Pope John Paul II Cultural Center of Washington, D.C." Thursday, April 17, 2008.

34. "Address of John Paul II to Hon. Richard B. Cheney, Vice President of the United States of America." Tuesday, January 27, 2004.

35. Jonathan Sarna, "The Cult of Synthesis in American Jewish Culture." *Jewish Social Studies* 5.1–2 (1999): 52–79

36. Central Conference of American Rabbis (CCAR) Responsa, "Reform Support for Orthodox Institutions."

37. *Siddur Sim Shalom: A Prayer Book for Shabbat, Festivals, and Weekdays.* Ed./ trans. Rabbi Jules Harlow (New York: The Rabbinical Assembly, The United Synagogue of America, 1985), 415; David Golinkin, ed., *The Responsa of Professor Louis Ginzberg* (New York: 1906), 54–55; *Festival Prayer Book* (New York: 1927), 201; *Sabbath and Festival Prayer Book* (New York: 1946), 130.

38. D&C 101: 80.

39. D&C 109: 54.

40. 1 Nephi 13: 14.

41. 1 Nephi 13: 30.

42. *Journal of Discourses,* 2:317.

43. Betty A. Dobratz, "The Role of Religion in the Collective Identity of the White Racialist Movement." *Journal for the Scientific Study of Religion* 40.2 (2002): 287–302 [299].

44. Louis Farrakhan, "A Vision for America" (reprinted from Farrakhan's book, *A Torchlight for America,* published in 1993).

45. Ibid.

46. Ibid.

47. FinalCall.com News, "Exclusive Interview with Minister Louis Farrakhan" (December 2007). (Emphasis added.)

48. Ibid.

49. Ibid.

50. Ibid.

51. Louis Farrakhan, "One Nation Under God" (February 25, 2007).

52. Omar Safi, ed., *Progressive Muslims: On Justice, Gender, and Pluralism* (Oxford: Oneworld Publications, 2003).

53. Omar Safi, "What is Progressive Islam?" *ISIM Newsletter* 13 (December 2003): 48–49 [48].

54. Andrew Rippin, e-mail dated August 13, 2008, to author.

55. Safi, "Progressive Islam?" 49.

56. Ibid., 49.

57. Ibid., 49.

58. Ibid., 49.

59. Ibid., 49.

60. Qtd. Ted J. Solomon, "The Response of Three New Religions to the Crisis in the Japanese Value System." *Journal for the Scientific Study of Religion* 16.1 (March 1977): 1–14 [11].

61. Dalai Lama, "Remarks by His Holiness the Dalai Lama to the Members of the United States Congress in the Rotunda of the Capitol Hill in Washington, D.C., 18 April 1991." Matthew E. Bunson, ed., *The Wisdom Teachings of the Dalai Lama* (New York: Plume, 1997), 226.

62. Dalai Lama, "Statement by His Holiness the XIV Dalai Lama on His Visit to the United States, September 1995." Bunson, *Wisdom Teachings,* 224.

63. Qtd. and trans. by Shoghi Effendi, *The World Order of Bahá'u'lláh* (Wilmette, IL: U.S. Bahá'í Publishing Trust, 1991 [1936]), 36.

64. Citing a text written by 'Abdu'l-Bahá on February 2, 1917, *Tablets of the Divine Plan* (Wilmette, IL: U.S. Bahá'í Publishing Trust, 1993), 62 (with a slightly different translation: "where the righteous will abide and the free assemble").

65. Citing a text written by 'Abdu'l-Bahá on February 2, 1917, in *Tablets of the Divine Plan* (Wilmette, IL: U.S. Bahá'í Publishing Trust, 1993), 62.

66. 'Abdu'l-Bahá, "Talk at Sanatorium of Dr. C. M. Swingle, Cleveland, Ohio, 6 May 1912. Notes by Sigel T. Brooks." *Promulgation of Universal Peace* (Wilmette, IL: U.S. Bahá'í Publishing Trust, 1982), 104.

67. 'Abdu'l-Bahá, *Promulgation of Universal Peace,* 104.

68. Ibid., 104.

69. Ibid., 104.

70. Ibid., 103.

71. 'Abdu'l-Bahá, "6 May 1912, Talk at Euclid Hall, Cleveland, Ohio." See *Promulgation of Universal Peace,* 103. However, this latter version has the word "democracy" instead of "people" at the end of the sentence, to wit: "This American nation is equipped and empowered to accomplish that which will adorn the pages of history, to become the envy of the world and be blest in the East and the West for the triumph of its democracy."

72. 'Abdu'l-Bahá, "20 April 1912, Talk at Orient-Occident-Unity Conference, Public Library Hall, Washington, D.C. Notes by Joseph H. Hannen." See *Promulgation of Universal Peace,* 36." See *Promulgation of Universal Peace,* 36. The text here states: "May this American democracy be the first nation to establish the foundation of international agreement. May it be the first nation to proclaim the universality [Shoghi Effend: "unity"] of mankind. May it be the first to upraise [Shoghi Effendi: "unfurl"] the standard of the Most Great Peace . . . ."

73. 'Abdu'l-Bahá, "16 April 1912. Talk at Hotel Ansonia to Bahá'í Friends of New Jersey, Broadway and Seventy-third Street, New York. Notes by Ahmad Sohráb." See *Promulgation of Universal Peace,* 19.

74. 'Abdu'l-Bahá, *Promulgation of Universal Peace,* 20.

75. Shoghi Effendi, *Citadel of Faith* (Wilmette, IL: U.S. Bahá'í Publishing Trust, 1980), 35, citing, in this final sentence: 'Abdu'l-Bahá, *Promulgation of Universal Peace,* 37. Thanks to attorney Brent Poirier for referring the author to this text. E-mail dated July 27, 2008 (Tarikh listserve).

76. See Roshan Danesh has further explored the Bahá'í Faith and internationalism in his journal article, "Internationalism and Divine Law: A Bahá'í Perspective." *Journal of Law and Religion* 19.2 (2003/2004): 209–242. However, Danesh does not directly address Bahá'í texts that bear on the destiny of America.

77. Dr. Martin Luther King, Jr., "Address Delivered at Poor People's Campaign Rally." March 19, 1968. Clarksdale, Mississippi. Qtd. by James H. Cone, *Risks of Faith: The Emergence of a Black Theology of Liberation, 1968–1998* (Boston: Beacon Press, 2000), 152, n. 20; Stanford University, "Martin Luther King, Jr., Papers Project."

78. See Christopher Buck, "Alain Locke." *American Writers: A Collection of Literary Biographies.* Supplement XIV. Ed. Jay Parini (Farmington Hills, MI: Scribner's Reference/The Gale Group, 2004), 195–219; idem, Chapter Ten: "Philosophy of Democracy: America, Race, and World Peace." *Alain Locke: Faith and Philosophy* (Los Angeles: Kalimát Press, 2005), 241–266.

79. Alain Locke, "Stretching Our Social Mind," in Christopher Buck and Betty J. Fisher, ed. and intro., "Alain Locke: Four Talks Redefining Democracy, Education, and World Citizenship." *World Order* 38.3 (2006/2007): 21–41 (forthcoming, 2008).

80. "Myths can also be understood as true stories." Eddie S. Glaude, "Myth and African American Self-Identity." *Religion and the Creation of Race and Ethnicity: An Introduction.* Ed. Craig R. Prentiss (New York: New York University Press, 2003), 29.

81. Richard T. Hughes, *Myths America Lives By.* Foreword by Robert N. Bellah (Champaign: University of Illinois Press, 2004).

82. The first two terms, "Exemplarism" and "Vindicationism," are borrowed from Jonathan Monten, "The Roots of the Bush Doctrine: Power, Nationalism, and Democracy Promotion in U.S. Strategy." *International Security* 29.4 (2005): 112–156 [112].

83. Henry Kissinger, *Diplomacy* (New York: Simon and Schuster, 1994), 18.

84. John Winthrop, "A Model of Christian Charity." *God's New Israel: Religious Interpretations of American Destiny,* 41.

85. Dean Hoge, "Theological Views of America among Protestants." *Sociological Analysis* 37.2 (1976): 127–139 [128].

86. Ibid., 128.

87. Ibid., 128.

88. Ibid., 128.

89. Thomas Heitala, *Manifest Destiny: Anxious Aggrandizement in Late Jacksonian America* (Ithaca, NY: Cornell University Press, 1985); Gene M. Brack, *Mexico Views Manifest Destiny, 1821–1846: An Essay on the Origins of the Mexican War* (Albuquerque: University of New Mexico Press, 1975).

90. Hoge, "Theological Views of America," 128.

91. Ibid., 128.

92. Robert N. Bellah. "Civil Religion in America." Special Issue: Religion in America. *Dædalus: Journal of the American Academy of Arts and Sciences* 96.1 (Winter 1967): 1–21 [1]. Reprinted in idem, *Beyond Belief: Essays on Religion in a Post-Traditionalist World* (Berkeley: University of California Press, 1991).

93. Bellah, "Civil Religion," 18

94. Ibid., 18

95. Ibid., 18

96. Paul Nathanson, *Over the Rainbow: The Wizard of Oz as a Secular Myth of America* (Albany: State University of New York Press, 1991), 398, n. 56.

97. Ibid., 398, n. 56.

98. Bellah, "Civil Religion," 21; James A. Mathisen, "Twenty Years After Bellah: What Ever Happened to American Civil Religion?" *Sociological Analysis* 50.2 (1989): 129–146.

99. Robert N. Bellah, "Religion in the Public Sphere: Is a Global Civil Religion Possible?" Emphasis added.

100. Pope John Paul II, "Address of John Paul II to Hon. Richard B. Cheney, Vice President of the United States of America." Tuesday, January 27, 2004.

101. *Siddur Sim Shalom: A Prayer Book for Shabbat, Festivals, and Weekdays.* Edited, with translations, by Rabbi Jules Harlow (New York: The Rabbinical Assembly, The United Synagogue of America, 1985), 415; David Golinkin, ed., *The Responsa of Professor Louis Ginzberg* (New York: 1906), 54–55; *Festival Prayer Book* (New York: 1927), 201; *Sabbath and Festival Prayer Book* (New York: 1946), 130.

102. See The Church of Jesus Christ of Latter-day Saints, "The Family: A Proclamation to the World" (September 23, 1995).

103. *"It is not a time for integration; it is a time for us to separate from our former slave-masters ...."* FinalCall.com News, "Exclusive Interview with Minister Louis Farrakhan" (December 2007). (Emphasis added.)

104. Louis Farrakhan, "A Vision for America" (reprinted from Farrakhan's book, *A Torchlight for America,* published in 1993).

105. Shoghi Effendi, *Citadel of Faith,* 126.

106. Ibid., 38.

107. Conrad Cherry, "Challenges Since Mid-Century." *God's New Israel: Religious Interpretations of American Destiny.* Ed. idem. Rev. ed. (Chapel Hill: University of North Carolina Press, 1998), 318.

108. John O'Sullivan, "America's Identity Crisis," *National Review* 46 (November 21, 1994): 36.

109. Roland Robertson, *Globalization: Social Theory and Global Culture* (London: Sage, 1992), 8.

110. Anthony Giddens, *The Consequences of Modernity* (Cambridge: Polity, 1990), 64.

111. Charles O. Lerche, "The Conflicts of Globalization." *International Journal of Peace Studies* 1.3 (January 1998): 47–66.

112. Fiona Robinson. "Rethinking Ethics in an Era of Globalization." *Sussex Papers in International Relations* no. 2 (January 1996): 4.

113. Sacvan Bercovitch, *Rites of Assent: Transformations in the Symbolic Construction of America* (New York: Routledge, 1993).

114. "Theodore Roosevelt: The Nobel Peace Prize 1906." See http://nobelprize.org /nobel_prizes/peace/laureates/1906/roosevelt-bio.html.

115. *The Letters of Theodore Roosevelt,* vol. 8, 853. Cited by Greg Russell, "Theodore Roosevelt, Geopolitics, and Cosmopolitan Ideals." *Review of International Studies* 32 (2006): 541–559 [557].

116. Theodore Roosevelt, *The Works of Theodore Roosevelt.* National ed., Ed. Herman Hagedorn (New York: Scribner, 1926), vol. 15, 268–269. Qtd. Greg Russell, "Theodore Roosevelt, Geopolitics, and Cosmopolitan Ideals," 557.

117. 'Abdu'l-Bahá, *The Secret of Divine Civilization* (Wilmette, IL: U.S. Bahá'í Publishing Trust, 1990), 64–65.

118. Pope John XXIII, *"Pacem in Terris:* Encyclical of Pope John XXIII on Establishing Universal Peace in Truth, Justice, Charity, and Liberty, April 11, 1963." *The Pope Speaks* 9 (1963), 13–48 [13].

119. Universal House of Justice, *The Promise of World Peace* (Haifa: Bahá'í World Centre, October 1985), 2.

120. Ibid., 4.

121. John Paul II, "Meeting with the President of the United States of America, Mr. Ronald Reagan. Address of John Paul II." Vizcaya Museum, Miami. Thursday, September 10, 1987.

122. Martin Luther King, Jr., "The World House." *Where Do We Go from Here: Chaos or Community?* (Boston: Beacon Press, 1968).

123. Shoghi Effendi, *The World Order of Bahá'u'lláh,* 193.

References

Aaron, David H. "Early Rabbinic Exegesis on Noah's Son Ham and the So-Called 'Hamitic Myth.'" *Journal of the American Academy of Religion* 63 (1995): 721–759.

'Abdu'l-Bahá. *'Abdu'l-Bahá on Divine Philosophy*. Ed. Isabel Fraser Chamberlain. Boston: The Tudor Press, 1917.

'Abdu'l-Bahá. *A Traveler's Narrative Written to Illustrate the Episode of the Báb*. Trans. Edward G. Browne, 2 vols. Cambridge: Cambridge University Press, 1891. Vol. 2.

'Abdu'l-Bahá. *Paris Talks: Addresses Given by 'Abdu'l-Bahá in Paris in 1911–1912*. 11th ed. London: Bahá'í Publishing Trust, 1969.

'Abdu'l-Bahá. "Prayer for America." *Bahá'í Prayers: A Selection of Prayers Revealed by Bahá'u'lláh, the Báb, and 'Abdu'l-Bahá*. Wilmette, IL: U.S. Bahá'í Publishing Trust, 1991. 25.

'Abdu'l-Bahá. *Promulgation of Universal Peace*. 2nd ed. Wilmette, IL: U.S. Bahá'í Publishing Trust, 1982.

'Abdu'l-Bahá. *The Secret of Divine Civilization*. Wilmette, IL: U.S. Bahá'í Publishing Trust, 1990.

'Abdu'l-Bahá. *Selections from the Writings of 'Abdu'l-Bahá*. Compiled by the Research Department of the Universal House of Justice. Translated by Marzieh Gail et al. Haifa: Bahá'í World Centre, 1982 [1978].

Ahmad, Imam Abu Laith Luqman. "Islam American Style." 2004. See http://www.imamluqman.com/Islam%20American%20Style.pdf. Hypertext version at http://www.imamluqman.com/Articles.htm.

Ahmadinejad. "Autobiography. 2006/08/08." See http://www.ahmadinejad.ir. Enter keywords "Great Satan" to access this particular blog.

Alexander, Michael. "The Meaning of American Jewish History." *Jewish Quarterly Review* 96.3 (2006): 423–432.

Alexander, Thomas G. *Things in Earth and Heaven: The Life and Times of Wilford Woodruff, a Mormon Prophet.* Salt Lake City: Signature Books, 1991.

Allen, James B. "The Significance of Joseph Smith's 'First Vision' in Mormon Thought." *Dialogue: A Journal of Mormon Thought* 1.3 (Autumn 1966): 29–44.

American Foreign Press. "Ahmadinejad: Britain, Israel, US to 'vanish like the pharaohs.' " (December 20, 2005). See http://www.breitbart.com/article.php?id=061220094102.ixs3bo81andshow_article=1.

American Jewish Historical Society. "Items Related to New York Congregation." *Publications of the American Jewish Historical Society* 27 (1920): 34–37.

Amstutz, Mark R. "Faith-Based NGOs and U.S. Foreign Policy." *The Influence of Faith: Religious Groups and U.S. Foreign Policy.* Ed. Eliott Abrams. Lanham: Rowman and Littlefield, 2001. 175–187.

Angrosino, Michael. "Civil Religion Redux." *Anthropological Quarterly* 75.2 (2002): 239–267.

Ansari, Ali M. "Iran and the US in the Shadow of 9/11: Persia and the Persian Question Revisited." *Iranian Studies* 39.2 (June 2006): 155–170.

Anti-Defamation League, "Warith Deen Mohammed Condemns the Nation of Islam." August 14, 2007. See http://www.adl.org/main_Nation_of_Islam/WD_Mohammed_NOI.htm.

"Aryan Nations." See http://www.aryan-nations.org.

"Aryan Nations Church of Jesus Christ Christian." See http://www.aryannations.org.

Associated Press. "Former Nation of Islam Leader Dies." *USA Today* (September 9, 2008). See http://www.usatoday.com/news/nation/2008-09-09-mohammed-obit_N.htm.

Auchincloss, Louis. *Woodrow Wilson.* New York: Viking Penguin, 2000.

Bahá'í International Community. "Baha'i Shrines Chosen as World Heritage Sites." See http://news.bahai.org/story/642.

Bahá'í International Community. "The Bahá'í Faith." See http://info.bahai.org.

Bahá'í International Community. "The Bahá'í World Community." See http://info.bahai.org/bahai-world-community.html.

Bahá'í International Community. "Closed Doors: Iran's Campaign to Deny Higher Education to Bahá'ís." See http://denial.bahai.org.

Bahá'í International Community. *The Search for Values in an Age of Transition* (New York: October 2005), par. 15(c). See http://statements.bahai.org/05-1002.htm.

Bahá'í International Community. "Sustainable Development and the Human Spirit." See http://www.bic-un.bahai.org/92-0604.htm.

Bahá'í World Centre. "The *Kitáb-i-Aqdas*: Its Place in Bahá'í Literature." *The Bahá'í World.* Haifa: Bahá'í World Centre, 1993.

Bahá'u'lláh, *The Hidden Words of Bahá'u'lláh.* Wilmette: Bahá'í Publishing Trust, 1985.

Bahá'u'lláh. *The Kitáb-i-Aqdas: The Most Holy Book.* Haifa: Bahá'í World Centre, 1992.

Bahá'u'lláh. "Queen Victoria." *The Summons of the Lord of Hosts*. Haifa: Bahá'í World Centre, 2002.

Bahá'u'lláh. "The Tablet of Unity." *Lawh-i Ittihád*. Trans. Moojan Momen. Provisional translation. See http://bahai-library.com/provisionals/ittihad .html.

Bahá'u'lláh. *Tablets of Bahá'u'lláh Revealed after the Kitáb-i-Aqdas*. Wilmette: Bahá'í Publishing Trust, 1978.

Barkun, Michael. "Racist Apocalypse: Millennialism on the Far Right." *American Studies* 31.2 (1990): 121–140.

Barkun, Michael. *Religion and the Racist Right: The Origins of the Christian Identity Movement*. Chapel Hill, NC: University of North Carolina Press, 1997.

Barone, Michael. "A Place Like No Other." Special issue: *Defining America: Why the U.S. Is Unique. U.S. News and World Report* (June 28, 2004).

Barreiro, J., ed. *Indian Roots of American Democracy*. Ithaca, NY: *Northeast Indian Quarterly* (1988).

Barrett, David B., ed. *World Christian Encyclopedia: A Comparative Study of Churches and Religions in the Modern World, A.D. 1900–2000*. Oxford and New York: Oxford University Press, 1982.

Beeman, William O. *The "Great Satan" vs. the "Mad Mullahs": How the United States and Iran Demonize Each Other*. Westport, CT: Praeger, 2005.

Beeman, William O. "Images of the Great Satan: Representations of the United States in the Iranian Revolution." *Religion and Politics in Iran: Shi'ism from Quietism to Revolution*. Ed. Nikki R. Keddie. New Haven, CT: Yale University Press, 1983, 191–217.

Beers, Charlotte. "Remarks at the National Defense University" (September 18, 2002). U.S. Department of State. See http://www.state.gov/r/us/18199.htm.

Bellah, Robert N. "Civil Religion in America." Special Issue: *Religion in America. Dædalus: Journal of the American Academy of Arts and Sciences* 96.1 (Winter 1967): 1–21. Reprinted in idem, *Beyond Belief: Essays on Religion in a Post-Traditionalist World*. Berkeley: University of California Press, 1991.

Bellah, Robert N. "Foreword." Richard T. Hughes, *Myths America Lives By*. Champaign: University of Illinois Press, 2004.

Bellah Robert N. "Religion in the Public Sphere: Is a Global Civil Religion Possible?" See http://www.ssrc.org/blogs/immanent_frame/2007/12/24/is-a-global-civil-religion-possible.

Benedict XVI. "Address of His Holiness Benedict XVI, 'Rotunda' Hall of the Pope John Paul II Cultural Center of Washington, D.C." (Thursday, April 17, 2008). See http://www.vatican.va/holy_father/benedict_xvi/speeches/2008/april/documents/hf_ben-xvi_spe_20080417_other-religions_en.html.

Beneke, Chris. *Beyond Toleration: The Religious Origins of American Pluralism*. New York: Oxford University Press, 2006.

Benson, Ezra Taft. "God's Hand in Our Nation's History." Fireside address was given at Brigham Young University on March 28, 1976. See http://speeches.byu .edu/reader/reader.php?id=6125.

Berbrier, Mitch. "Impression Management for the Thinking Racist: A Case Study of Intellectualization as Stigma Transformation in Contemporary White Supremacist Discourse." *Sociological Quarterly* 40.3 (1999): 411–433.

Bercovitch, Sacvan. "The Myth of America." *Puritan Origins of the American Self.* New Haven: Yale University Press, 1986. 136–186.

Bercovitch, Sacvan. "Rhetoric as Authority: Puritanism, the Bible, and the Myth of America." *Social Science Information* 211 (January 1982): 5–17.

Bercovitch, Sacvan. *The Rites of Assent: Transformations in the Symbolic Construction of America.* New York: Routledge, 1993.

Berlant, Lauren Gail. *The Anatomy of National Fantasy: Hawthorne, Utopia, and Everyday Life.* Chicago: University of Chicago Press, 1991.

Berman, Lila Corwin. "Mission to America: The Reform Movement's Missionary Experiments, 1919–1960." *Religion and American Culture* 13.2 (Summer 2003): 205–239.

Bernardin, Joseph Cardinal. *A Moral Vision of America.* Ed. John P. Langan. Washington, DC: Georgetown University Press, 1998.

Beyer, Peter. *Religion and Globalization.* London: Sage, 1994.

Blaya, Joaquin. "Testimony of Joaquin Blaya, Broadcasting Board of Governors, Before the Subcommittee on the Middle East and South Asia Committee on Foreign Affairs. May 16, 2007. See http://foreignaffairs.house.gov/sub_press_display.asp?sub_press=7&id=50 (accessed January 25, 2009).

Bloom, Harold. *The American Religion: The Emergence of the Post-Christian Nation.* New York: Simon and Schuster, 1992.

Blount, Marcellus. "The Preacherly Text: African American Poetry and Vernacular Performance." *PMLA: Publications of the Modern Language Association of America* 107.3 (May 1992): 582–593.

Bonham, G. Matthew, and Daniel Heradstveit. "The 'Axis of Evil' Metaphor and the Restructuring of Iranian Views Toward the US."*Vaseteh—Journal of the European Society for Iranian Studies* 1.1 (2005): 89–106.

Bottoms, Pam. "The Controversial, Subversive 'Broken Tongue' of Paul Lawrence Dunbar." *Midwestern Miscellany* 34 (Spring/Fall 2006): 6–26.

Brack, Gene. *The Diplomacy of Racism: Manifest Destiny and Mexico, 1821–1848.* St. Charles, MO: Forum Press, 1974.

Brack, Gene M. *Mexico Views Manifest Destiny, 1821–1846: An Essay on the Origins of the Mexican War.* Albuquerque: University of New Mexico Press, 1975.

Bringhurst, Newell G. *Saints, Slaves and Blacks: The Changing Place of Black People within Mormonism.* Westport, CT: Greenwood Press, 1981.

British Broadcasting Corporation News. "Iran's President Launches Weblog." August 14, 2006. http://news.bbc.co.uk/2/hi/middle_east/4790005.stm.

Broadcasting Board of Governors. "An Organization of U.S. International Broadcasters." See http://www.bbg.gov/bbg_aboutus.cfm.

Brooke, John L. *The Refiner's Fire: The Making of Mormon Cosmology, 1644–1844.* New York: Cambridge University Press, 1994.

Brown, Delwin. "Limitation and Ingenuity: Radical Historicism and the Nature of Tradition." *Tradition and Theories of Tradition: An International Discourse.*

Ed. Siegfried Wiedenhofer. Piscataway, NJ: Transaction Publishers, 2006. 213–228.

Browne, Edward G. "Introduction." In 'Abdu'l-Bahá. *A Traveler's Narrative Written to Illustrate the Episode of the Báb.* Trans. Edward G. Browne, 2 vols. Cambridge: Cambridge University Press, 1891. Vol. 2.

Brown v. Board of Education, 347 U.S. 483 (1954) (overruling *Plessy v. Ferguson* (1896)).

Brownson, Orestes. *The American Republic: Its Constitution, Tendencies, and Destiny.* New York: P. O'Shea, 1866. See http://terrenceberres.com/broame .html.

Brownson, Orestes. "Mission of America." *The Works of Orestes A. Brownson.* Ed. Henry F. Brownson. Detroit: T. Nourse, 1884. Vol. 11: 551–584.

Buck, Christopher. "Alain Locke." *American Writers: A Collection of Literary Biographies.* Supplement XIV. Ed. Jay Parini. Farmington Hills, MI: Scribner's Reference/The Gale Group, 2004. 195–219.

Buck, Christopher. "Alain Locke: Race Leader, Social Philosopher, Bahá'í Pluralist." Special Issue: Alain Locke: Dean of the Harlem Renaissance and Baha'i Race-Amity Leader. *World Order* 36.3 (2005): 7–36

Buck, Christopher. "Baha'i Faith and Social Action." *Encyclopedia of Activism and Social Justice.* Ed. Gary L. Anderson and Kathryn G. Herr. Thousand Oaks, CA: Sage Publications, 2007. Vol. 1, 208–213.

Buck, Christopher. "Discovering" [the Qur'an]. *The Blackwell Companion to the Qur'an.* Ed. Andrew Rippin. Oxford: Blackwell, 2006. 18–35. See http:// www.blackwellpublishing.com/content/BPL_Images/Content_store/Sample _chapter/9781405117524/1405117524_4_002.pdf.

Buck, Christopher. "The Eschatology of Globalization: Bahá'u'lláh's Multiple-Messiahship Revisited." *Studies in Modern Religions, Religious Movements and the Babi-Bahá'í Faiths.* Ed. Moshe Sharon. *Numen* Book Series: *Studies in the History of Religions,* 104. Leiden: Brill Academic Publishers, 2004. 143–178.

Buck, Christopher. "Islam and Minorities: The Case of the Bahá'ís." *Studies in Contemporary Islam* 5.1–2 (Spring/Fall 2003): 83–106. *Proceedings of the Twentieth Annual Conference of the American Council for the Study of Islamic Societies* (ACSIS), University of Victoria, Victoria, British Columbia, May 2–3, 2003. (Published June 2005.)

Buck, Christopher. "Melting Pot." *Encyclopedia of Race, Ethnicity, and Society.* Ed. Richard T. Schaefer. Thousand Oaks, CA: Sage Publications, 2008. 885–888.

Buck, Christopher. "Religious Minority Rights." *The Islamic World.* Ed. Andrew Rippin. London/New York: Routledge, 2008. 638–655.

Buck, Christopher. *Paradise and Paradigm: Key Symbols in Persian Christianity and the Bahá'í Faith.* Albany: State University of New York Press, 1999.

Buck, Christopher. "Philosophy of Democracy: America, Race, and World Peace" (Chapter Ten). *Alain Locke: Faith and Philosophy.* Los Angeles: Kalimát Press, 2005. 241–266.

Buck, Christopher. "*Plessy v. Ferguson.*" *Encyclopedia of Race, Ethnicity, and Society.* Ed. Richard T. Schaefer. Thousand Oaks, CA: Sage Publications, 2008. 1048–1051.

Buck, Christopher. "Religious Myths of America" (Michigan State University course syllabus). American Academy of Religion, "Syllabus Project," s.v. "Religions of America" and "Comparative Studies of Religion." See http://www.aarweb.org/Programs/Syllabus_Project/browse.asp.

Buck, Christopher. "A Unique Eschatological Interface: Bahá'u'lláh and Cross-Cultural Messianism." *In Iran.* Ed. Peter Smith. Los Angeles: Kalimát Press, 1986. 157–179.

Buck, Christopher, and Betty J. Fisher, ed. and intro. "Alain Locke: Four Talks Redefining Democracy, Education, and World Citizenship." *World Order* 38.3 (2006/2007): 21–41.

Bull, Malcolm and Keith Lockhart. *Seeking a Sanctuary: Seventh-day Adventism and the American Dream.* Bloomington, IN: Indiana University Press, 2006.

Burghardt, Walter J. "Foreword." John Courtney Murray. *We Hold These Truths: Catholic Reflections on the American Proposition.* Reprinted. Lanham MD: Rowman and Littlefield, 2005 [1960].

Burrows, Mark S. "The Catholic Revision of an American Myth: The Eschatology of Orestes Brownson as an Apology of American Catholicism." *Catholic Historical Review* 76 (1990): 18–43.

Burton, Richard. *Pilgrimage to Al-Madinah and Meccah.* 1855. Chapter 30. See http://ebooks.adelaide.edu.au/b/burton/richard/b97p/chapter30.html#2.

Bush, George W. "President Delivers State of the Union Address." Office of the Press Secretary. White House press release (January 29, 2002). See http://www.whitehouse.gov/news/releases/2002/01/20020129-11.html.

Bush, Lester E., Jr. "Mormonism's Negro Doctrine: An Historical Overview." *Dialogue* 8 (Spring 1973): 11–68.

Bushman, Richard L. *Joseph Smith and the Beginnings of Mormonism.* Urbana: University of Illinois Press, 1984.

Butler, Gregory S. "Visions of a Nation Transformed: Modernity and Ideology in Wilson's Political Thought." *Journal of Church and State* 39.1 (Winter 1997): 37–51.

Callicott, J. Baird. "Natural History as Natural Religion." *Encyclopedia of Religion and Nature.* Ed. Bron Taylor and Jeffrey Kaplan. London and New York Continuum, 2005. 2:1164–1169.

Cannon, Donald Q. "King Follett Discourse." *Encyclopedia of Mormonism.* New York: Macmillan, 1992. 791–792. See http://www.lib.byu.edu/Macmillan/.

Cannon, Donald Q. "The King Follett Discourse: Joseph Smith's Greatest Sermon in Historical Perspective." *Brigham Young University Studies* 18.2 (Winter 1978): 179–192.

Caplan, Eric. *From Ideology to Liturgy: Reconstructionist Worship and American Liberal Judaism.* Monographs of the Hebrew Union College Series, no. 26. Cincinnati: Hebrew Union College Press, 2002.

Carey, Patrick W. *Orestes A. Brownson: American Religious Weathervane.* Grand Rapids, MI: Wm. B. Eerdmans, 2004.

Carey, Patrick W., ed. *Orestes A. Brownson: Selected Writings.* Sources of American Spirituality. Mahwah, NJ: Paulist Press, 1991.

Carter, Ron. "Winds of Change Blowing Through the Nation of Islam." See http://www.wfial.org/index.cfm?fuseaction=artWorld.article_1.

Central Conference of American Rabbis (CCAR). *Responsa,* "Reform Support for Orthodox Institutions." See http://data.ccarnet.org/cgi-bin/respdisp.pl?file=92&year=narr (accessed January 25, 2009).

Central Conference of American Rabbis (CCAR). "A Statement of Principles for Reform Judaism." See http://ccarnet.org/Articles/index.cfm?id=44&pge_id=1606 (accessed January 25, 2009).

Century of Light. Prepared under the direction of the Universal House of Justice. Wilmette, IL: U.S. Bahá'í Publishing Trust, 2001 (2003 printing).

Chehabi, H. E. "Sport Diplomacy between the United States and Iran." *Diplomacy and Statecraft* 12.1 (2005): 89–106.

Cherry, Conrad. *God's New Israel: Religious Interpretations of American Destiny.* Ed. idem. Rev. ed. Chapel Hill: University of North Carolina Press, 1998.

Chiozza, Giacomo. "Love and Hate: Anti-Americanism in the Islamic World." Paper prepared for presentation in the Department of Politics, New York University, November 22, 2004. 1–58. See http://nyu.edu/gsas/dept/politics/seminars/chiozza_f04.pdf.

Church of Jesus Christ of Latter-day Saints. "The Family: A Proclamation to the World" (September 23, 1995).

Church of Jesus Christ of Latter-day Saints. Newsroom. "Statistical Information: Official 2007 Statistics about the Church of Jesus Christ of Latter-day Saints." See http://newsroom.lds.org/ldsnewsroom/eng/statistical-information.

Church of the Holy Trinity v. United States, 143 U.S. 457 (1892).

Churchill, Ward. "A Little Matter of Genocide: Sam Gill's *Mother Earth,* Colonialism and the Appropriation of Indigenous Spiritual Tradition in Academia." *Fantasies of the Master Race: Literature, Cinema, and the Colonization of American Indians.* Ed. M. Annette Jaimes. Monroe, ME: Common Courage Press, 1992. 187–213.

Clark, E. Douglas. *The Grand Design: America from Columbus to Zion.* Salt Lake City: Deseret, 1992.

Claussen, Martin P., ed. *The Journal of the Senate, including The Journal of the Executive Proceedings of the Senate, John Adams Administration, 1797–1801, Volume 1: Fifth Congress, First Session; March–July, 1797.* Wilmington, DE: Michael Glazier, Inc., 1977.

Clegg, Claude Andrew, III. *An Original Man: The Life and Times of Elijah Muhammad.* New York: St. Martin's Press, 1997.

Comparet, "Pastor" Bertrand L. "Man and Beast." See http://www.churchoftrueisrael.com/comparet/comp4a.html.

Cone, James H. *Risks of Faith: The Emergence of a Black Theology of Liberation, 1968–1998.* Boston: Beacon Press, 2000.

Corsbie-Massay, Charisse L'Pree. "International MTV and Globalization." See http://themediamademecrazy.com/papers-projects/mit-cms/mit-cms-internationalmtv.

Council on American-Islamic Relations. CAIR. "Islamophobia and Anti-Americanism Book Excerpts: Islamophobia." 2008. See http://www.cair.com/Issues/Islamophobia/Islamophobia.aspx.

Cowan, Douglas E. "Theologizing Race: The Construction of 'Christian Identity.'" *Religion and the Creation of Race and Ethnicity: An Introduction.* Ed. Craig Prentiss. New York: New York University Press, 2003. 112–123.

Creativity Movement. "CREATIVITY: Creed and Program." See http://www.rahowa.com/creativity12.html.

Creativity Movement. *Little White Book.* See http://creativitymovement.net/documents/LITTLEWH.PDF.

Csábi, Szilvia. "The Concept of America in the Puritan Mind." *Language and Literature* 10.3 (2001): 195–209.

Dalai Lama. "Buddhism, Asian Values and Democracy." *Journal of Democracy* 10.1 (January 1999): 3–7. Reprinted: *The Global Divergence of Democracies.* Ed. Larry Diamond and Marc F. Plattner. Baltimore: Johns Hopkins University Press, 2001. 18–22; *World Religions and Democracy.* Baltimore: Johns Hopkins Press, 2005. 70–74; *The Pluralist Paradigm: Democracy and Religion in the 21st Century.* Ed. Sondra Myers and Patrice Brodeur. Scranton, PA: University of Scranton Press, 2007.

Dalai Lama. *Constitution of Tibet.* Delhi: Bureau of His Holiness the Dalai Lama, 1963.

Dalai Lama. "His Holiness the Dalai Lama's Nobel Lecture, University Aula, Oslo, December 11th, 1989." See http://www.tibet.com/dl/nobellecture.html.

Dalai Lama. "Remarks by His Holiness the Dalai Lama to the Members of the United States Congress in the Rotunda of the Capitol Hill in Washington, D.C., 18 April 1991." See http://www.tibet.com/DL/caphill.html. Printed in Matthew E. Bunson, ed., *The Wisdom Teachings of the Dalai Lama.* New York: Plume, 1997.

Dalai Lama. "Statement by His Holiness the XIV Dalai Lama on His Visit to the United States, September 1995." See http://www.tibet.com/dl/hhus95.html. Printed in Bunson, ed., *The Wisdom Teachings of the Dalai Lama,* 224.

Dalai Lama. *The Wisdom Teachings of the Dalai Lama.* Ed. Matthew E. Bunson. New York: Plume, 1997.

Danesh, Roshan. "Internationalism and Divine Law: A Bahá'í Perspective." *Journal of Law and Religion* 19.2 (2003/2004): 209–242.

Dease, Dennis Joseph. *The Theological Influence of Orestes Brownson and Isaac Hecker on John Ireland's Americanist Ecclesiology.* Ph.D. dissertation: The Catholic University of America, 1978.

DeCaro, Louis A. *Malcolm and the Cross: The Nation of Islam, Malcolm X, and Christianity.* New York/London: New York University Press, 1998.

Diaz, Maria del Rosario Rodriguez. "Mexico's Vision of Manifest Destiny During the 1847 War." *Journal of Popular Culture* 35.2 (Fall 2001): 41–50.

Dobratz, Betty A. "The Role of Religion in the Collective Identity of the White Racialist Movement." *Journal for the Scientific Study of Religion* 40.2 (June 2001): 287–302.

Dobratz, Betty A., and Stephanie L. Shanks. *The White Separatist Movement in the United States: White Power, White Pride!* Boston: Johns Hopkins University Press, 2001.

Dolan, Charles. "America's Global Communications Efforts." Remarks to Public Relations Society of America, National Press Club, Washington, DC (October 31, 2002). Office of Electronic Information, Bureau of Public Affairs, U.S. Department of State. See http://www.state.gov/r/adcompd/rls/14885.htm.

Dorrien, Gary. *The Making of American Liberal Theology: Idealism, Realism, and Modernity, 1900–1950.* Louisville, KY: Westminster John Knox Press, 2003.

Doty, William. *Mythography: The Study of Myths and Rituals.* Tuscaloosa: University of Alabama Press, 2000.

Douglas, Norman. "The Sons of Lehi and the Seed of Cain: Racial Myths in Mormon Scripture and Their Relevance to the Pacific Islands." *Journal of Religious History* 8 (1974): 90–104.

Dunbar, Paul Laurence. "An Ante-Bellum Sermon." 1895. See http://www.dunbarsite.org/gallery/AnAnte-BellumSermon.asp.

Eisenberg, Carol. "Black Muslims Seek Acceptance from Fellow Americans, Adherents." *Seattle Times* (January 22, 2005). See http://seattletimes.nwsource.com/html/nationworld/2002157825_islam22.html.

Ellis, Monsignor John Tracy, ed. *Documents of American Catholic History.* Milwaukee, WI: Bruce Publishing, 1956.

Ellwood, Robert S. "East Asian Religions in Today's America." *World Religions in America.* Ed. Jacob Neusner. Louisville, KY: Westminster John Knox Press, 2000. 154–171.

Eschraghi, Armin. "'Undermining the Foundations of Orthodoxy': Some notes on the Báb's *shari'ah* (Sacred Law)." "A Most Noble Pattern: Essays in the Study of the Writings of the Bab." Ed. Todd Lawson (Oxford: George Ronald, forthcoming).

Farrakhan, Louis. "The Divine Destruction of America: Can She Avert It?" Speech delivered at Mosque Maryam, Chicago, 9 June 1996. Chicago: *Final Call Online* Edition. http://www.finalcall.com/artman/publish/article_4413.shtml.

Farrakhan, Louis. "One Nation Under God" (February 25, 2007). See http://www.walkwithfarrakhan.com/2007/03/one-nation-under-god-by-honorable.html.

Farrakhan, Louis. "A Vision for America." *A Torchlight for America.* (1993). See http://www.finalcall.com/artman/publish/article_4851.shtml.

Farrakhan, Louis. "A White Man's Heaven Is a Black Man's Hell." Video. See http://www.youtube.com/watch?v=cb8xKGaTJhg.

Feldberg, Michael, Karla Goldman, Scott-Martin Kosofsky, Pamela S. Nadell, Jonathan D. Sarna, and Gary P. Zola. *Three Hundred Fifty Years: An Album of American Jewish Memory.* New York: American Jewish Historical Society and the American Jewish Archives, 2005.

Fenton, William Nelson. "Chapter 2: This Island, the World on the Turtle's Back." *The Great Law and the Longhouse: A Political History of the Iroquois Confederacy.* Norman: University of Oklahoma Press, 1998. Revision of idem, "This Island, the World on the Turtle's Back." *Journal of American Folklore* 75, no. 298 (October–December 1962): 283–300.

Fenton, William Nelson, ed. *Parker on the Iroquois, Book III: The Constitution of the Five Nations.* Syracuse, NY: Syracuse University Press, 1968.

Fenton, William Nelson. "Seth Newhouse's Traditional History and Constitution of the Iroquois Confederacy." *American Philosophical Society Proceedings* 93.3 (1949): 141–158.

Ferber, Abby. "Of Mongrels and Jews: The Deconstruction of Racialised Identities in White Supremacist Discourse." *Social Identities* 3 (1997): 193–208.

Sabbath and Festival Prayer Book. New York: United Synagogue of America, 1946.

FinalCall.com News, "Exclusive Interview with Minister Louis Farrakhan. December 2007. See http://www.finalcall.com/artman/publish/article_4256.shtml.

Fogarty, Gerald P. "Americanism." *The New Dictionary of Catholic Social Thought.* Ed. Judith A. Dwyer. Collegeville, MN: The Liturgical Press, 1994. 39–42.

Fogarty, Gerald P. "The Vatican and the Americanist Crisis: Denis J. O'Connell, American Agent in Rome, 1885–1903." *Miscellanea Historiae Pontificiae,* 36. Rome Università Gregoriana Editrice, 1974.

Fradkin, Hillel. "America in Islam." *The Public Interest* no. 155 (Spring 2004): 37–55.

Franklin, Benjamin, ed. *Indian Treaties Printed by Benjamin Franklin, 1736–1762.* Ed. Carl Van Doren and Julian P. Boyd. Philadelphia, PA: The Historical Society of Pennsylvania, 1938. 41–79. Text and facsimile digitized by the Oklahoma State University Library Electronic Publishing Center, at http://earlytreaties.unl.edu/treaty.00003.html.

Franklin, Benjamin. *Not Your Usual Founding Father: Selected Readings from Benjamin Franklin.* Ed. Edmund S. Morgan. New Haven, CT: Yale University Press, 2006.

Franklin, Benjamin. "To James Parker" (Philadelphia, March 20, 1750). *The Writings of Benjamin Franklin. Vol. III, 1750–1759.* Collected and edited with a Life and Introduction by Albert Henry Smyth. New York: Macmillan, 1905. 40–45.

Frechette, Ann. "Democracy and Democratization among Tibetans in Exile." *Journal of Asian Studies* 66.1 (February 2007): 97–127.

Freeman, Gordon M. "The Conservative Movement and the Public Square." *Jewish Polity and American Civil Society: Communal Agencies and Religious Movements in the American Public Square.* Ed. Alan Mittleman, Robert A. Licht, and Jonathan D. Sarna. New York: Rowman and Littlefield, 2002. 235–260.

Friedlaender, Israel. "The Problem of Judaism in America." *Past and Present: A Collection of Jewish Essays.* Cincinnati, OH: Ark Publishing Co., 1919.

Friedland, Eric L. Review of *From Ideology to Liturgy: Reconstructionist Worship and American Liberal Judaism.* Monographs of the Hebrew Union College Series, no. 26. Cincinnati: Hebrew Union College Press, 2002. H-Judaic,

H-Net Reviews, June 2003. See http://www.h-net.org/reviews/showrev.cgi? path=180351058379318.

Fuchs-Kreimer, Nancy. "Seventy Years After Judaism as a Civilization: Mordecai Kaplan's Theology and the Reconstructionist Movement." *Jewish Social Studies* 12.2 (2006): 127–142.

Fulbrook, Mary. "Myth-making and National Identity: The Case of the G.D.R." *Myths and Nationhood*. Ed. Geoffrey Hosking and George Schöpflin. New York: Routledge, 1997. 72–87.

Gaines, James R., and Karsten Prager. "Rafsanjani's Advice to the 'Great Satan.' " *Time*. May 31, 1993. See http://www.time.com/time/magazine/article/ 0,9171,978611,00.html.

Gale, Rev. William P. *The Faith of Our Fathers*. See http://www.kelticklankirk.com/ GALE_Reverend_Colonel_William_P_Gale.htm.

Gale, Rev. William P. *Racial and National Identity: A Sermon*. See http:// www.kelticklankirk.com/Gale_Racial_and_National_Identity.htm.

Gardell, Mattias. "Countdown to Armageddon: Minister Farrakhan and the Nation of Islam in the Latter Days." *Temenos* 31 (1995): 253–262.

Gardell, Mattias. *In the Name of Elijah Muhammad: Louis Farrakhan and the Nation of Islam*. Durham, NC: Duke University Press, 1996.

Garr, Arnold K. *Christopher Columbus: A Latter-day Saint Perspective*. Provo, UT: Religious Studies Center, Brigham Young University, 1992.

Geertz, Clifford. "Religion as a Cultural System." *The Interpretation of Cultures*. Ed. idem. (New York: Basic Books, 1966). 87–125.

Gerasole, Vince (CBS). "Rare Wilmette Temple Makes Cut in '7 Wonders' List." April 30, 2007. See http://cbs2chicago.com/local/Baha.i.House.2.336767 .html.

Gerstle, Gary. "American Freedom, American Coercion: Immigrant Journeys in the 'Promised Land.' " *Social Compass* 47.1 (2000): 63–76.

Gibson, John Arthur. *Concerning the League: The Iroquois League Tradition as Dictated in Onondaga by John Arthur Gibson. Newly Elicited, Edited and Translated by Hanni Woodbury in Collaboration with Reg Henry and Harry Webster on the Basis of A. A. Goldenweiser's Manuscript.* Winnipeg, Manitoba: Algonquian and Iroquoian Linguistics, 1992.

Gibson, Chief John Arthur. *"The Deganawiidah Legend: A Tradition of the Founding of the League of the Five Iroquois Tribes."* English translation of text given by *John Arthur Gibson to J. N. B. Hewitt.* Ed. by Abram Charles, John Buck, Sr., and Joshua Buck (1900–1914). Trans. William N. Fenton and Simeon Gibson. 1941. National Anthropological Archives, Smithsonian Institution, Washington, DC, Bureau of American Ethnology, Nos. 1517b and 1517c.

Giddens, Anthony. *The Consequences of Modernity*. Cambridge: Polity, 1990.

Gill, Sam D. "The Academic Study of Religion." *Journal of the American Academy of Religion* 62 (Winter 1994): 965–975.

Gill, Sam D. *Mother Earth: An American Story*. Chicago: University of Chicago Press, 1987.

Ginzberg, Louis. *The Responsa of Professor Louis Ginzberg*. Ed. David Golinkin. Moreshet Series, Studies in Jewish History, Literature, and Thought, Volume XVI. New York: Jewish Theological Society Press, 1996 [1906].

Girgus, Sam B. *The New Covenant: Jewish Writers and the American Idea*. Chapel Hill, NC: University of North Carolina Press, 1984.

Girgus, Sam B. "The New Covenant: The Jews and the Myth of America." *The American Self: Myth, Ideology, and Popular Culture*. Ed. idem. Albuquerque: University of New Mexico Press, 1981. 105–123.

Glaude, Eddie S. "Myth and African American Self-Identity." *Religion and the Creation of Race and Ethnicity: An Introduction*. Ed. Craig R. Prentiss. New York: New York University Press, 2003.

Goldenberg, David M. *The Curse of Ham: Race and Slavery in Early Judaism, Christianity, and Islam*. Princeton: Princeton University Press, 2003.

Goldstein, Eric L. *The Price of Whiteness: Jews, Race, and American Identity*. Princeton, NJ: Princeton University Press, 2006.

Golinkin, David. "Prayers for the Government and the State of Israel Yom Haatzmaut 5766." *Insight Israel: The View from Schechter*. Second Series. Jerusalem: The Schechter Institute of Jewish Studies, 2006. 114–125 [121]. See http://www.schechter.edu/pubs/insight56.htm.

Golinkin, David, ed. *The Responsa of Professor Louis Ginzberg*. Moreshet Series, Studies in Jewish History, Literature, and Thought, Volume XVI. New York: Jewish Theological Society Press, 1996 [1906].

Graham, Troy. "Supremacist Pleads to Sale of Stolen Guns: Federal Investigators Also Are Examining Charges that He Gave an Informant an Explosive Compound." *Philadelphia Inquirer*. May 5, 2006. P. 1.

Grant, Susan-Mary. "Making History: Myth and the Construction of American Nationhood." *Myths and Nationhood*. Ed. Geoffrey Hosking and George Schöpflin. New York: Routledge, 1997. 88–106.

Greenberg, Gershon. "The Significance of America in David Einhorn's Conception of History." *American Jewish Historical Quarterly* 63 (December 1973): 160–184.

Grinde, Donald A., Jr. *The Iroquois and the Founding of the American Nation*. San Francisco: Indian Historian Press, 1977.

Grinde, Donald A., Jr. "Sauce for the Goose: Demand and Definitions for Proof Regarding the Iroquois and Democracy." *William and Mary Quarterly* 53.3 (July 1996): 621–636.

Grinde, Donald A., Jr., and Bruce E. Johansen. *Exemplar of Liberty: Native America and the Evolution of Democracy*. Native American Politics Series, No. 3. Los Angeles: American Indian Studies Center, University of California, 1991.

Gualtieri, Antonio R. "Founders and Apostates." *Journal of the American Academy of Religion* 61.1 (Spring 1993): 101–122.

Gurock, Jeffrey S., and Jacob J. Schachter, *A Modern Heretic and a Traditional Community: Mordecai M. Kaplan, Orthodoxy and American Judaism*. New York: Columbia University Press, 1997.

Hagy, James William. *This Happy Land: The Jews of Colonial and Antebellum Charleston.* Judaic Studies Series. Unnumbered. Tuscaloosa: University of Alabama Press, 1993.

Hale, Van. "The Doctrinal Impact of the King Follett Discourse." *Brigham Young University Studies* 18.2 (Winter 1978): 209–225.

Halim, Fachrizal. "Pluralism of American Muslims and the Challenge of Assimilation." *Journal of Muslim Minority Affairs* 26.2 (August 2006): 235–244.

Hanson, Louise G. "Columbus, Christopher." *Encyclopedia of Mormonism.* New York: Macmillan, 1992. 294–296. See http://www.lib.byu.edu/Macmillan/.

Harvey, Paul. " 'A Servant of Servants Shall He Be': The Construction of Race in American Religious Mythologies." *Religion and the Creation of Race and Ethnicity: An Introduction.* Ed. Craig R. Prentiss. New York: New York University Press, 2003. 13–27.

Hauptman, Laurence M. Chapter Three, "Speculations on the Constitution." *Tribes and Tribulations: Misconceptions about American Indians and their Histories.* Albuquerque: University of New Mexico Press, 1995.

Hawkins, Chester Lee. "Selective Bibliography on African-Americans and Mormons, 1830–1990." *Dialogue* 25 (Winter 1992): 113–131.

Heitala, Thomas. *Manifest Destiny: Anxious Aggrandizement in Late Jacksonian America.* Ithaca, NY: Cornell University Press, 1985.

"Herald of Truth." Archived broadcasts. See http://soundwaves2000.com/hot.

Herberg, Will. *Protestant–Catholic–Jew: An Essay in American Religious Sociology.* Chicago: University Of Chicago Press, 1983 [1955].

Herrera, Robert A. *Orestes Brownson: Sign of Contradiction.* Wilmington, DE: ISI Books, 1999.

Herrera, Robert. "Orestes Brownson's Vision of America." *Modern Age* 43.2 (Spring 2001): 133–145.

Hewitt, John Napoleon Brinton. *Constitution of the Confederacy by Dekanawidah, collected and translated from Mohawk by Chief Seth Newhouse 1898.* Manuscript 1343, Smithsonian Institution National Anthropological Archives, "copied 1936."

"Hezbollah Leader Nasrallah Supports Intifadah, Vows 'Death to America.' " Aired On Beirut *Al-Manar* Television, September 27, 2002.

Historica Foundation of Canada. "Peacemaker." Series: History by the Minute. *Historica Minutes: First Nations.* See http://www.histori.ca/minutes/minute.do?id=10120.

Hoge, Dean. "Theological Views of America among Protestants." *Sociological Analysis* 37.2 (1976): 127–139.

Holcombe, Randall G. "Constitutional Theory and the Constitutional History of Colonial America." *The Independent Review* 3.1 (Summer 1998): 21–36.

Hoonaard, Deborah K. van den, and Will C. van den Hoonaard. *The Equality of Women and Men: The Experience of the Bahá'í Community of Canada.* Winnipeg, MB: Art Bookbindery, 2006.

Horsman, Reginald. *Race and Manifest Destiny: The Origins of American Racial Anglo-Saxonism.* Cambridge, MA: Harvard University Press, 1981.

Howard-Pitney, David. *The Afro-American Jeremiad: Appeals for Justice in America.* Philadelphia: Temple University Press, 1990.

Huddleston, John. "The Spiritual Destiny of America and World Peace." *Processes of the Lesser Peace.* Ed. Babak Bahador and Nazila Ghanea. Oxford: George Ronald, 2002. 107–161.

Hughes, Richard T. *Myths America Lives By.* Foreword by Robert N. Bellah. Champaign: University of Illinois Press, 2004.

Hutchinson, Dawn L. *Antiquity and Social Reform: Religious Experience in the Unification Church, Feminist Wicca and the Nation of Yahweh* (Ph.D. dissertation: Florida State University, 2007). See http://etd.lib.fsu.edu/theses/available/etd-04092007-153203/unrestricted/hutchinson_dis.pdf.

Ikeda, Daisaki. "Faith for Attaining Buddhahood in This Lifetime: Advance Unerringly Along the Great Path of the Oneness of Mentor and Disciple." SGI-USA, *Buddhist Learning Review: 2007 Study Guide,* 62.

Ikeda, Daisaki. "The Humanism of the Middle Way—Dawn of a Global Civilization." See http://www.jha.ac/articles/a093.htm.

Ikeda, Daisaki. "On the Importance of Studying Buddhism: From the Human Revolution." SGI-USA, *Buddhist Learning Review: 2007 Study Guide.*

Ikeda, Daisaki. *Songs for America: Poems.* Mount Rainier, MD: World Tribune Press, 2000.

Ingram, Haroro J. "The Transformative Charisma Phenomenon in Islamic Radicalism and Militancy: Tracing the Evolutionary Roots of Islamic Terrorism." *Proceedings Social Change in the 21st Century Conference 2006.* See http://eprints.qut.edu.au/archive/00006343/01/6343.pdf.

Ireland, John. "The Church and Modern Society." *The Church and Modern Society: Lectures and Addresses.* New York: D. H. McBride, 1903. 27–65.

Ireland, John. "The Church in America." *Lecture and Addresses.* Vol. II. St. Paul, MN: Pioneer Press, 1905. 240–241.

Jacobs, Louis. *The Jewish Religion: A Companion.* Oxford and New York: Oxford University Press, 1995.

Jacobs, Renée. "Iroquois Great Law of Peace and the United States Constitution: How the Founding Fathers Ignored the Clan Mothers." *Native American Law Review* 16 (1991): 497–531.

Jefferson, Thomas. *Autobiography of Thomas Jefferson.* Mineola, NY: Dover, 2007. See http://avalon.law.yale.edu/19th_century/jeffauto.asp.

Jefferson, Thomas. "To Governor William H. Harrison Washington, February 27, 1803." *The Letters of Thomas Jefferson: 1743–1826.* See http://odur.let.rug.nl/~usa/P/tj3/writings/brf/jefl151.htm. University of Groningen.

Jefferson, Thomas. *The Writings of Thomas Jefferson.* 1903.

Jessup, Henry H. "The Religious Mission of the English Speaking Nations." *The World's Parliament of Religions: An illustrated and popular story of the world's first Parliament of Religions, held in Chicago in connection with the Columbian Exposition of 1893.* Vol. 2. Ed. John H. Barrows. Chicago: Parliament Pub. Co., 1893. 1122–1126.

Johansen, Bruce E. *Forgotten Founders: Benjamin Franklin, the Iroquois, and the Rationale for the American Revolution.* Ipswich, MA: Gambit, 1982.

Johansen, Bruce Elliott. "Dating the Iroquois Confederacy." *Akwesasne Notes* 1.3/4 (Fall 1995): 62–63.

Johansen, Bruce Elliott. *Forgotten Founders: How the American Indian Helped Shape Democracy.* Boston: Harvard Common Press, 1982.

Johansen, Bruce Elliott, and Barbara Alice Mann, eds., *Encyclopedia of the Haudenosaunee (Iroquois Confederacy).* Westport, CT: Greenwood Publishing, 2000.

John Paul II, Pope. "Address of John Paul II to Hon. Richard B. Cheney, Vice President of the United States of America" (Tuesday, January 27, 2004). See http://www.vatican.va/holy_father/john_paul_ii/speeches/2004/january/documents/hf_jp-ii_spe_20040127_vice-pres-usa_en.html.

John Paul II, Pope. "John Paul II on the American Experiment." *First Things* 82 (April 1998): 36–37.

John Paul II, Pope. "Meeting with the President of the United States of America, Mr. Ronald Reagan. Address of John Paul II." Vizcaya Museum, Miami. September 10, 1987. See http://www.vatican.va/holy_father/john_paul_ii/speeches/1987/september/documents/hf_jp-ii_spe_19870910_reagan-museo_en.html.

John Paul II, Pope. "Welcome Address of His Holiness John Paul II." International Airport of Miami. 10 September 1987." See http://www.vatican.va/holy_father/john_paul_ii/speeches/1987/september/documents/hf_jp-ii_spe_19870910_aeroporto-miami_en.html.

John XXIII, Pope. "*Pacem in Terris:* Encyclical of Pope John XXIII on Establishing Universal Peace in Truth, Justice, Charity, and Liberty, April 11, 1963." *The Pope Speaks* 9 (1963): 13–48.

Kaplan, Jeffrey. "The Context of American Millenarian Revolutionary Theology: The Case of the 'Identity Christian' Church of Israel." *Terrorism and Political Violence* 5.1 (Spring 1993): 30–82.

Kaplan, Mordecai Menahem. *Dynamic Judaism: The Essential Writings of Mordecai M. Kaplan.* Ed. Emanuel S. Goldsmith and Mel Scult. New York: Fordham University Press, 1991.

Kaplan, Mordecai Menahem. *The Greater Judaism in the Making: A Study of the Modern Evolution of Judaism.* New York: Reconstructionist Press, 1960.

Kaplan, Mordecai Menahem. *Judaism as a Civilization: Toward a Reconstruction of American-Jewish Life.* Philadelphia: Jewish Publication Society of America, 1994 [1934].

Kaplan, Mordecai M., Ira Eisenstein, and Eugene Kohn, eds. *The New Haggadah for the Pesah Seder.* Illus. Leonard Weisgard. New York: Behrman House, Inc., 1941; Newly Revised Edition, 1978.

Kaplan, Mordecai M., J. Paul Williams, and Eugene Kohn, eds. *The Faith of America: Readings, Songs and Prayers for the Celebration of American Holidays.* New York: Reconstructionist Press, 1951. Reprint: 1963.

Karp, Abraham J. *Jewish Continuity in America: Creative Survival in a Free Society.* Judaic Studies Series. Unnumbered. Tuscaloosa: University of Alabama Press, 1998.

Katz, Steven T. "Mordecai Kaplan's Theology and the Problem of Evil." *Jewish Social Studies* 12.2 (2006): 115–126.

Katzenstein, Peter J., and Robert O. Keohane, "Varieties of Anti-Americanism: A Framework for Analysis." *Anti-Americanism in World Politics.* Ed. Peter J. Katzenstein and Robert O. Keohane. Ithaca, NY: Cornell University Press, 2007.

Kauanui, J. Kehaulani. "Diasporic Deracination and 'Off-Island' Hawaiians." *The Contemporary Pacific* 19.1 (2007): 138–160.

Kaufmann, Eric. "American Exceptionalism Reconsidered: Anglo-Saxon Ethnogenesis in the 'Universal' Nation, 1776–1850." *Journal of American Studies* 33.3 (1999): 437–457.

Kehoe, Alice B. *North American Indians: A Comprehensive Account.* 3rd ed. Upper Saddle River, NJ: Prentice-Hall, 2006.

Kendrick, A. Clements. *Woodrow Wilson: World Statesman.* Lawrence: University Press of Kansas, 1987.

Kenney, Jeff. "The Politics of Sects and Typologies." *Nova Religio* 6.1 (October 2002): 137–146.

Khomeini, Ayatollah. *Imam's Will.* Tehran: Ministry of Islamic Guidance, 1989.

King, Martin Luther, Jr. "The World House." *Where Do We Go from Here: Chaos or Community?* Boston: Beacon Press, 1968.

Kingdom Identity Ministries. "Kingdom Identity Ministries Doctrinal Statement of Beliefs." See http://www.kingidentity.com/doctrine.htm.

Kissinger, Henry. *Diplomacy.* New York: Simon and Schuster, 1994.

Klassen, Ben. *Nature's Eternal Religion.* See http://www.resist.com/Natures_eternal_religion.pdf.

Klassen, Ben. *The White Man's Bible.* Milwaukee: The Milwaukee Church of the Creator, 1986.

Knock, Thomas J. *To End All Wars: Woodrow Wilson and the Quest for a New World Order.* Oxford: Oxford University Press, 1992.

Koester, Nancy. "The Future in Our Past: Post-millennialism in American Protestantism." *Word and World* 15.2 (Spring 1995): 137–144.

Koh, Harold Hongju. "Foreword: On American Exceptionalism." *Stanford Law Review* 55.5 (May 2003): 1470–1528.

Kohler, Kaufmann. "The Mission of Israel and its Application to Modern Times." *Yearbook of the Central Conference of American Rabbis* 29 (1919): 265–288 [discussion, 288–305].

Kolodziej, Edward A. "American Power and Global Order." *From Superpower to Besieged Global Power: Restoring World Order After the Failure of the Bush Doctrine.* Ed. Edward A. Kolodziej and Roger E. Kanet. Atlanta: University of Georgia Press, 2008. 3–30.

Krummel, Carl. "Catholicism, Americanism, Democracy, and Orestes Brownson." *American Quarterly* 6.1 (Spring 1954): 19–31.

Kuklick, Bruce. "Myth and Symbol in American Studies." *American Quarterly* 24 (October 1972): 435–450.

Laipson, Ellen. "The Absence of a U.S. Policy towards Iran and its Consequences." *The American Academy of Diplomacy Issues Brief* (September 21, 2004).

Langer, Ruth. "Theologies of Self and Other in American Jewish Liturgies." *CCAR Journal: A Reform Jewish Quarterly* (Winter 2005): 3–41.

Larson, Stan, ed. "The King Follett Discourse: A Newly Amalgamated Text." *Brigham Young University Studies* 18.2 (Winter 1978): 193–208.

"Latter-day Saints." *The HarperCollins Dictionary of Religion.* Ed. Jonathan Z. Smith. San Francisco: HarperSanFrancisco, 1995.

Leavitt, Michael F. Student Casenote: "*Keenan v. Aryan Nations,* No. CV-99-441. Idaho 2000." *Idaho Law Review* 37.3 (2001): 603–639.

Le Baron, E. Dale. "Mormonism in Black Africa." *Mormon Identities in Transition.* Ed. Douglas Davies. London and New York: Cassell, 1996. 80–86.

Lederhendler, Eli. "America: A Vision in a Jewish Mirror." *Jewish Responses to Modernity: New Voices in America and Eastern Europe.* New York: New York University Press, 1994. 104–139.

Leo XIII, "Concerning New Opinions, Virtue, Nature and Grace, with Regard to Americanism. *Testem Benevolentiae Nostrae.*" Encyclical of Pope Leo XIII promulgated on January 22, 1899. See http://www.papalencyclicals.net/Leo13/l13teste.htm.

Lerche, Charles O. "The Conflicts of Globalization." *International Journal of Peace Studies* 1.3 (January 1998): 47–66.

Letterbook, George Morgan. *American Commissioners for Indian Affairs to Delawares, Senecas, Munsees, and Mingos.* Pittsburgh, 1776. [Manuscript?]

Levy, P. A. "Exemplars of Taking Liberties: The Iroquois Influence Thesis and the Problem of Evidence." *William and Mary Quarterly* 53.3 (July 1996): 588–604.

Lewis, Bernard. "The Roots of Muslim Rage: Why so many Muslims deeply resent the West, and why their bitterness will not easily be mollified." *The Atlantic Monthly.* (September 1990): 1–10. *The Atlantic Online,* at http://www.theatlantic.com/doc/print/199009/muslim-rage.

Lewis, Kevin. "Nathanael West and American Apocalyptic." *Tradition and Postmodernity: English and American Studies and the Challenge of the Future.* Proceedings of the Eighth International Conference on English and American Literature and Language. Eds. Teresa Bela and Zygmunt Mazur. Krakow, Poland: Jagiellonian University, 1999. 435–443 [435].

Lieb, Michael. *Children of Ezekiel: Aliens, UFOs, the Crisis of Race, and the Advent of End Time.* Durham and London: Duke University Press, 1998.

Lincoln, Abraham. "First Inaugural Address" (March 4, 1861).

Lincoln, Abraham. "The Gettysburg Address" (November 19, 1863).

Lipset, Seymour Martin. *American Exceptionalism: A Double-Edged Sword.* New York: Norton, 1996.

Lipset, Seymour Martin. "A Unique People in an Exceptional Country." *American Pluralism and the Jewish Community.* New Brunswick, NJ: Transaction, 1990. 3–29.

Living the Life: A Compilation. London: Bahá'í Publishing Trust, 1974.

Locke, Alain. "Alain Locke: Four Talks: Redefining Democracy, Education, and World Citizenship." Ed. and intro. Christopher Buck and Betty J. Fisher. *World Order* 38.3 (2006/2007): 21–41. (Alain Locke, "The Preservation of the American Ideal"; "Stretching Our Social Mind"; "On Becoming World Citizens"; "Creative Democracy.")

Locke, Alain. "Alain Locke in His Own Words: Three Essays." Ed. Christopher Buck and Betty J. Fisher. Special Issue: Alain Locke: Dean of the Harlem Renaissance and Bahá'í Race-Amity Leader. *World Order* 36.3 (2005): ("The Gospel for the Twentieth Century" [39–42]; "Peace Between Black and White in the United States" [42–45]; "Five Phases of Democracy" [45–48]; see also idem, "The Moon Maiden" [37]).

Lopez, Robert Oscar. "The Colors of Double Exceptionalism: The Founders and African America." *Literature Compass* 5.1 (2008): 20–41.

Luce, Henry R. "The American Century." *Diplomatic History* 23.2 (2002): 159–171.

Luse, Christopher A. "Slavery's Champions Stood at Odds: Polygenesis and the Defense of Slavery." *Civil War History* 53.4 (December 2007): 379–412.

Madsen, Deborah L. *American Exceptionalism.* Edinburgh: Edinburgh University Press, 1998.

Makdisi, Ussama. " 'Anti-Americanism' in the Arab World: An Interpretation of a Brief History." *Journal of American History* 89.2 (September 2002). Reprinted in Joanne Jay Meyerowitz, ed. *History and September 11th.* Philadelphia: Temple University Press, 2003. 131–156.

Malcolm X, "Black Man's History." *The End of White-World Supremacy: Four Speeches by Malcolm X.* Ed. Benjamin Karim. New York: Little, Brown, 1971.

Malcolm X. "God's Judgement of America." *The End of White World Supremacy.* Ed. Imam B. Karim. New York: Seaver Books, 1971. 121–148. Also see http://www.malcolm-x.org/speeches/spc_120463.htm.

Malcolm X. "There's a Worldwide Revolution Going On." *Malcolm X: The Last Speeches.* Ed. Bruce Perry. New York: Pathfinder Press, 1989.

Mann, Barbara Alice. "Spirits of Sky, Spirits of Earth: The Spirituality of Chingachgook." *James Fenimore Cooper Society Miscellaneous Papers* No. 17 (September 2002): 1–5.

Marty, Martin E. *The Protestant Voice in American Pluralism.* George H. Shriver Lecture Series in Religion in American History, No. 2. Athens: University of Georgia Press, 2004.

Mathisen, James A. "Twenty Years after Bellah: What Ever Happened to American Civil Religion?" *Sociological Analysis* 50.2 (1989): 129–146.

Mattson, Ingrid. "How Muslims Use Islamic Paradigms to Define America." *Religion and Immigration: Christian, Jewish, and Muslim Experiences in the United States.* Ed. Yvonne Yazbeck Haddad, Jane Smith, and John Esposito. Walnut Creek, CA: Altamira Press, 2003. 198–215.

McConnell, Michael N. *A Country Between: The Upper Ohio Valley and Its Peoples, 1724–1774.* Lincoln and London: University of Nebraska Press, 1992.

McMullen, Michael. "The Religious Construction of a Global Identity: An Ethnographic Look at the Atlanta Bahá'í Community." *Contemporary American Religion: An Ethnographic Reader.* Ed. Penny Edgell Becker and Nancy L. Eiesland. Walnut Creek, London, New Delhi: Altamira Press, 1997. 236–237 and 227.

Mead, Sidney E. "American Protestantism Since the Civil War: I. From Denominationalism to Americanism." *Journal of Religion* 36.1 (January 1956): 1–16.

Merish, Lori. *Sentimental Materialism: Gender, Commodity Culture, and Nineteenth-Century American Literature.* Durham, NC: Duke University Press, 2000.

Meyer, Michael A. "America: The Reform Movement's Land of Promise." *Response to Modernity: A History of the Reform Movement in Judaism.* Oxford: Oxford University Press, 1988; Detroit: Wayne State University Press, 1995.

Miller, Hunter, ed. "Treaty of Peace and Friendship between the United States and the Bey and Subjects of Tripoli of Barbary, 1796–1797." *Treaties and Other International Acts of the United States of America.* Vol. 2. 1776–1818. Washington, DC: U.S. Government Printing Office, 1931.

Miller, Perry. *Errand into the Wilderness.* Cambridge: Belknap Press of Harvard University Press, 1956.

Moaddel, Mansoor. "Discursive Pluralism and Islamic Modernism in Egypt." *Arab Studies Quarterly* 24.1 (Winter 2002): 1–29.

Mohammed, Warith Deen. "A Message From: Imam Warith Deen Mohammed." February 25, 2000. *The Final Call Online,* at http://www.finalcall.com/columns/mlf/2000/imam_wdm2-25-2000.html.

Monten, Jonathan. "The Roots of the Bush Doctrine: Power, Nationalism, and Democracy Promotion in U.S. Strategy." *International Security* 29.4 (2005): 112–156.

Moore, Deborah Dash. "Judaism as a Gendered Civilization: The Legacy of Mordecai Kaplan's Magnum Opus." *Jewish Social Studies* 12.2 (2006): 172–186.

Moorhead, James H. "The American Israel: Protestant Tribalism and Universal Mission." *Many Are Chosen: Divine Election and Western Nationalism.* Ed. William R. Hutchison and Hartmut Lehmann. Philadelphia: Fortress Press, 1994. 145–166.

Moorhead, James H. " 'God's Right Arm'? Minority Faiths and Protestant Visions of America." *Minority Faiths and the American Protestant Mainstream.* Ed. Jonathan D. Sarna. Urbana/Chicago: University of Illinois Press, 1998. 335–361.

Morris, Richard B. "Benjamin Franklin's Grand Design: The Albany Plan of Union Might Have Made the Revolution Unnecessary." *American Heritage Magazine* 7.2 (February 1956). See http://www.americanheritage.com/articles/magazine/ah/1956/2/1956_2_4.shtml.

Muhammad, Elijah. Chapter 58, "The Mother Plane." *The Fall of America.* See http://www.seventhfam.com/temple/books/fall_america/amfall58.htm.

Murase, Miyeko. "Kuan-Yin as Savior of Men: Illustration of the Twenty-Fifth Chapter of the Lotus Sutra in Chinese Painting." *Artibus Asiae* 33.1–2 (1971): 39–74.

Murray, John Courtney. *We Hold These Truths: Catholic Reflections on the American Proposition.* Reprinted, Lanham MD: Rowman and Littlefield, 2005 [1960].

Nathanson, Paul. *Over the Rainbow: The Wizard of Oz as a Secular Myth of America.* McGill Studies in the History of Religion. Albany: State University of New York Press, 1991.

National Council of Churches. *The Yearbook of American and Canadian Churches.* 2008.

National Spiritual Assembly of the Bahá'ís of the United States. "The Destiny of America and the Promise of World Peace." *New York Times* (December 23, 2001), A29. Available at http://www.bahai.us/destiny-of-america. PDF of original full-page statement published in the *New York Times* available at http://www.sfbahai.org/documents/New%20York%20Times%20Ad%20.pdf.

National Spiritual Assembly of the Bahá'ís of the United States. "The Vision of Race Unity: America's Most Challenging Issue." 1991. See http://www.bahai.us/racism-in-america.

Neusner, Jacob. "Is America the Promised Land for Jews?" *The Washington Post.* 1987. Reprinted: Carol Diament, ed. *Zionism: The Sequel.* New York: Hadassah, 1998. 121–128.

Neusner, Jacob. "Judaism in the World and in America." *World Religions in America: An Introduction.* Ed. idem. Louisville, KY: Westminster John Knox Press, 2000. 107–123.

Neusner, Jacob. "Stranger at Home: 'The Holocaust.' " *Zionism, and American Judaism.* Chicago: University of Chicago Press, 1981.

Newhouse, Seth. *Constitution of the Confederacy by Dekanawidah.* 1897. Trans. by J. N. B. Hewitt. 1937. Smithsonian Institution, Bureau of American Ethnology Archives, No. 3490.

Newhouse, Seth. *Cosmogony of De-ka-na-wi-da's Government of the Iroquois Confederacy: The Original Literal Historical Narratives of the Iroquois Confederacy.* Manuscript. Public Archives of Canada, folder MG 19 F. 26, Ottawa.

Newhouse, Seth. *Mohawk Cosmogony of De-ka-na-wi-da's Government.* Photocopy. American Philosophical Society Library, 1885.

New York Morning News. "The True Title" (December 27, 1845).

New York Times. "Delegates Arrive for Hebrew Council; Representatives of 187 Congregations Gathering for the 22d Convention of the Union" (January 16, 1911).

New York Times. "The Hebrews of America; The Union of Congregations in Session at Richmond Discusses the Zionistic Movement" (December 8, 1898).

O'Connell, Marvin. *John Ireland and the American Catholic Church.* St. Paul: Minnesota Historical Society, 1988.

O'Driscoll, Cian. "Jean Bethke Elshtain's Just War Against Terror: A Tale of Two Cities." *International Relations* 21.4 (2007): 485–492.

Office of the Press Secretary. "In Their Own Words: What the Terrorists Believe, What They Hope to Accomplish, and How They Intend to Accomplish It." White House press release (September 5, 2006). See http://www.whitehouse.gov/news/releases/2006/09/20060905-7.html.

"The Old and the New." *Time* magazine. See http://www.time.com/time/magazine/article/0,9171,797618,00.html.

Oliver, William Hosking. *Prophets and Millennialists: The Uses of Biblical Prophecy in England from the 1790s to the 1840s.* Auckland: Auckland University Press, 1978.

Ostendorf, Rev. David. "Christian Identity: An American Heresy." *Journal of Hate Studies* 1.1 (2001/2002): 23–55. See http://guweb2.gonzaga.edu/againsthate/journal1/Ostendorf.pdf.

Ostling, Richard N., and Joan K. Ostling, *Mormon America: The Power and the Promise.* San Francisco: HarperSanFrancisco, 1999.

O'Sullivan, John. "America's Identity Crisis." *National Review* 46 (November 21 1994): 36–45.

O'Sullivan, John L. "Annexation." *The United States Magazine and Democratic Review* 17 (July–August 1845): 5–10 [5]. Emphasis added.

O'Sullivan, John L. "The Great Nation of Futurity." *The United States Democratic Review* 6.23 (November 1839): 426–430.

Oxford English Dictionary. 3rd Edition. John Simpson, Chief Editor. Oxford: Oxford University Press, 2008.

Parker, Arthur Caswell. "The Constitution of the Five Nations—or—the Iroquois Book of the Great Law." *New York State Museum Bulletin,* 184. Albany, NY: The University of the State of New York, 1916 (April 1, 1916).

Parker, Arthur C. "The Traditional Narrative of the Origin of the Confederation of the Five Nations Commonly Known as the Iroquois." *Parker on the Iroquois.* Ed. W. Fenton. Syracuse, NY: Syracuse University Press, 1968.

Payne, S. B. "The Iroquois League, the Articles of Confederation, and the Constitution." *William and Mary Quarterly* 53.3 (July 1996): 605–620.

Penzl, Herbert. "Paul Laurence Dunbar's Literary Dialects." *PMLA: Publications of the Modern Language Association of America* 108.1 (January 1993): 155–156.

Peterson, Thomas V. *Ham and Japheth: The Mythic World of Whites in the Antebellum South.* Metuchen, NJ: Scarecrow Press, 1978.

Pianko, Noam. "Reconstructing Judaism, Reconstructing America: The Sources and Functions of Mordecai Kaplan's 'Civilization.' " *Jewish Social Studies: History, Culture, and Society* 12.2 (Winter 2006): 39–55.

Pinheiro, John Christopher. *Crusade and Conquest: Anti-Catholicism, Manifest Destiny, and the United States–Mexican War of 1846–1848.* Ph.D. dissertation: University of Tennessee, 2001.

Portier, William L. "Heartfelt Grief and Repentance in Imperial Times." *Love Alone Is Credible: Hans von Balthasar as Interpreter of the Catholic Tradition.* Volume 1. Ed. David L. Schindler. Grand Rapids, MI: Eerdmans, 2008.

Pratt, Julius W. "The Origin of 'Manifest Destiny.' " *American Historical Review* 32.4 (July 1927): 795–798.

"Prayer for the Government." *Daily Prayer Book. Ha-Siddur Ha-Shalem.* Translated and annotated with an Introduction by Philip Birnbaum. New York: Hebrew Publishing Company, 1977. 380.

Prentiss, Craig R. "Coloring Jesus: Racial Calculus and the Search for Identity in Twentieth-century America." *Nova Religio* 11.3 (February 2008): 64–82.

Prentiss, Craig R. " 'Loathsome unto Thy People': The Latter-Day Saints and Racial Categorization." *Religion and the Creation of Race and Ethnicity: An Introduction.* Ed. Craig R. Prentiss. New York/London: New York University Press, 2003. 124–139.

"Proceedings of the Commissioners Appointed by the Continental Congress to Negotiate a Treaty with the Six Nations, 1775." *Papers of the Continental Congress, 1774–89, National Archives.* M247, Roll 144, Item No. 134, and cross-references to the Treaty Council at German Flats, New York, August 15, 1775.

Qutb, Sayyid. " 'The America I Have Seen': In the Scale of Human Values. 1951. Trans. Tarek Masoud and Ammar Fakeeh. *America in an Arab Mirror: Images of America in Arabic Travel Literature: An Anthology.* Ed. Kamal Abdel-Malek. New York: Palgrave Macmillan, 2000. 9–28.

Raboteau, Albert J. "African-Americans, Exodus, and the American Israel." *African-American Christianity: Essays in History.* Ed. Paul E. Johnson. Berkeley: University of California Press, 1994. 1–17 Reprinted in idem, *A Fire in the Bones.* Boston: Beacon Press, 1996. 17–36.

Ray, Stephen G., Jr. Review of *The Myth of Ham in Nineteenth-Century American Christianity: Race, Heathens, and the People of God. Conversations in Religion and Theology* 4.1 (2006): 36–38.

Reichard, Gladys A. "Literary Types and Dissemination of Myths." *Journal of American Folklore* 34, no. 133 (July–September 1921): 269–307.

Rejai, Mostafa. *Political Ideologies: A Comparative Approach.* 2nd ed. Armonk, NY, and London: M. E. Sharpe, 1995.

Research Department of the Universal House of Justice. *Conservation of the Earth's Resources: A Compilation of Extracts from the Bahá'í Writings.* London: Bahá'í Publishing Trust, 1990.

Ridgeway, James. *Blood in the Face: The Ku Klux Klan, Aryan Nations, Nazi Skinheads, and the Rise of a New White Culture.* New York: Thunder's Mouth Press, 1999.

Rieffer, Barbara-Ann J. "Religion and Nationalism: Understanding the Consequences of a Complex Relationship." *Ethnicities* 3.2 (2003): 215–242.

Rippin, Andrew. "Iblís." *Encyclopaedia of the Qur'an.* Ed. Jane Dammen McAuliffe. Vol. II. Leiden: E. J. Brill, 2002.

Rippin, Andrew. *Muslims: Their Religious Beliefs and Practices.* 3rd ed. London: Routledge, 2005.

"Robert A. F. Thurman." See http://www.bobthurman.com/biography.shtml.

Robertson, Roland. *Globalization: Social Theory and Global Culture.* London: Sage, 1992.

Robertson, Wilmot. *The Ethnostate: An Unblinkered Prospectus for an Advanced Statecraft.* Cape Canaveral, FL: Howard Allen Enterprises, 1992.

Robinson, Fiona. "Rethinking Ethics in an Era of Globalization." *Sussex Papers in International Relations* no. 2 (January 1996).

Rosenfeld, Alvin H. "Promised Land(s): Zion, America, and American Jewish Writers." *Jewish Social Studies* 3.3 (Spring/Summer 1997): 111–131.

Ross, Christopher. "American Public Diplomacy and Islam." *Ambassadors Review* (Spring 2003). See http://www.ciaonet.org/olj/ambrev/2003_spring/c.html.

Rouner, Leroy S. "Civil Religion, Cultural Diversity, and American Civilization." *The Key Reporter* 64.3 (1999): 1–6.

Russell, Greg. "Theodore Roosevelt, Geopolitics, and Cosmopolitan Ideals." *Review of International Studies* 32 (2006): 541–559.

Ryan, James Emmett. "Orestes Brownson in Young America: Popular Books and the Fate of Catholic Criticism." *American Literary History* 15.3 (2003): 443–470.

"SA: Racist Group Bases Website Activity in SA." *AAP General News Wire*. Sydney: January 31, 2006.

Sabbath and Festival Prayer Book. New York: United Synagogue of America, 1946.

Sabbath Prayer Book: With a Supplement Containing Prayers, Readings and Hymns and with a New Translation. New York: The Jewish Reconstructionist Foundation, Inc., 1945.

Safi, Omar, ed. *Progressive Muslims: On Justice, Gender, and Pluralism*. Oxford: Oneworld Publications, 2003.

Safi, Omar. "What Is Progressive Islam?" *ISIM Newsletter* 13 (December 2003): 48–49. See http://etext.lib.virginia.edu/journals/jsrforum/pdfs/SafiProgressive.pdf.

Salins, Peter D. *Assimilation, American Style*. New York: Basic Books, 1997.

Sarna, Jonathan. "Church-state Dilemmas of Jewish Americans." *Jews and the American Public Square: Debating Religion*. Ed. Alan Mittleman, Robert Licht, and Jonathan D. Sarna. Lanham, MD: Rowman and Littlefield, 2002.

Sarna, Jonathan. "Columbus and the Jews." *Commentary* 94:5 (November 1992): 38–41. Revised and expanded in idem, "The Mythical Jewish Columbus and the History of America's Jews." *Religion in the Age of Exploration*. Ed. Bryan F. Le Beau and Menahem Mor. Omaha: Creighton University Press, 1996. 81–95.

Sarna, Jonathan. "The Cult of Synthesis in American Jewish Culture." *Jewish Social Studies* 5.1–2 (1999): 52–79.

Sarna, Jonathan. "Early Prayers for the United States Government." *Prayer in America: Community Outreach Guide*. Public Broadcasting System, 2007. 111–124. See http://www.prayerinamerica.org/wp-content/downloads/get-involved/PRAYER-IN-AMERICA-Outreach-Guide.pdf.

Sarna, Jonathan. "A Forgotten 19th-Century Prayer for the United States Government: Its Meaning, Significance, and Surprising Author." *Hesed Ve-Emet: Studies in Honor of Ernest S. Frerichs*. Ed. Jodi Magness and Seymour Gitin. Atlanta, GA: Scholars Press, 1998. 431–440.

Sarna, Jonathan. "Free-Market Judaism." See http://www.beliefnet.com/story/142/story_14289_3.html.

Sarna, Jonathan. *Jacksonian Jew: The Two Worlds of Mordecai Noah*. New York: Holmes and Meier, 1981.

Sarna, Jonathan. "Jewish Prayers for the United States Government: A Study in the Liturgy of Politics and the Politics of Liturgy." *Moral Problems in American History: Essays in Honor of David Brion Davis.* Ed. Karen Halttunen and Perry Lewis. Ithaca, NY: Cornell University Press, 1998. 200–221. Reprinted in *Liturgy in the Life of the Synagogue: Studies in the History of Jewish Prayer.* Ed. Ruth Langer and Steven Fine. Duke Judaic Studies 2. Winona Lake, IN: Eisenbrauns, 2005.

Sarna, Jonathan. *Sacred Survival: The Civil Religion of American Jews.* Bloomington and Indianapolis: Indiana University Press, 1986.

Sarna, Jonathan. " 'Sacred Survival' Revisited: American Jewish Civil Religion in the New Millennium." *The Cambridge Companion to American Judaism.* Ed. Dana Evan Kaplan. Cambridge, MA: Cambridge University Press, 2005. 283–298.

Schaaf, Gregory. *The U.S. Constitution and the Great Law of Peace: A Comparison of Two Founding Documents.* Los Angeles: Center for Indigenous Arts and Cultures, 2004.

Scheske, Eric J. "Orestes Brownson: His Life, His Catholicism." *Logos: A Journal of Catholic Thought and Culture* 7.2 (2004): 137–164.

Scholnick, Robert J. "Extermination and Democracy: O'Sullivan, the *Democratic Review,* and Empire, 1837–1840." *American Periodicals: A Journal of History, Criticism, and Bibliography* 15.2 (2005): 123–141.

Schöpflin, George. "The Functions of Myth and a Taxonomy of Myths." *Myths and Nationhood.* Ed. Geoffrey Hosking and George Schöpflin. New York: Routledge, 1997. 19–35.

Seager, Richard Hughes. "Buddhist Chanting in Soka Gakkai International." *Religions of the United States in Practice.* Vol. II. Ed. Colleen McDannell. Princeton, NJ: Princeton University Press, 2001. 112–120.

"Seek the Welfare of the City." See http://www.ajhs.org/hai/entry.cfm?id=25.

Senate of the United States. S. Con. Res. 76/H. Con. Res. 331—*To Acknowledge the Contribution of the Iroquois Confederacy of Nations to the Development of the U.S. Constitution and to Reaffirm the Government-to-government Relationship between the Indian Tribes and the United States Established in the Constitution.* See http://www.senate.gov/reference/common/faq/Iroquois _Constitution.shtml.

Shannon, David T. " 'An Ante-bellum Sermon': A Resource for an African American Hermeneutic." *Stony the Road We Trod: African American Biblical Interpretation.* Ed. Cain Hope Felder. New York: Fortress Press, 1991. 98–123.

Shannon, Timothy J. *Indians and Colonists at the Crossroads of Empire: The Albany Congress of 1754.* Ithaca/Cooperstown: Cornell University Press and New York State Historical Association, 2000.

Sharpe, Tanya Telfair. "The Identity Christian Movement: Ideology of Domestic Terrorism." *Journal of Black Studies* 30.4 (March 2000): 604–623.

Shaw, Stephen. "Harassment, Hate, and Human Rights in Idaho." *Politics in the Postwar American West.* Ed. Richard Lowitt. Norman: University of Oklahoma Press, 1995. 94–105.

Shepard, William E. "Islam and Ideology: Towards a Typology." *International Journal of Middle East Studies* 19.3 (August 1987): 307–335.

Shipps, Jan. "Difference and Otherness: Mormonism and the American Religious Mainstream." *Minority Faiths and the American Protestant Mainstream.* Ed. Jonathan D. Sarna. Urbana/Chicago: University of Illinois Press, 1998. 81–109.

Shipps, Jan. *Mormonism: The Story of A New Religious Tradition.* Urbana/Chicago: University of Illinois Press, 1985.

Shipps, Jan. "The Reality of the Restoration and the Restoration Ideal in the Mormon Tradition." *The American Quest for the Primitive Church.* Ed. Richard T. Hughes. Urbana/Chicago: University of Illinois Press, 1988. 181–195.

Silverman, Rabbi Morris. "A Prayer for Our Country." *High Holiday Prayer Book.* Compiled and arranged by Rabbi Morris Silverman. Hartford, CT: Prayer Book Press of Media Judaica, 1951, 1962, 1979. P. 115.

Shoghi Effendi. *The Advent of Divine Justice.* Wilmette, IL: U.S. Bahá'í Publishing Trust, 1990 [1938].

Shoghi Effendi. *Citadel of Faith.* Wilmette, IL: U.S. Bahá'í Publishing Trust, 1980.

Shoghi Effendi. *Dawn of a New Day.* New Delhi: Bahá'í Publishing Trust of India, n.d.

Shoghi Effendi. *Directives from the Guardian.* New Delhi: Bahá'í Publishing Trust, 1973.

Shoghi Effendi. *God Passes By.* Wilmette: U.S. Bahá'í Publishing Trust, 1979 [1944].

Shoghi Effendi. *The Promised Day Is Come.* Rev. ed. Wilmette, IL: U.S. Bahá'í Publishing Trust, 1980 [1941].

Shoghi Effendi. *This Decisive Hour: Messages from Shoghi Effendi to the North American Bahá'ís, 1932–1946.* Wilmette, IL: U.S. Bahá'í Publishing Trust, 2002.

Shoghi Effendi. *The World Order of Bahá'u'lláh.* Wilmette, IL: U.S. Bahá'í Publishing Trust, 1991 [1936].

Shook, Somer, Wesley Delano, and Robert W. Balch. "Elohim City: A Participant-Observer Study of a Christian Identity Community." *Nova Religio* 2 (April 1999): 245–265.

Siddur Sim Shalom: A Prayer Book for Shabbat, Festivals, and Weekdays. Ed. and trans. Rabbi Jules Harlow. New York: The Rabbinical Assembly, The United Synagogue of America, 1985.

Skowronek, Stephen. "The Reassociation of Ideas and Purposes: Racism, Liberalism, and the American Political Tradition." *American Political Science Review* 100 (2006): 385–401.

Slotkin, Richard. "Myth and the Production of History." *Ideology and Classic American Literature.* Ed. Sacvan Bercovitch and Myra Jehlen. Cambridge, MA: Cambridge University Press, 1986. 70–90.

Smith, Anthony D. "Ethnic Election and National Destiny: Some Religious Origins of Nationalist Ideals." *Nations and Nationalism* 5.3 (1999): 331–355.

Smith, Anthony D. "The 'Sacred' Dimension of Nationalism." *Millennium: Journal of International Studies* 29.3 (2000): 791–814.

Smith, Ethan. *View of the Hebrews: Or, the Tribes of Israel in America.* Poultney, VT: Smith and Shute, 1823.

Smith, Jonathan Z., ed. *The HarperCollins Dictionary of Religion.* San Francisco: HarperSanFrancisco, 1995.

Smith, Joseph. *The Articles of Faith of the Church of Jesus Christ of Latter-day Saints.* See http://scriptures.lds.org/a_of_f/1.

Smith, Joseph. "The King Follett Discourse." See http://mldb.byu.edu/follett.htm.

Smith, Joseph. "The King Follett Discourse: A Newly Amalgamated Text." Ed. Stan Larson. *Brigham Young University Studies* 18.2 (Winter 1978): 193–208.

Smith, Joseph. *Times and Seasons* 5.8 (April 15, 1844): 510.

Smith, Joseph Fielding. *Essentials in Church History.* Salt Lake City: Deseret, 1972.

Smith, Joseph Fielding, ed. *Teachings of the Prophet Joseph Smith.* Salt Lake City: Deseret, 1993.

Smith, Joseph, Jr., ed. *The Papers of Joseph Smith. Vol. 1, The Autobiographical and Historical Writings.* Ed. Dean C. Jessee. Salt Lake City: Church of Jesus Christ of Latter-day Saints, 1989.

Snow, Lorenzo. *The Teachings of Lorenzo Snow, Fifth President of the Church of Jesus Christ of Latter-day Saints.* Ed. Clyde J. Williams. Salt Lake City: Bookcraft, 1984.

Snyder, Gary. "For All." *Deep Ecology for the Twenty-First Century.* Ed. George Sessions. Berkeley: Shambhala, 1995. 462.

Snyder, Gary. "For All." *The Gary Snyder Reader: Prose, Poetry, and Translations.* Washington, DC: Counterpoint, 2000. 504.

Soka Gakkai International-USA, *Buddhist Learning Review: 2007 Study Guide.* Santa Monica, CA: SGI-USA, 2007. See http://www.sgi-usa-study.org/BLR_2007 _webres.pdf.

Soka Gakkai International–USA. "What Is Nam-myoho-renge-kyo? How Does Chanting Work?" http://www.sgi-usa.org/newmembers/resources/faqs/ whatisnammyohorengekyo.php (accessed January 25, 2009).

Solomon, Arnold M. "Reform Judaism and the Mission unto the Nations." *The Chosen People in America: A Study in Jewish Religious Ideology.* Bloomington: Indiana University Press, 1983. 53–72.

Solomon, Norman. *Judaism: A Very Short Introduction.* Oxford and New York: Oxford University Press, 1996.

Solomon, Ted J. "The Response of Three New Religions to the Crisis in the Japanese Value System." *Journal for the Scientific Study of Religion* 16.1 (March 1977): 1–14.

Southern Poverty Law Center. "Aryans Without a Nation." *Intelligence Report* (Fall 2000). See http://www.splcenter.org/intel/intelreport/article.jsp?aid=216.

Southern Poverty Law Center. "Elder Statesman: A Life of Hate, and the Future in the Balance." *Intelligence Report* (Summer 1998). See http://www.splcenter.org/ intel/intelreport/article.jsp?pid=709.

Starna, W. A., and G. R. Hamell. "History and the Burden of Proof: The Case of Iroquois Influence on the U.S. Constitution." *New York History* 77 (1996): 427–452.

State of Louisiana. *The Joint Legislative Committee on Un-American Activities, Report No. 3*, 98–99 (n.d.).

Steigerwald, David. *Wilsonian Idealism in America*. Ithaca, NY: Cornell University Press, 1994.

Stephanson, Anders. *Manifest Destiny: American Expansionism and the Empire of Right*. New York: Hill and Wang, 1995.

Stern, Chaim, ed. *Gates of Prayer: The New Union Prayer Book*. New York: Central Conference of American Rabbis, 1975.

Stevens, Rabbi Elliot L. "The Prayer Books, They Are A'Changin'." *Reform Judaism* (Summer 2006). See http://urj.org/Articles/index.cfm?id=10575.

Stewart, Kathleen. "Bad Endings: American Apocalypsis." *Annual Review of Anthropology* 28 (1999): 285–310.

Stockman, Robert. "Redeemer Nation Revisited: The American Bahá'í Sacred History of America." Chapter 7. *The Bahá'í Faith and American Protestantism*. Th.D.: Harvard University, 1990.

Stockman, Robert. *Thornton Chase: The First American Bahá'í*. Wilmette, IL: Bahá'í Publishing Trust, 2001.

Storch, Neil T. "John Ireland's Americanism after 1899: The Argument from History." *Church History* 51.4 (1982): 434–444.

Strong, Josiah. *Our Country: Its Possible Future and Its Present Crisis*. Astor, NY: American Home Missionary Society, 1885. An edited edition of *Our Country* was later published as follows: Josiah Strong, *Our Country: Its Possible Future and Its Present Crisis*. Ed. Jurgen Herbst. Cambridge, MA: Belknap Press, 1963.

Stuckey, Mary E., and Joshua R. Ritter. "George Bush, 'Human Rights,' and American Democracy." *Presidential Studies Quarterly* 37.4 (December 2007): 646–666.

Swift, Wesley A. "The Children of the Beast." See http://www.churchoftrueisrael.com/swift/swchildbeast.html.

Swift, Wesley A. "Church of True Israel" (Sermons of Wesley A. Swift). See http://www.churchoftrueisrael.com/swift.

Swift, Wesley A. "The Coming Liberation of America." January 30, 1966. See http://www.israelect.com/reference/WesleyASwift/sermons/66-01-30.htm.

Swift, Wesley A. "What Really Happened in the Garden of Eden?" See http://www.churchoftrueisrael.com/swift/sw-what-happened.html.

Talbot, David. "Terrorists Increasingly Turn to the Internet." M.I.T. See http://www.technologyreview.com/Infotech/16385/?a=f.

Talmage, James. *A Study of the Articles of Faith: Being a Consideration of the Principal Doctrines of The Church of Jesus Christ of Latter-day Saints*. Salt Lake City: Church of Jesus Christ of Latter-day Saints, 1976 [1890].

Tareen, Sophia. "A Spry Farrakhan Sings Obama's Praises." Associated Press, February 24, 2008. See http://www.breitbart.com/article.php?id=d8v13imo1andshow_article=1.

Taylor, Bron. "Environmental Ethics." *Encyclopedia of Religion and Nature, 1*: 597–608.

Taylor, Wayne. "Premillennium Tension: Malcolm X and the Eschatology of the Nation of Islam." *Souls* 7.1 (Winter 2005): 52–65.

Teague, Tom. "From Farrakhan to New Philadelphia: Vibert White Embraces History at Every Crossroad." *Illinois Heritage* 5.2 (March/April 2002): 6–10. See http://www.lib.niu.edu/2002/ih020306.html.

"Tefilah Lememshalah/Prayer for the Country." *Kol Hanesshamah: Shabbat Vehagim.* Wyncote, PA: Reconstructionist Press, 1994. P. 418 [Hebrew, 419]. (Prayer from Rabindranath Tagore [Adapted] on p. 419.)

[Tefilot Yisra'el]. *Prayers of Israel, with an English Translation.* 5th ed. New York: Henry Frank, 1856. 198–199.

Terrill, Robert E. "Protest, Prophecy, and Prudence in the Rhetoric of Malcolm X." *Rhetoric and Public Affairs* 4.1 (2001): 25–53.

"Theodore Roosevelt: The Nobel Peace Prize 1906." See http://nobelprize.org/nobel_prizes/peace/laureates/1906/roosevelt-bio.html.

Thibodeaux, Raoul. "Al-Qaeda Hires Blackwater." *Avant News* (October 30, 2007). See http://www.avantnews.com/modules/news/article.php?storyid=354.

Thomas, Rhondda Robinson. *Exodus: Literary Migrations of Afro-Atlantic Authors, 1760–1903.* Ph.D. dissertation: University of Maryland, 2007.

Thompson, John A. *Woodrow Wilson.* London: Longman, 2002.

Thurman, Robert. "Christian Experiences with Buddhist Spirituality: A Response." *Buddhist-Christian Studies* 21.1 (2001): 69–72.

Thurman, Robert. *Inner Revolution: Life, Liberty, and the Pursuit of Real Happiness.* New York: Putnam/Riverhead Books, 1998.

Tibet.com. "The Dalai Lama's Biography." See http://www.tibet.com/dl/biography.html.

Toll, William. "Horace M. Kallen: Pluralism and American Jewish Identity." *American Jewish History* 85.1 (1997): 57–74.

"Top Ten LDS News Stories of 2007." *Deseret News,* Thursday, January 17, 2008. See http://www.mormontimes.com/people_news/newsmakers/?id=2573 (accessed January 25, 2009).

"Torah Service. *Siddur Sim Shalom,* page 139." See http://www.ohebshalom.org/docs/2008transtorah.pdf.

Tuveson, Ernest Lee. *Redeemer Nation: The Idea of America's Millennial Role.* Chicago: University of Chicago Press, 1968.

Underwood, Grant. "Early Mormon Perceptions of Contemporary America: 1830–1846." *Brigham Young University Studies* 26 (Summer 1986): 49–61.

Underwood, Grant. *The Millenarian World of Early Mormonism.* Urbana/Chicago: University of Illinois, 1993.

Underwood, Grant. "Mormons and the Millennial World View." *Mormon Identities in Transition.* Ed. Douglas J. Davies. London: Cassell, 1996. 135–142.

Universal House of Justice. *The Constitution of the Universal House of Justice.* Haifa: Bahá'í World Centre, 1973.

Universal House of Justice. *Letter to the National Spiritual Assembly of the Bahá'ís of the United States* (April 10, 2001). See http://bahai-library.com/uhj/feast.html.

Universal House of Justice. *The Promise of World Peace.* Haifa: Bahá'í World Centre, October 1985.

Varacalli, Joseph A. *Bright Promise, Failed Community: Catholics and the American Public Order.* Lanham, MD: Lexington Books, 2000.

Varacalli, Joseph A. "On Being Catholic American." *Homiletic and Pastoral Review.* August–September 2004. See http://ignatiusinsight.org/features2005/varacalli_amcatholic_may05.asp.

Vecsey, Christopher. *Imagine Ourselves Richly: Mythic Narratives of North American Indians.* New York: Crossroad, 1988.

Vecsey, Christopher. "The Story and Structure of the Iroquois Confederacy." *Journal of the American Academy of Religion* 54.1 (Spring 1986): 79–106.

Vysotsky, Stanislav. "Understanding the Racist Right in the Twenty First Century: A Typology of Modern White Supremacist Organizations." Unpublished, Northeastern University (January 10, 2004). 9. See http://home.comcaSt.net/~vysotsky.s/Understanding.pdf.

Wallace, Mike. *The Hate That Hate Produced.* Television documentary, 1959. See http://www.archive.org/details/PBSTheHateThatHateProduced.

Wallace, Paul A. W. "Dekanahwideh." *Dictionary of Canadian Biography Online.* Based on the *Dictionary of Canadian Biography/Dictionnaire biographique du Canada.* Ed. John English. Toronto and Montreal: University of Toronto and Université Laval, 1959.

Wallach, Glenn. *Obedient Sons: The Discourse of Youth and Generations in American Culture, 1630–1860.* Amherst: University of Massachusetts Press, 1997.

Walzer, Michael. "Who Is an American Jew?" *Occasional Papers on Jewish Civilization, Jewish Thought and Philosophy.* Washington, DC: Program for Jewish Civilization, Georgetown University, 2007. 8–15.

Ward, Allan L. *239 Days: 'Abdu'l-Bahá's Journey in America.* Wilmette, IL: U.S. Bahá'í Publishing Trust, 1979.

Weaver, Jace, ed. *Defending Mother Earth: Native American Perspectives on Environmental Justice.* Maryknoll, NY: Orbis Books, 1996.

Webb, Stephen H. *American Providence: A Nation with a Mission.* New York: Continuum, 2004.

Wenger, Beth S. "Making American Civilization Jewish: Mordecai Kaplan's Civil Religion." *Jewish Social Studies* 12.2 (2006): 56–63.

West, Robin. "Ennobling Politics." "Law and Democracy in the Empire of Force." Ed. H. Jefferson Powell and James Boyd White. Ann Arbor, MI: University of Michigan Press, forthcoming. See http://www.press.umich.edu/titleDetailDesc.do?id=360278.

White, Donald W. *The American Century: The Rise and Decline of the United States as a World Power.* New Haven and London: Yale University Press, 1996.

White, Donald Wallace. *The American Century: The Rise and Decline of the United States as a World Power.* New Haven and London: Yale University Press, 1996.

White, Richard. *The Middle Ground: Indians, Empires, and Republics in the Great Lakes Region.* Cambridge: Cambridge University Press, 1991.

White, Vibert L. *Inside the Nation of Islam: A Historical and Personal Testimony by a Black Muslim.* University Press of Florida, 2000.

Wilber, Dr. Donald N. "Overthrow of Premier Mossadeq of Iran." Washington, DC: Central Intelligence Agency, March 1954. First published in an article written by James Risen of *The New York Times* in its editions of April 16 and June 18, 2000. See http://www.nytimes.com/library/world/mideast/iran-cia-intro.pdf, with hyperlinks to each of the chapters.

Williams, Ray C., ed. *"By the Hands of Wise Men": Essays on the U.S. Constitution.* Provo, UT: Brigham Young University Press, 1979.

Wills, David W. "The Central Themes of American Religious History: Pluralism, Puritanism, and the Encounter of Black and White." *Religion and Intellectual Life* 5 (1987): 30–41. Reprinted in Timothy E. Fulop and Albert J. Raboteau, eds., *African-American Religion: Interpretive Essays in History and Culture.* New York/London: Routledge, 1997. 7–20.

Wilson, Woodrow. "Presenting the Treaty for Ratification Address to the Senate of the United States. July 19, 1919." *God's New Israel: Religious Interpretations of American Destiny.* Ed. Conrad Cherry. Rev. ed. Chapel Hill: University of North Carolina Press, 1998. 279–288.

Winn, Kenneth H. *Exiles in a Land of Liberty: Mormons in America, 1830–1846.* Studies in Religion. Chapel Hill, NC: University of North Carolina Press, 1989.

Winthrop, John. *Life and Letters of John Winthrop, Governor of the Massachusetts-Bay Company at Their Emigration to New England, 1630.* Ed. Robert Charles Winthrop. Boston: Ticknor and Fields, 1864–1867. 18–20.

Winthrop, John. "A Model of Christian Charity." *God's New Israel: Religious Interpretations of American Destiny.* Ed. Conrad Cherry. Rev. ed. Chapel Hill: University of North Carolina Press, 1998.

Wise, Isaac Mayer. "Our Country's Place in History." *God's New Israel: Religious Interpretations of American Destiny.* Ed. Conrad Cherry. Rev. ed. Chapel Hill: University of North Carolina Press, 1998. 224–234.

Woocher, Jonathan S. "Spirituality and the Civil Religion." *Secularism, Spirituality, and the Future of American Jewry.* Ed. Elliott Abrams and David G. Dalin. Washington, DC: Ethics and Public Policy Center, 1999. 19–25.

Woodruff, Wilford. *Conference Report* (April 1898).

Woodruff, Wilford. *The Discourses of Wilford Woodruff.* Ed. G. Homer Durham. Salt Lake City: Bookcraft, 1946.

World Heritage Committee. "World Heritage Site: Bahá'i Holy Places." See http://www.worldheritagesite.org/sites/bahaiholyplaces.html.

Yazdani, Enayatollah, and Rizwan Hussain. "United States' Policy towards Iran after the Islamic Revolution: An Iranian Perspective." *International Studies* 43 (2006): 267–289.

Zagorin, Adam. "Khatami: American 'Conceit and Pride' Led to Iraq Mess." *Time.* September 8, 2006. See http://www.time.com/time/world/article/0,8599,1533026,00.html.

Zakaria, Fareed. *From Wealth to Power: The Unusual Origins of America's World Role.* Princeton: Princeton University Press, 1998.

Zimmerman, John. "Sayyid Qutb's Influence on the 11 September Attacks." *Terrorism and Political Violence* 16.2 (April–June 2004): 222–252.

Ziolkowski, Eric J. Review of *The World's Parliament of Religions: An illustrated and popular story of the world's first Parliament of Religions, held in Chicago in connection with the Columbian Exposition of 1893*. Ed. John H. Barrows. Chicago: Parliament Pub. Co., 1893. *Journal of the American Academy of Religion* 64.3 (Autumn 1996): 662–664.

Index

'Abdu'l-Bahá (Bahá'í Faith): compares interracial meeting to "a beautiful cluster of precious jewels," 188–189; in public addresses in America (1912), promoted interracial harmony, interrreligious reconciliation, and ideal international relations, 176; likens spiritual destiny of Canada to America's destiny, 180; predicts that America "will lead all nations spiritually," 173, 175, 181, 217, 220, 225; presages the advent of "true civilization," 228; propounds ethic of interracial unity in Bahá'í Emancipation/Civil War Myth, 186–189; propounds ethic of world unity in Bahá'í Wilsonian Myth, 189–190; son of, successor to, interpreter of Bahá'u'lláh (Prophet-Founder of the Bahá'í Faith), 173–200; speaks in Rankin Chapel, Howard University (1912), 186–188; states that "consciousness of the Oneness of Mankind" is distinguishing feature of the Bahá'í Faith, 174

"African American Exodus Counter-Myth" (Protestantism): "An Ante-Bellum Sermon" (1895) exemplifies how the Exodus narrative was analogized to the new Egypt, America, 41–43; an incipient African American theology of liberation, 40–44; "Many uses of religious myths among African Americans reject identification with America," 40; "No single story [Exodus] captures more clearly the distinctiveness of African-American Christianity," 41; preeminent African American counter-myth is the Exodus story, 40; under the Exodus myth, America's mythic role is reversed, 41

African Americans: "African American Exodus Counter-Myth," 40–44; "An Ante-Bellum Sermon" (1895) exemplifies how the Exodus narrative was analogized to the new Egypt, America, 41–43; "Black Man's History" (Malcolm X's December 1962 anti-White sermon), 126–127, 220; experience of African American Muslim after 9/11, 135; Imam Luqman Ahmad, African American Muslim, 153–154; Nation of Yahweh (goal of "dismantling the power structure of the persecutors of African-Americans"), 4; "Religious myths remain central to the making of a new African American self," 40